The Librarian's Guide to

GRAPHIC NOVELS FOR ADULTS

David S. Serchay

Neal-Schuman Publishers, Inc.
New York   London

Published by Neal-Schuman Publishers, Inc.
100 William St., Suite 2004
New York, NY 10038

Printed and bound in the United States of America.

The paper used in this publication meets the minimum requirements of American National Standard for Information Sciences—Permanence of Paper for Printed Library Materials, ANSI Z39.48-1992.

Library of Congress Cataloging-in-Publication Data

Serchay, David S., 1971-
    The librarian's guide to graphic novels for adults / David S. Serchay.
        p. cm.
    Includes bibliographical references and indexes.
    ISBN 978-1-55570-662-3 (alk. paper)
    1. Libraries—Special collections—Graphic novels. 2. Graphic novels—United States.
I. Title.

Z692.G7S469 2010
025.277415'973—dc22

                                                            2009041011

For My Family

Contents

List of Exhibits and Figures

Foreword

When graphic novel adaptations appear of Proust, Poe, Jane Austen, and Shakespeare, when the *New York Times* puts out not one but three graphic novel bestseller lists, when a graphic novel wins a Pulitzer Prize and another is voted book of the year by *Time* magazine—how can anyone still believe that comics are (only) for kids?

Even after the graphic novel and manga explosion across genres and readerships over the past five years, even just this year in 2009 I read reports of library staffers refusing to set up separate collections and shelving areas for adult graphic novels. The teen and juvenile collections, they maintain, are fine. "Comics are trite," "graphic novels are a fad," and "this type of material is not uplifting"—all different ways of saying that graphic narrative is inherently incapable of conveying serious, quality content fit for adults.

When we house quality art in museums and quality writing in libraries, what is it about combining art with writing that sets these people off? Perhaps they forget that nineteenth-century adult books quite normally boasted plentiful illustrations. Charles Dickens' *Pickwick Papers* was originally commissioned simply as text for Robert Seymour's drawings, and the original printing of William Makepeace Thackeray's *Vanity Fair* included nearly 200 illustrations by Thackeray himself. Comics are simply illustrated books taken to the next level and can show as wide a range of quality and content as any medium.

So David Serchay's new book serves two functions. It gives detailed and excellent guidance for setting up adult graphic novel collections, of course. But as the first on the topic, it also stakes out the territory, saying, *See? Graphic novels for adults exist, and in considerable quantity and quality*—indeed, enough to fill an entire book. And here it is.

I first became acquainted with David through his posts on GNLIB-L, the e-list for librarians working with graphic novels. Then I had the fortunate opportunity to review his first book: *The Librarian's Guide to Graphic Novels for Children and Tweens*. Now I was impressed. David's writing displayed both a range and a level of detail that I had rarely seen previously in books about graphic novels in libraries.

In staking out the new territory of adult graphic novels, David has brought the same broad scope as well as detailed discussion of the fine points: how graphic novels are made, types of editions and collections, genres popular with adult readers, special characteristics of manga, vendor programs, major publishers catering to adults, theft and censorship issues, hundreds of suggested titles for purchase. Such content provides essential background for librarians.

Especially innovative and therefore valuable are those sections addressing collection development policies, comics in academia, internal library censorship, comics traditions elsewhere in the world, and "how adult is too adult?"

No book can offer the last word on a subject, including this one. Eventually, we should hope, there will be many more guides to graphic novels for adults. Industry surveys from Diamond Comics Distributors report an average comics readership aged 29 to 34. Perhaps many do not currently use the library for their favorite reading material, but if the titles are there, they will come. Certainly, the teens now gobbling up ninja and high school romance manga in library-based young adult collections will soon be eager for a broader range of content. For these future guides, *The Librarian's Guide to Graphic Novels for Adults* sets a high standard.

Martha Cornog, MA, MLS
Graphic novel columnist
Library Journal

Preface

"Comics are for kids!" This idea has been around for decades. A prosecuting attorney in Texas even used it in convicting a man for selling an adult comic book *to an adult*.[1] It's also been used by librarians in choosing graphic novels for their libraries. Well, these people are all wrong. Saying "comics are for kids" is the same as saying "movies are for kids." Some movies are for kids, but adults enjoy G- and PG-rated films as well, and some movies that younger children should not watch are perfectly fine for adults to view. The same applies to comics and graphic novels. All comics are fine for adults but not all are fine for children. Or, as W. H. Auden put it, "There are good books which are only for adults, because their comprehension presupposes adult experiences, but there are no good books which are only for children."[2]

This is one of the reasons that I wrote *The Librarian's Guide to Graphic Novels for Adults*. Another is to show that there is a substantial adult readership for graphic novels, and not just for those in the superhero genre such as *Batman, Spider-Man*, and the *X-Men* but for all genres—those that appeal to young and old alike and those made specifically for an older audience. The latter are being produced not only by comic book companies but also by mainstream book publishers as well, and many have gone on to acclaim, awards, and popularity. *Sandman, Watchmen, Road to Perdition, V for Vendetta, Persepolis*, and *American Splendor* are just a few of these.

In some graphic novels, fairy tale characters live in our world, the mayor of New York is a former superhero, and one man is the only male left in a world of women. Other graphic novels deal with regular people—their lives, families, loves, and losses—while others are autobiographies, histories, adventure stories, or works of horror, science fiction, romance—every genre out there.

Some of you may already know about graphic novels and even have a collection for your younger patrons (and may have previously read this volume's companion work, *The Librarian's Guide to Graphic Novels for Children and Tweens*), but for those of you who are starting a collection (especially an adult collection) from scratch and who know very little about the subject, this book discusses all aspects of graphic novels and libraries and provide answers to the following questions:

- What exactly are graphic novels? (Chapter 2)
- What is manga? (Chapter 4)

- Why should I purchase graphic novels for my library? (Chapter 1)
- Why should I purchase adult-specific titles? (Chapter 1)
- How do I purchase them? (Chapter 5)
- What are my cataloging and shelving options? (Chapters 7 and 8)
- How can I make them last longer? (Chapter 7)
- How can I promote them? (Chapter 8)
- What genres do graphic novels come in? (Chapter 3)
- What problems might I have with my graphic novel collection? (Chapter 8)
- Why would a university library need graphic novels? (Chapter 9)
- What programs can I provide with graphic novels? (Chapter 8)
- What is the difference between a graphic novel for adults and an adult graphic novel? (Chapter 6)
- And, most important, what should I purchase for my collection? (Chapter 6)

To address what to purchase, I offer a list of "mature audience" titles as well as discussion of some of the more popular "younger ages" titles. Appendix A, "An Annotated List of Selected Graphic Novels," features an annotated list of over 600 graphic novels ranging from original graphic novels, to series of books, to works by a particular author or publisher or in a particular genre or subject. These titles are rated so that you know which ones can also be put into a collection for teens or younger readers, which ones are best for the adult section of the library, and which are most definitely "adults only." In addition, Appendix B, "Recommended Additional Books for Your Collection," lists a large number of graphic-novel-related books that you can also purchase for your library. These include other books on graphic novels in libraries and nonfiction works that range from scholarly books on the subject to those that are just fun. Appendix C, "Recommended Online Sources for Information and Purchasing," provides a list of online sources for more information, including publisher Web sites, sites for news and information, and various online mailing lists that you can join.

Rounding out the book are two indexes that will help you quickly locate information both in the main text and in the appendixes. First is the title/creator/publisher index that includes bold page numbers for titles in both Appendix A and Appendix B, so you can easily locate the annotated entries. This is followed by a broad subject index covering topics discussed throughout the book.

Some points to remember as you read this book:

- Graphic novels are a format, not a genre.
- Many adults read graphic novels.
- Certain graphic novels are created for an adult audience.
- Adults also like to read the same graphic novels that are enjoyed by children, tweens, and teens.

Graphic novels are a wonderful addition to any library's collection, providing the library with high circulation figures and its patrons with entertainment. Comic books and graphic novels aren't just for kids anymore—in fact, they never were.

Notes

1. *Texas v. Jesus Castillo*. See Exhibit 8-1 for more on this and similar cases.
2. Auden, W. H. 1973. *Forewords and Afterwords* (p. 291). New York: Random House.

Acknowledgments

I have to give thanks to everyone who helped to create this book, especially Carole Fiore; my editors at Neal-Schuman, Amy Knauer, Kathy Blake, Paul Seeman, and Charles Harmon; the people at GNLIB-L; the people on the Grand Comic-Book Database list; the people on the comixscl-l list; as well as Andrea Greenbaum, Karen Green, Jackie Estrada, Georgia Higley, Adam Johnson, Martha Cornog, Daniel Berry, Gail de Vos, Lance Eaton, Andrew Friedenthal, Carl Gerriets, Diana Green, Travis Langley, Allison Mandaville, Leonard Rifas, Robin Brenner, Mike Pawuk, Eva Volin, and the various publishers, editors, and creators who answered my questions and/or provided me with materials for review. I would also like to thank everyone who purchased my first book, and I would especially like to thank my wonderful wife, Bethany, who has put up with several years of deadlines and having books and papers piled up around the house.

PART I

Understanding the Value and Types of Graphic Novels

Chapter 1

Why Offer Graphic Novels for Adults in Your Library?

By now most public librarians understand that they need to include graphic novels in their collections (and for those who do not, this chapter presents some reasons to include them). However, the perception still exists that graphic novels should go only into the young adult (YA) or juvenile sections and that the ones offered in the YA section are enough for those adults who do read them. Neither perspective is true.

Adults *do* read graphic novels. One study put out by Diamond Distributors found that the average graphic novel reader is 29 years old (*The Public Librarian's Guide to Graphic Novels*, 2003). What some librarians have not yet realized is that many graphic novels are written specifically for adults. Sometimes these books contain explicit material, such as nudity and sexual language, making it inappropriate to house them on the same shelves as books aimed for children or younger teens. In other cases, the books may simply have been written for an older audience—having no objectionable content—but simply not of interest to younger readers. Just as a novel by John Grisham or James Patterson should be shelved in the adult area, so too should certain graphic novels.

Unfortunately, combining the words "adult" and "graphic" can give the wrong impression at first. For example, when you explain to someone that your library keeps the children's DVDs in one corner and the adult DVDs in another you are not implying that your library carries X-rated material. While some comics can be considered truly pornographic, or at least "adults only," when used in this book, the term "adult" means "for older readers"—in other words, for readers who are adults (or at least in their late teens), who enjoy books written specifically for them, but who may also enjoy works written for younger readers.

These older readers are coming into the library to get graphic novels, ranging from the superhero adventures of Batman and the X-Men, to the "graphic memoirs" of Harvey Pekar and Joe Matt, to the vampire stories of Steve Niles, and to all the other genres discussed in more detail in Chapter 3. A failure to purchase graphic novels for your adult readers would deprive your patrons of the chance to read some excellent stories, and would deprive your library of the following advantages of having graphic novels in your collection.

Increased Circulation

One advantage to purchasing graphic novels—one that may help to convince reluctant superiors—is that having graphic novels in the collection increases circulation, as has been proven time and again. Another common finding is that those who check out graphic novels come back, not only for more of the same but for other books as well. While most studies focus on young adult collections and how circulation can increase two to four times when graphic novels are added (*The Public Librarian's Guide to Graphic Novels*, 2003), some of the data are applicable to adult collections as well.

Mainstream Appeal and Recognition

Comic book publishers aren't the only ones putting out graphic novels. As Chapter 6 will show, many mainstream publishers (e.g., Simon & Schuster, HarperCollins, Ballentine Books, Houghton Mifflin) are now publishing original works. These publishers realize that a market exists for graphic novels for adults, and they have responded accordingly. Many of them now have booths at major comics conventions alongside the better-known publishers of comics and graphic novels such as DC and Marvel. In some cases, publishers are even creating special imprints for their graphic novel lines, such as Roaring Brook's award-winning imprint First Second.

Book awards also reflect the growing acceptance of graphic novels by mainstream audiences. While comics have had their own awards since the 1960s, some have also won, or at least been nominated for, the same awards as prose titles. Some of the most notable include 1986's *Watchmen*, which won a special Hugo Award (the Hugos finally added a graphic novels category in 2009) and 1986's *Maus*, which was awarded a Pulitzer Prize Special Award in 1992 and has long been used as an example of a "respectable" graphic novel. Gene Luen Yang's *American Born Chinese* (2007), a book for younger readers, was a finalist for the National Book Award and also the first graphic novel to win the American Library Association's (ALA) Michael L. Printz Award. *Fun Home* was a finalist for the National Book Critics Award and the winner of many others, and several graphic novels, including *Palestine* (1996), *Jimmy Corrigan* (2001), and *Jimbo's Inferno* (2007) have received the American Book Award. Unfortunately, such occasions still spark controversy. In 1991, the story "A Midsummer Night's Dream" from issue 19 of *Sandman* (September 1990) won the World Fantasy Award for best short story. Soon after the rules were changed so that comic book stories could win only in a "special award" category, and as of 2009 they have not been changed back.

Comic books and graphic novels have also found greater respectability in the mainstream media. *Time, Entertainment Weekly*, and other publications often include reviews of graphic novels along with other book reviews and treat them with the same level of respect. *Time* magazine placed *Watchmen* on its list of the 100 best English language novels since 1923 and named *Fun Home* as the best book of 2006. *Entertainment Weekly* has also included graphic novels in its "best of" lists, most notably its "New Classics" list of the 100 best books since 1980. On the list were *Maus* (7),

Watchmen (13), *Persepolis* (37), *Sandman* (46), *Jimmy Corrigan* (54), and *Fun Home* (68). The Pulitzer Prize–winning "nongraphic" novel *The Amazing Adventures of Kavalier and Clay*, which was about the early years of comic books, came in at #53 (Reese, 2008).[1] *Publishers Weekly* has a regular column in its print edition as well as a weekly report via e-mail and owns the comics-themed news blog *The Beat* (http://pwbeat.publishersweekly.com/blog; see Appendix C for more Web sites). Many newspapers also carry positive articles on and reviews of graphic novels. Unfortunately, some do still feel the need to use the campy sound effects from the 1960s *Batman* television show in headlines like "Pow! Bam! Guess What? Grown-ups Read Comics Too!"

Bookstores have also helped graphic novels gain new respectability. At one time, bookstores were unaccustomed to shelving books in this format. When Will Eisner's *Contract with God* came out in 1978, one of the first bookstores to carry it was Brentano's in New York City. However, after removing it from the "new title" table and shelving it with religious books, they received a complaint that it didn't belong with the religious books because it was a "cartoon book." So they put it in with the other cartoon books, such as the collections of *Peanuts*, and got complaints about having "a comic book that shows a naked lady in with the *Beetle Bailey Books*." Eventually, not knowing what to do with it, the manager put the remaining copies into a box and stored it in the basement (Andleman, 2005: 291–292).

As more and more graphic novels started to appear in bookstores, they were mainly shelved either in the cartoon/comics section or with the science fiction and fantasy novels. They can still often be found in or near those areas of the store. In 2003, however, the Book Industry Systems Advisory Committee of the Book Industry Study Group, Inc., gave graphic novels their own shelving classification (MacDonald, 2003). This new classification allowed the subject term "graphic novel" to be added to the back of paperbacks, sometimes along with genre designations such as "drama," "biography," "horror," "romance," and so on.

The presence of graphic novels in bookstores has allowed them to be featured on the regular book bestseller lists. For example, *The 9/11: A Graphic Adaptation* made it to #6 on the *New York Times* nonfiction paperback list.[2] They have also become so popular that in 2009 the *New York Times* began putting a weekly graphic books bestseller list on their "Artsbeat" Web page (http://artsbeat.blogs.nytimes.com). This list is divided into hardcover, softcover, and manga titles, and figures are compiled in the same way as on the other bestseller lists. Due to readers' interest in the *Watchmen* movie, both that title as well as other material by its author, Alan Moore, were prominent on the early lists.

Library organizations and publications are also dealing with graphic novels for all ages. In 2002, Young Adult Library Services Association (YALSA), the young adult branch of the American Library Association, sponsored a preconference on graphic novels for that summer's ALA Summer Conference. The best-attended preconference of that year, it featured talks by Neil Gaiman, Colleen Doran, Jeff Smith, and Art Spiegelman, as well as representatives from various comic book companies. A few years later, Doran, who spoke about manga, recounted the event:

> It was magnificent, the librarians were so positive. All of them were saying, "Graphic novels in libraries—this is the best thing that has happened in years. The graphic novels circulate better than any of our other books for young adults. We're so happy to have you here. It's the best preconference ever. You guys are great." We were all kind of walking around going, "No shit? Really? Us? Thanks!" It was fantastic. I couldn't believe how well it went. It was the most enthusiastic audience. I got up there and said, "You know, when I was a kid, my teachers would take my comic books and throw them in the trash. They were certain they would rot my brain. And here I am speaking before all of you today." The irony was obvious. (McCabe, 2004: 109)

Neil Gaiman has also discussed the importance of the conference:

> They knew that there was a demand for graphic novels and they came to us and said, "Tell us what we need to know. People want these and we don't know what they are." At that point, I remember standing out in the rain in Atlanta. Art Spiegelman took out a cigarette and I said, "Everything's changed. This is not the world we were in last week." And it really was suddenly the world in which we'd won. The battle to get comics taken seriously and to become part of the world had just been won in that moment. (Daniell, 2009)

YALSA also puts out "The Best Graphic Novels for Teens" lists, and a number of titles are actually more appropriate for adults than for younger teens. In addition, ALA has a grant for a lecture program called "Let's Talk About It: Jewish Literature—Identity and Imagination," and one theme of this program is "Modern Marvels: Jewish Adventures in the Graphic Novel" (see Chapter 8 for more on this program).

Besides the preconference, graphic novels have had a presence at the ALA conference for years, with a special "Graphic Novel Alley" in the exhibiter's hall and occasional programming on the topic. Other library conferences and related events, such as Book Expo America, have had some similar programs as well. Conversely, many comic book conventions have had programs on graphic novels in libraries or academic studies on the topic. These programs feature librarians, scholars, and often people in various areas of the comics industry, including writers and artists. The New York Comic Con even has a conference the day before it officially starts that is attended by librarians, creators, retailers, and publishers (see Chapter 6 for more on conventions).

Film Adaptations and Genre Crossovers

Does your library carry DVDs?

If so, does it have these movies: *Atonement, No Country for Old Men, LA Confidential,* and *The Cider House Rules*?

Does it have the books that they were based on?

Now, does your library have these movies on DVD: *Persepolis, Ghost World, From Hell, Road to Perdition*, and *A History of Violence*?

Do you have the graphic novels that they were based on?

Many films are based on comic books and graphic novels, and while some, such as many of the superhero genre, are based on several stories, others are based on a specific title. Many are adapted from adult graphic novels. Two of them—*Ghost World* and *A History of Violence*—were nominated for the Academy Award for best adapted screenplay (see Exhibit 1-1 for more adult graphic novels that have been turned into feature films). Of course comics in the superhero genre have been adapted into radio, film, and television programs for over 60 years, ranging from the *Superman* theatrical cartoon shorts in the early 1940s to 2010's *Iron Man 2* and *Jonah Hex*.

Exhibit 1-1. Film Versions of Adult Graphic Novels			
Film	Based On (X)	Starring	Notes
The Punisher (1989)	Loosely based on *The Punisher* comic book	Dolph Lundgren	New versions in 2004 and 2008
The Crow (1994)	*The Crow* (1989)	Brandon Lee	Several sequels and television series
Judge Dredd (1996)	Character and world introduced in 2000 AD #2 (1977)	Sylvester Stallone Max Von Sydow	Many changes to original story
Spawn (1997)	*Spawn* comic book (1992–), primarily the early issues	Michael Jai White John Leguizamo Martin Sheen	Also animated series on HBO
Blade (1998)	Marvel comics character	Wesley Snipes	Sequels and television series
From Hell (2001)	*From Hell* (1991–1996)	Johnny Depp Heather Graham	Directed by the Hughes Brothers
Ghost World (2001)	*Ghost World* trade (originally serialized in Eightball)	Thora Birch Scarlett Johansson Steve Buscemi	Academy Award nomination for best adapted screenplay
Road to Perdition (2002)	*Road to Perdition* (1998)	Tom Hanks Paul Newman	Academy Award for cinematography and nominated for five others
The League of Extraordinary Gentleman (2003)	*The League of Extraordinary Gentleman* (1999–2000)	Sean Connery Peta Wilson	Many changes to original story
Hellboy (2004)	Various *Hellboy* comic stories (1993–)	Ron Pearlman Selma Blair	Live action and animated sequels
			(Cont'd.)

Exhibit 1-1. Film Versions of Adult Graphic Novels *(Continued)*			
Film	Based On (X)	Starring	Notes
Constantine (2005)	Various *Hellblazer* stories (1988–)	Keanu Reeves Rachel Weisz Shia LaBeouf	Partly based on the story *Dangerous Habits*
Sin City (2005)	*Sin City* stories *That Yellow Bastard, The Hard Goodbye,* and *The Big Fat Kill*	Bruce Willis Mickey Rourke Clive Owen Jessica Alba Rosario Dawson	Partly directed by comic writer Frank Miller, with sequels planned
A History of Violence (2005)	*A History of Violence* (1997)	Viggo Mortenson Ed Harris William Hurt	Academy Award nomination for best adapted screenplay
V for Vendetta (2006)	*V for Vendetta* (1982–1988)	Hugo Weaving Natalie Portman John Hurt	Adapted by the Wachowski Brothers
30 Days of Night (2007)	*30 Days of Night* (2002)	Josh Hartnett	Other volumes may be adapted
300 (2007)	*300* (1998)	Gerard Butler	Director also adapted *Watchmen*
Persepolis (2007)	*Persepolis* graphic novels (2003–2005)	Voice of Catherine Deneuve	Jury Prize at Cannes Film Festival
Wanted (2008)	*Wanted* (2003–2004)	James McAvoy Angelina Jolie	Changes from a group of supervillains to a group of assassins
Watchmen (2009)	*Watchmen* (1986–1987)	Billy Crudup Jackie Earle Haley	Some minor changes
The Surrogates (2009)	*The Surrogates* (2005–2006)	Bruce Willis	Science fiction film
Whiteout (2009)	*Whiteout* (1999)	Kate Beckinsale	Adapts first book only
Jonah Hex (2010)	Various *Jonah Hex* stories (2005–)	Josh Brolin	Set in the Old West

As is often the case when a novel is adapted for the screen, readers show a greater interest in the original work. When the first trailer for the *Watchmen* feature film came out in 2008, sales of the original title skyrocketed. Despite being over 20 years old and the movie not coming out for another eight months, *Watchmen* found itself among the top ten titles on Amazon.com, leading DC Comics to produce an additional new printing of one million copies (Brady, 2008), with interest in the title continuing after the film came out.[3] Libraries with *Watchmen* in their collection also saw a greater demand for the title. New editions of graphic novels are usually put out to coincide with the theatrical release, and in cases where the films are not based on any one particular story (as is often the case with superhero films), new collections featuring both the heroes and the villains of these stories are often created.

As with films adapted from nongraphic literature, film versions of graphic novels include changes that make them different from the original works. For example, while the graphic novel version of *From Hell* kept Jack the Ripper as its central character, the makers of the film version wanted to keep his identity a secret and so turned the main focus onto Inspector Abberline (Johnny Depp), a supporting character in the original work. In *Constantine*, based on the comic book series *Hellblazer*, the title character was changed from a blond Liverpool-born Englishman to a black-haired American played by Keanu Reeves. Again, as with other film adaptations, the original writer may have little or no involvement in the writing of the film (though, in one interesting situation, Max Allan Collins wrote the novelization of *Road to Perdition*, adapting the script that David Self had himself adapted from Collins's 1998 graphic novel).

Film and television versions of comic books can also have an effect on the original work, most often with superhero titles. For example, the history of the relationship between Superman and his archenemy Lex Luthor has changed in recent years to become closer to that of the *Smallville* television show. In addition, characters and elements first introduced in a show or film may later become part of the comic book continuity, such as Renee Montoya, a police officer who first appeared in *Batman the Animated Series* and later became a regular character in the various Batman-related comics (and is currently the latest incarnation of the superhero The Question).

Similar to screenplays, some prose books for adults adapt comic book stories, use characters who have appeared in comic books, or have similar themes. Adapted works include novel versions of the limited series *Infinite Crisis* and *52* or storylines such as the Batman story *Knightfall*. Examples of comic book characters in novels include the novels based on the *30 Days of Night* titles and the *Queen and Country* stories as well as books featuring existing superheroes. Some of the superhero-themed novels include new takes on classic characters, such as Tom DeHaven's *It's Superman* (2005). Some novels are superhero themed with new twists, such as *Soon I Will Be Invincible* by Austin Grossman (2007), or are about comic book creators, most notably Michael Chabon's *The Amazing Adventures of Kavalier and Clay*.

Many nonfiction books deal with comics and graphic novels, including general histories, books on specific characters titles and creators, collections of essays, and even humorous works. Chapters 6 and 9 discuss more of the related fiction and non-fiction books, and some suggested titles can be found in Appendix B. As will be shown in Chapter 3, novels that adults read also are adapted into comic books, both directly and indirectly, with elements of the books being used for new stories. These include works by such authors as Stephen King, Laurell K. Hamilton, and Orson Scott Card.

Several graphic novel and comic book writers are also authors of prose novels, and many novelists have written comics. Historical examples include Patricia Highsmith,

Otto Binder, and Alfred Bester. Modern examples are listed in Exhibit 1-2. That writers of comic books also write novels is an additional reason to purchase graphic novels, especially in a public library. After all, if the library will purchase a prose novel by Neil Gaiman, Brad Meltzer, Eric Jerome Dickey, etc., why not also purchase a graphic novel by those same authors? In 2006, a "first" occurred when Brad Meltzer simultaneously had both the number one bestselling novel (*The Book of Fate*) and the number one bestselling comic book (*Justice League of America*, Vol. 2, #0), a comic book that included an excerpt from the novel (MacDonald, 2003). Among both "book" and comic readers, reaction to a writer going to another format can sometimes be harsh. When authors whose primary work has been in comics go on to write prose novels, some will attack them for trying to be a "real writer" (McCabe, 2004: 109), while some comic readers may think that bringing in a popular novelist is nothing more than a stunt to boost sales and that a more experienced comic writer would create a better story.

Many comics people are involved as writers, producers, directors, and even creators of films and television shows, and, again, the reverse is true. The creators of such shows as *Babylon 5* and *Buffy the Vampire Slayer* have also written the adventures of Spider-Man, X-Men, and other well-known characters. These and others are also listed in Exhibit 1-2.

Exhibit 1-2. Genre Crossover Writers		
The following list includes some of the people who write comic books as well as novels and/or film and television scripts.		
Creator	Comic Work Includes	Other Work Includes
Peter David	*Fallen Angel, The Incredible Hulk, Supergirl, X-Factor*	*Star Trek* novels (including his *New Frontier* series) and the *King Arthur* and *Sir Apropos* books
Neil Gaiman	*Sandman, Marvel 1602, Eternals*	*American Gods, Anansi Boys,* and *Smoke and Mirrors*
Paul Dini	*Detective Comics*	Writer on the Batman and Superman animated series and writer/story editor on *Lost*
J. Michael Straczynski	*Amazing Spider-Man, Fantastic Four*	Creator and head writer of *Babylon 5*
Brad Meltzer	*Identity Crisis, Justice League of America*	*New York Times* best-selling writer
Jeph Loeb	*Batman: The Long Halloween, Superman for All Seasons,* etc.	Writer on *Smallville, Lost,* and other shows
Joss Whedon	*Astounding X-Men, Runaways, Buffy the Vampire Slayer*	Creator of *Buffy the Vampire Slayer* and *Angel*

(Cont'd.)

Exhibit 1-2. Genre Crossover Writers *(Continued)*		
Creator	Comic Work Includes	Other Work Includes
Michael Chabon	*The Amazing Adventures of the Escapist*	Award-winning and best-selling writer
Orson Scott Card	*Ultimate Iron Man*	Award-winning writer of *The Tales of Alvin Maker* and other series
Eric Jerome Dickey	*Storm*	Best-selling author
Javier Grillo-Marxuach	*Middleman, Annihilation*	Creator/writer *Middleman* television show and writer on *Lost* and other shows
Allan Heinberg	*Young Avengers*	Writer on *Grey's Anatomy, The O.C.,* and other shows
Reginald Hudlin	*Black Panther*	Movie director and BET President of Entertainment
Jim Butcher	*Dresden Files*	*Dresden Files* and *Codex Alera* book series
Dwayne McDuffie	*Static, Firestorm, Fantastic Four*	Various animated series
Frank Miller	*300, Sin City*	Director of *The Spirit*
David Morrell	*Captain America: The Chosen*	*Rambo*
Tamora Pierce	*White Tiger*	Various fantasy novels
Greg Rucka	*Whiteout, Queen and Country, Gotham Central*	*Atticus Kodiak* series and other books
Kevin Smith	*Green Arrow, Spider-Man,* and *Black Cat*	Writer/Director of *Clerks, Chasing Amy* and other films
Brian K. Vaughan	*Y: The Last Man, Ex Machina*	Writer on *Lost*
Jodi Picoult	*Wonder Woman*	Various novels

Educational Uses

Libraries that offer educational programs, be they adult literacy or ESL classes, can make use of graphic novels. While most studies have examined the educational use of comics and graphic novels in regard to children, tweens, and teens, the same facts can apply to adults. Studies have shown that comics and graphic novels can lead to increased vocabulary. The combination of pictures and text common to these works can make understanding context much easier. In addition, for someone struggling to learn to read, these mixed-media pages are far less intimidating than full pages of text.

The same can be said for non-English speakers seeking to learn the language. Comics provide visual clues that "increase the amount of comprehensible input and [boost] reading comprehension" and reduce the anxiety and frustration some students feel because the text is in an unfamiliar language (Cary, 2004: 13). In addition, comic books and graphic novels will introduce recent immigrants to America to "non-standard" words and phrases that are often not found in "text" books. Comics will contain American slang, idioms, abbreviations, and even onomatopoeia that are different from their native language (such as a dog going "guau guau" in Spanish and "bow wow" in English). If the graphic novel is in a common setting, readers can gain some cultural knowledge about their new home (Chow, n.d.). Because some English language comics are available in Spanish (and occasionally in French or other languages), having editions in each language in your collection could also help. Additional information can be found in Cary's *Going Graphic* (2004).

Foreign language comics can also be used to teach English speakers other languages. For example, the books *Kana de Manga* and *Japanese the Manga Way* use comic art to teach the reader to read and write simple Japanese words and phrases. In his book, Cary (2004) mentions that when he was looking at comics in Mexico, the visuals "reduced the amount of text that he had to 'tackle' and provided comprehension clues that made learning Spanish vocabulary and structures easier." He also picked up "colloquialisms and pop culture knowledge" that he was immediately able to use in his travels. He found that "for the first time, second language reading was fun, manageable, and best of all, useful" (Cary, 2004: 3–4). The "fun factor" has been given as a reason that using comics—which many people find fun—helps in learning. In his book *A Celebration of Neurons: An Educator's Guide to the Human Brain*, author Robert Sylvester pointed out that emotion drives attention and attention drives learning. The more emotionally connected students feel to a piece of material, the more concepts and skills they are able to learn (Cary, 2004). In addition, foreign language comics have been shown to aid children of immigrants or immigrant children who grew up speaking English. It keeps reading in their "heritage" language fun and increases their competence in the language without any fear of misspeaking while in a public setting (Cho, Choi, and Krashen, 2005).

Graphic novels have even been used to teach language in college environments at least as far back as the 1970s, when Dr. Rufus K. Marsh of Indiana's University of Evansville used comics as a supplement to the reading and grammar texts. He first used French translations of American comic strips, such as *Peanuts*, followed by French comics with American and British themes, such as the Old West adventures of *Calamity Jane*, *Tintin en Amerique* (*Tintin in America*), and *Asterix chez les Bretons* (*Asterix in Britain*). Marsh used these works for lessons in vocabulary and expression, grammar and composition, and conversation, as well as for examining cultural content. He found these conveyed an "authenticity of French language and culture," and that the students "experience[d] the adaptation of French to a familiar popular medium" that "conform[ed] immediately to the liveliness of the language and . . . the distinctive character of French Culture." He also found that "the verification of these qualities" made the comics "a powerful additional tool of language instruction" (Marsh, 1983: 112).

Of course teaching foreign languages is not the only use of comics and graphic novels in schools today. Many schools now offer classes on the subject, often as a literature, art, or library science course, and they have been incorporated into other classes and programs as well. Some academic conferences have graphic novel themes, such as the yearly program at the University of Florida, and Comic-Con International and other conventions have had "comic scholarship" program tracks. A number of books on the subject have also been written by college professors, and university-based publishers, such as the University Press of Mississippi, have put out notable books. Chapter 9 presents more on the use of graphic novels in academics.

A final thought on why libraries should carry graphic novels comes from Scott McCloud, the author of *Understanding Comics* and other works, who said that "the benefits of libraries collecting comics are the same benefits as reading comics." He noted:

> Comics are a valid medium and can hold their own against the great works of traditional literature and can provide the same enrichments as prose and poetry. Certainly if libraries include video and sound collections comics should also be included. Comics are probably closer to the mission statements of libraries than either of the previous two. And libraries can be in the forefront of educating the public that there's more to comics than guys in tights beating each other up. (cited in Weiner, 1996: 40)

Notes

1. Alison Bechdel, creator of *Fun Home*, did a four-page comic story about reading titled "Life Drawing" for the same issue (Bechdel, 2008).

2. One of the first graphic novels on the *New York Times* bestseller lists was a 1979 adaptation of the movie *Alien*.

3. Regularly one of the best-selling trades, *Watchmen* sold 100,000 copies in 2007.

References

Andleman, Bob. 2005. *Will Eisner: A Spirited Life*. Milwaukee, WI: M Press.

Bechdel, Alison. 2008. "Life Drawing." *Entertainment Weekly* (June 27): 110–113.

Brady, Matt. 2008. "Watchmen: One Million Copies in 2008." Available: www.newsarama.com/comics/080814-WatchmentOneMillion.html (accessed August 22, 2009).

Cary, Stephen. 2004. *Going Graphic: Comics at Work in the Multilingual Classroom*. Portsmouth, NH: Heinemann.

Cho, Grace, Hong Choi, and Stephen Krashen. 2005. "Hooked on Comic Book Reading: How Comic Books Made an Impossible Situation Less Difficult." *Knowledge Quest* 33, no. 4 (March/April): 35–38.

Chow, Natsuko K. n.d. "Comics: A Useful Tool for English as a Second Language (ESL)." Diamond Bookshelf. Available: http://bookshelf.diamondcomics.com/public/default.asp?t=1&m=1&c=20&s=182&ai=37714&ssd=. (accessed August 22, 2009).

Daniell, Mark. 2009. "T.O. Surprises Don't Stop for Neil Gaiman." Available: http:/ jam .canoe.ca/Books/2009/06/22/9890516-ca.html (accessed August 22, 2009).

MacDonald, Heidi. 2003. "Bookstore Revolution: Graphic Novels Get Their Own Category." *Pulse News*, January 20. Retrieved from (no longer available): www.comicon.com/ubb/ ultimatebb.php/ubb/forum/f/36.html.

Marsh, Rufus K. 1983. "Teaching French with the Comics." In James L. Thomas (Ed.), *Cartoons and Comics in the Classroom*. Littleton, CO: Libraries Unlimited.

McCabe, Joseph (Ed). 2004. *Hanging Out with the Dream King: Conversations with Neil Gaiman and His Collaborators*. Seattle: Fantagraphics Books.

The Public Librarian's Guide to Graphic Novels. 2003. Lexington, KY: Book Wholesalers.

Reese, Jennifer, et al. 2008. "The New Classics: Books." *Entertainment Weekly* (June 27): 96–107.

Weiner, Stephen. 1996. *100 Graphic Novels for Public Libraries*. Northampton, MA: Kitchen Sink Press.

Chapter 2

What Are Comic Books and Graphic Novels?

Now that you know why you need to have graphic novels at your library, you may still be wondering, *What exactly is a graphic novel?* The answer to that question (as well as to what is not a graphic novel) is the focus of this chapter. The answers to these questions have been a source of debate among readers, librarians, and scholars. Definitions range from the scholarly to the slightly humorous, including those by Alan Moore (*Watchmen, From Hell*, etc.), who called it a "big expensive comic book," and Art Spiegelman (*Maus*), who called it "a comic book that needs a bookmark" (Rollins, 2006: 8).

For this book, the definition of a graphic novel will be the one given by author and educator Gail de Vos (2005) "bound books, fiction and nonfiction, which are created in the comic book format and are issued an ISBN," though a few titles discussed in the book and listed in Appendix A do not fully meet this criterion. Also for this book, the term "graphic novel" will be used as an "umbrella term" that covers original graphic novels, trade editions (which collect and reprint stories from comic books), and manga and related works (see Chapter 4).

Some people do not like the term "graphic novel." Alan Moore has called it just a marketing term (Kavanagh, 2000) used to get away from the "stigma" of the term "comic book." In his "Graphic Novel Manifesto," posted on the *Comic Journal*'s message board in 2004, writer/artist Eddie Campbell (*From Hell, Fate of the Artist*, etc.) raised the following points:

- "Graphic novel is a disagreeable term, but we will use it anyway on the understanding that 'graphic' has nothing to do with graphics and that 'novel' does not mean anything to do with 'novel.'"
- "Graphic novel signifies a movement rather than a form."
- "The goal of the graphic novelist is to take the form of the comic book, which has become an embarrassment, and raise it to a more ambitious and meaningful level."

The term itself was first used by Richard Kyle in 1964 for an article for the second issue of *Capa-alpha*, a comics-themed amateur press association publication, and it first appeared on books in the 1970s. Others have used alternate terms for their books, such as Daniel Clowes whose *Ice Haven* (2001) is a "comic-strip novel," Seth who called his *It's a Good Life, If You Don't Weaken* (2003) a "picture novella," and Alison Bechdel who subtitled her award-winning *Fun Home* (2006) "a family tragicomic." Besides terminology, disagreements also arise over what constitutes a graphic novel. Some, for example, would like the term used only for original works and not for collections of comic books, even though many sources, such as this book, do so (e.g., most references to the source of the 2009 film version of *Watchmen* call it a graphic novel when it originated as a 12-issue comic book limited series). For this book, with a few exceptions, collections of comic strips will not be considered graphic novels, even if they are published by comic book companies such as Fantagraphics (*The Complete Peanuts*), Drawn & Quarterly (*Gasoline Alley*), or IDW (*Dick Tracy*). Books that have a few pages of comic art interspersed throughout, such as Jodi Picoult's *The Tenth Circle*, will not be considered graphic novels, unless they are the "hybrid" type of graphic novel, a more recent version that is part text and part graphic novel, with the "graphic" parts actually continuing the story instead of simply illustrating the text.

De Vos's (2005) definition mentions the "comic book format," but what does that mean? Will Eisner in his *Graphic Storytelling & Visual Narrative* (1996: 6) defines comics as "the printed arrangement of art and balloons in sequence, particularly in comic books." This "arrangement" allows for the graphic narrative—"a generic description of any narration that employs image to transmit an idea." The work may be in black and white or in color, have dialogue or be silent, and have artwork that is realistic or exaggerated. Also, in some works, the words for narration or dialogue appear outside of the panel instead of inside a balloon or text box.

Comics Creators

A "graphic story," being composed of both text and art, requires people to fill various roles: writer, penciler, and inker, for example, and, when needed, a letterer and colorist. In a number of the works discussed in this book, one individual handles both the writing and the artwork. In other cases, a writer-artist team is used, with one person handling all of the artistic needs. In the reverse case, multiple writers or artists may work together on a single work. For the following sections, it should be assumed that each role is performed by a different person.

Writers, Pencilers, and Inkers

The writer is, obviously, the individual who writes the script. The penciler is the "first part of the art team" (O'Neil, 2001: 22) who draws the story in (of course) pencil. The inker adds India ink to the penciled pictures to make them easier to print. The inker's work adds texture, shading, shadows, and the illusion of depth to the penciled drawings (O'Neil, 2001). This work is important because inking can improve or ruin the penciler's work.

When they are different people, the writer and the penciler share the storytelling chores. The working relationship between them can vary from work to work. The main options are creating the comic/graphic novel using a "full script" style or by using a "plot first" script.

With full script, the writer creates a detailed script in which the contents of every panel on every page are described in full. This method helps to put the writer in the "driver's seat." The writer controls the story and can make any desired changes prior to submitting it to the artist (Chinn, 2004). When using this approach the writer must have the ability to convey properly through words the desired visuals, since a story has passed to the artist and been drawn on the pages, it cannot be changed. Sometimes to avoid this, the writer will create a "layout," or "drawn" script, that provides rough preliminary sketches to guide the artist (Chinn, 2004).

Exhibit 2-1. Comic Book Terms

border: The outline of the panel. The border does not necessarily need to be a rectangular shape.

caption: A sentence or sentence fragment that appears in a panel but not in a balloon. Captions are usually in a box at the top or bottom of a panel and can be used for several reasons. The first is to establish time or place (e.g., New York, one hour later). The second is to convey dialogue for "off-camera" people, usually when the panel is set in a different location than the previous one. For example, the dialogue in the first panel is "After all, what could go…" and panel two has a box with "wrong?" while the panel shows exactly what went wrong. Panels are also used to show the thoughts of the title's main character, sometimes done in a "voice-over narration" style.

panel: The box that contains a given scene. A comic book page can have any number of panels, though six to nine tend to be the most common.

speech balloon: Also called "word balloon" or just "balloon." Used to convey speech. A part called the "pointer" or "tail" indicates the speaker. The shape of the balloon can be used to indicate the way something sounds. For example, a "burst" or "electric balloon" is a balloon with jagged edges that can indicate either volume or stress or that the source is from a broadcast or over the telephone. If the balloon is drawn with dashes it indicates the speaker is whispering. The size of the letters can also indicate how loud or low the speaker is talking. Other techniques include showing the balloon looking "icy" to show the person is speaking in a cold tone of voice and an oddly shaped balloon showing the speaker "under the influence." Some artists choose instead to indicate the speaker with a dash going from the words to the speaker. An accent can also be indicated in the dialogue provided in the balloon. In "wordless comics," a question mark may be used to indicate that a character is asking a question, without actually having dialogue. An exclamation point or symbols such as "$" may also be used to further convey what the character is "saying."

splash page: Usually the first page of a comic book, containing one or two images that incorporate the title, logo (if needed), credits, etc. It does not need to be the first page. A splash page is slightly different from a full page show, which is simply a picture that takes up the entire page.

thought balloons: Similar to a speech balloon but "scalloped" with a series of circles acting as the tail to show what a character is thinking. An early version was a normal balloon with the "thoughts" in parenthesis.

tier: Row of panels on the page.

Source: Based on information from *Comics & Sequential Art* by Will Eisner (1989) and *The DC Comics Guide to Writing Comics* by Dennis O'Neil (2001).

In the plot first method, the writer gives the penciler a script containing the basic content of the issue and describing the plot, action, and any other elements that the writer wants to ensure are in the finished work. The penciler draws the issue and sends the finished work back to the writer. This method, also called the "Marvel Method" after Stan Lee's approach to writing many of the Marvel Comics titles in the early 1960s, gives the artist a greater say in the storytelling process. On the other hand, some artists feel that this method forces them to do the writer's job (Gertler and Leiber, 2004). Another possible flaw in this method is that the artist's work may not fit the writer's vision, moving the emphasis away from what the writer intended or dramatically altering the pace (Chinn, 2004). The writer may be able to remedy this with dialogue or captions or, in some circumstances, may be inspired by the art to further develop the story (O'Neil, 2001), but this can also adversely affect the story. When Lee used this method, he had artists such as Jack Kirby and Steve Ditko with a talent for "graphic storytelling," but this may not always be the case and can result in a conflict between the writer and artist.

Modern technology has made it easier for writers and artists to work together. These days the writer, the penciler, and the inker can live on separate continents and yet be in closer contact than their predecessors who may have lived only a few hours apart. There are creative teams who have closely collaborated on hundreds of pages together without ever meeting in person until long after the work is completed. Whether the Internet, which allows the instant sending of script changes or early previews of artwork, has helped to prevent conflicts among the creative team remains to be seen.

The Letterer

After the artwork is complete and, if necessary, the writer has revised the dialogue, the pages are turned over to the letterer. The job of the letterer is to draw all word/thought balloons and captions (see Exhibit 2-1) and to write the scripted words into them in the appropriate style. The letterer will also add words/letters to any books, signs, newspapers, and so forth that may appear in the panel. Important tasks for the letterer are to place the balloons in a way that does not block any meaningful artwork and also so that the reader will know the proper "reading order" of the dialogue (one reason for the delayed appearance of translated manga to America—more on this in Chapter 4). In recent years, lettering has been done with the use of a computer.

The Colorist

When needed, the final artistic role is that of the colorist. Like the letterer, much of the colorist's work is currently done with the help of a computer. This allows for much more color options than in the old days of the traditional "four-color printing" that used the primary colors, or cyan, magenta, yellow, and black in the printing.

While all of the individuals involved in creating a comic or graphic novel currently are named in the credits or on the cover/title page, this was not always the case. For several decades, either no credit was given or perhaps just to the writer and/or the artist. Comic scholars, such as the contributors to the Grand Comic-Book Database (www.comics.org; see Chapter 9), must use old records and sometimes guesswork to determine the proper credits and reprints of older material, such as DC's Archive Editions, and include statements such as the following:

> Until the 1970s it was not common practice in the comic-book industry to credit all stories. In the preparation of this Archive, we have used our best efforts to review any surviving records and consult any available databases and knowledgeable parties. We regret the innate limitations of this process and any missing or mis-assigned attributions that may occur. (*DC Comics Rarities Archive*, 2004: 6)

Original Graphic Novels

As mentioned, this book uses the term "graphic novel" as an umbrella term for original graphic novels, trade editions, and manga. Manga, along with other foreign works, will be covered in Chapter 4, and both comic books and trades will be discussed later in this chapter. First, let's take a look at original graphic novels (OGNs).

OGNs can be referred to as such since, for the most part, the material in them has not appeared anywhere else, especially not in any comic book form. OGNs can be one full story or contain several short stories. They come out in both hardcover and softcover, in color or black and white, and in various shapes, sizes, and page lengths. Some OGNs are relatively short while others are longer than many "text" novels. For example, Dash Shaw's *The Bottomless Belly Button* is 720 pages long.

Much as the proper definition of the term "graphic novel" is debated so, too, is the origin of the first one. Prototypes include several wordless books, such as 1918's *25 Images de la Passion d'un Homme* (*The Passion of Man*) by Frans Masereel and Lynd Ward's *Wild Pilgrimage* (1932), which were both produced by woodcuts instead of drawings, and Milt Gross's illustrated *He Done Her Wrong* (1930). Perhaps the first example of a graphic novel as we know it today is 1950's *It Rhymes with Lust*. Published by St. John Publishing Company, this digest-sized book was billed as "An Original Picture Novel" and was most definitely created for adult readers.

Arnold Drake, who along with Leslie Waller wrote *It Rhymes with Lust* under the pseudonym Drake Waller, said this about the book's creation:

> The attitude about comics then was, because you started reading them as a child, they were a thing you were supposed to outgrow. The attitude was, for an adult to read a comic book was a mark of ignorance. A lot of people thought that way, including a lot of people within the craft. But [Waller] and I knew we were geniuses, so we thought we would simply change the world. Our goal was to create a kind of Warner Brothers low-budget film-noir action-romance on paper in words and pictures. We told St. John that, because we wanted this to be a link between a comic book and *book* book, it should be in black and white, so the reading public would recognize it as being closer to "*lit*-er-a-*ture*." (Hadju, 2008: 165–167)

It Rhymes with Lust cost 25 cents, the same as many "pulp" novels at the time, but did not do well. However, it did contain panels, word balloons, and captions and was not previously in comic book form—all criteria for an OGN. One other item of note is that the penciler on the work was Matt Baker, who was one of the first, if not the first, African Americans to work in mainstream comics. *He Done Her Wrong* was reprinted by Fantagraphics in 2006, and *It Rhymes with Lust* was reprinted by Dark Horse in 2007. The two woodcut novels are included in 2007's *Graphic Witness: Four Wordless Graphic Novels* (see Appendix A).

Several notable OGNs appeared in the 1970s. *Blackmark* (1971), a sword and sorcery/science fiction paperback by Archie Goodwin and Gil Kane, was called a "paperback comics novel" when given an award by the Academy of Comic Arts. Three 1975 books actually had the words "graphic novel" either on the cover or on an interior page: *Bloodstar* by Richard Corben, *Chandler: Red Tide* by Jim Sterenko, and *Beyond Time and Again* by George Metzger, which was actually a trade collection (Arnold, 2003). In 1978, Will Eisner's *A Contract with God* was published. While the words "graphic novel" did not appear on the original hardcover version, which did not have a dust jacket, they were on the paperback version, and the term eventually moved into common usage. While *Contract* was not the first graphic novel, it has at times (incorrectly) been identified as such and is the best known of the early graphic novels.

Actually composed of four "graphic short stories," *A Contract with God* being the first one, this was Eisner's first new comic work in years and the first of the 18 OGNs that he would write. After finishing the rough draft of the work, Eisner looked for a publisher. Believing that his potential audience would be inclined to go to bookstores instead of comic stores, he sought out a noncomics publisher, in this case Bantam Books. He called Bantam's president Oscar Dystel, who wanted to know what Eisner had produced. Thinking that Dystel would hang up if he said it was a comic, he called it a "graphic novel." Interested by that phrase, Dystel asked Eisner to stop by, but when he looked at what Eisner had brought, he told him, "Call it what you will, but this is still a comic book. I'm surprised at you, Will. Go find a small publisher." Eisner then turned to Baronet Books, who published it (Andleman, 2005: 290–291). Later editions would be put out by comics publishers Kitchen Sink and DC, and it is currently being published by W.W. Norton.

Several other original works began to appear, and by the early 1980s the larger companies such as DC and Marvel were putting out original works in both hardcover and softcover. These works featured both new and established characters. Notable works by Marvel, which often published them in a 10" × 7" paperback format, included their first one, *The Death of Captain Marvel* (1982) and *God Loves, Man Kills* (1982), which was one of the sources for the second *X-Men* movie and has been reissued on several occasions. Other companies followed with OGNs and today they are being published by both comic book and mainstream publishers.

Comic Books and Trade Editions

As mentioned earlier, trade editions collect and reprint stories that have already appeared in comic books. American comic books are also known as "comics," "comic magazines," and, more recently, both "floppies" and "pamphlets," to differentiate them from the booklike graphic novels.

The majority of comic books today are $6\frac{5}{8}''$ × $10\frac{1}{8}''$, between 24 and 64 pages, and cost between $2.00 and $7.00 dollars, with $2.99 to $3.99 being the most common range. The type of paper varies from book to book, and they generally have a stapled binding called "saddle stitch." The inside of a comic book may have one story or multiple stories, or even a full issue of one-page "pinups." Besides the stories, the average issue may also contain advertisements, text pages, and/or letters' pages. Advertisements include promotions for other comics, movies, and various products, ranging from candy to automobiles. Text pages are currently used primarily for "what's going on at our company" information, including promotions for upcoming works, but may also include works of fiction, something that dates back to the 1930s. Letters' pages, which print reader comments about previous issues, have also been around for years, with some future comics professionals starting off as "letterhacks." Letters' pages also allowed fans around the country to get in touch with one another, which aided in the creation of organized comics fandom. In these days of message boards, some titles no longer have letters' pages, but others have embraced both formats.

Both text and letters' pages have a common origin. For decades, comic books were forced to include at least two pages of text to qualify for the same second-class bulk mailing rate that was given to other periodicals like magazines and newspapers. The publishers first used text stories and then later letters from readers, which was better for the publishers since, of course, they didn't have to pay anyone to write them (though some were made up by the editor). The second-class rate was replaced in 1996 by a "periodical rate," which comics qualify for, but the old standards still remain (Cronin, 2006).

The whole thing is fronted by the cover, which has the name of the comic (but generally not of the story), often with a distinct logo, the publisher's name, the cost, and often the month and year it came out. It has long been the practice for the date to be several months ahead of the actual date, and any references to an issue's date in this book will reflect that. The interior art team will often also take care of the cover, but this is not always the case. Sometimes the artists may be wonderful storytellers but might not be the best at creating eye-catching covers. Comic books are occasionally published with different covers known as "variants." These are often done by a different artist, or even with a "photo cover." Sometimes the quantity of issues produced for a book with cover "A" is the same as the number of issues for cover "B," but other times cover "B" (or "C," "D," etc.) is on a smaller percentage of comics, which makes them more appealing to collectors. On some occasions the variant is used to indicate a new printing of the issue. Many "iconic" covers over the years are often paid homage to or parodied, including the cover from *Action Comics* #1 (1938, first Superman),

Detective Comics #27 (1939, first Batman), *Fantastic Four* #1 (1961), and *Crisis on Infinite Earths* #7 (1985, death of Supergirl). The various *Marvel Zombies* (2006–) limited series have included "zombified" versions of classic Marvel comics, drawn by Arthur Suydam, and various Marvel titles in recent years have had "zombie" variant covers.

Some comic books have different formats and layouts than the standard sort or have different paper or stronger covers. While most are still in the "floppy" format, a few are occasionally produced in "bookshelf" format. Also called "prestige format," comics published in bookshelf format are printed with glossy paper, use the more durable "cardstock" covers, and have spines similar to books. Therefore, unlike regular comic books, they can stand up on a bookshelf. One-shots (discussed later in this section) produced in a bookshelf format can be, and have been, purchased for libraries and shelved with other books. Limited series in this format (though none are produced this way) could also be purchased by libraries, but if any one issue is lost, damaged, or stolen, the story would remain incomplete. Technically speaking, some of the "one-shot" comics in bookshelf format can be considered to be OGNs.

Kinds of Comics

Series

A comic book series can best be described as an open-ended run of a comic book title. Issues in a series generally come out monthly, bimonthly, or quarterly, or on some other regular schedule. Some also come out biweekly or weekly, though this is usually for a short period. Comics that are self-published or from a smaller company may come out on a more irregular basis, and certain series may also have large time spans between issues due to the work schedule of the creators. As with most television series, a comic book series generally has no planned last issue. Just as a series with high ratings can go on for years, a comic series that is selling well can last for a long time. On the other hand, just as a low-rated show can be cancelled in a matter of weeks, a poor selling comic book series can end after only a few issues.

Currently, the oldest comic book series still being published is the Batman title *Detective Comics* that began in 1937, though Batman was not introduced until 1939. However, due to a more frequent publishing schedule and a 42-issue weekly run in the 1980s, the Superman book *Action Comics*, which debuted in 1938, has put out about 21 more issues, though both are past issue 850. Two related comics, *Superman* and *Batman*, have also been continuously published since 1939 and 1940, respectively. It will still be several decades, however, before any of them pass the issue count of the Dell Comics anthology series *Four Color Comics*. Even though the series ran for only 23 years (1939–1962), multiple issues were put out each month, and while the exact number of issues is unknown, best estimates put it at over 1,300 issues. Some foreign series have also passed 1,000 issues. Australia's *Phantom* comics, which comes out twice a month and mainly reprints the comic strip about the jungle hero, has been running since 1948 and has around 1,400 issues as of 2009. The British weekly science fiction comic *2000 AD* (1977–2000) had over 1,600 issues (called "progs"). Foreign comics and graphic novels are discussed in Chapter 4.

Poor sales are not the only reason to end a series. Sometimes a publisher wishes to restart a title at issue #1. Marvel Comics has restarted Captain America four times since 1996, and as seen in Exhibit 2-2, DC has done various things with *The Legion of Super-Heroes*. Just as some television shows begin with the creators preplanning on a particular number of seasons or episodes (such as *Babylon 5*'s "five-year arc"), some comic book series creators have a basic idea of when they want to end the book. The best example would be *Cerebus* (1977–2004), whose creator had said that he wanted to end at 300, over 20 years before that issue came out. A smaller example is *Ex Machina* (2004–2010), which began the year *Cerebus* ended and whose creator has worked out a 50-issue storyline. Additional "negative" items that lead to the end of a series are, in the case of licensed or creator-owned materials, that the publisher loses the license or the creator decides to go elsewhere. In the worst-case scenario, the series ends because the publisher goes out of business.

Exhibit 2-2. Unusual Aspects of Comic Books

A number of libraries, especially those in universities, collect comic books (explored further in Chapter 9). Some libraries catalog them as periodicals or series and others catalog them in different ways. However, comic books have some unusual aspects that collectors should understand.

Renamed and Restarted Series
Over the years many series have changed their titles. Sometimes this is due to a total change in the theme of the comic book. For example, *All-Star Comics*, a 1940s' superhero title, changed to *All-Star Western*. Another book from that era started as *Moon Girl and the Prince* and became *Moon Girl* with the second issue, then *Moon Girl Fights Crime* with #7, and then *A Moon a Girl…Romance* with #9 and *Weird Fantasy* with #13. After #17, the numbering restarted at #6 and then merged with *Weird Science* to become *Weird Science-Fantasy*, which went to the final title of *Incredible Science Fiction*.

Sometimes a book will change its title because a second book with the same characters is starting up. In 1987, *Superman* became *The Adventures of Superman* so that a new *Superman* could begin. However, in 2006, the second *Superman* book ended and the original book reclaimed its title. So would you move all of the books from the first series to the "A's" and then back to the "S's" when the title changed back? While it didn't have a new book created when it changed its name, Marvel's *Journey into Mystery* spent 30 years as *Thor* before switching back.

In some cases, two series from the same publisher will have the same title. This may happen for a number or reasons: the previous title was canceled years ago and now the publisher is bringing it back, the publisher wants to retain a copyright and the new book is only tangentially connected to the earlier one, or, as mentioned, the publisher is starting the book over at issue #1. This last approach may be taken as a way to boost sales since collectors may prize a first issue over an issue #158 for example, or as a way to give the title a "fresh start," often with a new creative team or direction.

One of the odder cases of both renaming and restarting is DC Comics' futuristic superteam, the Legion of Super-Heroes. After years of appearing in various titles, they began to appear in *Superboy*, which had begun in 1949. The Boy of Steel had long been a member, traveling 1,000 years into the future to join them, and they soon became the main feature of the original title, which then became *Superboy and the Legion of Super-Heroes*. When Superboy left the team to

(Cont'd.)

Exhibit 2-2. Unusual Aspects of Comic Books *(Continued)*

end up in a new book, the comic became simply *The Legion of Super-Heroes* (LSH). This was actually the second LSH book, the first being an early 1970s reprint title. In 1984, DC created a third, simultaneous volume of LSH and volume 2 became *Tales of the Legion of Super-Heroes*, ending in 1987. Volume 3 ended in 1989 to be quickly replaced by volume 4, which ran until 2000. This was replaced by series called *Legion* and several limited series, until 2005 when volume 5 began, which, during the middle of the run, changed to *Supergirl and the Legion of Super-Heroes* before going back to the original title (and ending in 2009). So we have five Legions, two of which changed the title at least once, plus two additional *Superboy* series, one of which changed its name as well. We also have the three volumes of LSH annuals, related limited series, specials, one-shots, five books called *Supergirl*, and a related title called *L.E.G.I.O.N* that ran from 1989–1994 and would change its title every year to reflect the new date.

Confused about cataloging? Easy to understand—with so many changes and crossovers, organizing your collection can seem a Herculean task. See Chapter 9 for some options to assist in this effort.

Unusual Numbering

While title changing can cause confusion, so can some of the more unusual aspects of comic book numbering. While most are #1, #2, #3, etc., that is not always the case.

First are the "zero" issues. Some new ongoing titles will include an issue zero to act as a prequel to the series, sometimes after a few issues have already come out and other times as "pre-first" first issues. But in 1994, DC Comics had "Zero Month" to tie in with the *Zero Hour* limited series in which nearly every title that month was issue zero. Not to be outdone, in 1997 Marvel Comics had a "Flashback Month" in which nearly every title was numbered "–1" with a story that took place prior to issue #1. At least with an issue #0 or #–1, the titles can be easily placed at the beginning, but in 1998 DC had its "One Million" month to cross over with the *DC One Million* limited series. Most DC titles that month listed the issue number as "1,000,000." To complicate things further, several DC titles had that issue as their last. While these titles were short lived, technically they can say that they ended with issue #1,000,000.

An interesting combination of restarting and unusual numbering began in the mid-1990s when Marvel Comics restarted several of its titles. Beginning in 2003, however, Marvel realized that, had they not restarted, several of their titles would be reaching the milestone issue of 500. So starting with *Fantastic Four*, they added the number of issues from the original series, the 1996 restart, and the 1998 restart, and once the total reached 500 they went back to the original numbering system. This means that in 2003 the issues went #68, #69, #70, #500, #501, etc. Other books soon followed this pattern.

Besides other odd forms of numbering, including an issue number "X" or a series whose first issue had "alpha" and "omega" versions, there is also the unusual circumstance of numbering that goes backward, including *Zero Hour* (#4 to #0), *Countdown* (#51 to #1), and *Marvel: The Lost Generation* (12–1), which at least had the excuse of a story that was told chronologically backward as well.

Limited Series

A limited series is the equivalent to a television miniseries. It is known from the beginning how many issues there will be, with the covers often proclaiming something along the lines of "issue X of Y." Limited series have the same publication schedule possibilities as ongoing series. They are also known as "mini-" or "maxi-" series, depending on the number of issues, though the number of issues in which a "mini" becomes a "maxi" is unclear. While there is technically no highest number, most limited series do not exceed 12 issues (a number considered a maxiseries). The first original (nonreprint) work to be a considered a limited series is 1979's *World of Krypton*, a sort of *Roots* meets Superman. The 1982 *Marvel Superheroes Contest of Champions*—various heroes competed with one another—was the first title actually called a limited series. Also in that year *Camelot 3000*, which put Arthurian characters into the far future, became the first maxiseries.

On a few occasions, a limited series will continue being published as a regular series, such as Marvel's *Transformers*, which started in 1984 as a limited series and ended seven years later with the words "#80 in a 4-issue limited series" printed across the cover. Some limited series will add or subtract a planned issue due to various reasons, and in very rare occasions, such as *Sonic Disrupters* (1987–1988), the title is cancelled before the story ends. Some debate whether a series with a planned ending, such as *Ex Machina*, could technically be counted as a limited series. The lines get even more blurred with three DC titles—*52* (2006–2007), *Countdown* (2007–2008), and *Trinity* (2008–2009)—that each had 52 weekly issues.

Limited series may feature established characters, including those who appear in other titles, or they may feature new characters. They may be set in the same "universe" as other titles, or they may be in a world of their own. It might even act as a "pilot" for an ongoing series. A limited series may be one complete story, several different stories, or even an anthology. Some limited series may have sequels, and in other cases, instead of an ongoing series, there will just be a large number of limited series with the same characters or idea. The *30 Days of Night* titles are an example of this. In almost every case, by the time the last issue comes out, at least one complete story has been told, with a beginning, ending, and plot resolution.

In the world of superhero comics, mainly those of DC and Marvel, there is the "event" limited series in which the storyline affects stories in other comic books. Beginning in the 1980s with titles like *Marvel Superheroes Secret Wars* and *Crisis on Infinite Earths* and continuing to today with *Secret Invasion* and *Final Crisis* and other recent works, the stories that begin in the "prime" title can continue or be referenced in various ongoing series. They might even lead to additional, simultaneous, limited series and other related works. Chapter 6 discusses how "events" can affect your purchasing decisions.

Annuals and Specials

As the word implies, annuals are comic books that come out on an annual basis. They tend to be at least twice as long as an issue of a series and are almost always tied into an existing series (e.g., *Batman Annual*, *X-Men Annual*, etc.). They have been around since the 1940s, and, like series and limited series titles, they can contain more than one story. Sometimes the events in an annual may directly relate to the events in the series, and there even have been "event" storylines that continue between annuals. The term "special" can be applied to a number of kinds of comics. The most obvious have the word "special" in the title. Sometimes they are similar in size to an annual, but unlike annuals, they come out on a more irregular basis. Other times they have the same page count as the regular series and limited series comics. Many specials have more than one issue, but not all. However, a one-issue special is not necessarily the same as a one-shot, the topic of the next section.

One-Shots

A one-shot is a comic book, usually but not always, 32 pages in length, with only one planned issue of the title. On some occasions, several one-shots with a similar theme will come out over several weeks, such as Marvel's "What If?" one-shots. DC Comics has published stories told in a series of one-shots, with a two-issue limited series acting as bookends.

Reprints

Reprints are comics that reprint older comic book stories. Sometimes an issue of an ongoing series will contain a reprinted story in addition to or in place of a new one. Reprints have also been published as one-shots and limited series, and there have even been long-running ongoing series in which older material is reprinted, including the Spider-Man title *Marvel Tales* (1966–1992). Reprints also can clean up mistakes, such as fixing the story in *Amazing Spider-Man* #3 (1963) in which Dr. Octopus calls Spider-Man "Superman." All subsequent reprints of this issue include Spider-Man being called by his proper name. Another form of reprints, one that you will be getting for your library, is covered in the next section.

Trade Editions

Trade editions, also called trade paperbacks (TPBs) when they are in softcover (which the majority of them are), graphic albums (a European term), or collected editions, are comic book stories that have been collected into book form. They are the comics equivalent of a collection of a serialized novel, a collection of short stories, or a television show that has been collected on DVD. Like books, trade editions have ISBN numbers and a spine and come in a variety of sizes. They can be under 100 pages long or over 1,000. In some cases, the pages of the trade are larger or smaller than they were in the original comic book. This is especially true with the digest-size TPBs, which are growing in popularity. Despite the shrinking of the images, these digests are helpful for libraries that purchase graphic novels since they are much cheaper than the full-sized books. DC has also put out various high-priced Absolute Editions with enlarged artwork.

Besides enlarging or shrinking the pages, additional changes between the original comic book and the trade edition include improvements and even the occasional change to artwork. In some other cases, most notably Marvel's Essential line and DC's Showcase books, stories that were originally in color are reprinted in black and white, often to save on printing costs. As mentioned earlier, these are not graphic novels in the truest sense, since graphic novels are mainly original works and trade editions are reprints. However, for simplicity's sake, they will be referred to as trades, trade editions (TEs), or TPBs when discussing them in the specific, but as graphic novels when discussing them in general terms.

Although once rare, trades have proliferated, with hundreds of titles coming out each year. It is almost expected that a comic book will be reprinted in book form, sometimes less than two months after the "newest" story in the collection was published. This has led to some debate among comic readers over whether they should spend money on the individual comic book issues or just "wait for the trade." This is the equivalent to not watching a television series and instead waiting until the DVD collection comes out. Just as the DVD leaves out the commercials and any onscreen logos or pop-ups, the collected trade has no ads or text or letters' pages, and just like the DVD compiles an entire season that can be watched in a few days instead of several months, the trade condenses months worth of reading stories into just a few hours. An advantage is that if the story turns out bad, you will not have wasted months of time and money getting to the ending. An additional reason that some prefer to wait for the trade is that, because it is in book form, it will easily fit on a bookshelf, unlike a comic book, which needs a different form of storage. And of course there's a strong chance that instead of having to purchase it, the trade will be available for free at the library.

The downside of waiting for a trade is that if sales of the comic book are poor, then there might not even be a trade edition. From the opposite view, some people will not purchase the trade if they've already purchased the original comic book issues. To counter this, trades will sometimes include extras to entice the buyer, much as special edition DVDs are made to entice those who have already purchased a copy of a particular film. Trade extras (see Exhibit 2-3) include scripts, additional artwork, covers (including all of the variants), essays and "behind the scenes" information, extra stories (such as a related one-shot), and even deleted scenes.

The practice of collecting comic stories into books had long been popular in Europe. The earliest American collections came out in the 1960s, but, like the early OGNs, were generally not published by comic book publishers. One of the first was *The Great Comic Book Heroes*, an anthology of reprints put together by Jules Feiffer in 1965. At the time, Fieffer, who had worked in comics in the 1940s, including working as Will Eisner's assistant, had a regular comic strip in the *Village Voice*. Besides essays by Fieffer, this hardcover anthology included reprints of stories from the 1940s,

---

Exhibit 2-3. *Squadron Supreme*

Perhaps the most unusual "extra" was in the 1997 collection of Marvel's 1985–1986 *Squadron Supreme* maxiseries. When writer Mark Gruenwald died in 1996, his will stipulated that he wanted to be cremated and have his ashes mixed in with printer's ink and used in a comic book. Since *Squadron Supreme* was considered by many to be his best work, it was decided that this trade paperback would be the perfect place for using the ashes. This resulted in many examples of black humor on the comics-related Usenet groups: "I've heard of an author throwing himself into his work but this is ridiculous" and "Who do we use if there's a second printing?" As it turns out, the trade has seen multiple printings (with the rest of the creators still healthy) that include a note on the text page about Gruenwald: "X Printing: Contains no ashes." See Appendix A for the listing for a new version of *Squadron Supreme*.

including stories featuring The Spirit and Captain Marvel, who were not well known to 1960s readers. The book sold well, and the essay portions were later reprinted by Fantagraphics Books in 2003. Fantagraphics has also published collections of Fieffer's short stories and cartoon stories.

Soon afterward, Ballantine Books put out two paperback books, *The Autumn People* (1965) and *Tomorrow Midnight* (1966), which reprinted the Ray Bradbury adaptations from *Tales from the Crypt*, *Weird Science*, and other EC Comics titles from the early 1950s. The reprints were in black and white and reprinted vertically, with two panels per page, so that the reader had to turn the book onto its side to read it. Other classic ECs were among the earlier reprints as well as the 53-volume *Complete EC Library* (Cochran 1979–1989).

Superhero comics were often reprinted in the 1970s, including *Superman from the Thirties to the Seventies* (Crown Publishing, 1971), *Wonder Woman* (Holt, Rinehart and Winston, 1972), and Simon & Schuster's *Origins of Marvel Comics* (1974) and its sequels. The 1981 *A Smithsonian Book of Comic-Book Comics*, published by Smithsonian Institution Press and Harry N. Abrams, featured comics from various genres. Some of the adult "underground" comics from the 1960s and 1970s were also among the early works to be collected, including the two-volume *Best of the Rip Off Press* (1973–1974), *The Apex Treasury of Underground Comics* (Quick Fox, 1974), *The Best of Bijou Funnies* (Links Books, 1975), and various collections of the works of R. Crumb.

More trades were produced in the 1980s, with a number coming from comics publishers. The trend grew in the 1990s and increases year after year. Not every new comic book is being collected, but a large percentage of titles are. And as seen in Chapter 6, it is not just recent material being collected, as many trades that reprint older works are also being published.

The majority of trade editions fall into at least one of the four categories covered in the following sections: limited series, chronological, storyline, and theme.

Collected Limited Series

The collected limited series trade is just what it sounds like, a comic book limited series collected together in (usually) one volume. Some of the earliest trades that were published by the originating comic book company were of this sort (such as *Batman: The Dark Knight Returns*). Most limited series are written as a one full story, so a collected limited series will allow the reader to get the complete story with (again, usually) no additional subplots that would have to be resolved in another volume (not counting sequels). On some occasions, when the limited series is long, the publisher will release the collection as multiple volumes, with 12-issue limited series being broken up into two or three trades.

Chronological Collections

Generally, a chronological trade simply collects issues X–Y of a comic book series. The next volume produced in the series then begins with the issue after "Y." For example, the first collection of *Y: The Last Man* collects issues 1–5, the second 6–10, the third 11–17, and so forth, until the end of the series. Many ongoing series that began in the past ten years have their complete run (or for still-running titles most of the run up to the present issue) collected. Some older, cancelled series have also had their entire run collected. One of the most notable older collections is *Cerebus*. One of the first ongoing series to be collected, the 16 200–400 page books, known to fans as "phone books" due to the size and the quality of the paper, have collected all but three issues of the 300-issue series. Interestingly, *High Society*, which reprinted issues 26–50 and is considered the second volume, came out first (a similar thing happened with *Sandman*).

Other long-running series that are still around have some, but not all, of their issues collected. *Hellblazer* (1986–) still has over eight years worth of stories uncollected as of 2009. And titles that go back to the 1960s, such as *Uncanny X-Men*, or to the 1930s/1940s, such as *Superman*, have even more gaps, though they are being filled. Sometimes only part of an older comic is collected. For example, while the *Action Comics Archives* collected the Superman stories from the 1930s and 1940s, the stories from those issues without Superman (with characters like Congo Bill and Zatara) are not included. On other occasions, even with recent works, a collection might skip an issue so that a volume may contain, for example, issues 8–10 and 12–15. There are various reasons for this, including the missing issue being put into a different collection. Of course, there is still much that has not been collected.

The second type of chronological collection occurs when the reprinted stories are still in chronological order but are not necessarily from the same title. This is usually seen with reprints of older material, such as in the Showcase and Essential books and their color, hardcover counterparts, Archive Editions and Marvel Masterworks. For example, the volumes of DC's *Showcase Presents Supergirl* include stories from six different titles. Those which include stories from the 1980s onward may also include annuals, limited series, and stories from other comics that continue from and/or are continued in other titles. *Essential X-Men*, Vol. 6, includes not only 14 issues of the comic but nine other stories as well. Marvel has also begun new hardcover *Omnibus* editions that collect large chronological runs of series or appearances.

Collected Storylines

The collected storyline type of trade collects a multipart comic book story in one (or more) volume. When the reprinted issues are all from the same comic book, then the volume is also the first kind of chronological collection (examples include the works of Joe Matt collected from *Peepshow*), though some chronological collections will also contain both a multipart story along with "one-shot" or shorter "two-part" stories. Some storylines also cross over into other comics, though this primarily occurs in superhero comics that take place in the same fictional "universe." These are sometimes in the same "family" (such as all of the Superman or X-Men titles) and other times go into other books. The books that tie in to an "event" limited series can be this sort, but usually it occurs when the story beginning in one comic title continues in another and then goes back either to the original book or to a third title. The collections of these stories can also technically be the second type of chronological collection.

Another version of collected storyline is what comics writer Denny O'Neil calls a "Megaseries." This is a very large mega-crossover that usually is in the same "family" and, when finally collected, is in several volumes. The example that O'Neil uses in his book *The DC Comics Guide to Writing Comic* is "No Man's Land," a year-long story that ran though nine regular titles and six related comics, including specials and one-shots. When collected into five volumes (simply *Batman: No Man's Land*, Vols. 1–5), the megaseries was 1,449 pages long (O'Neil, 2001).

Both crossovers and event storylines can cause problems. For example, a writer may have a multi-issue story arc planned, only to have it interrupted time and again by a company-wide story that was imposed by the publisher. In other cases, a delay in the main limited series can cause a delay in some of the crossover titles whose publication is prevented to avoid spoiling a "surprise" found in the limited series. For the librarian, event storylines can also be a cause for concern when, among other things, deciding how many of the related titles should be purchased. This is discussed further in Chapter 6.

Theme Trades

Theme trades are usually anthologies. The comic books reprinted in theme trades are often from several different titles and may span decades. Some of the early trades of the 1970s were of this type. A "text" equivalent to this would be a collection of short stories, whether by different authors (such as a *Year's Greatest* collection) or a single author. In these cases, the works have been originally published elsewhere and now are collected in a single place. While many of them are superhero titles, others are not.

Theme trades can contain reprints of comics from a particular period (*Superman in the Sixties*), comics dealing with a particular character (*The Greatest Flash Stories Ever Told* and *Life's a Bitch*), stories with a common theme (*Women of Marvel* and *Mammoth Book of Best War Comics*), the work of a particular writer or artist (*DC Universe: The Stories of Alan Moore*, *Marvel Visionaries: John Buscuema*, and Joe Sacco's *Notes from a Defeatist*), and more. Some of these trades with multiple volumes, such as *The Complete Crumb*, can also be chronological.

Other Examples

Of course, a few trades do not fall easily into any of these categories. For example, the *Hellblazer* collection *Rare Cuts* contains reprints from random issues of the series, with no story or theme linking them together (other than they were from the same title and had been uncollected). Trades are also occasionally rereleased in new formats, such as "Definitive Editions" or Absolute versions. The latter, used for DC titles such as *Watchmen* and *The League of Extraordinary Gentlemen*, reprint those works in a larger format usually along with extra material. Some works that had originally been printed with just the stories may be reprinted with extras, and some new collections will reprint material in one volume that has previously been collected in two or more books. The children's graphic novel *Bone* had the material from its nine trades collected in one 1,332 page omnibus. The three volumes of the *Queen & Country Definitive Editions* collects what was originally in eight trades (or 32 issues). The four-volume *Absolute Sandman* titles include improved art and stories printed elsewhere along with scripts and other extras. These "collections of collections" can be very helpful when building a graphic novel collection or when replacing a book whose original volume is out of print.

Trade editions have also been helpful to comic book publishers. By putting comics in book form, they have been able to get them into libraries, bookstores, and other places where they will be seen by people who don't frequent comic book shops (see Chapter 5). In fact, in some cases, the trades have sold better than the original comics, and successful sales of the trades has been credited on more than one occasion with preventing a series from being cancelled.

A Brief History of Comics

The use of pictures to tell a story—sequential art—goes back thousands of years. Prehistoric artwork, hieroglyphics, ancient pottery found in the Middle East and the Mediterranean all told stories using artwork. For example, a 17,000-year-old Paleolithic cave painting at Lascaux is described by the NYC Museum of Natural History as possibly portraying a single deer "plunging into a stream, swimming across and emerging on the other side" (McCloud, 2000: 216).

Slightly closer to our time is the Bayeux Tapestry, which is a 230-foot-long needlework embroidery thought to commissioned by Odo of Bayeux, the brother of William the Conqueror, and created in the late eleventh century. The story tells of William's victory in 1066 in a "flow of sequential images and text" (Talbot, 2007: 87–88). With the rise of moveable-type printing presses in the 1400s and 1500s, more and more were being printed, and these included broadsheets using comic art to illustrate the story or the intentions of the writer. Comic scholar Eric Caren has called this "The Pioneer Age" of comics. Many of these broadsheets used multiple panels to tell the story in chronological order. For example, a 1589 work showing the murder of King Henry III of France has four images, starting with the stabbing of the King and ending with his killer's execution (Caren, 2007). The earliest sequential comic "panel" strip created in the English language was "God's Revenge for Murder" by John Reynolds and an unknown artist in 1656 (Beerbohm et al., 2007).

In the mid-eighteenth century, British artist William Hogarth would tell stories using either a single illustration or a series of prints. These works were meant for adult audiences and often dealt with the social issues of the day. Some of his best-known work includes *The Harlot's Progress* (1731), its "sequel" *The Rake's Progress* (1735), the 12-print *Industry and Idleness* (1747), *The Four Stages of Cruelty* (1751), and the twin 1751 works *Beer Street* and *Gin Lane*, which contrasted the "happy" beer drinkers with the "drunk and wretched" gin drinkers. Hogarth was among the earliest artists to use panel borders with cartoons, creating the first interdependent combination of words and pictures seen in Europe. In 1754, Benjamin Franklin created what was perhaps the first American political cartoon, the famous "Join, or Die" that appeared in the May 9, 1754, edition of *Pennsylvania Gazette* (Caren, 2007). Franklin created several other cartoons over the years, as did another famous figure of that era, Paul Revere (Beerbohm et al. 2007).

The nineteenth century brought the next steps that led to the modern comic book. In 1827, the Swiss artist Rodolphe Töpffer created *Historie de M. Vieux Bois* ("The Story of Mr. Wooden Head"). The humorous story was 30 pages long, with each page containing anywhere from one to six drawn panels with a caption or narration on top, and was produced through "autography," a kind of lithography that let Töpffer draw with a pen on specially prepared paper, providing an easier and quicker method than the engravings used for printing at the time. Interestingly he did not create it for the purpose of publication, but after being convinced by his friends (including the writer Goethe), he finally did so in 1837. Töpffer's story became popular in Switzerland and elsewhere, including the United States, where on September 14, 1842, an unauthorized translation appeared as a supplement in the New York newspaper *Brother Jonathan Extra* under the title *The Adventures of Obadiah Oldbuck*. When the images were reformatted to fit the style of the paper, it made it very similar to the modern comic book, with 40 pages containing 195 panels. This is considered by many to be the first American comic book. Other works soon followed, coming from England and elsewhere.

The following year, the British humor publication *Punch* published a series of five drawings that satirized the government, which they called "Mr. Punch's Cartoons." Prior to this, the term "cartoon" meant a rough drawing used as a sample of a planned work. This came from the Italian word "cartone," the card on which Italian fresco painters and tapestry designers would draw a full scale "rough draft" before beginning the main work, which would be harder to change. At that time in London when competitive exhibition featuring similar "roughs" was going on, the artists at *Punch* were inspired to create their own. *Punch* first called these pictures "pencilings," but it soon applied the term "cartoon" to any humorous drawing, be it political satire or just regular humor. This caught on with other British publications as well as the American imitators of *Punch*—*Puck* (1871), *Judge* (1881), and *Life* (1883; no relation to the later publication)—which were sometimes referred to as "comic weeklies" (Harvey, 2001).

The period from the early 1880s to the early 1930s has been referred to as the "Platinum Age of Comics." Some of the early works at that time included *The Mischief Book* (1880), *The Evolution of a Democrat—A Darwinian Tale* (1888), and *The Girl Who Wouldn't Get Married* (1890), In 1897, *The Yellow Kid in McFadden Flats* was published. This 196-page hardcover (cardboard) book reprinted the popular strip in the *New York Journal*. The term "comic book" was coined here, printed on the back cover (Russell, 2005). This book was soon followed by additional titles that collected not only *The Yellow Kid* but also *Buster Brown, Mutt and Jeff, The Katzenjammer Kids*, and *Little Nemo in Slumberland* as well as other titles that are still known 100 years later.

Additional comics from the first 30 years of the twentieth century, some of which were for older readers, include *The Adventures of Willie Winters* (1912), which was published by Kellogg's, *Foxy Grandpa Visits Richmond* (1920), a hotel giveaway featuring a well-known comic strip character, and many others. These were often "one-shot" titles, and while some had new material, many of them were collections of comic strips. In 1922, *Comic Monthly* debuted and was the first magazine format collection of comic strips to come out on a regular basis. Containing such strips as *Barney Google*, this black-and-white title cost a dime and lasted for 12 issues (Goulart, 2004).

Seven years later *The Funnies* was another step to the modern comic book. It was in color, though the format was more like the Sunday comics supplement of the time. It originally ran for a year, but a revised version ran in one form or another from 1936–1962. Another step was the "Big Little Books" put out by Western Publishing's Whitman division; these were 4" × 4" × 1½" books with cardboard covers and ran anywhere from 240–320 pages of pulp paper. The books, which alternated between a page of text and a page of art, featured both new material and reprints of comic strips with the word balloons removed and the "text" page telling the story and dialogue.

In 1933, Procter & Gamble created a comic book that its customers could get for free with a coupon. *Funnies on Parade* was wildly successful, and while it contained reprints of Sunday color comics, it is considered to be the first modern comic book. The following year, *Famous Funnies* from Eastern Publishing began. Another reprint title, this was the first ongoing series in the modern comic form and ran for 218 issues with good sales (Inge, 1990).

In 1935, Major Malcolm Wheeler-Nicholson's National Allied Publishers (the forerunner of today's DC Comics) developed the idea of publishing original material and created *New Fun* (Inge, 1990). The series was at first oversized in black and white, sold for a dime, and contained stories in a variety of genres (including "Don Nogales, Cattle Rustler," "Sandra of the Secret Service in the Gavonian Affair," "2023: Super Police," an adaptation of Ivanhoe, and "Oswald the Rabbit"). The first issue of *New Fun*, which with some title changes would run until 1947, is generally considered to be the start of the "Golden Age" of comics, which ended around 1949.

During the 1930s and 1940s, many comic book companies were formed, including the companies that would become DC and Marvel (see Chapter 6), Quality, Fox, Fawcett, Lev Gleason, MLJ, Fiction House, Harry "A" Chesler, Dell, and many more. The vast majority of the titles were for younger readers, but some were read by adults. During World War II, many soldiers found comic books included in their care packages (and modern-day soldiers have had special comics made for them), and following the war, interest in comics by adults led to some stories being written for older audiences. For example, Prize Comics' title *Young Romance* (1947) has printed on the cover "Designed for the More ADULT Readers of COMICS" (emphasis theirs) (Goulart, 2004: 367). Stories for older readers also appeared in crime and horror comics, and this ended up leading to problems.

In 1940, literary critic Sterling North wrote an article in the *Chicago Daily News* titled "A National Disgrace" in which he attacked comic books as having an adverse effect on children. Throughout the 1940s, the subject of how good or bad comics were for children was debated on the radio and in articles in a wide range of publications, including *Library Journal* and *Wilson Library Journal*. The debate continued into the 1950s, with 1954 bringing three important events: a book written by psychiatrist Fredric Wertham called *Seduction of the Innocent*, in which he, among other things, blamed juvenile delinquency on horror and crime comics; the formation of a special Senate Subcommittee on Juvenile Delinquency headed by Senator Estes Kefauver, which held hearings on the topic of how comic books affected juvenile delinquency (this followed hearings and the creation of censorship laws on local and state levels); and the creation of the Comics Code Authority.

While the comics industry had attempted self-regulation in the 1940s, the new version of the code was a broader attempt begun by the Comics Magazine Association of America, formed the previous year. The code had specific rules as to what could and could not appear in a comic book, and those that were approved would get the Comics Code Authority's seal placed on the issue.[1] While membership in the association was purely voluntary, most publishers of non-code-approved comics found that vendors would not sell their titles for fear of incurring the wrath of either local government or local anti-comics organizations, which might boycott or otherwise disrupt their business. At a time when there were church- and school-sponsored burnings of comic books, this was not an unreasonable fear.

The rules of the code most adversely affected crime and horror comics (more in Chapter 3) and comics aimed at adult readers mostly faded away. Several companies were also negatively affected by the code, most notably EC Comics (*Tales from the Crypt*, *Crime SuspenStories*, etc.). EC Publisher William Gaines had appeared in the Senate hearings, and EC had even made fun of those who blamed comics for social issues in the 1953 story "The Reformers" (*Weird Science* #20). Unfortunately, they had multiple problems with the code's censors and the proverbial straw that broke the camel's back was a story in *Incredible Science Fiction #33* (January–February 1956), which reprinted a story from 1953 titled "Judgment Day." The story dealt with racism and showed an astronaut from Earth who visited a world of robots to judge if they were ready to join the Galactic Republic; he decided they were not because the orange robots discriminated against the blue ones. The code wanted EC to cut the final panel that revealed the astronaut to be black. Gaines called them bigots, printed it as is, and then cancelled all of the remaining EC titles, except for *Mad*, which was turned into a magazine (Thompson and Lupoff, 1973/1998).

But even with the code new and better changes were happening in comics. In 1956, DC put out *Showcase Comics* #4, which introduced a new version of the Flash. This comic marks what many comic historians have deemed the Silver Age of Comics. Depending on whom you talk to, the Silver Age ended anywhere between 1969 and 1985. The names and periods of the other ages have been debated among comic fans and historians. As comics moved into the 1960s, more developments occurred, including the beginning of the modern Marvel Comics. There were adults who enjoyed comic books, but when it came to comics written specifically for adults, the 1960s were important due to the rise of the Underground Comics Movement.

Also referred to as "Comix," the Undergrounds were also a part of the counter-culture movement of the era. By 1965, innovations in offset printing technology made it easier to print your own small tabloid paper for a relativity small price, and papers such as *Los Angeles Free Press*, *Berkeley Barb*, *San Francisco Oracle*, *Chicago Seed*, *Fifth Estate* (in Detroit), and New York's *East Village Other* featured both writing and art (Callahan, 2004). Cartoonists would also have their works appear in magazines such as *Help!*, and artists like Robert Crumb created such characters as Fritz the Cat and Mr. Natural. In 1968, Crumb would create the first ongoing underground comics series, *Zap Comics*.

Zap was printed by two Bay Area poets, Don Donahue and Charlie Plymell, and while the exact print run is unknown, sources (including Donahue and Plymell) place the total as anywhere from 1,000 to 5,000 copies. On February 25, 1968, they, along with Crumb and his wife, sold the comic by walking around the Haight-Ashbury district of San Francisco, with Crumb pushing a baby carriage full of the comics (Callahan, 2004).

Many more titles appeared from Crumb and others, including Gilbert Shelton, Trina Robbins, Lynda Barry, Frank Stack, Art Spiegelman, and more. Some of the underground works of the 1960s and 1970s have been collected in one form or another (certain titles can be found in Appendix A). Comix would be sold in various ways, including at "head shops," where they appeared among the drug paraphernalia and other material for the counterculture movement.

Of course, because Underground comics included a great deal of sex and drug-themed stories, they did face the occasional legal problem. An incest themed story in *Zap* #4[2] led to that issue being seized by the police in San Francisco and banned in New York (Pilcher and Kannenberg, 2008). The 1972 comic *Tits & Clits* led to the owner of the San Francisco bookstore Fahrenheit 451 being arrested and the creators Joyce Farmer and Lyn Chevely forced to go into hiding (Pilcher and Kannenberg, 2008). More about Underground Comics can be found in Charles Hatfield's *Alternative Comics: An Emerging Literature* and other titles listed in Appendix B.

As the years progressed comics and graphic novels for adult readers moved into the mainstream. The Comics Code was twice revised and is barely a factor these days. With graphic novels, "mature audience" lines of comics, public acceptance, and more, the concept of comics being just for children is starting to fade, with the recognition of them as something for adults being on the rise.

Notes

1. A listing of the 1954 version of the Comics Code can be found on several Web sites, but for a history of the code as well as its changes over the years, see Nyberg's *Seal of Approval* (1998). For additional information on the anticomics feelings of the 1940s and 1950s, see Hajdu's *The Ten-Cent Plague* (2008).
2. This story can be found in the *R. Crumb Handbook*. See Appendix A.

References

Andleman, Bob. 2005. *Will Eisner: A Spirited Life*. Milwaukee, WI: M Press.

Arnold, Andrew D. 2003. "The Graphic Novel Silver Anniversary." *Time* (November 14). Available: www.time.com/time/columnist/arnold/article/0,9565,542579,00.html (accessed September 11, 2009).

Beerbohm, Robert, Richard Samuel West, and Richard D. Olsen. 2007. "Comic Strips and Books 1646–1900." In Robert Overstreet, *Overstreet Comic Book Price Guide*, 37th edition (pp. 318–338). New York: House of Collectibles/Gemstone.

Callahan, Bob. 2004. "No More Yielding but a Dream." In *The New Smithsonian Book of Comic-Book Stories*. Washington, DC: Smithsonian Books.

Campbell, Eddie. 2004. "Graphic Novel Manifesto." Available: www.donmacdonald.com/archives/000034.html (accessed August 22, 2009).

Caren, Eric. C. 2007. "The American Comic Book: 1500–1828." In Robert Overstreet, *Overstreet Comic Book Price Guide*, 37th edition (pp. 308–317). New York: House of Collectibles/Gemstone.

Chinn, Mike. 2004. *Writing and Illustrating the Graphic Novel*. New York: Barron's.

Cronin, Brian. 2006. "Comic Book Urban Legends Revealed #39." Available: http://goodcomics.comicbookresources.com/2006/02/23/comic-book-urban-legends-revealed-39/ (accessed August 22, 2009).

DC Comics Rarities Archive, Vol. 1. 2004. New York: DC Comics.

de Vos, Gail. 2005. From "ABCs of Graphic Novels." *Resource Links* 10, no. 3. Retrieved from (no longer available): www.resourcelinks.ca/features/feb05.htm.

Eisner, Will. 1989. *Comics & Sequential Art*. Tamarac, FL: Poorhouse Press.

Eisner, Will. 1996. *Graphic Storytelling & Visual Narrative*. Tamarac, FL: Poorhouse Press.

Gertler, Nat, and Steve Lieber. 2004. *The Complete Idiot's Guide to Creating a Graphic Novel*. New York: Alpha Books.

Goulart, Ron. 2004. *Comic Book Encyclopedia: The Ultimate Guide to Characters, Graphic Novels, Writers, and Artists in the Comic Book Universe*. New York: HarperCollins.

Hajdu, David. 2008. *The Ten-Cent Plague: The Great Comic-Book Scare and How It Changed America*. New York: Farrar, Straus, and Giroux.

Harvey, Robert C. 2001. "Comedy at the Juncture of Word and Image: The Emergence of the Modern Magazine Gag Cartoon Reveals the Vital Blend." In Robin Varnum and Christina T. Gibbons (Eds.), *The Language of Comics: Word and Image* (pp. 77–78). Jackson: University Press of Mississippi.

Inge, M. Thomas. 1990. *Comics as Culture*. Jackson: University Press of Mississippi.

Kavanagh, Barry. 2000. "The Alan Moore Interview." Blather.net (October 17). Available: www.blather.net/articles/amoore/northampton.html (accessed August 22, 2009).

McCloud, Scott. 2000. *Reinventing Comics: How Imagination and Technology Are Revolutionizing an Art Form*. New York: HarperCollins.

Nyberg, Amy Kiste. 1998. *Seal of Approval: The History of the Comics Code*. Jackson: University Press of Mississippi.

O'Neil, Dennis. 2001. *The DC Comics Guide to Writing Comics*. New York: Watson-Guptill Publications.

Pilcher, Tim, and Gene Kannenberg, Jr. 2008. *Erotic Comics: A Graphic History from Tijuana Bibles to Underground Comix*. New York: Harry N. Abrams.

Rollins, Prentis. 2006. *The Making of a Graphic Novel*. New York: Watson-Guptill Publications.

Russell, Michael. 2005. "History of Comic Books Part II." Available: http://ezinearticles.com/?History-of-Comic-Books---Part-II&id=114701 (accessed August 22, 2009).

Talbot, Bryan. 2007. *Alice in Sunderland: An Entertainment*. Milwaukie, OR: Dark Horse.

Thompson, Don, and Dick Lupoff. 1973/1998. *The Comic-Book Book*, Revised edition. Iola, WI: Krause Publications.

Chapter 3

What Genres Do Graphic Novels Cover?

I f those who promote graphic novels in libraries had an official slogan, it would be "Remember, graphic novels are a format, not a genre." Graphic novels come in all genres, both fiction and nonfiction—superhero, adventure, mystery, science fiction, fantasy, crime, true crime, horror, romance, historical fiction, historical nonfiction, biography, autobiography, memoir, and more. Any genre that you will find in "text" fiction and many that are found in nonfiction can also be found in the graphic novel format. Most themes and plotlines found in fiction can also be found in graphic novels.

This chapter discusses some of the genres found in adult graphic novels within general categories, as some books can belong to more than one genre. For example, *Jonah Hex*, *Dead West*, *Daisy Cutter*, *Lone*, and the manga series *Priest* all have elements of the Western genre, but all but the Jonah Hex stories have either a science fiction or horror element to them (and in the uncollected 1985–1986 series *Hex*, the character was transported into the future). On the other hand, modern superhero books have been set both during World War II and in the far future, but this would not necessarily put them into the historical or science fiction genres. The following sections discuss some of the more popular comic book and graphic novel genres.

Superhero

When someone mentions comic books or graphic novels, the image that will appear in the heads of most noncomics readers is that of a superhero.[1] The vast majority of trades are in the superhero genres, with over 70 years worth of stories available. If your library serves all ages, then the majority of your superhero titles will probably be placed in the young adult section, though adult readers would also show interest in them. Most of these titles are not included in Appendix A, except for some with older material (for the "nostalgia factor"), and those which are more geared toward adult readers. Chapter 6 elaborates more on what to buy.

Superheroes are on television and in movies. They are on our clothes, our walls, and even on our postage stamps. It is hard to say what exactly makes a superhero. Fighting crime or injustice is usually a requirement, as is a costume, which is generally used to hide one's "secret identity." While many have superhuman abilities, this is not always the case. Some may have special equipment (such as Iron Man or Green Lantern), but others are just ordinary people who rely on their brains, brawn, and the occasional weapon or device (Batman being the best example).

Superheroes have many antecedents. Hercules can be considered a superhero (and in Marvel Comics actually is), as can Samson and Gilgamesh. Robin Hood wore a distinctive outfit, used an alias, and had skill with a bow and arrow better than that of the evil Sheriff's men. The Scarlet Pimpernel (created in 1905) and Zorro (created in 1919) both had secret identities through which they pretended to be weak and "foppish" to fool others, something adopted by many comic book heroes, especially in the case of Batman, whose origins have connections to Zorro. The 1930 novel *Gladiator* told the story of Hugo Danner who gained superstrength from experiments conducted by his father, and The Shadow appeared both on the radio and in magazines, fighting evil with "the power to cloud men's minds."

The first modern original character that could be considered a superhero was The Clock, introduced in 1936.[2] While he had no powers, former District Attorney Brian O'Brien fought criminals clad in a three-piece suit and fedora with a black mask totally covering his face. Two years later, Superman made his debut as the first original superpowered crime fighter. Soon more heroes, powered and not, debuted, and while many first fought ordinary criminals and during the war years spies and saboteurs, superpowered and/or costumed villains began to become more prevalent as well. The early 1940s brought several comic book mainstays, including the first superhero team (the Justice Society in 1940), the first teen sidekick (Robin, also in 1940, who was soon followed by Bucky, Speedy, and others), and even the first superhero death (the Comet in 1942, and like many of those who would follow, he eventually came back from the dead). The genre went into decline at the end of the 1940s but rebounded at the beginning of the Silver Age and remains popular to this day.

Most superheroes are part of the "shared universe" of their publisher. For example, Batman, Superman, and Wonder Woman live in the same world filled with other DC Comics characters, while Spider-Man, Iron Man, and the Hulk live in the "Marvel Universe." They may interact with the other characters in their universe, and events in one title can affect events in another. They also tend to exist in what is called a "sliding-scale" time line, so while teenager Peter Parker became Spider-Man in 1962, in the Marvel Universe he is in his midtwenties, not his midsixties. Technology and cultural references are also updated, so when a character remembers the past he or she remembers it in an "updated" way (what was once a Beatles concert is now a Justin Timberlake show).

Because of this sliding scale, sometimes a character must be changed to be updated. Known as "retcons," for retroactive continuity, these changes can be minor or major. The term, which can refer to the act of "retconning" or to the change itself, can be something as simple as a newly revealed piece of the character's history, an alteration of a character's history to modernize him or her (Iron Man's origin is now tied to the Middle East instead of Vietnam), or, in the most extreme method, a total revamp of a character. DC Comics did this to several characters in the 1980s, including Superman, Wonder Woman, and Hawkman (as well as their villains and supporting casts). This affected other characters in the DC Universe. For example, when recounting the history of the superteam Justice League, the activities of those three characters had to be taken on by other characters.

At times, even the retcons will be retconned, sometimes going back to the original version, in what comic writer Peter David calls a "stetcon." Some elements removed when Superman was retconned have been brought back, though occasionally slightly altered. Wonder Woman, who had been retconned into *not* being a founding member of the Justice League, again is one. Because of changes over the years, older readers who are now just coming back to comics may find some of their favorite characters strangely altered. With the increase of older material being collected, multiple incarnations of the same character may be next to one another on the shelf and, in the case of a decade-spanning "theme" trade, together in the same book.

However, stories aimed at teens and younger children are not the only graphic novels in the superhero genre. Many are written for adults or at least take a new look at the genre. This had been done in books, such as Robert Mayer's 1977 novel *Superfolks*, but 1986's *Watchmen* was one of the first comics to "deconstruct" the superhero concept. Many other books have taken new looks at the genre. For example, *The Authority* has superbeings who try to fix the world's problems no matter who says different. *The Boys* shows a superteam more interested in merchandising than saving the world. *After the Cape* has a superhero that goes bad after being down on his luck. *Brat Pack* is among those that parody some of the popular "archetypes." *The Rookie* and the *Top Ten* books show superbeings as police officers, the latter set in a city where everyone has powers, while *Powers* looks at the "normal" police who must monitor the superbeings. From the opposite side is *Wanted*, which is about the supervillains who have taken over the world. Of course not every nontraditional superhero story is a "grim and gritty" one. Some are humorous or just lighthearted. These include *Dr. Blink Superhero Shrink*, *Empowered*, and *Love and Capes*, the latter being the story of a Superman-like hero and his girlfriend.

Biography, Autobiography, and Memoir

Biographical comics have been around since the 1940s, but at that time, as with many of them today, they were generally written for children. Now, however, we have some for adults too, even if they may occasionally share the same subject matter as the juvenile biographies and are generally less in-depth and less analytical than "text" biographies. Recent subjects of adult-level graphic biographies include Ronald Reagan, Malcolm X, Neils Bohr, Emma Goldman, and Canadian historical figure Louis Riel. Of note is *King*, Ho Che Anderson's "warts and all" biography of Martin Luther King that was originally collected in multiple volumes. Lesser-known individuals have also been the subject of biographies. For example, both Emmanuel Guibert and Harvey Pekar have done books on soldiers who fought in World War II and Vietnam, respectively. Ann Marie Fleming did one on her great-grandfather, the magician Long Tack Sam, while Raymond Briggs did one on his parents, who were just an ordinary English couple. Other books about family members include their dealing with illness (*Mom's Cancer*, *Epileptic*) or their experiences during the Holocaust (*We Are On Our Own*, *Maus*). Often when the subject matter is a family member, the author is also a "character" in the book.

Autobiographical, or at least semiautobiographical graphic novels, are a genre that is growing in popularity. However, as many of them deal with only a portion of the subject's life and not his or her entire life, "graphic memoir" may be a more accurate way to describe these books. They can range from a significant event in the author's life (the Holocaust, illness, combat, etc.), life-shaping events from his or her youth, or just regular life events, including love life or lack thereof. The stories may be slightly fictionalized, and some names may be changed, but they are primarily based on the author's life.

Art Spiegelman credits Justin Green with inventing "confessional autobiographic comix" (Spiegelman, 1995: 4) with his 1972 underground comic *Binky Brown Meets the Holy Virgin Mary* published by Last Gasp. With "Binky" being a stand-in for Green, the comic told the story of his youth and how his religious beliefs combined with a disorder now recognized as obsessive-compulsive disorder caused problems for him as a youth. The comic cost 50 cents (more than twice the cost of the "mainstream comics" of the time), sold around 40,000 issues, and was later collected in *Justin Green's Binky Brown Sampler* (1995). Green isn't the only author to use an alias for the memoir comics. Will Eisner used a character based on himself in such semiautobiographical works as *The Dreamer*; Michel Rabagliati's "Paul" is based on the author, as is Eddie Campbell's "Alec"[3]; and despite the title, the main character in Peter Kuper's *Stop Forgetting to Remember: The Autobiography of Walter Kurtz* (2008) is Kuper.

Around the same time that Green was doing *Binky Brown*, in Japan, artist Keiji Nakazawa created *Ore wa Mita* (*I Saw It*), describing how as a young boy he had witnessed the results of the atomic bomb hitting Hiroshima.[4] This would become the basis of one of the most famous manga, *Barefoot Gen*. Memoirs and biographies of civilians who have lived through war and its aftermath are discussed in a separate section later in this chapter. Another hardship that people have written about is their fight with illness, especially cancer, including Harvey Pekar and Joyce Brabner's *Our Cancer Year*, *Cancer Vixen* (2006) by cartoonist Marisa Acocella Marchetto and Miriam Engleberg's *Cancer Made Me a Shallower Person* (2006), which is subtitled *A Memoir in Comics*. The traumas of sexual abuse have also been told in autobiographical graphic novels, including Phoebe Gloeckner's 2000 work *A Child's Life* (via her "proxy" Minnie) and *Daddy's Girl* (2008) by Debbie Drechsler.

A large number of memoir graphic novels do not deal with illness or war or anything that is necessarily bad or traumatic. Instead they recount a "this is my life, the good, the bad, and the mundane" story. One of the best examples of this is Harvey Pekar's *American Splendor* stories. While he has discussed his illness and his past (*The Quitter*) and written about other people, most of the *Splendor* stories are simply Pekar dealing with everyday events, such as work, family, bills, and so forth. *American Splendor* began in 1976 and over the years has been self-published by Pekar (16 issues between 1976–1991) or published by various comic companies and book publishers. The comics created popularity for Pekar, which led to, among other things, appearances on *Late Night with David Letterman*. These appearances were later recounted in the comic. Pekar is just the writer of the stories, with the artwork done by a number of different artists, including R. Crumb, Alison Bechdel, Chester Brown, and Eddie Campbell. Pekar's history was recounted in the award-winning 2003 film *American Splendor*, and the making of and reaction to were recounted in the graphic novel *Our Movie Year* (2004).

The "regular guy" memoir is also tackled by creators such as Jeffrey Brown, who often covers his romantic life; Tom Beland, whose *True Story Swear to God* tells how he met and later married his wife; Joe Matt, whose books come from the comic *Peepshow*; and Chester Brown, whose works are from *Yummy Fur* (Matt and Brown appear in each other's books along with fellow creator Seth). Some of these stories also deal with the author's childhood. The works that Ariel Schrag first did in high school started off talking about her life in general but later expanded to cover her emerging lesbianism. Alison Bechdel's *Fun Home* covers her relationship with her father.

Other memoirs cover more interesting parts of the author's life. Marijan Starapi's *Persepolis* books, which were also made into a film, tell of growing up in Iran during the Islamic Revolution and her later experiences in and out of the country. Percy Carey has recounted his time as rapper MC Grimm who, among other things, spent time in jail. Caldecott winning artist David Small covers life with his family, especially when an operation removed one of his vocal cords. Guy Delisle has told about going to North Korea and China to work. Josh Neufeld, Craig Thompson, and Ted Rall have all discussed their travels to other countries, K. Thor Jensen has told of how he traveled around America by bus, and Joe Sacco's *But I Like It* tells of his travels as the roadie for a punk rock band.

In discussing comic book memoirs, comics scholar Rocco Versaci has said that "as a representation of the life of its author, the comic book memoir achieves what Will Eisner calls a 'special reality' that explores issues of autobiographical writing in ways unavailable in prose alone" (Versaci, 2007: 37). However, not everything that seems to be an autobiographical graphic novel actually is. Seth's *It's a Good Life, If You Don't Weaken* features his quest to find out about a cartoonist, and even features Chester Brown and Joe Matt, but is at least partially fictional. In one memorable scene from *Our Cancer Year*, Pekar, sick after chemotherapy, says, "Tell me the truth. Am I some guy who writes about himself in a comic book called *American Splendor* or am I just a character in that book?" (Pekar and Brabner, 1994).

Adaptations and Licensed Works

Comics and graphic novels that adapt or expand works from other sources have been around since at least 1921, when a comic book version of *Swiss Family Robinson* was produced. Decades of students used *Classics Illustrated* and its imitators to help with book reports. Literary adaptations for younger readers are also among the graphic novels becoming popular, both highly abridged and close to the full work, including manga versions of Shakespeare. Other adaptations are usually found in the adult fiction section of the library, often works of science fiction, fantasy, or horror, possibly because many comic readers are interested in that genre, but that is not always the case. *Bloodstar*, one of the early graphic novels, adapted an Edgar Rice Burroughs story. During the 1990s, many of the works of Anne Rice and Clive Barker were adapted into comic book form, and Dark Horse produced a series adapting the works of Harlan Ellison. Many of Neil Gaiman's novels and short stories have been adapted, sometimes by Gaiman himself. Stephen King, Laurell K. Hamilton, Orson Scott Card, and George R. R. Martin, and others have recently seen their works adapted into a monthly comic book series that is later collected into a trade edition. One notable series of graphic novels from Eureka Publications adapts stories by prominent older authors, often containing lesser-known works. Even the Bible has graphic adaptations.

Besides simply adapting the literary works, some comics are used to create prequels and sequels, and occasionally the original author even writes them. Jim Butcher created a new *Dresden Files* story for comics, Max Brooks created a comic based on his popular zombie titles, and David Brin expanded one of his short stories to create *The Life Eaters*. Literary characters such as Tarzan and Doc Savage have long had their adventures continued in comic book form, and some literary characters are even made part of a particular comic book universe. Dracula, for example, has become part of the Marvel Universe and has fought the X-Men and other heroes. Some of the most interesting literary characters in comics are in Alan Moore's *League of Extraordinary Gentlemen* stories, the main characters of which are from Victorian literature, including Captain Nemo, Mr. Hyde, and the Invisible Man. As is discussed in Chapter 6, Moore also used other famous literary characters in a much different way.

Of course, unless the character is in the public domain, the comic company must license the character. A publisher may later decline to renew the license, or the owner may not allow it to be renewed and offer it to another company. For example, the rights to Robert E. Howard's Conan the Barbarian was first licensed to Marvel Comics but then to Dark Horse. Besides allowing Dark Horse to publish new Conan stories, this also meant that they were the only ones who could collect the stories that Marvel had published. This has also prevented Marvel from even reprinting superhero stories in which Conan has appeared. Similar issues have occurred with comics that are based on film and television shows.

While television shows and movies have been based on comic books, the reverse is also true, dating back to the early years of the modern comic book. Again, while the better-known ones have tended to be in the "fantastic" genre, this is not always the case. Westerns and sitcoms have been made into comic books. Although some are direct film-to-comic adaptations, most are new adventures. One of the best examples are the comics based on the *Star Wars* films. As with *Conan*, the rights were first given to Marvel, but since 1991 Dark Horse has put out over 100 original graphic novels and trade collections, including reprints of the original Marvel series. Like the *Star Wars* tie-in novels, the comics take place in various eras in the Star Wars Universe, ranging from 25,000 years before the time of the 1977 film to decades after *Return of the Jedi*. Other films that have resulted in recent comics and graphic novels include the *Evil Dead/Army of Darkness* series, *Friday the 13th*, *Nightmare on Elm Street*, *The Texas Chainsaw Massacre*, *28 Days Later*, *Final Destination*, and *Seven*. Some of these have even led to ongoing series or multiple limited series.

The television show that has been in comics the most is *Star Trek* and its various sequels. As expanded on in Exhibit 3-1, *Star Trek* comics have been published by six different companies (not counting Checker, which simply reprinted other companies' works), with some companies losing and then regaining the property (IDW is the current publisher of *Star Trek* comics). During the early 1990s, DC Comics gained the rights to the original series and *Star Trek: The Next Generation*, while Malibu Comics had the rights to *Star Trek: Deep Space Nine*. A similar thing is currently happening with *Buffy the Vampire Slayer*, which is licensed to Dark Horse, and its spin-off *Angel*, which is licensed to IDW. As is often the case with tie-in novels, the events in the comic books are not considered part of the show's internal continuity, though there are exceptions. The current *Buffy* comic book, *Buffy the Vampire Slayer Season Eight*, is considered to be "official continuity," and many issues were written by show creator Joss Whedon and other writers from the show. Other recent television shows with comic book tie-ins include *Supernatural*, *Chuck*, *Doctor Who*, *24*, *The Simpsons*, and *Battlestar Galactica*, which has comics based on both the original and "reimagined" versions.

Exhibit 3-1. *Star Trek* and Comic Books: A History

Star Trek has had comic book incarnations almost as long as it's been around. The first was in 1967, the year after the original series premiered, and was published by Gold Key. This version ran irregularly for 61 issues until 1979 and is best known for the art mistakes of the early issues, including portraying the African Lt. Uhura as being Caucasian. This series would later be collected by Checker BPG as *Star Trek: The Key Collection* (2004–).

In 1979, *Star Trek: The Motion Picture* brought the characters to the big screen, and the following year Marvel began its own *Star Trek* comic that ran for 18 issues and continued where the movie left off. DC acquired the license in 1984 and its *Star Trek* began shortly after the events of 1982's *Star Trek II: The Wrath of Kahn*. This 56-issue series incorporated the events of 1984's *Star Trek III: The Search for Spock* (including the destruction of the Starship Enterprise) and 1986's *Star Trek IV: The Voyage Home* (the introduction of a new Enterprise). DC also put out adaptations of the two movies as well as annuals and a two-issue *Who's Who in Star Trek*, created in 1986 honor of the show's twentieth anniversary. Some issues of the first DC series have been collected.

(Cont'd.)

Exhibit 3-1. *Star Trek* **and Comic Books: A History** *(Continued)*

After *Star Trek V: The Final Frontier* came out in 1989, DC began a new ongoing series as well as a second series based on the new spin-off *Star Trek: The Next Generation* which has debuted in 1987 and had a DC limited series published in 1988. Both ongoing series lasted for 80 issues and had several annuals. During the run of the series, DC also put out several limited series, an adaptation of 1991's *Star Trek VI: The Undiscovered Country*, and the original graphic novel *Star Trek: Debt of Honor*. Stories from these series have been collected by DC, Titan Books, and others.

In 1993 a second spin-off television series, *Star Trek: Deep Space Nine*, premiered, and while the DC titles were still being published, it was Malibu who purchased the rights to the newest show. Over the next three years, Malibu put out an ongoing series as well as annuals, specials, limited series, and one-shots. In 1994, DC and Malibu co-published a limited series that teamed up the characters of *The Next Generation* with those of *Deep Space Nine*. That same year, DC put out an adaptation of the film *Star Trek: Generations*.

In 1996 the film *Star Trek: First Contact* came out and Marvel reacquired the license, publishing its own *Deep Space Nine* book as well as a new title based on *Star Trek: Voyager* (which debuted the previous year on the new channel UPN) and *Star Trek Unlimited* that featured characters from the first two shows. Marvel also created new titles that were only partly connected to the television programs: *Star Trek: Starfleet Academy*, *Star Trek: The Early Years*, and *Star Trek: Untold Voyages*. Besides other limited series and one-shots, Marvel also publishes *Star Trek/X-Men* (1996) and *Star Trek/X-Men: Second Contact* (1998) in which Marvel's mutant team encountered both the original and *Next Generation* crews. The latter was continued in a paperback book. But by 1998, the year that the ninth film, *Star Trek: Insurrection*, came out, Marvel has again lost the license and its titles were cancelled, several with storylines left unresolved.

In 2000 The DC Comics imprint Wildstorm got the license and published several limited series and specials (some in "bookshelf" format) covering the various *Star Trek* shows. One notable title is *Star Trek: The New Frontier—Double Time*, based on the series of books by Peter David (who also wrote the issue). Over the next few years, a fourth series, *Star Trek: Enterprise (2001–2005)* would come out (but as of 2009 it has yet to have a comic based on it) and *Star Trek: Nemesis* would come out, but there was not much in the way of comics. This has changed in recent years.

Since 2006 Tokyopop has produced several original English language manga *Star Trek* stories with authors that include the writers of *Star Trek Novels* and *Next Generation* actor Wil Wheaton. The following year, IDW obtained the license and has been putting out many limited series with both the original and *Next Generation* characters. Other books by them focus on various alien races, adventures based on the 1960s episode "Assignment Earth," *The New Frontier* (again by David), and the evil "Mirror Universe." When the "rebooted" *Star Trek* film came out in 2009, IDW created a best-selling prequel title. Most of IDW's stories have been collected, and in 2009 they began putting out the *Star Trek Archives* and *Star Trek Omnibus* volumes that collect the earlier DC, Marvel, and Malibu comic books (see Appendix A for titles).

War Comics

Wars have long been a topic in comics, covering everything from historical wars to wars still being fought to wars to come. In the 1950s, EC Comics put out *Frontline Combat*, an anthology title that included stories set in Korea while the war was still being fought there, and while many stories written during World War II stereotyped the enemy soldiers, those in the 1950s showed the other side as "human." DC has produced a number of titles over the years, including *Our Army at War*, *GI Combat*, and *Star Spangled War Stories*. These books include stories featuring Sgt. Rock and

Easy Company, the high-flying paramilitary group the Blackhawks (originally published by Quality), master of disguise the Unknown Solder, and the Enemy Ace, a World War I German air ace. Some of their stories took on science fiction and fantasy elements, especially those featuring the adventures of the Haunted Tank, GI Robot, and the Creature Commandoes and those set in "The War That Time Forgot." A more recent work, the limited series *The Other Side*, takes place in Vietnam and deals with both an American and a Viet Cong soldier. Marvel's titles have ranged from the World War II adventures of Sgt. Fury and His Howling Commandoes, which had time continuity with their Superhero stories, to *The 'Nam*, to the nonfiction limited series *Combat Zone: True Tales of GIs in Iraq*.

Other works are set in the near future. The title character in Dark Horse's *Lives and Times of Martha Washington* fought in several twenty-first-century wars. The OGN *Shooting War* is set in Iraq a few years from now.[5] DC's *Army@Love* books, which take place in the fictional country of "Afbaghistan," take a satirical look at war, while another DC series, *DMZ*, is set in a Manhattan torn apart by a modern civil war between the United States and the "Free States." Stories dealing with nuclear war cover a range from science fiction (DC's Atomic Knights stories of the 1960s), humorous (*Apocalypse Nerd*), and even touching (Raymond Briggs' wonderful *When the Wind Blows*).

The effects and aftermath of war on the civilian population are also covered in graphic novels. Two manga titles, *Barefoot Gen* and *Town of Evening Calm, Country of Cherry Blossoms*, both deal, in one way or another, with the dropping of the atomic bomb. The Holocaust has been a subject of many works, both memoir and fictional (see Exhibit 3-2). The events in the former Yugoslavia during the past 20 years and the effect on the people there have been chronicled in a number of works, including *Fax from Sarajevo*, *Macedonia*, Joe Sacco's *The Fixer*, *Safe Area Gorazde*, *War's End*, and *Regards from Serbia*, which was done by Serbian cartoonist Aleksandar Zograf.

Exhibit 3-2. The Holocaust in Comics

The Holocaust has been a topic in a number of comics and graphic novels, both real and fictional. One of the earliest examples was the story "Master Race" in 1955's *Impact* #1 from EC Comics. The subject has also come up in superhero comics. The X-Men character Magneto, who has been both a hero and a villain, is a Holocaust survivor. Of all of the true stories, the best known is Art Spiegelman's *Maus*. The story of his parents' experiences, *Maus* began life as a three-page story published in the Underground title *Funny Animals* in 1971(which can be found in 2008's *Breakdowns: Portrait of the Artist As a Young %@&*!*). An expanded version was later serialized in Spiegelman's comic magazine *Raw* beginning in 1980. It was later collected into two volumes—*My Father Bleeds History* (1986) and *And Here My Troubles Began* (1991)—and currently is also available as a single volume and in a CD-ROM version that includes additional information, interviews, and even the notes Spiegelman used when interviewing his father. *Maus* won a special Pulitzer Prize in 1992 and was one of the first graphic novels to be taken seriously by the general public. *Maus* has appeared on reading lists and has been taught in classrooms and has even been the subject of

(Cont'd.)

Exhibit 3-2. The Holocaust in Comics *(Continued)*

the academic work *Considering Maus: Approaches to Art Spiegelman's "Survivor's Tale" of the Holocaust*.

Other memoirs dealing with the Holocaust include *We Are On Our Own*, in which the author tells of how, as a young child in 1944 Hungary, she and her mother were able to avoid being sent to the camps, and *Mendel's Daughter*, in which the author tells the story of how his mother was saved by people in her town who thought well of her father. Although not even a hybrid graphic novel, *I Was a Child of Holocaust Survivors* has a few comics pages. Works of fiction that deal with the Holocaust include the manga series *Adolf*, the French book *Auschwitz*, which is inspired by actual events, and Joe Kubert's *Yossel April 19, 1943*, which told what his life might have been like had his parents not emigrated from Poland in the 1920s.

Horror and the Supernatural

While the horror and supernatural genres have long appeared in comics, in books, they have seen resurgence in recent years. During the 1950s, titles such as EC's *Tales from the Crypt* and *Vault of Horror* were popular but were also made targets during the anti-comics fervor of the time. The introduction of the Comics Code (see Chapter 2) also put restrictions on what could be shown. Still a number of titles were being published, especially anthology series, such as *House of Mystery*, *House of Secrets*, and *Strange Tales*. During the 1960s, Warren Publications was able to bypass the Comics Code by publishing comics in a black-and-white magazine format, including *Creepy*, *Eerie*, and *Vampirella*. The loosening of the some of the code's restrictions brought more titles from the mainstream publishers. Marvel, for example, produced comics featuring Dracula, the Frankenstein Monster, the demonic Ghost Rider, a zombie character, and the "Werewolf by Night." Other publishers who were not part of the Comics Code also put out horror titles. These days, while all aspects of horror are appearing in comics and graphic novels, the "hottest" kinds deal with two aspects of the "walking dead": vampires and zombies.

The original version of the Comics Code forbid the use of vampires, but the 1970s revisions made it easier to show them, especially if presented in a classical manner, such as with Dracula. And beginning with Dracula, Marvel Comics created a host of related characters who worked with and against Dracula, including the vampire-hunter Blade. Besides *Tomb of Dracula* and adaptations of the Bram Stoker novel, other literary vampires who have appeared in comics include Anne Rices's Lestat and the vampires created by Laurell K. Hamilton (with the vampires of *Twilight* appearing soon). Vampires from film and television include both the evil vampires slain by Buffy and her allies (and spin-off characters) Angel and Spike.

DC and Marvel had other vampire stories in the 1980s, including the regular feature "I . . . Vampire" in *House of Mystery* and the early Marvel graphic novel *Greenberg the Vampire*. One of the biggest vampire stories in recent years was IDW's *30 Days of Night*, which told the story of a town in northern Alaska where, during the winter, the sun did not shine for an entire month—something that is irresistible to a gang of vampires. The original limited series has led to a number of follow-up titles as well as a feature film.

Vampire stories are told in many other ways. *Bite Club* has vampires living out in the open, with some of them involved in organized crime; *CVO* has vampires as government operatives; *Life Sucks* has a vampire who was turned so that he can work the night shift at a convenience store; Joann Sfar's *Vampire Loves* takes a humorous look at a nice-guy vampire; *Dark Hunger* features a romance between a vampire and a werewolf; and *Damn Nation* involves a United States overrun by them.

Zombies were also banned by the Comics Code. Marvel tried to get around this in their superhero titles by calling them "zuvembies" that were just mind controlled by a Voodoo priest instead of actually being dead. They also published the noncode comic magazine *Tales of the Zombie* that featured Simon Garth, a businessman who was killed and raised as a zombie but still retained some control. *Tales* has been collected in a Marvel *Essential* volume, and a revamped version character has appeared in recent limited series for their adult "Max" line. However, Marvel's biggest contribution to the recent zombie craze was the limited series *Marvel Zombies*. Spun off from a storyline in *Ultimate Fantastic Four*, *Marvel Zombies* and its sequels took place on an alternate world in the Marvel Universe where the heroes have been turned into people-eating monsters. The title is a pun on a term used to describe fanatical Marvel Comics fans.

While there have been comic book adaptations of many popular zombie films, the biggest serious take on zombies in comics has been the ongoing Image series *The Walking Dead* (2003–), which deals with a group of people in a world overrun with zombies. Boom! Studios, IDW, and Dark Horse have also published various limited series and collections (some with one story and others that are anthologies). Another anthology, *Zombies*, features stories from the United Kingdom both serious and humorous. A slightly humorous take on the topic was the story *Living with the Dead*, in which two friends are able to survive among the zombies simply by putting on scary masks and going "*braaains.*" *Dead West* puts Zombies in the old West, while *Xombie*, based on an online series, is set in a postzombie apocalyptic future. *Recess Pieces* has a group of elementary school children dealing with zombies, while in *Crawl Space: Xxxombies* it's the crew of 1970s porn films and mobsters who are trapped by the hungry creatures.

Crime

In addition to the 70 years worth of comics featuring costumed characters catching criminals, sometimes with aid of superpowers and paraphernalia, there also is a history of stories in which the characters are stopped by members of law enforcement, private investigators, or even, in some cases, not stopped at all. Two years before Batman made his debut, *Detective Comics* lived up to its title by featuring stories with such "hard-boiled" detectives as Slam Bradley, and others soon followed, including some characters taken from other works of fiction.

The best known of the early crime comics is *Crime Does Not Pay*, which was published by Lev Gleason Publishers from 1942–1957. The title recounted the exploits of real criminals, including their occasionally gruesome fates. The stories, often by Charles Biro, were very popular and led to both high sales and many imitators, such as *Headline Comics, Official Crime and Cases, Crimes by Women, True Crime Comics*, and *Crime SuspenStories*. These titles gained popularity with older teens as well as adults, and the stories began to take on more adult themes, including implied sex, drug use, and an increase in violence. A classic image from the time is from a story in *True Crime Comics* #2 (1947) called "Murder, Morphine, and Me" in which, during a dream sequence, the main character imagines a hypodermic needle about to be stabbed into her eye. This image was seized on by Dr. Frederic Wertham and others when discussing the negative impact of comics. Along with the horror titles, the crime comics caught the attention of the 1950s congressional hearings. One notable exchange occurred between Senator Kefauver and EC's William Gaines over artist Johnny Craig's cover for *Crime SuspenStories* #22 (May 1954) that showed an image which Kefauver found particularly disturbing.

> **KEFAUVER:** Here is your May issue. There seems to be a man with a bloody axe holding a woman's head up, which has been severed from her body. Do you think that's in good taste?"
>
> **GAINES:** Yes, sir I do—for the cover of a horror comic. A cover in bad taste, for example, might be defined as holding the head a little higher so that blood can be seen dripping from it. (Goulart, 2004: 101–102)

Crime comics was one of the genres greatly affected by the Comics Code. The code covered them in its first section with 12 rules, including "crimes shall never be presented in such a way as to create sympathy for the criminal, to promote distrust of the forces of law and justice, or to inspire others with a desire to imitate criminals," and "if crime is depicted it shall be as a sordid and unpleasant activity." Even the titles of the comics were affected; the code forbid the solo use of the word "crime" on a cover and included recommendations that publishers show restraint in any usage of the word in the title or subtitle. As with horror comics, this helped to generally eliminate crime-themed comics during that period.

Modern times offer many crime-themed comics and original graphic novels. One of the most notable "true-crime" series of OGNs is Rick Geary's *Treasury of Victorian Murder* from NBM, which covers not only the famous killers and victims of the 1800s, such as Jack the Ripper and the two assassinated presidents, but some who are lesser known, including H. H. Holmes and Mary Rogers, who were the subjects of recent nonfiction works.[6] Geary has also begun a series of twentieth-century murders starting with the Lindbergh baby kidnapping.

Fictional crime and detective stories have taken many forms, with a number having a criminal as a protagonist. Those set in the 1800s include *The Black Diamond Detective Agency* and *The Long Haul*. Titles dealing with the gangsters of the 1920s and 1930s include *Road to Perdition*, the source of the film, and *Jew Gangster*, which goes well with *Brownsville*, a book based on real characters. Modern mob and criminal activities appear in *A History of Violence*, the series *Criminal*, and some volumes of Frank Miller's *Sin City* series. Some stories involving detectives and criminals also mix with other genres. The *Stonehaven* books take place in an alternate world with magical beings. *The Damned* features a 1920s gangster who has to deal with demons, and *Black Cherry* has a modern gangster who must deal with both demons and aliens. The *Criminal Macabre* series features Cal McDonald, a private detective who deals with the supernatural.

Other Examples of Nonfiction

Comics have been sources of nonfiction information for adults for a long time as well as for instructional methods, propaganda, information on current events, and politics (see Exhibit 3-3). These are usually specially produced titles not produced by standard comics companies. Some of the more interesting (and odd) ones include various antidrug comics, a comic on fetal alcohol syndrome, the World War II Army's "How to Spot a Jap" (by *Terry and the Pirates* creator Milton Caniff), the invasion of Granada, Martin Luther King and the Montgomery Bus Boycott, and comics on birth control and sexually transmitted diseases.[7]

Exhibit 3-3. Politics and Comics

Prior to the 2008 elections, two comic book publishers, IDW and Antarctic Press, put out comic book biographies of Barack Obama and John McCain. This was not the first time that comics mixed with politics, as these comics were not the first to feature a person running for office. Harry Truman had a comic book published about him when he was running for re-election in 1948, as did Dwight Eisenhower in 1956. When running for governor in the early 1960s, George Wallace put out a comic book that highlighted how he stood up to integrationists. Even in 2008, some candidates for office used comic books to try to get their message out.

Sitting presidents have occasionally interacted with comic book characters, sometimes giving heroes assignments or even being saved by them. The most famous presidential appearance was in *Action Comics* #285 in which John F. Kennedy helped Superman by disguising himself as Superman's secret identity of Clark Kent so that Superman and "Clark" could be seen together. "After all," says Superman to Kennedy, explaining why he revealed his secret to him, "if I can't trust the President of the United States, who can I trust?" Unfortunately, this issue came out only a few weeks before JFK's assassination. A second planned story, in which Superman helps with Kennedy's "Presidential Fitness Program," was shelved at first, but at the request of the White House it was published as a tribute in *Superman* #170 (1964) (this first story can be found in *Showcase Presents Superman*, Volume 3, while the second is in Volume 5).

Since his election, Barack Obama has appeared in several comic books, most notably was *Amazing Spider-Man* #583 (2009), which was so popular that Marvel put out five printings, all of which had high sales (this story can be found in *Spider-Man: Election Day* [2009]). He appeared in titles from other publishers as well, including parodies that portray him like Conan (Devil's Due's *Barack the Barbarian*) and as a Zombie Fighter (Antarctic Press's *President Evil*). The topic of President Obama and comic books will be included in a book about Obama and popular culture to be called *Obama-Mania: Critical Essays on Representations of President*

(Cont'd.)

Exhibit 3-3. Politics and Comics *(Continued)*

Barack Obama in Popular Culture. Additional comic book biographies have also been created, including the *Female Force* titles from Bluewater Productions, which are comics about Hilary Clinton, Sarah Palin, Michelle Obama, and other women in politics. Even Obama's dog got a comic book. On a more serious note, Michael Crowley and Dan Goldman created the nonfiction graphic novel, *08 Graphic Diary of the Campaign Trail* (Three Rivers Press).

Fictional presidents and politicians have also appeared in comics over the years, sometimes even as bad guys. DC's science fiction title *Transmetropolitian* had the president causing a lot of trouble for the title's protagonist Spider Jerusalem. In the 1970s DC had a comic called *Prez* about a teenager elected president, and in the DC Universe itself, Superman's enemy Lex Luthor was president for a time, changing the normal circumstances of having the "real world" president being president there as well. In 2008, DC also had a limited series, *DCU: Decisions*, in which superheroes began to endorse presidential candidates. While these candidates were all fictional, Image Comics' Savage Dragon endorsed Obama on a variant cover for issue #137 of his book. The manga series *Eagle: The Making of an Asian-American President* tells the story of Democratic Senator Kenneth Yamaoka who runs for president in 2000. The five-volume series, which originally ran in Japan from 1997–2001, also features President "Bill Clydon" and his wife "Ellery" who has her own political ambitions. On a lower level, the ongoing series *Ex Machina* is about a former superhero who becomes mayor of New York City.

One of the best-known usages of comics to teach adults was the U.S. Army publication *PS Magazine*. Originally called *Army Motors*, it changed its name during the Korean War. Subtitled *The Preventive Maintenance Monthly*, it helped to provide up-to-date information that could appear faster (and cheaper) in the magazine than in a revised army manual. In addition, it was in a format that "entices soldiers/mechanics to pick up the publication and use its information to keep Army materiel working" (Whitworth, 2006). This format included cartoons and comic strips, including the character of Joe Dope, created by Will Eisner (the magazine's creative director 1951–1971), who was used as an example of what *not* to do. Eisner would travel to places like Korea and Vietnam to learn more about the soldiers' activities, and it was one of these trips that inspired a story in his graphic novel *Last Day in Viet Nam*. The Eisner-directed issues of *PS Magazine* can be found online in the digital collections of Virginia Commonwealth University at dig.library.vcu.edu.

When it comes to nonfiction graphic novels, one of the most diverse creators is Larry Gonick, whose *Cartoon History* and *Cartoon Guide* books have covered such topics as U.S. and world history, computers, genetics, chemistry, statistics, and even sex. Two publishers have produced a series of "For Beginners" books on topics such as Sigmund Freud, anarchism, the Olympics, and Karl Marx. Besides the graphic biographies, war, and true crime books, other nonfiction items covered in graphic novels for adults include the history of the Students for a Democratic Society, the hoax of the *Protocols of the Elders of Zion*, the U.S. Constitution, the creation of the atomic bomb, a history of Jews in America, and the 9/11 attacks.[8] Chapter 7 discusses options in cataloging the nonfiction graphic novels in your collection.

Diversity in Comics and Graphic Novels

Comics and graphic novels have a great deal of diversity in terms of religion, ethnicity, and sexuality. This was not always the case, and during the 1940s non-Caucasians were often drawn stereotypically. Religion was usually relegated to characters cele-brating Christmas (unless it was a specifically religious comic), and there was not even the slightest hint that anyone was anything but heterosexual. But things have changed, and today mainstream comics feature characters of varied races, religions, and sexual orientations. This is especially true with graphic novels, and this diversity can be helpful when using graphic novels in book displays and discussions (see Chapter 8) or in the classroom (see Chapter 9).

A large of number of titles for both adults and younger ages feature characters who are of various religions (which sometimes is important to the story, while other times it is just who the character is), ethnicities (both as a "hyphenated" American or their country of origin), and sexualities. In all three cases, this variety is seen in both the lead characters and the supporting ones (for example, the *Sandman* collection *A Game of You* features both lesbian and transgender characters).

Lists of characters of various ethnicities, religions, and sexualities appear on various online sites. There is also much diversity among the creators, including those who have written autobiographical and semiautobiographical works. In addition, the stories told in the titles listed in Appendix A take place on every continent (including Antarctica) and, as the next chapter shows, creators and graphic novels come from all over the world. The titles listed in Appendix A cover many other genres as well: Westerns, romance (which covers love, sex, and even sexuality), science fiction, fantasy, adventure, historical, and simple stories of everyday life.

Notes

1. The term can also be written as "super-hero" or "super hero." DC Comics and Marvel Comics jointly own the trademark for the term, at least as it applies to the title of any publi-cations or merchandising.

2. It is unclear if The Clock first appeared in *Funny Pages* #6 or *Funny Picture Stories* #1 because they both came out in the same month.

3. Campbell wrote his first story with the character of Alec MacGarry in the late 1970s. In September 2009 Top Shelf put out *Alec: The Years Have Pants*, which collected all of the Alec stories.

4. This story is reprinted in *The Mammoth Book of War Comics*. See Appendix A.

5. Written in 2007, *Shooting War* incorrectly predicted that John McCain won the 2008 election.

6. Holmes' story was told in Eric Larson's award-winning *The Devil in the White City: Murder, Magic and Madness at the Fair That Changed America* (2003), while the story of Rogers' murder and its influence on the work of Edgar Allan Poe was recounted in *The Beautiful Cigar Girl: Mary Rogers, Edgar Allan Poe, and the Invention of Murder* (2006).

7. These and several other odd comics can be found at www.ep.tc/intro.html.

8. Speaking of 9/11, following the events of September 11, 2001, several comic book companies produced comic books and graphic novels about it, usually with proceeds going to charities. These included the graphic novel anthology *9-11: September 11, 2001 (Artists Respond)*, Volume 1, published jointly by Dark Horse Comics, Image Comics, and Chaos! Comics; its companion book *9-11: September 11, 2001 (The World's Finest Comic Book Writers & Artists Tell Stories to Remember)*, Volume 2, from DC Comics; and the similarly themed *9-11: Emergency Relief* from Alternative Comics. Marvel Comics put out several 9/11-themed comic books, including a special issue of *Amazing Spider-Man*. The following year, the Library of Congress had a special exhibition on 9/11 and comics along with a panel that included Will Eisner who had contributed to several of the anthologies.

References

Goulart, Ron. 2004. *Comic Book Encyclopedia: The Ultimate Guide to Characters, Graphic Novels, Writers, and Artists in the Comic Book Universe.* New York: HarperCollins.

Pekar, Harvey, and Joyce Brabner. 1994. *Our Cancer Year.* New York: Four Walls Eight Windows.

Spiegelman, Art. 1995. "Symptons of Disorder/Signs of Genius," in *Justin Green's Binky Brown Sampler.* San Francisco: Last Gasp.

Versaci, Rocco. 2007. *This Book Contains Graphic Language: Comics as Literature.* New York: Continuum.

Whitworth, Jerry. 2006. *A Case for Comics: Comic Books as an Educational Tool Part Three.* Available: www.sequentialart.com/article.php?id=234 (accessed August 22, 2009).

Chapter 4

What Is Manga and Where Else Do Graphic Novels Come From?

While only in recent years have graphic novels become "acceptable" for adults in the United States, elsewhere in the world they have been mainstream for decades. Some aimed at younger readers, such as the Franco-Belgian *Tintin* and *Asterix*, have been around for decades. Newer works from the United Kingdom, France, Japan, South Korea, and other countries in Europe, Asia, and other parts of the world are now being brought to America. Many of these titles are written for adult readers, and both they, and those for younger readers, are becoming very popular. However, in terms of sales and popularity, the biggest kind of "foreign import" when it comes to graphic novels is manga.

Manga around the World

Go into any bookstore with a decent graphic novel section and you will see shelves full of manga, with possibly more volumes than those of Western comics. While technically the term "manga" applies to only comics from Japan, it has also been used to describe manhua (from China), manhwa (from South Korea), Original English Language (OEL) manga (also known as Amerimanga), and manga-style works from other non-Asian countries, sometimes referred to as "Original Global Manga (OGM)." In addition, all types of manga can be described as being "graphic novels."

Manga in Japan

The word "manga" (pronounced "mahn-ga"), is the Japanese word for "comics," though it can also refer to comic strips, caricatures, and other similar works and was taken from the Chinese ideograms for "Man" (involuntary) and "Ga" (picture). It can also be literarily translated as "whimsical sketches" or "lighthearted pictures." An early usage of the term appeared in *Hokusai Manga* (*Random Sketches by Hokusai*), a multivolume series of sketches created by the Japanese woodblock-print artist Hokusai beginning in 1814.

Japan has a long history of comic art that dates back to ancient times. The Edo Period in which Hokusai lived saw an increase in comic pictures, and with the opening of Japan to the West, Japanese artists were exposed to the Western style of art (and introduced the West to the work of Hokusai and others). At the beginning of the twentieth century, newspaper comics and cartoons increased this exposure. Following World War II, the Japanese people were eager for inexpensive entertainment and turned to two kinds that involved using pictures to aid storytelling.

The first was the outdoor storytelling known as "kami-shibai" (paper plays), in which storytellers would travel around neighborhoods with hand-painted and varnish-covered cardboard story sheets that were presented in sequence while the narrator provided sound effects and the story to accompany them. The storytelling was free, but members of the audience were expected to buy sweets sold by the storyteller. From the end of the war to the year 1953, when television broadcasts began, an estimated 10,000 people made a living as kami-shibai narrators and 5 million people watched one show a day.

The second kind of entertainment was manga. Early after the war, some artists created self-contained comic stories for professional book lenders/pay libraries called "kashibonya" that loaned out hardcover comics for a small fee. Other artists worked on different kinds of published manga, including one kind that was printed in red ink and known as "akabon" (red books). One of the most popular stories featured in these books was *Shin Takarajima* (*New Treasure Island*), created by a 19-year-old medical student named Osamu Tezuka. His second published work, it sold over 400,000 copies, initiated a national craze for manga (Kinsella, 2000), and helped launch Tezuka's career (see Exhibit 4-1).

In 1959, the first weekly manga publication, *Weekly Shonen Magazine*, began. Manga was becoming popular for all ages and receiving critical respect. One notable work at the time was *Ninja Bugeichō* (*Ninja Military Chronicles*), which ran from 1959–1962 and told the story of ninja who fought against corrupt feudal lords on behalf of the people. This story became very popular with student protestors who had their own problems with the government (Thompson, 2007). This period also saw the rise of the gekiga (dramatic pictures) type of manga, which were "darker" stories aimed at adults. This was the equivalent to the "underground" or "alternative" movement in the United States. Examples of gekiga in Appendix A include *Golgo 13* and the works of Yoshihiro Tatsumi. Manga magazines that were primarily for adults began to appear at this time as well, including *Garo* (1964), *Com* (created by Tezuka in 1967), and *Biggu Komikku* (*Big Comic*), which began in 1968 and is still being published.

Manga's popularity grew even more over the next several decades. In Japan, manga is currently a multibillion dollar industry, and sales of many individual magazine titles—about 300 each month—are roughly equivalent to those of such major American magazines as *Time* and *Newsweek*. Close to 40 percent of all materials printed in Japan are manga magazines and books, and manga magazines account for one-sixth of the Japanese magazine industry (Brenner, 2007). Manga has also become part of

---

Exhibit 4-1. Osama Tezuka

A pioneer in both comics and animation (anime), Osamu Tezuka (1928–1989) has been referred to as "the father of manga," the "god of manga," and "the Walt Disney of Japan" (a term also bestowed upon director Hayao Miyazaki). He has also been compared to such influential American artists as Will Eisner and Jack Kirby. His 40+ year career produced works for both children and adults in all genres, some of which have only recently been translated into English. The young Tezuka was a fan of the works of Walt Disney and copied the "cute" look of big eyes and wide mouths for his work, a style that still influences the artwork in manga and anime (Pilcher and Brooks, 2005). In 1946 he created his first comic, *Manchan no Nikkicho* (*Manchan's Diary*), for the children's magazine *Mainchi Shogakusei Shinbun* (*Mainichi Newspaper for Elementary School Students*), and the following year *Shin Takarajima* (*New Treasure Island*), inspired by the Robert Louis Stevenson story, was published. Other manga by Tezuka that were based on or adapted from Western literary works included *Faust* (1949), *Pinocchio* (1952), and *Crime and Punishment* (1953).

In 1950 he created *Jungle Taitei* (*Jungle Emperor*) for *Manga Shonen*, which ran until 1954 and was turned into a cartoon series. The cartoon was soon dubbed into English and shown on NBC as *Kimba the White Lion* (which would also influence the Disney film *The Lion King*). The following year he created Atomu Taishi (Ambassador Atom), later changed to *Tetsuwan Atomu* (*Mighty Atom*), which led to the animated series known in America as *Astro Boy*. The cartoon for *Astro Boy* predated *Kimba* and in fact was the first animated show in Japan. In 1953, he created *Ribon no Kishi* (*Princess Knight*), considered to be the first modern shojo manga (Thompson, 2007). By the time of his death in 1989, he had won a number of major awards and produced over 160,000 pages of work.

Many of Teuzka's works were for adults and may include such elements as nudity and other adult themes. Seven of Tezuka's works—*Apollo's Song* (*Apollo no Uta*, 1970), *Ode to Kirihoto* (*Kirihito Sanka*, 1968–1971), *Black Jack* (1973–1983), *Buddha* (1972–1983), *MW* (1976–1978), *Adolf* (1983–1985)—are included in Appendix A. Two additional titles of note are *Metropolis* (1949), a science fiction story about a private investigator who must take care of a robot child after its creator is killed, and *Phoenix* (*Hi no Tori*, 1956–1989), a story, set throughout time, of people's quest for immortality, which was described by by Tezuka as his "life's work" (Thompson, 2007: 270).

Japanese society. In 1984, questions about manga were incorporated into an entrance exam to a public university. Ten years later, the Japanese government began producing white papers in manga form (Kinsella, 2000).

While currently in Japan an estimated two-thirds of boys and one-sixth of girls under 18 read manga, it is also not uncommon to see adult businessmen reading thick manga magazines on the train while going to and from work. These large magazines, which range from titles aimed at children like *Weekly Shonen Jump* to adult titles like *Biggu Komikku*, have squared backs, come out weekly or biweekly, are between 240 and 400 pages, and cost about 250 to 300 yen. This is roughly equivalent to the price of a single American comic that runs only 32 pages. These magazines often contain up to 10 to 40 stories, many of which are part of a serialized story, as well as articles, columns, interviews, and promotions. There are also monthly magazines that range in size and price but can be up to 1,000 pages and cost 700 yen. The stories tend to be in black and white, though occasionally some color appears at the beginning of the story.

While the magazines are printed on cheap paper and are often tossed out when finished, many of the story chapters are collected in the manga equivalent of the trade edition, called "tankōbon." The standard tankōbon is softcovered with a dust jacket, costs about 400 yen, and contains about 184 pages of a serialized story. They often have multiple printings and a long shelf life, and the most popular are further reprinted in smaller "pocket" editions called "bunkoban" or larger ones known as "kazenban," both of which tend to have more pages than the tankōbon.

Both the magazines and books are very popular, though in 2005 the total amount of tankōbon sales was greater than that of magazine sales for the first time (Thompson, 2007). This may be the Japanese equivalent to American readers "waiting for the trade," especially since readers may be interested in only a certain story and not the others found in the weekly magazines. As in America, people can be seen standing around in bookstores reading manga (the Japanese term for this is "tachiyomi"), and Japan also has places called manga kissa, cafés where for around 400 yen an hour people can sit and read books from a manga library. Some of these cafés also offer food, drink, video games, Internet access, and even a place to sleep. Manga can even be purchased from vending machines.

The creators of manga are known as "manga-ka." Over 3,000 manga-ka work in Japan, and while the vast majority of them barely make a living at it, the top creators are well rewarded for their work, especially if they retain some of the rights to their characters and get good royalties. Rumiko Takahashi, the creator of *Ranma 1/2*, *InuYasha*, and other popular titles, has been listed as one of the ten richest people in Japan (Pilcher and Brooks, 2005).

Manga Comes to America

The first known manga in the United States was *The Four Immigrants Manga*, aka *The Four Students Manga* (*Manga yonin shosei*) created in 1931 by Japanese immigrant Henry (Yoshitaka) Kiyama. This autobiographical work was created while Kiyama was living in San Francisco. He had it printed while visiting Japan and then self-published it when back home in America. The book contained a foreword by prominent locals, including the consul general of Japan, and was written primarily in Japanese but with dialogue spoken by Americans in English. A full translation was published over 60 years later by Stone Bridge Press (Schodt, 1998).

Not until the 1980s would translated manga begin to appear regularly in America. The expense of relettering the word balloons and sound effects, signs, etc., was cost-prohibitive. One notable exception was Keiji Nakazawa's semiautobiographical *Barefoot Gen* (see Exhibit 4-2), which was translated and published in 1978 by Project Gen, a group made up of Japanese and American volunteers (Gravett, 2004). In 1983, *Manga Manga* by Frederik Schodt (who would later translate *The Four Immigrants Manga*), became the first English language book on the subject. But it was in 1987 when a number of manga titles were translated and released in comic book form by American comic book publishers. These included *Lone Wolf and Cub* from First

---

Exhibit 4-2. *Barefoot Gen*

On August 6, 1945, six-year-old Keiji Nakazawa was living in Hiroshima when the atomic bomb was dropped. He was a little over a kilometer away from the bomb, standing at the back gate of Kanzaki Primary School, and was saved because he was in the building's shadow. However, most of his family was killed (Nakazawa, 2004). He grew up to become a creator of manga, and after his mother's death he felt that he had to tell the story (Gravett, 2004) using young Gen Nakaoka as a substitute for himself.

As mentioned in Chapter 3, he first wrote the manga short story "Ore wa Mita" ("I Saw It") and then began to serialize *Hadashi no Gen* in the children's magazine *Weekly Shonen Jump*. The story ran from 1972–1973 and was later collected into 10 volumes. A few years after Project Gen, translated volumes were published by New Society Publishing. Recently, Last Gasp published the previously untranslated volumes.

Comics (currently published by Dark Horse), *Area 88*, *The Legend of Kamui*, and *Mai the Psychic Girl* jointly published by VIZ and Eclipse (though under Eclipse's name), and, in the following year, *Akira* from Marvel's Epic Comics imprint. Even noncomics publishers produced manga works at this time, such as the University of California Press's 1988 publication of *Japan Inc: An Introduction of Japanese Economics*.[1] More titles appeared, with Dark Horse Comics and VIZ Media publishing the majority of them. The increased popularity of black-and-white comics with American readers in the 1980s furthered the popularity of these books. Manga's popularity was also helped by a growing American interest in anime. One recent sign of manga's increased popularity was that in 2006, the term was added to the *Merriam-Webster's Dictionary*.

Eventually manga published in the United States began to take the form that we know today, with one volume containing several chapters of a manga story. Besides VIZ, companies such as Tokyopop, Go! Comi, Digital Manga Publishing, and Vertical exclusively publish manga, while DC, Dark Horse, and "text" book publisher Del Rey have manga lines (see Chapter 6). Recent years have seen a great increase in the amount of translated manga, due in part to the increasing popularity of the format. Some extreme manga fans who can't wait for the American translations to catch up to Japanese publications, with the use of a scanner and knowledge of Japanese, create unauthorized "scanslations" (also called "scanlations") that are sent to fans via the Internet. However, recent economic problems have also hit the comics industry, and this, along with an oversaturation of the market, has hurt sales. This has caused some publishers to go out of business and others to make cuts in staff and reduce their output—in some cases by over 20 percent ("Broccoli Books Shuts Down," 2008).

Translations are usually done by native English speakers, and some manga will have a "notes" section in the back of the book that explains certain cultural or historical references. But language isn't the only difference between Japanese and American editions. In Japan, the order of the pages, the panels, and even reading order of the word balloons is right to left, so for American publications they have to be "flopped," so that they appear in the manner to which American readers are accustomed, which adds an extra expense to the publisher. Now, however, unflopped manga is becoming more popular and many publishers are choosing to release the translated material in the "authentic" layout. Many publishers will print a "warning" (often tongue-in-cheek style) at what American readers would consider the "front" of the book (though it's really the back), often with diagrams explaining how the book should be read. Some examples:

> Stop! This is the back of the book. You wouldn't want to spoil a great ending! This book is printed "manga-style," in the authentic Japanese right-to-left format. Since none of the artwork has been flopped or altered, readers get to experience the story as the creator intended. (From Tokyopop's *Chobits*, Vol. 1)

> Tomare! [stop]. You are going the wrong way! Manga is a completely different type of reading experience. To start at the beginning, go the end! That's right! Authentic manga is read the traditional Japanese way—from right to left, exactly the opposite of how American books are read. It's easy to follow: Just go to the other end of the book, and read each page—and each panel—from right side to left side, starting at the top right. Now you're experiencing manga as it was meant to be. (From Del Rey's *Mu Shi Shi*, Vol. 1)

> Wrong Way! Japanese books, including manga like this one, are meant to be read from right to left. So the front cover is actually the back cover, and vice-versa. To read this book, please flip it over and start in the top right-hand corner. Read the panels, and the bubbles in the panels, from right to left, then drop down to the next row and repeat. It may make you dizzy at first, but forcing your brain to do things backward makes you smarter in the long run. We swear. (From Vertical's *To Terra*, Vol. 1)

Deciding which is the actual "front" and "back" of a manga volume can be tricky not only for readers but also for librarians who must decide where to put the "date due card" pocket, barcodes, or anything else added during processing. See Chapter 7 for more on processing decisions.

Both the art and writing style of manga is different from that of American comics. For example, many characters have large eyes, and "speed lines" are often used to show rapid movement. In addition, the pacing of the stories tends to be slower, with many more panels that have art but no dialogue. This is in part because many readers, especially businesspeople on a long train ride to and from work, tend to skim a manga page in only three seconds.

One other aspect of manga stories that is different from many Western titles is that they often are one long story that eventually ends, whereas many American series continue for years with many different stories. In other words, many manga resemble an American "limited series" more than on ongoing series. With collected manga, there are some one-volume books, some that are finished in five to ten books, and others that continue even longer. Some of the longest-running translated series of books include the *Dragon Ball* titles (42 volumes), *Ranma 1/2* (38 volumes), and the still-running *Nartuo*, which will have over 47 volumes by the time it ends. In Japan, the longest-running manga in terms of number of volumes is *Kochira Katsushika-ku*

Kôen-mae Hashutsujo (*This Is the Police Station in Front of Kameari Park in Katsushika Ward*) by Osamu Akimoto. Appearing in *Weekly Shonen Jump* since 1976, its over 1,400 chapters have been collected in more than 160 volumes since 1977. This is an exception to the "continuing-story" rule, however, being more like a "sitcom" than one basic story (Thompson, 2007). As is covered in later chapters, because most manga series are one extended story in which every volume is needed, this can affect both your purchasing and your weeding decisions.

Manga in Other Parts of the World

Manga from Korea is called "manhwa." Although heavily influenced by Japanese comics, it is printed left to right, American style, so it does not need to be flopped. The first major manhwa title published in the United States was *Redmoon*, produced by the now-defunct publisher ComicsOne. Several manga publishers also produce manhwa, and one publisher, Ice Kunion, is a joint venture of three major Korean publishers. Manhua, also published in America and originating from Taiwan and Hong Kong, comes from a different artistic tradition than manga or manhwa. Among its various genres, martial arts stories are common, and these are often published in color. Manhua has been published in America since the 1980s, with DrMaster and HK Comics being among the domestic publishers.

Manga-style comics are also being created all around the world, and they are commonly referred to as original global manga (OGM). Italy, France, Germany, and Australia are among the manga-producing countries, with some of their titles also appearing in America. Manga created in the United States used to be known as "Amerimanga" but is now referred to as OEL (original English language) manga. Tokyopop, Antarctic Press, and Seven Seas are among the comics publishers that produce OEL manga, along with other publishers, such as HarperCollins. Tokyopop has held several "Rising Stars of Manga" competitions for American creators. Unfortunately, financial difficulties can cause a publisher to forgo OEL stories in favor of licensed translated material that is cheaper and easier to produce (Yaoi Press, 2008).

Other publishers of mainstream comics also attempt to copy the manga style. Some examples are Marvel's "Mangaverse" and "Tsunami" lines of comics and DC's *Teen Titans Go!* comic, based on the animated series that had an "anime" look to it.

Some think that it is not "true" manga unless it comes from Japan, or at least from Asia, but whether called a manga or a comic, it is still a very popular kind of book and one that will probably circulate well at your library. And there is at least one notable person in Japan who enjoys non-Japanese manga: Tarō Asō, Prime Minister from 2008–2009.[2] In 2007, as Minister of Foreign Affairs, Asō created a "Nobel Prize of Manga" that was awarded to a foreign artist whose work "best contributes to the spread of manga worldwide" ("Japan Plans," 2007). During its first year, the award attracted 146 entries from 26 countries (China had the most with 24, followed by England with 15 and Germany with 14 while the United States submitted 5). The winner was Hong Kong creator Lee Chi Ching for a manga about the creator of *The*

Art of War, with the runners-up being China's Kai (*1520*), Malaysia's Benny Wong Thong Hou (*Le Gardenie*), and Australia's Madeleine Rosca, whose *Hollow Fields* was released in America by Seven Seas (Anime News Network, 2007).

Manga Genres and Popular Storylines

Manga comes in a larger range of genres than in American comic books (see Exhibit 4-3). While many are "fantastic" stories with science fiction, fantasy, and horror themes, and some are mystery, crime, and romance books, others are about subjects that might be considered mundane. For example, some manga feature people playing games or sports or involved in hobbies and other leisure activities. Besides well-known titles like *Prince of Tennis*, *Eyeshield 21* (about American football), and *Hikaru No Go* (about the Japanese board game *Go*) there are stories and even whole manga magazines that focus on fishing (called tsuri manga), the popular pinball-like game Pachinko, and mah-jongg. In 2006, the publisher Japanime produced *The Manga Guide to Sudoku* that contained a 40-page story followed by 40 pages of puzzles.

Other manga are about ordinary people in various professions, such as teachers (*GTO*) and firefighters (*Firefighter: Daigo of Fire Company M*). Another popular

---

Exhibit 4-3. Examples of Popular Manga Storylines

The following are some examples of the storylines of various manga aimed at different ages:

- After falling into a cursed spring, a boy turns into a girl whenever splashed with cold water (*Ranma 1/2*).
- High school students are sent to an island where it is kill or be killed (*Battle Royale*).
- A Japanese-American senator runs for President of the United States (*Eagle: The Making of an Asian-American President*).
- A magic notebook causes the death of anyone whose name is written in it (*Death Note*).
- A fictional version of the life of Cesare Borgia (*Canterella*).
- A froglike alien is supposed to be part of an invasion but ends up living with a human family (*Sgt. Frog*).
- A person who is male on top and female below the waist becomes part of a strange dream experiment (*After School Nightmare*).
- A strange virus causes suicides and gives some teens special abilities (*Alive*).
- The semiautobiography tells the story of life after the dropping of the atomic bomb (*Barefoot Gen*).
- The 7-Eleven comes to Japan (*Project X*).
- A sword and sorcery epic tells the story of a lone warrior (*Berserk*).
- Aliens are possessing people so they can eat other humans (*Parasyte*).
- An assassin becomes the leader of a mafia family (*Crying Freeman*).
- Parents must learn to deal with an autistic child (*Within the Light*).
- In Feudal Japan, a samurai turned assassin must protect his infant son (*Lone Wolf and Cub*).
- Two men fall in love after meeting in school (*Ichigenme*).
- A newly married and inexperienced married couple must learn about sex (*Manga Sutra*).
- A mysterious pet shop offers its customers not only what they want, but what they deserve (*Pet Shop of Horrors*).
- The happenings at the strangest high school in Japan are shared (*Cromartie High School*).
- After an accident, a boy is mistakenly given the face of the girl he has a crush on (*Pretty Face*).

genre referred to as "salaryman" manga first appeared in the 1960s, often as comic strips in weekly newsmagazines and major newspapers, and the stories were often about the common low-ranked employee in a white-collar job (comparisons have been made to *Dilbert*). By the 1980s, these manga had become about the idealized businessman who is moving up the corporate ladder and doing things because it helps the company, not his own career. Another version of the genre featured the businessman who actually cares more about his family or hobbies than his job. Some salaryman manga can also be about true businesspeople, including the *Project X* series, an all-ages title that covers subjects such as the creation of the Cup Noodles, and a biography of Warren Buffet (Thompson, 2007).

Interestingly, Japan has very little in the way of superhero comics, at least not in the same "costumed crimefighter" vein that is common in America. Some American comics (called "amecomi") have been translated into Japanese, but they tend to sell only to hard-core fans. Most American characters are better known from video games and movies, though some American heroes have appeared in manga, including Spider-Man and Batman. Television offers more superhero stories, especially those in the Tokusatsu (special effects) genre, such as *Ultraman* and *Cyborg 009*.

Manga has a strong tie to anime, with manga being based on anime and anime adapting the manga stories (including live action versions as well). Anime came to the United States much earlier than manga because it is much easier to dub than to reletter. Most appeared on television, including *Kimba the White Lion*, *Gigantor*, *Speed Racer*, *Battle of the Planets*, *Star Blazers*, *Pokemon*, and *Sailor Moon*.[3] The latter helped to increase the number of female manga fans in the 1990s. The rise of the Cartoon Network also introduced many anime series to U.S. audiences. One of the first major anime shown in movie theaters was the adaptation of *Akira*, and films directed by Hayao Miyazaki, such as *Princess Mononoke* and *Spirited Away*, garnered box office success and awards.

Manga for Different Ages and Sexes

Various terms are used for manga to describe both the age level and sex for which they are being written as well as for the nature of the content (see Exhibit 4-4). For the younger readers, there is shōnen (or shounen) for boys, shōjo (or shoujo) for girls, and kodomo for readers under ten. Many shōnen and shōjo are also read by adults and make up about half of the manga published in Japan, but, as in America, many are specifically created for older readers.

Seinen (young men) manga are aimed at men in their older teens through adulthood. Arising from gekiga in the 1960s, with manga magazines that included *Manga Action* and *Big Comic*, two basic types of seinen are published. The first type, referred to as "Young," a word that often appears in the magazines' titles, is aimed at males in late high school and college. These tend to be rowdy and raunchy in nature, along with some stories aimed at otaku ("fanboys") that feature science fiction, fantasy, horror, action, and so on. The other type, also known as "dansei" (adult men), is aimed at adult

Exhibit 4-4. Manga Terms

The following is a quick list of manga terms, some of which are defined elsewhere in this chapter.

bara: "Rose"; manga written for homosexual men.

bishônen: "Beautiful boy"; male characters with handsome though slightly androgynous looks.

dojinshi: Self-published works aimed at other fans. The popular manga collective Clamp started off as a dojinshi group. A group is known as a "circle," and each member contributes to the story. These works are tolerated by publishers in most cases and there are even dojinshi conventions.

fanservice: Also known as a "service cut" or even "service," this is sexually suggestive eye candy or even nudity that adds nothing to the story. For example, a "panty shot" during an action scene or a picture that focuses on a female character's breasts or behind.

gekiga: "Dramatic pictures"; term used by some manga-ka as an alternative type.

hentai: Used by English-speaking fans to indicate pornographic anime and manga.

josei: Manga aimed at adult women.

Lolicon: Short for "Lolita Complex," a Japanese trend since the 1980s that refers to sexually suggestive material involving female characters who are or at least look young. Includes adult characters drawn with "cute" faces and childlike features. A related term is "Moe," which means "to sprout," and is a more platonic version focusing on cute for cuteness sake. The male equivalent is "Shota" or "shotcan," which is named after a character in *Tetsujin 28-go*, better known in America as *Gigantor*.

manga-ka: A manga creator. Some manga titles are credited not to an individual writer or artist but to artistic teams.

mecha: A genre that refers to all machines from real ones to giant robots.

otaku: The Japanese equivalent to the American "fanboy." The stereotype otaku is smart but has poor social skills and hygiene as well obsessive collection tendencies and is heavily into science fiction, fantasy, toys, anime, etc. There is also a stereotype that otaku are heavily into pornography, which was reinforced when a man was arrested for kidnapping, molesting, and killing three preschool-age girls, and a search of his apartment revealed horror and porno Lolicon anime. This caused the term to become derogatory for a time and created a moral panic, leading to restrictions of the sale of adult anime and manga in Japan. The term has since reclaimed its older meaning.

redicomi: Ladies' comics. While once part of josei the term now indicates sex comics aimed at women.

seinen: "Young man"; manga aimed at males in their late teens and older. Depending on how it is written in Japanese, it could also refer to sexual themed comics.

shōjo (or shoujo): Manga written for girls and young women ages 12 through 18.

shōnen (or shounen): Manga aimed at boys.

shōnen-ai: "Boys' love"; romances between males, often written by women for a female readership. The female version is sh_jo-ai.

tankobon: Collected volumes of manga stories. The Japanese equivalent of a trade edition. Other versions of collected editions include bunkoban, kazenban, and aizoban.

yaoi: In Japan the term applies to "slash fiction," while in America it is more graphic sh_nen-ai. The female version is yuri ("lily").

Source: Information for these definitions came from several sources, but primarily from Thompson's *Manga: The Complete Guide* (2007, pp. 258–259 [otaku] and 495–502).

male readers, including those in middle age. These stories may be violent or risqué but are also about adults and appeal to adult readers. Many of these stories are adapted into live action films (Thompson, 2007). Dansei genres often include salaryman, crime, and political drama and include such stories as *Golgo 13*, *MW*, and *Ode to Kirihito*.

The female equivalent to seinen is "josei," which is aimed at college-aged to middle-aged women. The writing is often sophisticated and mainly deals with work, family, and romance (Thompson, 2007). Josei generally began to appear in the late 1970s; before this, shojo made up almost all of the female-themed manga. The genre took off in the 1980s, with stories aimed at female office workers. Stories at this time focused on sexual themes and were about taboo love affairs and erotic fantasies. This caused josei to begin to gain a bad reputation, and eventually the genre split into "regular" josei and the more erotic and sexual "redicomi" manga. By the late 1980s, josei began to focus on "younger, hipper" women, including professionals. Only a small percentage of josei titles have been translated so far (though the number is growing), with notable titles including *Antique Bakery*, *Nana*, *A Perfect Day for Love Letters*, and a line of romance stories produced by Harlequin.

One type of manga that has gained increased popularity is yaoi ("yah-oi"), which deals with romantic and often sexual relationships between two men. Yaoi is primarily written by women for women and originates partly from dojinshi (self-published manga created by fans), stories about two previously existing male characters in a relationship. Dojinshi is the equivalent to the American genre of fan fiction known as "slash," which takes its name from how the protagonists' names are written (e.g., Kirk/Spock). Yaoi is credited with attracting thousands of Japanese women to self-published comics (Thompson, 2007).

The term "yaoi" has no actual Japanese translation; it comes from the first syllables of the words in the phrase "yamanashi, ochinashi, iminashi," or "no climax, no conclusion, no meaning," and is actually used more in the United States than in Japan, where it generally referred to as shonen-ai or "boys' love." Stories about teen boys in love began in the 1970s in Japan, though the emphasis was on a more idealized form of love. More recent books of this type with less sexual content are also referred to as shonen-ai by American fans. Many of these "tamer" stories deal with bishonen, or "beautiful boys," male characters drawn with a handsome, but slightly androgynous look. Often in these stories, the character does not think of himself as gay; he just happens to be attracted to another male (Thompson, 2007).

Yaoi has gained popularity in the United States, though it was not regularly published until 2004. Many of the regular American publishers have yaoi titles, though some publish the stories under a different imprint: Tokyopop has Blu; Digital Manga Publishing has a line called June, with yaoi being the main product of its sister company 801 Media; the now-defunct Broccoli had a Boysenberry line; and Aurora Publishing uses the imprint Deux Press (with a redicomi published under the Luv Luv Press imprint). Also of note is Yaoi Press, which publishes yaoi not only from Japan but also from Italy, the first major American publisher to do so.

Female versions of shonen-ai and yaoi do exist—shojo-ai and yuri—but even in Japan this is a small subgenre. Unlike "boys' love" stories that are written for women and not gay men (though there is manga for that group as well, called "bara"), many yuri stories tend to appeal more to lesbians (though the term can apply to "girls' love" stories that appeal to male readers as well). There is even a female version of bishonen called "bishojo." Yuri is just beginning to be published in America by companies like Seven Seas and Aurora (Thompson, 2007).

While some yaoi can be explicit and other seinen, redicomi, and so forth, can skirt the line between "for adult" and "adult," pornographic manga stories exist as well. Purely "sex comics," these are known in Japan as ero-manga but, creating a case of translation confusion, can also be called "seinen" (which, while pronounced the same as the word meaning "young men," is written with a different kanji, the Japanese written character) or written as "seijin." Icarus Publishing is one of the few American publishers that sells translated ero-manga.

Another type, hentai, contains even more graphic sex, often featuring scenes of rape, bondage, and "dirty" sex. This term is generally used in America, as in Japan it is a derogatory term for "weirdoes" and "perverts" and basically means "abnormal." The term "etchi," based on the Japanese pronunciation of the letter *H*, is also used to describe sexual material.

Chapter 6 discusses what sort of graphic novels to add to your adult collection as well as the ratings applied to manga, and Chapter 8 discusses how even manga with an age rating below "mature" may be inappropriate for certain ages.

Comics Traditions Elsewhere in the World

Japan, China, and Korea aren't alone in having a comics tradition. Comics are created all around the world (see Pilcher and Brooks' *The Essential Guide to World Comics* [2005] for a broader overview), and only a handful of these have been published in the United States, with the majority coming from France and the United Kingdom. Some notable foreign creators whose works have been brought to America (many of whom have works listed in Appendix A) include Malaysia's Lat, Switzerland's Frederik Peeters, Norway's Jason,[4] Sweden's Max Andersson and Lars Sjunnesson, South Africa's Joe Daly, Spain's Max, Israel's Rutu Modan, New Zealand's Dylan Horrocks, and Gabriel Bá and Fábio Moon, twin brothers from Brazil. Canadian writers whose works often appear in the United States (mainly in books published by Fantagraphics and the Canadian-based Drawn & Quarterly) include Seth, Chester Brown, Julie Doucet, and Michel Rabagliati. Many creators from other countries work on American comic books, while other creators born in one foreign country will have their work published in another. For example, Marguerite Abouet from Cote d'Ivorie, Guy Delisle from Canada, and Marjane Satrapi from Iran have all had work first published in France.

Comics are highly respected in France, where one in every eighth book sold is a comic book (*Cinebook Catalog* #6). French comics are commonly known as bandé dessinée or BD (pronounced bay-day), which means drawn strip. The format has also been known as "The Ninth Art" since 1964, when film critic and Sorbonne professor Claude Beylie said that it, along with television (the eighth art), should be added the *Reflections of the Seven Arts* that was created in 1923 by Italian critic Ricciotto Canudo. This equated comics with painting, sculpture, music, and other forms of art.[5] France is also home to the Festival International de la Bande Dessinée d'Angoulême (Angoulême International Comics Festival), the second largest comics convention in the world. French comics can more accurately be described as "Franco-Belgian," as many notable creators come from Belgium, including Georges Prosper Remi aka Hergé, whose children's comics character Tintin is known all around the world.

In 1974 comic writers Jean-Pierre Dionnet and Bernard Farkas and artists Jean Giraud and Philipe Druillet created a science-fiction-themed comic magazine for adults called *Métal Hurlant* as well as a publishing company Les Humanoïdes Associés. *Métal Hurlant* inspired an English-language counterpart *Heavy Metal* that at first included work by both American and French creators. This led to some French creators gaining fame in America, most notably Giraud, who went by the pen name Moebius. The publishing company is still around, though with new owners, and an American counterpart, Humanoids Publishing, was created in 1998. Humanoids has published translated works of such creators as Yugoslavia-born Enki Bilal as well as work by American writers that first appeared in France. They have also entered into partnerships with American publishers such as DC Comics and Devil's Due.

Another major creator-founded publishing house is l'Association, begun in 1990 by seven creators, with Lewis Tronheim and David B. being the best known to American readers. One of the most interesting books published by l'Association is *Comix 2000*, which was over 2,000 pages long and featured work by 324 creators from around the world. Other notable French creators include Joann Sfar, Philippe Dupuy, Charles Barberian, and Emmanuel Guibert. Drawn & Quarterly, First Second, and NBM are among the publishers who have produced translated Franco-Belgian comics in America. A newer company, the UK-based Cinebook, has been publishing Franco-Belgian works in English and calls itself "The 9th Art Publisher."

As covered in the history section of Chapter 2, Great Britain has a long history of comics art, including the works of William Hogarth, the periodical *Punch*, and even the usage of the word "cartoon" as meaning a humorous drawing. Other early British protocomics included *Funny Folks* in 1874 and *Comic Cuts* in 1890. In the early part of the twentieth century *Film Fun* (1920) sold over 1.7 million copies a week, and *The Beano*, which began in 1938 and is still published, holds the record for being the longest-running weekly comic with over 3,400 issues. As in the United States, the United Kingdom had its own "comics scare" in the 1950s, with similar results among the publishers of horror comics, as well as its own underground movement. A good overview of comics from the United Kingdom can be found in Gravett and Stanbury's *Great British Comics* (2006).

Like American comics, British comics have come in all genres, and many American comics have been reprinted in British publications. Of note is Marvel UK, which had been set up in 1972 to reprint Marvel Comics but then began to create new comics for British readers. Writers for these stories included Alan Moore, Dave Gibbons, Grant Morrison, and other writers and artists who would later become very well known to American audiences for their work on American comics. Some Marvel UK characters, such as Captain Britain, were incorporated into the regular "Marvel Universe," and a line of "Marvel UK" comics was sold in America in the 1990s.

One of the executives at Marvel UK was Derek "Dez" Skinn, who in 1982 created a comic magazine for older readers, *Warrior Magazine*. Though it lasted for only 26 issues, it won many awards and contained work by many notable writers and artists. One of the best-known stories that began in *Warrior* was *V for Vendetta*, written by Alan Moore with art by David Lloyd. The story was finished as a DC Comics limited series, collected, and made into a movie in 2006.

Another publication for adults was the science fiction magazine *2000 AD* that began in 1977. Like *Warrior* and the original Marvel UK titles, such writers and artists as Moore, Morrison, Bryan Talbot, Garth Ennis, and Neil Gaiman, had some of their earliest work published here. One of the best-known characters introduced in *2000 AD* was Judge Dredd, whose adventures were loosely adapted into the 1995 Sylvester Stallone film of the same name. Dredd also appeared in two titles from DC Comics. DC Comics also published trade editions of other *2000 AD* stories, including *Strontium Dog* and *Robo Hunter*. Dynamite Entertainment will also be reprinting notable *2000 AD* titles as well as new stories with Judge Dredd and other *2000 AD* characters.

One notable figure in original British graphic novels is Raymond Briggs. His children's title *Father Christmas* (1973) was told in comics form and his *Gentlemen Jim* (1980) was written for an adult audience. The main characters in Gentlemen Jim, Jim and Hilda Bloggs, were later featured in his nuclear war story *When the Wind Blows*, which has been adapted into stage and radio versions as well as animated film. The Bloggs were modeled after his own parents who were the subject of his award-winning biographical work *Ethel and Ernest*. The work of British writers and artists can be found in a number of American comic books, and original works are published in the United States by First Second, Dark Horse, Drawn & Quarterly, Pantheon, and others.

While books that originated in other countries will be treated the same in your library as far as purchasing goes, Chapter 7 discusses how their country of origin may affect how they are cataloged and Chapter 8 will show how this affects their shelving.

Notes

1. *Japan Inc. (Manga Nihon Keizai no Nyūmon)* was created by Ishinomori Shôtarô and published in Japan by the financial broadsheet *Nohon Keizai Shinbun* in autumn of 1986. It

sold over 550,000 copies during its first year. It was based on a series of previous published seminars on the economy that, among other subjects, covered the Japanese economic systems in regard to foreign imports. *Japan Inc.* became the prototype for adult informational manga that, at least at first, was produced by publishers who were not part of the manga industry (Kinsella, 2000). Shôtarô would also work with 50 academic specialists to create a 48-volume history of Japan in manga called *Manga Nihon no Rekishi*.

2. The year 2008 seems to have been the year for world leaders who are comic readers. After Barack Obama's election, articles came out discussing how he was a fan of Spider-Man and Conan comic books.

3. Many of these were altered to make them more "acceptable" to younger viewers. For example, for *Battle of the Planets* (known in Japan as *Kagaku ninja tai Gatchaman*), violent scenes were altered by either cutting them or having a robot character (created especially for the new version) explain that, unlike in the original version, the destroyed cities had been evacuated and that the destroyed armies consisted solely of robot troops. In *Sailor Moon*, dialogue has been changed so that the two female characters who were romantically involved in the original versions are now simply cousins.

4. Norway is also known for original Disney comics that were later translated for publication in America. The weekly *Donald Duck and Co.* magazine sells about 1 million copies a week, and that's in a country of 4.8 million people.

5. Canudo originally named six arts in 1911. Along with painting, sculpture, and music, there was architecture, dance, and cinema. He added poetry in 1923.

References

Anime News Network. 2007. "Hong Kong Artist Wins Japan's 1st Manga Nobel Prize." Available: www.animenewsnetwork.com/news/2007-06-30/hong-kong-artist-wins-japan's-1st-manga-nobel-prize (accessed August 22, 2009).

Brenner, Robin. 2007. *Understanding Manga and Anime*. Westport, CT: Libraries Unlimited.

"Broccoli Books Shuts Down." 2008. Available: www.icv2.com/articles/news/13785.html (accessed August 22, 2009).

Cinebook Catalog #6, Winter/Spring 2009. 2008. Canterbury, Kent, UK: Cinebook. Available: www.cinebook.co.uk/cinebook_catalogue_dec08.pdf (accessed September 11, 2009).

Gravett, Paul. 2004. *Manga: Sixty Years of Japanese Comics*. London: Laurence King Publishing.

Gravett, Paul, and Peter Stanbury. 2006. *Great British Comics*. London: Aurum Press.

"Japan Plans 'Nobel Prize of Manga'." 2007. CNN.com, May 23. Retrieved from (no longer available): www.cnn.com/2007/SHOWBIZ/books/05/22/manga.nobel.ap/index.html.

Kinsella, Sharon. 2000. *Adult Manga: Culture and Power in Contemporary Japanese Society*. Honolulu: University of Hawaii Press.

Nakazawa, Keiji. 2004. *Barefoot Gen: A Cartoon Story of Hiroshima*. San Francisco: Last Gasp.

Pilcher, Tim, and Brad Brooks. 2005. *The Essential Guide to World Comics*. London: Collins and Brown.

Schodt, Frederik L. 1998. "Henry Yoshitaka Kiyama and *The Four Immigrants Manga*." Available: www.jai2.com/HK.htm (accessed August 22, 2009).

Thompson, Jason. 2007. *Manga: The Complete Guide*. New York: Ballentine Books.

Yaoi Press. 2008. "Yaoi Press Blog." Available: www.yaoipress.com/2008/10/yaoi-press.html (accessed August 22, 2009).

PART II

Creating and Working with Your Graphic Novel Collection

Chapter 5

How Can You Purchase Your Graphic Novel Collection?

G raphic novel publishers are well aware that they have a new market in libraries. According to ICv2, which bills itself as "the top source for information on the business of pop culture products,"[1] libraries are the source of up to 10 percent of retail sales for graphic novels (Twiddy, 2007). But how do libraries purchase graphic novels? You can create and add to your collection using a number of sources, such as the same vendors you use for other books or local stores that specialize in selling comic books and graphic novels.

Before you decide on your method(s) of purchasing graphic novels, however, you will need to determine what to buy and how to pay for it. "What to buy" is discussed in Chapter 6, and some of the methods presented here may depend on what your library allows in terms of approved vendors or purchase methods. The other issue to consider is whether you want graphic novels to be a separate "line" in your budget or included as part of the overall book budget. If it is the former, than you will also need to decide what percentage of the budget will go to graphic novel purchases.

If you are creating a collection from scratch or greatly increasing the number of titles in your existing collection, then the initial percentage will be high the first year, and you will definitely want to include it in a special area of the budget. Some libraries apply for and receive grants to allow them to do this. If you continue to add to the initial collection, the subsequent percentages will be less. If graphic novels are a separate area of the budget and you have juvenile and teen collections as well, you will also need to decide whether one graphic novel budget covers all ages or whether you need separate percentages from the different juvenile, teen, and adult budgets.

You may also want to consider having someone familiar with graphic novels choose the titles for the library, even if not technically part of that person's regular position. On the other hand, if the graphic novels are just part of your regular order, then you can treat them the same as anything else (as in "We'll order the new James Patterson, a book on Barack Obama, and the latest *Hellblazer* collection").

Library Vendors

Many libraries get their graphic novels from the same vendors who supply them with the other books for their collections. Most of these vendors recognized early on the growing interest of libraries in the graphic novel format and created special sections on their Web sites and special publications dedicated to graphic novels. They have also sent representatives to library conferences and comics conventions. Getting your graphic novels from a book vendor has several advantages. For example, your library may have existing business relationships with them, with the proper paperwork already in place on both sides. From a budgetary point of view, most of the titles will be available from vendors at discounted prices, and they may also provide good deals on shipping. In addition, as discussed in Chapter 7, many of the vendors also provide processing services for the books, in terms of both cataloging and the addition of proper stamps and stickers as well as reinforcement, including turning a paperback book into a hardcover. Libraries can also set up "standing orders" with vendors so they will automatically send the latest volume of a manga or the newest trade of an ongoing series. In addition, some will also allow libraries to preview books before committing to a purchase. The following are some of the more common vendors.

Brodart

Brodart's subscribers site, Bibz, contains monthly lists, including suggestions for adult-level titles, compiled by *Voice of Youth Advocate*'s (*VOYA*) graphic novel reviewer Kat Kan. Brodart's public graphic novel Web page (www.graphicnovels.brodart.com) primarily covers children's titles but also includes articles written by librarians or from library publications and links to graphic novels in library-related sites. Another part of Brodart is McNaughton, which provides a book-leasing service to libraries, an approach often used when a library needs a large number of a "hot" title (the new Nora Roberts book, for example, or one mentioned on *Oprah*) and doesn't want to get stuck with hundreds of copies when interest wanes. Through leasing, the library is able to return a large percentage of the titles, keeping only a small number for their collection. More common with graphic novels, however, is purchasing smaller amounts for the "permanent" collection. Many of the graphic novel titles offered by McNaughton are aimed at older readers, though some are also suitable for younger readers, including titles in the superhero genre. In addition, any book that is released as a paperback is turned into a hardcover.

Baker & Taylor

Baker & Taylor puts out a biannual (fall and spring) publication on graphic novels called *Imagery* that includes lists of new and upcoming books divided into children's graphic novels, comics and cartoons, graphic novels (divided into non-series, series, and manga), nonfiction, and superheroes titles, with age recommendations. *Imagery* is available both in print and online at www.btol.com. Baker & Taylor has also participated in conferences on graphic novels.

Book Wholesalers, Inc. (BWI)

BWI's online catalog Titletales has a special section on graphic novels that includes bibliographies containing award winners, recommended titles, upcoming titles, and kinds of manga. Users can also do a keyword search on graphic novels. As with some of the other vendors, reviews from *Library Journal*, *Publisher's Weekly*, and similar works are also found on the Web page, along with information from an in-house reviewer. Among its others publications is *The Public Librarian's Guide to Graphic Novels*, which, besides listing some of the graphic novels BWI offers, also discusses such graphic novels in libraries issues as genres, mature content, shelving, cataloging, and dealing with challenges.

Ingram

As with the others, Ingram has a graphic novel publication, which can be found at www.ingrambook.com/programs/catalogs/supplements.asp. A graphic novel section can also be found in Ingram's trade publication *Advance*.

By going through a vendor, you can order titles months before they are due to be released, but this can also cause problems. Delays in publication can occur due to various reasons, such as when the final issue of a limited series does not come out on time, which causes the collected edition to come out at a later date than originally announced. Other problems at the vendor's end may also prevent a book from getting onto your library shelves until months after it came out in stores, perhaps even after the next volume in the series has been delivered to your library.

Comic Book Shops

Another source for purchasing graphic novels may just be a short drive from your library—your local comic book shop. This source will not provide help in cataloging and processing and possibly not a discount, but it can often provide advice and maybe even get the books quicker than any other source.

Also called comic book stores or comic book specialty shops, local comic shops (LCSs) can not only provide the books but also give you a better idea of what to buy (or what not to buy). They can also be helpful in regard to programming, helping to promote your programs, and being the source of items to purchase for the programs (and on some occasions, even the source of free comic books). Some libraries use comic book shops in addition to other sources, and others, such as Columbia University, use their LCS as the primary or even only source of graphic novels. While comic shops may not have every graphic novel available, they should have most or all of the newer titles and usually can get what is not already on the shelf. In addition, a comic shop may have a copy of a book that is now out of print, which is especially helpful when you have to replace a lost or damaged title (see Chapter 7). Even if the book is in print, if it is available at the comic shop, then the lost/damaged book can be replaced much faster than if you went through a vendor, especially if you do in-house processing.

Up until the 1960s, comic books were primarily sold on newsstands and in drugstores and supermarkets. Some bookstores sold them and a few, like the Kansas store owned by Harvey "Pop" Hollinger, would stock older comics and actively buy and sell older issues. However, no stores included comic books as their primary sales item. On April 1, 1968, Seven Sons Comic Books opened in San Jose, California. Owned by seven partners, including the then 16-year-old Bud Plant, who even today is a seller of comic art, Seven Sons is considered to be the first "true" comic book store. Shortly afterward, San Francisco Comic Book Company opened up. Besides selling comics, the store, which is still around, was also a publisher of Underground Comics, including *Bogeyman Comics* and *Moonchild Comics*. Additional stores soon opened around the United States.

The early comic shops purchased their comics from the same periodical distributors as the newsstands and drugstores. However, in 1972, Phil Seuling formed Seagate Distribution, a wholesaler created specifically to sell comic books directly to comic book shops. This led to what is known as the direct market. The direct market retailers could offer a much larger discount than their former distributors because, unlike with the older distributors whose unsold material could be returned, with the direct market owners were stuck with unsold merchandise. This larger discount offered a larger profit to the store's owner but with greater risk. However, as they had to keep the unsold books anyway, the stores would put them in a "back issue" bin (with prices raised as the demand or the collectability of the title allowed). This was a boon to collectors and, in the days before most books were collected into trades, to anyone else who wanted to read older stories.

Eventually, more distributors appeared and more and more shops opened up. Thanks to the direct market, comic shop owners would get the new comic book issues sometimes weeks before the drugstores, newsstands, etc. The direct market also allowed comic shops to get every issue of a comic series and in the amount that they requested. They could increase or decrease the number of issues of a title as demand indicated. In previous years, people who bought their comics from newsstands and other such outlets did not know if their preferred store would get enough copies of the issue that they wanted or even get it at all. Some comic book readers would have to visit several stores in an attempt to procure all of the titles that they wanted.

Publishers also took advantage of the direct market and of the growth of comic shops. Many of the smaller publishers began to distribute their titles through only the direct market. The black-and-white boom of the 1980s was full of direct-market-only titles. Some publishers whose books went to newsstands, including the "big two," DC and Marvel, also began to create titles purely for the direct market, including the first maxi-series, DC's *Camelot 3000*.

By the late 1980s/early 1990s the comic book market was booming, and around 7,000 comic shops could be found around the country and over 700 titles came out each month. Besides the regular comic book readers and those who considered themselves collectors, speculators—people who purchased comics simply as an investment—

began purchasing comics that they thought would increase in value. Some comics companies aimed their marketing at these speculators with techniques such as multiple and "enhanced" covers and the overuse of popular characters. For example, Wolverine and the Punisher "guest-starred" in many Marvel Comics titles in an attempt to make them more desirable to collectors.

Yet with every boom comes a bust, and that bust came in the mid-1990s. Speculators stopped buying, sales went down, and some comic companies even went out of business. This affected comic book stores as well, and today there are, at best, about half the number of comic shops than at their peak. During this time, the direct market went through some shakeups. Before 1995, many distributors existed, and each one offered comic book titles from most, if not all, of the comic publishers. But 1995 brought a period of exclusivity in which a particular publisher—mainly the major publishers—would allow only one particular distributor to send their books to comic shops.

First Marvel, which had purchased the distributor Heroes World, said that only that company would distribute their titles. Then DC signed an exclusive agreement with Diamond Distributors (see Exhibit 5-1). Many of the other companies (known as "Independents") went with Diamond or a third company, Capital City, though not always on an exclusive basis. This caused problems for the comic shop owners who had to deal with several distributors with different distribution rates to get the popular titles. To put things in perspective, imagine if, when your library was ordering books, it could only get Penguin's books from BWI, Random House's from Brodart,

---

Exhibit 5-1. Diamond Distributors

Founded by Steve Geppi in 1982, Diamond Comic Distributors is the largest comics distributor in North America, sending the products of most of the comic book publishers to stores and even to libraries. Diamond publishes a catalog called *Previews*, which comic book stores and the stores' subscribers use to order merchandise. Dark Horse, DC, and Image have special places in the front of *Previews* (Marvel has a separate insert), followed by the other independents in alphabetical order. While mainly upcoming titles are listed, backlists of older graphic novels and trade editions are often included as well, and besides comics and graphic novels, *Previews* also includes listings for books, action figures, magazines, and much more. The listings in *Previews* are just solicitations, however, and are not reviews. A subscription is $150.00 a year, so if you want to purchase a copy for your library, it is best to do so from a comic book store, where you can buy one for $4.50.

Diamond has also recognized the inroads that graphic novels have made into libraries. Its Web page at bookshelf.diamond.com has a section for libraries that includes news and information, a list of print and online resources, reviews by Kat Kan, a list of recommended titles, and suggestions for setting up the collection and for cataloging. A print version contains a sample of available books categorized by age, with adult listings divided into action-adventure, drama, fantasy, humor, and literature as well as reference material. It also has a top-ten listing of recommended titles for older (16+) teens and one for adults. The latter includes *A Contract with God*, *Watchmen*, *Fun Home*, and *Buddha*. Diamond has also participated in library events and conferences, including being in ALA's "graphic novel alley." While Diamond does provide a discount, the company does not provide any binding or cataloging services.

and Simon & Schuster's from Baker & Taylor. Things settled down only after Marvel shut down Heroes World and went back to Diamond, who by then had taken over Capital City.

Currently, Diamond has gone on to become the main supplier for comic book shops. Among the few other distributors still remaining are Last Gasp Publishing, which distributes and occasionally publishes "underground" titles, and Haven Distribution, which in 2008 took over another distributor, Cold Cut. Haven specializes in providing comics and graphic novels from small presses and "independent" publishers to retailers.

The rise in graphic novels from non-comics publishers has also led to a new method for comic shops to purchase graphic novels, and that's by doing it the same way as many libraries. Shops have started to use BWI, Baker & Taylor, and other vendors, as they are more familiar with these publishers than with the companies who work with the direct market. One advantage for shops in using these vendors is that they can reorder titles that have sold out without having to pay the reordering fee that Diamond and others may charge (Rosen, 2006).

Some libraries are close to several comic shops, while others have only one or even none within an easy traveling distance. The best way to locate stores in your area is to look in the Yellow Pages (print or online), usually under bookstores. Diamond provides another option through its comic shop locator, which can be reached by phone at 1-800-Comic-Book or online at www.comicshoplocator.com. Also online is The Master List of Comic Book & Trading Card Stores, located at www.the-master-list.com. While not 100 percent complete or up to date, these sources should help you to find a store in your area.

Many comic shops sell more than just comic books and graphic novels, though they are often products that appeal to comics fans. These include collectable cards (ranging from sports cards to cards for games like *Magic: The Gathering*), role-playing games such as *Dungeons and Dragons*, books, DVDs (especially anime, foreign films, comics-related movies and television shows, and cult films), toys, posters, statues, materials for the storage and preservation of comic books (long and short boxes, plastic bags, and acid-free boards), and more. Many stores also offer a subscription service for their regular customers, which could include a library. The customers pre-order particular titles, usually by looking through *Previews* (see Exhibit 5-1) or by having a standing order for an ongoing series, and the shop ensures that the books are ordered, "pulled" from the weekly delivery, and held for them. This way, the regulars do not have to worry about missing a title if they can't make it in every Wednesday, the day new books usually come out. Many stores also offer discounts to subscribers and will occasionally have sales and special events, including book signings by writers and artists.

Some people have a stereotypical view of comic shops, including that they are staffed by people like "Comic Book Guy" from *The Simpsons*, filled with "geeks," and are not female friendly. Admittedly, some stores are like this, but it is not the case with the majority. There are no nationwide chains of comic book shops, though some do have multiple locations and others are known outside of their local area, due in part to events they hold or mentions in the comics-related press. Such shops include Midtown Comics and Jim Hanley's Universe in New York City, Mile High Comics in Colorado, The Beguiling in Toronto, and Golden Apple Comics in Los Angeles. A branch of one Salt Lake City store, Night Flight Comics, is even located in the same building as a library. The Eisner Awards (see Chapter 6) give out a "Spirit of Comics Retailer Award" to the shop that has "done an outstanding job of supporting the comics art medium both in the community and within the industry at large," and one of the criteria for judging is "community activity," which includes "maintaining relationships with schools/libraries" ("Will Eisner Spirit of Comics Retailer Award," 2008). See Chapter 8 for ways that you can work with your local comic book shop.

Other Sources

Bookstores are also a good local source for you to purchase graphic novels, especially the large chain stores that often have rows of bookshelves filled with graphic novels. As discussed in Chapter 1, over the years, most graphic novels have gone from being found in the comics/cartooning or science fiction/fantasy section to a location of their own. Depending on the store, some titles, especially the nonfiction ones, may be found in other sections. Some stores have discounts for libraries and educators and can also request certain titles for you. The larger stores also tend not to mind when people want to browse the contents of the books, which can be helpful in your selection process (see Chapter 6).

Bookstores are also working with mainstream publishers to help with distribution of comics companies' works. For example Simon & Schuster has distributed VIZ's books, HarperCollins handles Tokyopop's, and some of Fantagraphics' titles have been distributed by W.W. Norton. Diamond also has a separate book division that works with bookstores.

Chapter 8 covers shelving issues in libraries, but bookstores have similar issues to deal with in accommodating the popularity of graphic novels. While graphic novels do have their own shelving area, most bookstores will separate the manga from the other titles but keep the shelves next to each other. In addition, bookstore shelves rarely feature any segregation by age. An all-ages title might be on the shelf right next to one containing nudity, foul language, and ultraviolent images. The large amount of titles, especially in the case of multivolume manga series, has caused some readers to be concerned that certain titles, especially those by smaller publishers, will be "squeezed out" of the shelves in favor of the more popular titles.

For those libraries without nearby comic shops or large bookstores, online sources are also a possibility. Amazon.com, DeepDiscount.com, and the online counterparts of the chain stores will ship directly to your library, often at a discount and possibly even with free shipping. A number of comic shops, including Mile High, Midtown, and Golden Apple, offer a mail-order service. Several publishers also have online stores that could be used to purchase titles without having to go through a "middle-man."[2] Of course, if you are purchasing from a comic shop, a bookstore, or an online source, any sort of processing will have to be done in-house. As Exhibit 5-2 will explain, many of these sources are also good if you wish to order comic books for your library.

There is no one perfect source when it comes to purchasing graphic novels for your library. Each has its own advantages and disadvantages, and what is right for one library may not be right for another. Some sources will take care of your processing needs, while others will not. Some allow you to have the books in your library quickly, while others take longer. Some offer discounts, while others require you to pay the full price. Some charge for shipping, while others offer it for free with a large enough order. Some sources are thousands of miles from your library, while others may be five minutes away. Some libraries will use only one method, and others may go with multiple sources to get the best value possible. In choosing your methods, you will need to consider the needs of your library as well as which methods are the most practical in setting up and maintaining your graphic novel collection.

Notes

1. Short for Internal Correspondence version 2, ICv2 provides information on five areas of pop culture—anime/manga, comics/graphic novels, games, movies/television licensed products, and toys—through a Web site (www.icv2.com) and retailer guides. ICv2 has taken an

---

Exhibit 5-2. Purchasing Comic Books for Your Library

For libraries seeking to purchase actual comic books, as something either to be displayed with the other periodicals or to be collected and archived, several possibilities exist. Ebsco and a few other vendors provide some comics that can be ordered in the same manner as a periodical, such as *Time*, *Newsweek*, etc. Some bookstores carry comic books, but it would be difficult to guarantee any consistency as to what issues would be available at any given time. Many comic book companies offer subscriptions, though often just for ongoing titles and not for such things as limited series and one-shots. Others offer individual issues via their Web sites, though sometimes sales are through a third party. Comic shops, whether online or a physical store, may be the best way of acquiring titles on a regular basis, especially if they offer a subscription service. As *Previews* allows comics to be ordered several months in advance, a purchase order for what you wish to buy could be ready by the time that the books arrive at the store. If your library is looking to archive the comics, then the shop can also be a place where you can purchase the materials that will best preserve them.

If interested in older issues, some can be purchased from the publisher, but most comic shops will have them. The back issues usually cost more, with prices generally determined by various price guides, including the popular *Overstreet* guide (an annual publication first put out by Robert Overstreet in 1970, with listings dating back to the Platinum Age). Many shops also have a box full of cheaper comics, some less than a dollar, that can be purchased, though they are often placed in a more random order than the back issues. These books can also be good if you simply want cheap comics that you can leave out for patrons to read and not have to worry if they are stolen or damaged. There are also a number of online sources for older comics, even places that may seem unlikely, including eBay and Amazon.com.

interest in the area of graphic novels in libraries, sponsoring discussions, reporting on panels, and using librarian as reviewers.

    2. Of course, if you want to purchase *The Middleman* from the publisher, you can go to www.vipercomics.com.

References

Rosen, Judith. 2006. "Comics Shops Turn to Book Distributors for Graphic Novels." *PW Comic Week—Publisher's Weekly* (July 18). Available: www.publishersweekly.com/article/CA6354132.html (accessed August 22, 2009).

Twiddy, David. 2007. "Pictures Causing Problems." *[Cedar Rapids–Iowa City] Gazette*, January 14: 5L.

"Will Eisner Spirit of Comics Retailer Award." 2008. Available: www.comic-con.org/cci/cci_eisners_spirit.shtml (accessed August 22, 2009).

Chapter 6

How Do You Decide What to Purchase and What Is Available?

Y ou now know why you should buy graphic novels for adults and how to buy them, so we turn now to the next question: "What should I buy?" Over 2,000 original graphic novels, trade editions, and manga volumes come out each year, with content that ranges from all ages to adults only, and with prices ranging from under $10.00 to over $100.00 (see Exhibit 6-1).

As with other matters, you should treat the purchase of graphic novels the same as you would for any other book in your collection. While you want the best possible book in terms of story and art quality, you will also want titles that will circulate. With luck, these elements will coexist in the same works, but, unfortunately, as every librarian knows, some works of dubious quality have long waiting lists, and some high-quality works are just "shelf-sitters." And because public libraries must serve the needs and wants of the general public, they often shelve more copies of the former. Review sources, awards, promotional material, and even word-of-mouth sources (including over the Internet) can be very helpful in making your final decision.

Knowing *who* publishes *what* is an important first step in this decision because there are dozens of graphics novels publishers, some who also produce comic books, and others who are better known for producing "text" books. So we begin in this chapter with a look at both mainstream and independent comic book and graphic novel publishers.

The "Big Two" Publishers: DC and Marvel

With soft drinks it's Coke and Pepsi, with fast food it's Burger King and McDonald's, and with comic books it's DC and Marvel. They are oldest of the current publishers, have a greater monthly output than the others, and their characters are known around the world.

The home of Superman, Batman, Wonder Woman, and other famous characters, DC Comics is actually the result of several publishers coming together. The earliest incarnation was begun in 1934 by Major Malcolm Wheeler-Nicholson as National

Exhibit 6-1. December 2008 Graphic Novel Releases

This is a list of the number and cost of graphic novels that came out in December 2008 according to the New Comic Book Release List (www.comiclist.com).

Comic	Issues Released	Price ($)	Comic	Issues Released	Price ($)
Alterna Comics	2	22.90	Image Comics	10	365.86
Amaze Ink/Slave Labor Graphics	1	12.95	Last Gasp	1	29.95
			Look Out Monsters	1	12.95
Ammo Books	1	49.95	Marvel Comics	30	765.71
Antarctic Press	1	14.95	Moonstone	1	12.95
Archie Comics	1	9.95	NBM & Papercutz	4	56.80
Aurora	4	47.80	Netcomics	5	49.95
Barrons	1	8.95	Oni	1	13.95
Boom! Studios	6	92.94	Paizo Publishing	1	12.95
Buenaventura Press	1	125.00	Penny Farthing	1	14.95
Checker BPG	1	99.00	Poison Press	1	15.00
Cinebook	5	75.75	Radical	2	39.90
Conundrum Press	1	15.00	Rampart Press	1	24.95
Dark Horse	12	330.45	Raw Junior	1	12.95
DC Comics	23	375.77	Rebellion	1	30.99
Del Rey Manga	5	56.91	Red Eye Press	1	14.95
Devil's Due Publishing	1	18.95	Running Press	1	15.95
Digital Manga Publishing	6	77.70	Seven Seas	3	32.97
Do Gooder Press	1	15.99	Sofawolf Press	1	29.95
Drawn & Quarterly	2	26.90	Sterling Publishing	1	27.95
Dynamite Entertainment	7	199.94	Titan Books	1	19.95
Fanfare/Potent Mon	1	25.00	Tokyopop	15	153.86
Fantagraphics	3	68.97	Top Shelf	1	10.00
Forcewerks Productions	1	15.99	Undercover Fish Books	1	14.95
Gemstone	3	25.97	Underwood Books	1	27.95
Go! Comics	2	21.98	Vertical	1	21.95
HarperCollins	2	16.98	VIZ	36	359.52
I Box Publishing	1	15.99	Yaoi	1	12.95
IDW	9	158.41	Yen Press	7	75.93

(Cont'd.)

Exhibit 6-1. December 2008 Graphic Novel Releases *(Continued)*

This list includes original graphic novels, collected reprints, and manga. The 226 titles range from books aimed at younger readers to those intended for adults, with prices ranging from $6.99 (the children's book *Warriors Tigerstar & Sasha*, Volume 2) to $125.00 (the anthology *Kramers Ergot*, Volume 7) for a prediscount total of $4305.68. Some publishers did not put out any books in December, while others released a greater or lesser amount of titles than they do in other months, and some of the titles released that month have been or will be released in a different format with a higher or lower price. In addition, the list does not reflect any books about comics that you may wish to purchase (see Appendix B) or even the hundreds of actual comic books that were released that month. Even if you narrow your focus to a particular age range, there will still be a large amount of titles available each month, and you will still need to make decisions about which ones to purchase for your library.

Allied Publications, later called National Comics and then National Periodical Publications. In February of the following year they published the first issue of *New Fun*.[1] This was soon followed by what became the long-running *Adventure Comics* (1935–1983) and *Detective Comics*, which began in 1937, introduced Batman in 1939, and *Action Comics* (1938), both of which are still being published. Some of the characters published by National (and related companies) at the time included the "Golden Age" versions of the Flash, Atom, Green Lantern, Wonder Woman, and, of course, Superman. As far back as 1940, National used a logo with the words "A DC Publication" (with DC standing for Detective Comics) on the cover, and long before it became the company's official name, the company was being referred to as "DC Comics." Hyping its other popular character, several of the later logos also included Superman's name or image.

As mentioned in Chapter 2, DC's *Showcase* #4 is considered by many to be the start of the "Silver Age of Comics." This issue introduced a new version of the super-fast hero the Flash, replacing the one introduced 16 years earlier. Many other Golden Age heroes were revamped, often with a more science-fiction-based origin, which was at least partially influenced by editor Julius Schwartz (who, among his other accomplishments, was a pioneer in science fiction fandom and was the agent for such writers as Ray Bradbury, Robert Bloch, and H. P. Lovecraft). For example, where the original Atom was simply short, the new version was a scientist who invented a method of shrinking himself, and Green Lantern went from being an engineer with a magic ring to a test pilot who got his ring from a dying alien so that he could join an intergalactic police force.

DC began publishing work for mature audiences in the early 1980s. Titles such as *Camelot 3000* and *Thriller* had stories that appealed to older readers, and as the decade went on, more titles emerged in which the cover clearly said that they were for mature audiences. These were often direct market only, printed on a different kind of paper, and were more expensive than books published for younger ages. These were also not Comics Code approved. Notable titles from this period include *Swamp Thing*, *Doom Patrol*,[2] *Animal Man*, the still-published *Hellblazer*, and, most notably,

Sandman (see Exhibit 6-2). Many of these books were written by some of the British creators mentioned in the previous chapter.

These titles led to the creation of DC's mature audience imprint, Vertigo, in 1993. The six existing titles continued, and over the past 15-plus years, more than 200 titles appeared, including ongoing series, limited series, one-shots, and original graphic novels. These works covered all genres, with such notable titles as *Books of Magic*, *Army@Love*, *Y: The Last Man*, *Sandman Mystery Theater* (featuring a character created in the 1940s), *100 Bullets*, *Transmetropolitan*, and *Preacher*. Stories in Vertigo comics may contain foul language, nudity, and adult themes.

Some older mature audience titles have been put under the Vertigo Banner when reprinted, including *V for Vendetta* and *A History of Violence*, which was originally published under Paradox Press, an earlier mature audiences imprint.[3] Harvey Pekar has also brought some of his autobiographical works to Vertigo, including new *American Splendor* stories. The Vertigo imprint has also included several sub-imprints, the most recent being "Vertigo Crime," which includes a *Hellblazer* story by popular author Ian Rankin. In 2008, publisher Dorling Kindersley (DK), who had previously published illustrated encyclopedias for Superman, Spider-Man, and other superheroes, published *The Vertigo Encyclopedia* with entries on Vertigo's titles and characters.

Exhibit 6-2. *Sandman*

Created by Neil Gaiman, *Sandman* is one of Vertigo's flagship titles and perhaps the one that is known best, even to those who may not normally read comics. The original series ran for 75 issues from 1989–1996, has been collected in various ways (see Appendix A), has inspired sequels, spin-offs, a book of short stories, and nonfiction and other scholarly works. It has won a number of awards and has been praised by many sources, including Norman Mailer who called it "a comic strip for intellectuals" (Anderson, 2001).

The main character of the comic is Dream, also known as Morpheus (and by a thousand other names), the actual personification of dreams. He and his siblings make up The Endless, whose number also includes his brother Destiny, his sister Death, and his androgynous sister-brother Desire. The stories told in *Sandman* included both ongoing storylines and one-shots. In some of them Dream was the main character, while others involved mortals (and other beings) who eventually interact with him or his family. Stories included a man who meets Dream in a tavern every 100 years, how Lucifer abdicated ruling Hell and let Dream decide who gets it, a convention for serial killers, and how the dreams of 1,000 cats may change the world. Characters who appeared in *Sandman* included figures from mythology (such as Odin, Thor, and Orpheus), history (such as Augustus, Shakespeare, and the "Emperor of the United States" Joshua Norton), and from the DC Universe. The latter includes previous characters known as "Sandman" as well as Cain and Abel, the "hosts" of two long-running horror anthology series *House of Mystery* and *House of Secrets*.

An additional character who appeared in many issues was Lucian. Like Cain and Abel, he "hosted" a horror anthology, but his was very short lived. In *Sandman*, his main responsibility is to run the Library of Dreams. This is a very unusual library as it contains every book that has ever been dreamt of. This includes the unwritten works of Poe, Dickens, and every other author, as well as that book that you have always said you would write one day. Books that have actually been written are located in a "small" annex of the library (other librarians in comics include Barbara Gordon, who has been known as both Batgirl and Oracle, and "super-librarian" Rex Libris).

Another source of mature-audience titles for DC is Wildstorm (also written as WildStorm), which was founded by creator Jim Lee in 1992 as part of Image Comics (see the following section) and has produced such titles as *Stormwatch*, *Gen 13*, and *WildC.A.T.s.* (which was made into a cartoon series). Wildstorm also had its own imprints, including Cliffhanger and Homage comics, which produced such works as *Astro City*, *Leave It to Chance*, and *Danger Girl*. In 1998, Wildstorm was purchased by DC, though its titles, for the most part, remained separate from the "DC Universe."

Also acquired with Wildstorm was a new imprint, America's Best Comics (ABC), created by Alan Moore. ABC's titles, which at first were written solely by Moore, include *Tom Strong*, *Promethea*, *Top Ten*, and the first three volumes of *The League of Extraordinary Gentlemen*. Today Wildstorm has its own page on DC's Web site, and its more notable books include new versions of *Gen 13*, *Danger Girl*, and *Astro City* as well as *Ex Machina*, *Planetary*, the *Stormwatch* spin-off *The Authority*, and comics based on various horror films.

DC also publishes manga under the CMX imprint and has a "child friendly" line of books that includes titles based on various cartoons. From 2007–2008 DC's Minx imprint published original graphic novels aimed at teenaged girls, and along with Paradox Press, DC had another mature audience imprint, Piranha. In the past, DC was also one of the publishers of Will Eisner's graphic novels (and they still license the rights to his character the Spirit) and, for a time, was the U.S. distributor for books from France's Humanoids Publishing and England's *2000 AD*. DC had even published two titles featuring Judge Dredd.

Marvel Comics, which is home to Spider-Man, the X-Men, the Hulk, and other popular characters, has been around in several incarnations for over 70 years. It was founded as Timely Comics in 1939 by pulp-magazine publisher Martin Goodman. Its first title, *Marvel Comics* #1, introduced both the android version of the Human Torch and the aquatic hero The Sub-Mariner. Captain America was introduced two years later in *Captain America Comics* #1, which is notable for having a cover in which Captain America is punching Hitler, even though it came out before the United States entered the war. During the 1950s, it was known as Atlas and, along with other genres, produced crime, science fiction, fantasy, war, and western titles.

By 1961, the name had changed to Marvel Comics, and with the first issue of *Fantastic Four*, the "Marvel Universe" had begun. Existing titles such as *Tales of Suspense*, *Journey Into Mystery*, and *Tales to Astonish* became superhero comics, with name changes to *Captain America*, *Thor*, and *The Incredible Hulk*. With writers like Stan Lee and artists such as Jack Kirby and Steve Ditko, Marvel titles grew in both number and popularity. A notable aspect of Marvel Comics' superheroes was that they had problems, and their lives were more than "How do I stop the bad guy without my girlfriend figuring out my secret identity?" Spider-Man may be able to stop Dr. Octopus, but afterward he has to deal with not being able to pay the bills. The X-Men had to defend a world that "hates and fears them" and have always been a metaphor for people who face prejudice due to their race, religion, or sexual orientation. Due in part to its "psychedelic" art style, the mystical character Dr. Strange was also popular with college students in the mid-1960s. A 1965 Jefferson Airplane concert in San Francisco was even called "A Tribute to Dr. Strange."

Marvel also has had a number of imprints over the years, including some that specialize in stories for older readers. In the 1970s, Curtis Magazines published black-and-white magazines that featured comic stories that were free of Comics Code restrictions, including various horror titles. Epic Comics ran from 1982–1996 and got its name from Marvel's anthology magazine *Epic Illustrated*. Epic's titles included both creator-owned work and characters from the Marvel Universe. Some of their better-known comics included *Dreadstar*, *Groo the Wanderer*, *The Trouble with Girls*, *Elektra: Assassin*, *Sachs and Violence*, and a translation of the manga *Akira*. Some of these had come from other publishers and others would continue or be reprinted elsewhere.

Two other imprints, Marvel Edge (1995–1996) and Marvel Knights (1998–), featured existing characters such as Spider-Man, Daredevil, and the gun-toting vigilante the Punisher in stories that were "edgier" but not for mature audiences only. This designation was given to Marvel Max (2001–). These stories included some existing characters, including the Punisher, Blade, and a new version of the Squadron Supreme, and, like Vertigo, sometimes featured foul language and nudity. Another Marvel imprint that may include stories for older readers is Icon Comics, a creator-owned imprint that includes such titles as *Powers*, about police who monitor super-heroes, and *Criminal*, which, as the title indicates, is about various criminals. Other imprints include the "Ultimate" line, which has new versions of the Marvel Universe characters, the "kids" line Marvel Adventures, and Marvel Illustrated, which adapts works of classic literature.

The Independent Publishers

DC and Marvel may be as ubiquitous as Burger King and McDonald's, but plenty more places make burgers and plenty more companies produce comics and graphic novels. While their output may not be as great as the "Big Two," they can rival DC and Marvel in terms of popularity and, more important, sales. Collectively, they are referred to as "Independents." This section takes a look at some of them.

Boom! Studios

One of the newer comic book publishers, Boom! produces comics in various genres, including superhero, science fiction, and horror.

Dark Horse

Founded in 1986, Dark Horse Comics is one of the major Independents. Among their publications are a number of licensed properties, including *Buffy the Vampire Slayer*, *Conan the Barbarian*, and *Star Wars*. Original titles include *300*, the *Sin City* titles, *The Umbrella Academy*, *Criminal Macabre*, *Rex Mundi*, and the *Hellboy* books. Dark Horse also has a line of manga, published since 1988, with such notable titles as *Lone Wolf and Cub*, *Blade of the Immortal*, and the *Harlequin Manga* titles, as well as some titles published with Digital Manga Publishing.

Devil's Due Publishing (DDP)

Devil's Due publishes comic versions of many licensed properties, such as GI Joe, *Dragonlance*, and *Xombie*, as well as original works such as *Drafted*. They also reprint comics from Humanoids Publishing.

Digital Manga Publishing

Digital Manga publishes manga for all ages, including some copublished with Dark Horse. Notable titles include *The Ring*, *Trigun*, and the *Project X* books. A sister company 801 Media also publishes yaoi.

Dynamite Entertainment

A newer publisher, Dynamite produces original works such as *The Boys* and *Project Superpowers* as well as a number of licensed properties including *Battlestar Galactica* (both series), *Red Sonja*, *Army of Darkness*, *Highlander*, and *Xena: Warrior Princess*.

Fantagraphics Books

The publishers of *The Comics Journal*, Fantagraphics has produced myriad work for adults, including *Ghost World*, *King*, *Jimmy Corrigan*, books by Norwegian artist Jason, reprints of the works of R. Crumb, works by Joe Sacco, and books in the *Love and Rockets* series. They also publish "truly" adult works (under the Eros imprint) and various collections of classic comic strips, including *Peanuts*, *Pogo*, *Popeye*, and comic work done by Jules Feiffer.

Go! Comi

This publisher of manga is home to such titles as *Afterschool Nightmare*, *The Devil Within*, and *Canterella*.

IDW Publishing

A division of Idea and Design Works, IDW is known for its horror comics (*30 Days of Night*, *CVO*, *Bigfoot*) and licensed properties (*CSI*, *Angel*, *Star Trek*, *Dr. Who*) as well as ongoing series such as *Fallen Angel*, original graphic novels, and several collections of works from defunct companies.

Image Comics

Another major Independent, Image Comics was founded in 1992 by former Marvel Comics artists, including Todd McFarlane, Rob Liefeld, and Eric Larsen. Each of the partners formed their own studio. Their longest running titles are *Spawn* and *Savage Dragon*, both of which have been around since the early 1990s and have been made into animated series and/or movies. Other popular titles include *Witchblade*, *After the Cape*, *Age of Bronze*, *Elephantmen*, *Wanted*, *True Story Swear to God*, and *The Walking Dead*. The last title is written by Robert Kirkman, who is the only non-founder to currently be a partner in the company.

NBM Publishing

The New York–based Nantier Beall Minoustchine Publishing has been publishing graphic novels since 1976, often translating works from France and Belgium. Titles include *Boneyard*, *Brownsville*, adaptations of operas, and the *Treasury of Victorian Murder* series of books. Many of their titles for older readers are in their "ComicsLit" line, and they have also published books on the subject of graphic novels. They also publish titles for younger readers, as does their sister company Papercutz. On the opposite end of the spectrum, they also publish adult-only graphic novels through lines called either Amerotica and Eurotica depending on the source of the material.

Oni Press

Founded in 1997, the Oregon-based Oni publishes comics and graphic novels for all ages. Titles that appeal to older readers include *Queen and Country*, *Whiteout*, *Barry Ween*, *Maintenance*, *Resurrection*, *Capote in Kansas*, *Scott Pilgrim*, and *Wasteland*.

Slave Labor Graphics (SLG)

Slave Labor publishes such popular oddball titles as *Milk and Cheese* and *Gloom-cookie*. Other works include *Paris* and *Rex Libris*, which is about a super-librarian. Its Amaze Ink imprint is for titles that are more appropriate for younger readers.

Tokyopop

Tokyopop is one of the major publishers of manga in America. Originally called Mixx, Tokyopop was founded in 1997, incorporated in Japan, and has branches in the United States (headquartered in Los Angeles), Germany, and the United Kingdom. Besides a handful of OEL manga, Tokyopop also publishes such Japanese titles as *Sgt. Frog*, *Fake*, *Gravitation*, *Priest*, and various yaoi titles (often under the "Blu" imprint) as well as mature audience titles such as *Manga Sutra*.

Top Shelf Productions

Founded in 1997, the Georgia-based Top Shelf is the home of such notable graphic novels as the multiple award winning *Blankets*, the "adults only" *Lost Girls*, *Essex County*, *The Surrogates*, *From Hell*, and works by Jeffrey Brown and Alex Robinson.

VIZ Media

Another major manga publisher, the San Francisco–based VIZ, which is jointly owned by two of Japan's largest publishers of manga, is the home of such books as *Ranma 1/2*, *Golgo 13*, *Pretty Face*, *Strawberry 100%*, *The Drifting Classroom*,

Vagabond, and *Death Note*. VIZ also publishes the manga magazine *Shonen Jump* and distributes anime.

Other independent publishers of note include Alternative Comics, AiT/Planet Lar Bongo Comics, Fox Atomic, Archaia, Arcana, ADV Manga, Adhouse Books, Zenescope Entertainment, Titan Books, Cinebook, Moonstone Books, Checker BPG, Antarctic Press, Big Head Press, Dork Storm Press, Drawn & Quarterly, and Dabel Brothers Productions (which at times has distributed its products, often literary adaptations, through Image, Marvel, and other publishers). Creator-owned publishers include Batton Lash's Exhibit A, which publishes *Supernatural Law*, Terry Moore's Abstract Studio, the home of *Strangers in Paradise*, Paul Sizer's Café Digital, Jim Ottiviani's GT Labs, and Aardvark-Vanaheim, which Dave Sim used to publish *Cerebus*. Some creator-owned publications have gone to or been collected by other publishers. *Strangers in Paradise* was briefly published by Image (Wildstorm); the earliest issues of *American Splendor* were self-published by Pekar before they were collected by various book and comic publishers.

Book Publishers and Graphic Novels

Some book publishers produce graphic novels along with other materials. Sometimes a special division or imprint is created, while on other occasions the graphic novel is released under the regular publisher name. Some smaller publishers include Manic D, Stickman Graphics, Soft Skull, Vertical (which publishes manga, including many works by Osumu Tezuka), and Last Gasp. Founded in 1970 in San Francisco, Last Gasp has been the publisher of a number of "underground" and "alternative" comics as well as the manga *Barefoot Gen*.

Among the larger book publishers who also produce some comics and graphic novels are the following:

- Hatchette, which has put out books under the Grand Central Publishing and Yen Press imprints, the latter which produces manga
- W.W. Norton, which has been reprinting the works of Will Eisner and is also a distributor for Fantagraphics
- Random House, which also includes Villard, Ballentine, Pantheon, Del Rey, and Del Rey Manga
- Houghton Mifflin Harcourt
- Penguin
- HarperCollins
- Simon & Schuster (along with their Touchstone imprint)
- Macmillan (part of Holtzbrinck Publishing), who is the parent company of both Farrar, Straus, and Giroux (a distributor for Drawn & Quarterly and whose division Hill and Wang publishes a line of "Novel Graphics") and Roaring Brook Press, which has the award winning graphic novel imprint First Second Books

Publisher Crossovers and Changes

Since the 1970s, there have been comic books in which characters owned or licensed by one publisher meet characters owned/licensed by another. DC and Marvel have participated in most of these, ranging from *Superman vs. the Amazing Spider-Man* (1976) to *JLA/Avengers* (2003). Others of interest include *Marvel Zombies vs. Army of Darkness* (Marvel/Dynamite), *New Avengers/Transformers* (Marvel/IDW), *Superman and Batman vs. Aliens and Predator* (DC/Dark Horse), *Freddy vs. Jason vs. Ash* (DC/Wildstorm/Dynamite), and, one of the strangest crossovers ever, *The Punisher Meets Archie* (Marvel/Archie).[4]

Other times a comic book or character published by one company will later move to another company or sometimes a work published by one company will be collected or reprinted by another. There are three main reasons for this. The first is that the property is owned by the creators and not the publisher, and for one reason or another, the creator decides to take it elsewhere. Recent examples include *The Boys* (which moved from DC/Wildstorm to Dynamite), *Rex Mundi* (Image to Dark Horse), *Fallen Angel* (DC to IDW), and *True Story Swear to God* (AiT/Planet Lar to Image). Terry Moore's *Strangers in Paradise* started first at Antarctic Press, restarted at Moore's Abstract Studio, and restarted again at Image, only to move back to Abstract after a few issues. Alan Moore and Eddie Campbell's *From Hell* began at Spiderbaby Graphix and then went to Tundra and Kitchen Sink (all now defunct). It was first collected in a trade by Campbell's own company and then by Top Shelf. Sergio Aragones' *Groo the Wanderer* has appeared over the years in comics by Pacific Comics, Eclipse Comics, Marvel Comics (Epic imprint), Image Comics, and Dark Horse Comics (over 150 issues combined). This applies to non–comic book publishers as well. Ariel Schrag's autobiographical works were first published in the 1990s by Slave Labor but have recently been reprinted by Simon & Schuster's Touchstone imprint. Many of Will Eisner's works have been published by both comics and book publishers, starting with *A Contract with God*, which began at Baronet Books, then went to Kitchen Sink, then on to DC, and currently with W.W. Norton.

The second reason is that it is a licensed property. As discussed in Chapter 3, the granting and revoking of rights has led to comics based on one particular literary work, television show, or movie to be published by several different companies. This has even applied to trade editions where books published by one company contain works originally published by another, such as Dark Horse's collection of *Star Wars* and *Conan* comics put out by Marvel and IDW's collections of *Star Trek* stories from DC and Marvel. In another case, the rights to a translated work may go from one publisher to another. Tezuka's *Black Jack* was first put out by VIZ but is currently published by Vertical.

A third reason is that the original publisher has gone out of business (see Exhibit 6-3). Another company will then purchase some or all of its characters and work to do with as they see fit. DC purchased characters from Fawcett, Quality, and Charlton and has continued the adventures of, or reinvented, characters like the Marvel Family,

Plastic Man, and the Blue Beetle. DC has also reprinted stories with these characters from the 1940s to 1970s. In addition, sometimes the copyright to characters will expire, placing them in the public domain. Dynamite's recent *Project Superheroes* stories feature characters from several long defunct publishers, and Fantagraphics' *I Will Destroy All the Civilized Planets* and its sequels reprint the long out-of-print works that writer/artist Fletcher Hanks created over 65 years ago. At times it is a combination of the three. Checker has reprinted Gold Key's *Star Trek* comic, and after First Comics went out of business, both licensed *and* creator-owned works were collected and reprinted by other publishers.

Exhibit 6-3. Notable Defunct Comic Book Publishers

Broccoli Books (2003–2008). A U.S. publisher of Manga series including *Kamui, My Dearest Devil Princess*, and *E's*. Broccoli also had a line of yaoi titles under its Boysenberry Books imprint.

Charlton Comics (1946–1986). This Connecticut-based publisher's characters included Blue Beetle, Captain Atom, Peacemaker, The Question, and a number of titles based on television shows as well as war comics. Their superhero characters were purchased by DC, who revamped them, giving several their own series in the 1980s. DC has also reprinted certain Charlton stories in their *Action Hero Archive Editions*.

Comico (1982–1997). This was the original home of Matt Wagner's Grendel stories (now published by Dark Horse) and his *Mage* stories (now published by Image). Other Comico titles included adaptations of *Robotech*.

Crossgen (1998–2004). Also called Cross Generation Entertainment, this Florida-based company published many major writers and artists including George Perez, Mark Waid, and Ron Marz. Many of their titles were fantasy or science-fiction based, often tying in to a common shared universe. Much of their previously uncollected work has been collected and put out by Checker BPG (including *Sigil*, *Sojourn*, and *Negation*) with a few properties purchased by Disney.

Dell Comics (1928–1973). Part of Dell Publishing, Dell Comics was the creator of *The Funnies*, one of the first comics with all original material. Their titles mainly consisted of licensed properties, especially animated characters from Warner Brothers, Disney, and elsewhere, and they were the publisher of *Four Color*. A number of their licensed properties came from Western Publishing who later broke away to form Gold Key.

Dreamwave Production (1996–2005). Besides original works, Dreamwave also put out comics featuring various licensed properties including the Transformers (who had once been licensed to Marvel and are now licensed to IDW).

Eastern Color Printing (1933–1955). Eastern was one of the first comic book companies, and it was the publisher of the early titles *Funnies on Parade* and *Famous Funnies*. After it got out of comics, it continued for several decades as a printing company.

EC Comics (1944–1956). Also known as Educational Comics and Entertaining Comics, EC produced many of the influential titles of the late 1940s/early 1950s, including *Tales from the Crypt, Weird Science, Frontline Combat, Two-Fisted Tales, Crime SuspenStories*, and the humor comic *Mad*. After dealing with the problems of the anticomics feeling of the 1950s (see Chapter 2), EC got out of the comics business, with the exception of *Mad*, which was turned into a magazine. The company was later sold to the same company that owned DC Comics. Collections of the old EC stories have been put out by various publishers, most recently by Gemstone.

(Cont'd.)

Exhibit 6-3. Notable Defunct Comic Book Publishers *(Continued)*

Eclipse Comics (1978–1993). The publisher of *Sabre*, one of the pre–*Contract with God* graphic novels, as well as of such notable titles as *DNAgents*, *Espers*, *Zot!*, *Ms. Tree*, and the first American production of the British books *Modesty Blaise* and *Miracleman*. Eclipse was also the publisher of *Mai the Psychic Girl*, one of the first complete manga series to be reprinted in English.

Fawcett Comics (1939–1980). Fawcett Comics is best known for the original Captain Marvel aka young Billy Batson who would transform into the adult hero by saying the magic word "Shazam!" He battled evil throughout the 1940s along with the rest of the "Marvel Family" and other heroes such as Bulletman, but a perceived similarity to Superman brought a lawsuit from DC's predecessor National Comics. Fawcett eventually got out of superhero comics by the mid-1950s, and DC Comics later purchased Fawcett's superhero characters. The 1940s comics have been reprinted into various Archive Editions.

First Comics (1983–1991). First was the home of many creator-owned titles ,including Howard Chaykin's *American Flagg*, Mike Baron's *Nexus* and *Badger*, John Ostrander and Tim Truman's *GrimJack*, Mike Grell's *Jon Sable*, and the translated manga series *Lone Wolf and Cub*. Many of First's titles have either continued elsewhere or have been reprinted by other publishers include Dark Horse, Image, and IDW.

Gold Key (1963–1984). Created by Western Publishing (home of the "Little Golden Books") after breaking with Dell, Gold Key put out a number of original and licensed titles, including the first *Star Trek* series. An affiliated imprint, Whitman, was known for packaging multiple issues of DC and Marvel comics for sales in stores.

Harvey Comics (1941–1986). Harvey is best known for being the home of Casper the Friendly Ghost, Hot Stuff, the Little Devil, and Richie Rich among others. In 2007, Dark Horse began reprinting their works in the *Harvey Comics Classics* series of trades.

Kitchen Sink Press (1969–1999). Founded by Dennis Kitchen, KSP began as a publisher of underground comics. Its better known works include *Omaha, the Cat Dancer*, and *Megaton Man*, and both reprints and original stories featuring Will Eisner's *Spirit*, some by Eisner and others by various writers and artists. It also published several of Eisner's graphic novels and was the second publisher of *A Contract with God*. Some of Kitchen Sink's titles have gone to other companies including DC, NBM, W.W. Norton, and Image.

Lev Gleason Publications (1941–1955). The publisher of the first and perhaps best known "crime" comic of the 1940s, *Crime Does Not Pay*.

Malibu (1986–1994). Malibu published a number of superhero titles as well as science fiction, fantasy, and licensed properties including *Star Trek: Deep Space Nine*. They were purchased by Marvel in 1994.

Pacific Comics (1981–1983). The original home of such characters as Groo the Wanderer and the Rocketeer. Several of their titles found homes at other publishers for both original stories and collected reprints.

Quality Comics (1939–1956). The works of this early publisher included comics created by Will Eisner. Some of their better known characters include Plastic Man, The Blackhawks, Uncle Sam, The Black Condor, and the Ray. DC purchased the company in the 1950s, and many of the characters have continued to appear in comics, though some have been "revised." Reprints of Quality's titles can be found in DC's Archive Editions for Plastic Man and the Blackhawks.

Topps Comics (1993–1998). A division of the popular trading card maker Topps' lineup including a handful of original works, some based on ideas by Jack Kirby, and a number of licensed properties including *Xena: Warrior Princess* (now licensed to Dynamite) and *The X-Files* (now licenced to DC/Wildstom), reprints of which have been collected by Checker.

Tower Comics (1965–1969). While short-lived, Tower Comics is best remembered for Wally Wood's *T.H.U.N.D.E.R. Agents* which has since been collected by DC in six Archive Editions.

While many foreign-language graphic novels are translated before publication in the United States, others are distributed in their original language, and American and international graphic novels are also translated into Spanish and other languages and sold in the United States. Public Square Books is one of the largest publishers of Spanish-language graphic novels in the United States, with titles for both juvenile and adult audiences. Translated titles for older readers include *Sin City*, *Strangers in Paradise*, *Hellboy*, and *Queen and Country* and works by Peter Bagge and Charles Burns. They also publish manga that has been translated into Spanish as well as other works that were originally in non-English languages, including *Persepolis* and *The Rabbi's Cat*. Some titles available from Public Square and other publishers were originally in Spanish or another language and have not yet been translated into English. Having Spanish-language graphic novels in your collection can help to attract native Spanish speakers to your library and could even be helpful in programs that teach both English and Spanish (see Chapter 8).

Publisher Offerings

As hinted at by Exhibit 6-1, there are thousands of original graphic novels, trade editions, and volumes of manga published each year. When planning to get the trades for an ongoing series or the volumes of a manga title, the frequency of these volumes must be taken into account. Most ongoing series will produce a trade edition two or three times a year. In addition, some of these will be released in hardcover with a soft-cover edition coming out either later that year or the following year. Most manga titles will come out six times a year, but sometimes multiple volumes will be released within a short time. The frequency of a title can affect your decisions both for budgetary and shelving reasons.

In recent years, more and more collections are reprinting older material. Over 30 percent of DC's and Marvel's recent output have been collections containing material that first appeared prior to 2000, ranging from a book that was from one particular year or decade to books that contain works from multiple decades.[5] A ten-year-old boy can go into a library and read a recently created Superman story, then read one that came out when his father was ten, then go on to one published when his grandfather was ten, and finish up with a story that his ten-year-old *great*-grandfather had read. All four stories might even be in the same volume. And it's not just these two publishers. As Exhibit 6-4 shows, a library could stock 70+ books reprinting 70+ years worth of stories without repeating either the book or the comic that it came from.

The items on that list include works that range from the obscure to the well known and from works written for younger readers to those intended for older audiences. However, just because some works are intended for a younger crowd does not mean that adults would not also be interested in them. Some adults enjoy reading stories for all ages, and there is also the "nostalgia" factor: "Hey, I had that issue when I was kid!"

Exhibit 6-4. Comic Book Stories from 1938–2009 and Trade Edition Reprints

The following provides a list of various comic book stories that were originally printed between 1938–2009 (one comic per year) and of the trade editions in which they have been reprinted (most of which are found in Appendix A). The Superman stories that the ten-year-old might have read are in bold. The 1938 story is not the oldest currently being reprinted, as stories from 1936–1937 are included in Fantagraphics' 2009 collection *Supermen!*.

Year	Comic Book	Reprinted In
1938	*Action Comics #1*	*Superman Chronicles,* Vol. 1
1939	*Detective Comics #27*	*Batman Archives,* Vol. 1
1940	*Big 3 #2*	*I Shall Destroy All the Civilized Planets*
1941	*Captain America Comics #1*	*Marvel Masterworks: Golden Age Captain America,* Vol. 1
1942	*Human Torch #8*	*Marvel Masterworks: Golden Age Human Torch,* Vol. 2
1943	*Military Comics #17*	*Blackhawk Archives,* Vol. 1
1944	*Leading Comics #9*	*Seven Soldiers of Victory Archives,* Vol. 3
1945	*Sensation Comics #33*	*Wonder Woman Archives,* Vol. 4
1946	*World's Finest Comics #25*	*Batman: The World's Finest Archives,* Vol. 2
1947	*Flash Comics #86*	*Black Canary Archives,* Vol. 1
1948	*Police Comics #77*	*Plastic Man Archives,* Vol. 8
1949	*All-Star Comics #46*	*All-Star Comics Archives,* Vol. 10
1950	*Marvel Boy #1*	*Atlas Era Heroes*
1951	*Tales from the Crypt #22*	*EC Archives: Tales From the Crypt,* Vol. 1
1952	*Shock SuspenStories #1*	*The EC Archives: Shock SuspenStories,* Vol. 1
1953	*Journey Into Mystery #6*	*Atlas Era: Journey into Mystery,* Vol. 1
1954	*Menace #1*	*Agents of Atlas*
1955	*Strange Adventures #56*	*Showcase Presents Strange Adventures,* Vol. 1
1956	*Showcase #4*	*Showcase Presents: The Flash,* Vol. 1
1957	*Blackhawk #110*	*Showcase Presents: Blackhawk,* Vol. 1
1958	*Adventure Comics #247*	*Legion of Super-Heroes Archives,* Vol. 1
1959	*Tales to Astonish #4*	*Atlas Era Tales to Astonish,* Vol. 1
1960	*Superman #140*	*Showcase Presents: Superman,* Vol. 2
1961	*Fantastic Four #1*	*Fantastic Four Masterworks,* Vol. 1
1962	*Our Army At War #118*	*Showcase Presents: Sgt. Rock,* Vol. 2
1963	*Amazing Spider-Man #1*	*Fantastic Four/Spider-Man Classic #1*

(Cont'd.)

	Exhibit 6-4. Comic Book Stories from 1938–2009 and Trade Edition Reprints *(Continued)*	
Year	Comic Book	Reprinted In
1964	Sgt. Fury #13	Marvel Masterworks Sgt. Fury, Vol. 1
1965	Modeling With Minnie	Marvel Visionaries: Roy Thomas
1966	G.I. Combat #120	Showcase Presents: The Haunted Tank, Vol. 2
1967	Star Trek #1 (Gold Key)	Star Trek: The Key Collection, Vol. 1
1968	Justice League of America #64	Crisis on Multiple Earths, Vol. 2
1969	Wonder Woman #185	Diana Prince, Wonder Woman, Vol. 2
1970	Conan the Barbarian #1	Chronicles of Conan, Vol. 1
1971	Avengers #89	Avengers: Kree Skrull War
1972	The Demon #1	Jack Kirby's the Demon Omnibus
1973	Dracula Lives #1	Essential Tomb of Dracula #1
1974	The Brave and the Bold #115	Batman: The Strange Deaths of Batman
1975	Werewolf by Night #28	Essential Werewolf by Night, Vol. 2
1976	Captain America #200	Captain America and the Falcon: Madbomb
1977	Cerebus #1	Cerebus
1978	What If #10	What If? Classic, Vol. 2
1979	Godzilla #24	Essential Godzilla, Vol. 1
1980	Daredevil #163	Hulk vs. the Marvel Universe
1981	Iron Man #150	Iron Man vs. Dr. Doom
1982	New Teen Titans (Vol. 1) #23	New Teen Titans Archives, Vol. 4
1983	John Sable, Freelance #1	The Complete John Sable Freelance, Vol. 1
1984	Saga of the Swamp Thing #25	Saga of the Swamp Thing, Vol. 1
1985	Crisis of Infinite Earths #1	Crisis on Infinite Earths
1986	**Man of Steel**	**Superman: The Man of Steel, Vol. 1**
1987	Concrete #1	The Complete Concrete
1988	Hellblazer #1	Hellblazer: Original Sins
1989	Sandman #8	Sandman: Preludes and Nocturnes
1990	Hate #1	Buddy Does Seattle
1991	From Hell #1	From Hell
1992	Yummy Fur #28	I Never Liked You
1993	Palookaville #4	It's a Good Life, If You Don't Weaken
1994	Naughty Bits #14	Life's a Bitch

(Cont'd.)

	Exhibit 6-4. Comic Book Stories from 1938–2009 and Trade Edition Reprints *(Continued)*	
Year	Comic Book	Reprinted In
1995	*Skrull Kill Krew #1*	*Skrull Kill Krew*
1996	*Berlin #1*	*Berlin: City of Stones*
1997	*Zombieworld: Champion of the Worms #1*	*Zombieworld: Champion of the Worms*
1998	*Buffy the Vampire Slayer #1*	*Buffy the Vampire Slayer Omnibus,* Vol. 3
1999	*Age of Bronze #5*	*Age of Bronze: A Thousand Ships*
2000	*100 Bullets #6*	*100 Bullets,* Vol. 2: *Split Second Chance*
2001	*Hellboy: Conqueror Worm #1*	*Hellboy: Conqueror Worm*
2002	*Y: The Last Man #1*	*Y: The Last Man,* Vol. 1: *Unmanned*
2003	*Fables #7*	*Fables: Animal Farm*
2004	*Michael Chabon Presents the Amazing Adventures of the Escapist #1*	*The Amazing Adventures of the Escapist,* Vol. 1
2005	*Fallen Angel* (Vol. 2) *#1*	*Fallen Angel,* Vol. 1: *To Serve in Heaven*
2006	*Strangers in Paradise* (Vol. 3) *#83*	*Strangers in Paradise Pocket Book #6*
2007	*True Story Swear to God* (Vol. 2) *#1*	*True Story Swear to God,* Vol. 1
2008	*Walking Dead #50*	*Walking Dead,* Vol. 9: *Here We Remain*
2009	**Final Crisis: Superman Beyond #2**	**Final Crisis**

Besides the occasional "theme" trade, some trade editions reprint older materials in multiple volumes. These include DC's Showcase Presents, Archive Editions, and Chronicles books and Marvel's Masterworks and Essential lines. And it is not only the best-known characters, such as Batman or the X-Men, who are having their stories reprinted. Lesser-known characters, such as Metamorpho, the Creeper, and Killraven, are having their appearances (sometimes in conjunction with new appearances) collected, as are older comics series that have not previously been collected. The increase in the availability of older material is also helpful to comic scholars (see Chapter 9) who have the opportunity to view these stories without having to track down old comic books. Neil Gaiman has said that readers are now in a "Golden Age"

> not just because there's some good stuff being produced, but [also because,] for the first time ever, there is this astounding multiplicity of everything good that's ever been produced. It's out there. You want to read *Little Nemo* comics the same size as they were when they were done by Winsor McKay? They're out there! You want to read *Peanuts* in glorious editions, three to a page and then a Sunday? They're out there. You want to read Jack Cole Plastic Mans? They're out there. And all the Archive Editions, and so on and so forth? I think it's amazing. So one of the things that's happened is we're in a world in which books like *Maus* and *Dark Knight* and

Watchmen kind of changed everything. Because the idea when they were published that [they] would be in print and occasionally creeping up on to bestsellers lists 22 years after they were published . . . could you have imagined that, then? I couldn't have done. (Baker, 2009)

Purchasing for Adult Collections

So the question becomes, at least for libraries that serve all ages, what specifically should be purchased for an adult collection? What counts as "adult?" Since the average age of comic book readers is in their twenties, even titles that collect new materials and are suitable for teens or younger ages might circulate well in an adult collection. However, for budgetary reasons, you may wish to have such titles purchased by the children/teen departments as long as your adult patrons still have access. As discussed in Chapter 8, you may even want an integrated collection, in which titles for all ages and titles for mature readers are in the same general area.

So how do you know which titles definitely should be cataloged as "adult"? Sometimes the imprint will be a clue. Books from DC's Vertigo line, Marvel's Max titles, or the yaoi imprints of certain manga publishers should, in almost all cases, go into the adult area; for the exceptions, it is probably better to shelve them first in the adult section and then "downgrade" them once you have examined them. Factors such as nudity and foul language can also apply, though many young adult titles have foul language, and PG-13 movies feature nonsexual nudity (*Titanic*, for example). In many cases, it will simply be that the story will be of more interest to adult readers than younger ones, as with a large number of books in any adult collection. Many "adult" titles listed in Appendix A are perfectly acceptable for teen and, in some cases, even "tween" readers.

Ratings

One helpful way of finding out the publisher's target audience is the ratings systems that many publishers have created for themselves. For example, Marvel's ratings, as listed on their Web site, follow:

ALL AGES: Appropriate for readers of all ages.

A: Appropriate for ages 9 and up.

T+ TEENS & UP: Appropriate for most readers 13 and up; parents are advised that they may want to read before or with younger children.

PARENTAL ADVISORY: 15+ years old, similar to T+ but featuring more mature themes and/or more graphic imagery. Recommended for teen and adult readers.

MAX: EXPLICIT CONTENT: 18+ years old; most Mature Readers books will fall under the MAX Comics banner (created specifically for mature content titles). MAX and Mature-themed titles will continue to be designed to appear distinct from mainline Marvel titles, with the "MAX: Explicit Content" label very prominently displayed on the cover. MAX titles will NOT be sold on the newsstand, and they will NOT be marketed to younger readers. (Marvel, n.d.)

Tokyopop's ratings include "content indicators" developed by librarian Michele Gorman. Many other manga publishers have a system similar to this:

A: All Ages. May contain cartoon violence and potty humor.

Y: Youth (10+). May contain mild language, fantasy violence, and bullying.

T: Teenage (13+). May contain infrequent and mild profanity, mild violence and gore, crude humor, mild sexual language and themes, nondescript nudity, and mild fanservice, as well as references to tobacco, alcohol, and illegal drug use.

OT: Older Teen (16+). May contain profanity and strong language, moderate violence and gore, moderate sexual themes and sexual violence, nudity, moderate fanservice, and alcohol and illegal drug use.

M: Mature Ages (18+). May contain excessive profanity and language; intense violence; excessive gore; explicit sexual language, themes, and violence; and explicit fanservice. (Tokyopop, n.d.)

Of course, sometimes the ratings may not be 100 percent accurate. As VIZ mentions on its ratings Web page, ratings "are based on . . . internal subjective assessments and are meant for general guidance only. We cannot guarantee uniform application and they should not be considered the equivalent of any regulatory standard" (VIZ media, n.d.).

Readers and librarians have found at times that the ratings are inaccurate and that an ongoing series will "jump up" a rating level, making what was once acceptable for teens better for adults. This is not necessarily a problem, however, when your selections are already for older readers. Of course, the opposite can also happen. Marvel's *Supreme Power* had a "Max" rating but its sequel, *Squadron Supreme*,[6] has a "parental advisory" rating, but because someone reading *Squadron Supreme* will probably also have an interest in *Supreme Power*, it is probably best to catalog both titles as adult. Because the rating indicator is sometimes covered by stickers or bar codes during processing (as discussed in the next chapter), having them properly cataloged can be helpful for people looking for—or looking to avoid—a certain type of book.

Review Sources

Another great way to find out if a book should be only in the adult area is to consult reviews. You may automatically receive titles for an ongoing series or from a particular writer whose works you have purchased in the past, but you may need some help when deciding which new series, other trades, and original graphic novels to purchase for your libraries. Luckily, a large number of sources, both in print and online, review comics and graphic novels.

Unfortunately, many graphic novels do not have review copies available prior to publication (though this is changing), so it is unlikely that you would see most reviews prior to publication. With trades, the individual issues may have been reviewed, and while this may not provide all of the information, it can give you a basic idea of the quality of the work. However, unlike the new Danielle Steel or John Grisham book, or a work that has been mentioned on television, there is rarely immediate heavy demand for a particular graphic novel, and this luxury of time allows you to pick and choose your purchases properly.

For print reviews, most of the sources that you consult for other book reviews will also review graphic novels. In fact, several have regular columns that specifically cover the format. The first publication for librarians to do so was *VOYA* (*Voice of Youth Advocates*), which has published Kat Kan's "Graphically Speaking" since 1994, with the column appearing in every issue since October 2002. Also in 2002, *Library Journal* began a bimonthly column by Steve Raiteri, who was joined by Martha Cornog in 2006. *Booklist, School Library Journal,* and other library-related publications also print reviews in special columns or articles or mixed in with the other reviews.

Publications such as *Entertainment Weekly* and the *New York Times Book Review* will occasionally review graphic novels, and many comic-book-related publications offer reviews as well as interviews, articles, and information on upcoming works. Some of the better-known publications are *Wizard, The Comic Buyer's Guide,* and *The Comics Journal,* which also have online presences. Other online sources that you can use for reviews range from the professional to ones set up by fans or even by librarians.

Some Web pages and/or e-newsletters of interest include *Publishers Weekly* PW Comics Week and GraphicNovelReporter.com, which is part of bookreporter.com. "The Beat," hosted by *Publisher's Weekly,* and *The Comic Journal's* "Journalista" contain links to news and reviews from sites all around the Internet and can be helpful in finding reviews and "best of the year" type lists. Some of the sites that sell graphic novels, such as Diamond, Booklist, and BWI, will also have reviews, some done in-house and others taken from periodicals.

Of course, sometimes it helps to have the opinion of another librarian, and that's where GNLIB-L comes in. Created in October 1999 by Steve Miller, this e-mail list is dedicated to the subject of graphic novels in libraries and counts among its participants librarians from all around the world as well graphic novel creators and representatives from publishers and vendors. A number of people on the list have also written books on the subject, regularly do reviews, and/or have created Web sites including Kat Kan, Steve Raiteri, Michele Gorman, Robin Brenner, and Michael Pawuk (the latter two are also co-moderators). From the list's beginning, librarians have used it to get recommendations for titles as well as answers to questions of cataloging, shelving, preservation, programming, challenges, and age-appropriate titles. For subscriber information and other online resources, see Appendix C.

Another electronic source for reviews is H. W. Wilson's "Graphic Novels Core Collection: A Selection Guide" database. Features of this database (available by subscription by itself or with other Wilson products) include reviews by Kat Kan and the ability to search in various areas, including genres, subjects, awards, and age appropriateness. This database, along with many of the review sites, can also be helpful if you are starting a collection and want to add older material or if you have received a request from a patron that your library carry certain older titles.

A number of books also discuss older works. Besides the various books that include booklists as part of a discussion of libraries and graphic novels, two helpful graphic novel guides are Pawuk's *Graphic Novels: A Genre Guide* (2006) and Thompson's *Manga: The Complete Guide* (2007). For other helpful titles, see Appendix B.

Awards

As is usually the case when it comes to "text" books, a graphic novel that wins an award is something that you should purchase for your library. As mentioned in Chapter 1, a number of comics, such as *Fun Home, Maus, Palestine, Jimmy Corrigan, Watchmen*, and *Sandman* have won or been nominated for mainstream awards, but comic books have long had their own awards, both fan created and from professional groups. Some of the earlier ones include the Alley Awards (1961–1969), created by some of the early members of comics fandom, and the Shazam! Award, which was given out by the Academy of Comic Book Arts from 1971–1975. *Wizard, The Comics Buyer's Guide*, and other magazines have had awards that fans could vote for, and when online fandom began, the fans created their own awards.

Currently, the two major awards in the comics industry are the Eisners and the Harveys, which both originated from a common source. In 1985, the Jack Kirby Awards were created by several individuals at Fantagraphics who wanted to "create a set of awards that could generate genuine respect, ones that would be actively sought after by creators and publishers alike [and that] the world outside the comic book industry could look to for quality reading" (Olbrich, 2008b). However, a dispute over ownership led Kirby to request that his name be taken off the award out of respect for both parties (Olbrich, 2008a), and in 1988 the award was split.

The Will Eisner Comic Achievement Award, presented yearly at Comic-Con International, is considered to be the "Oscar" of the comic book industry.[7] The categories cover both the actual comics and graphics novels as well as the creators, with nominees coming from a five-person panel of judges and the actual winner voted on by creators, publishers, retailers, distributors, and others in the industry. Foreign works have their own category, and recently Japanese comics were given a category separate from that. Until his death in 2005, Eisner took part in the ceremonies and also won five Eisners of his own.

In 2005, librarian Kat Kan was chosen as an Eisner Judge. Since then several others have been judges, including Robin Brenner, Eva Volin, and Mike Pawuk. Eisner coordinator Jackie Estrada said that she decided to make a librarian a judge after meeting more and more librarians who are enthusiastic about graphic novels at book industry events and also after noticing that more librarians were reviewing graphic novels. She has also found them to be "especially knowledgeable about manga and books geared to younger audiences, which really helped fill in the gaps in knowledge from the other judges," and she considers having a librarian as a judge a "win-win situation" (Estrada, personal communication, January 19, 2009).

The Harvey Awards are named for Harvey Kurtzman, whose works have included early issues of *Mad*, other early EC titles, and even the *Playboy* comic strip *Little Annie Fanny*. They are co-coordinated by Fantagraphics, and while at first they were presented at various conventions, since 2005 they have been given out at the Baltimore Comic-Con. Nominees are voted for by people in the industry, who receive mailed ballots on which they can nominate up to five entries per category. The top five nominees are then put on the final ballot that is then voted on by creators and publishers. The categories are similar to those on the Eisners, and both awards also have a Hall of Fame.

Another notable award is the Ignatz Award, which is for small-press and creator-owned works. The award is named after a character in George Herriman's famous comic strip *Krazy Kat* and is voted on by attendees of the Small Press Expo. Others include the Eagle Awards, presented by fans in the United Kingdom; the Lulu Awards, for female creators or stories with female protagonists; the Reuben Awards, from the National Cartoonists Society); the Joe Shuster Award (named for Superman's co-creator) for work by Canadian creators; and the Glyph Comics Awards for black creators and characters (see Exhibit 6-5).

Exhibit 6-5. Selected List of Award Winners and Nominees

These are some of the titles in Appendix A that have won or have been nominated for awards.

100 Bullets	Exit Wounds	Kings in Disguise	The Rabbi's Cat
300	Fables	Last Day in Vietnam	Safe Area Gorazde
Abandon the Old in Tokyo	Fax from Sarajevo	Last Musketeer	Sandman
Acme Novelty Library	The Fixer	The League of Extraordinary	Sin City
	From Hell	Gentlemen	Stagger Lee
Age of Bronze	Fun Home	The Left Bank Gang	Stuck Rubber Baby
Aya	Ghost World	Life and Times of	Swallow Me Whole
Berlin	Hellboy	Martha Washington	Three Fingers
Black Hole	Hicksville	in the Twenty-First	The Ticking
Blankets	Hutch Owen:	Century	To the Heart of the
Blue Pills	Unmarketable	Lone Wolf and Cub	Storm
Box Office Poison	I Killed Adolf Hitler	Louis Riel	Tricked
Buddha	I Shall Destroy All the	Love and Rockets	Twentieth Century
Carnet De Voyage	Civilized Planets!	Maus	Eightball
The Cartoon History	It's a Good Life, If You	Misery Loves Company	The Umbrella
of the Universe	Don't Weaken	The Name of the Game	Academy
Cerebus	James Sturm's America:	The Originals	Understanding
Clyde Fans	Gods, Gold, and	Our Cancer Year	Comics
Creepy Archives	Golems	Persepolis	Watchmen
Criminal	Jimbo's Inferno	Powers	Whiteout
Curses	Jimmy Corrigan	Pride of Baghdad	Why Are You Doing
Epileptic	Julius Knipl, Real Estate	The Push Man and	This?
Ex Machina	Photographer:	Other Stories	Wimbledon Green
	Stories		Y: The Last Man

Conferences and Conventions

While you can examine publishers' Web sites and sometimes even e-mail them for additional information, at times you can also talk to them in person. Many graphic novels publishers have appeared at the American Library Association's annual conference for several years. There is even a designated "Graphic Novel Alley" where publishers' representatives are available to answer questions and provide catalogs and review copies, and where creative personnel may even do signings. Although they do not set up in the Alley, the "mainstream" book publishers should also be in the exhibit hall and may have a special table for their graphic novel imprints. Related events, such as BookExpo America, also have a graphic novel presence, and many include programs on graphic novels in libraries. There are also various academic conferences (see Chapter 9) and other events, such as Splat!—a graphic novels symposium sponsored by the New York Center for Independent Publishing.

Another way to interact with publishers and creators is at a comic book convention. At most conventions, fans attend panels, meet creators, get their comics signed, get sketches by artists, and purchase back issues, original artwork, and other collectables. Only a few hundred fans went to the first ever convention, held on July 27, 1964, in New York City. The handful of guests for that "con" included artist Steve Ditko and Flo Steinberg, Stan Lee's personal secretary. More conventions followed, growing in size, duration, guest list, and attendance. Today conventions are held all around the world, and people travel across the country and even internationally to attend. Besides comics, many of these conventions also include actors and writers from science fiction, fantasy, and horror-themed television shows and films.

Some of the notable comics-themed conventions in the United States include Small Press Expo, New York Comic Con, Mid-Ohio Con, Baltimore Comic-Con, Wizard World in Chicago, Emerald City ComiCon in Seattle, Heroes Convention in Charlotte, Wondercon and the Alternative Press Expo in San Francisco, and the Motor City ComiCon in Detroit. But the biggest of them all in North America is Comic-Con International, held each year in San Diego.

Also known as San Diego Comic-Con, the grounds were laid for the first convention with a "mini-con" held on March 21, 1970, in the basement of the U.S. Grant Hotel. This raised funds and tested the waters for the San Diego's Golden State Comic-Con held later that year on August 1–3 at the hotel. That event had only about 300 attendees, who came to see people like Jack Kirby and Ray Bradbury, but it grew and grew, changing names and locations until the 2009 convention filled the entire San Diego Convention Center with over 126,000 attendees (and, for the second year in a row, it sold out before it began). Besides the guests, attendees included over 12,000 people from the comic book and entertainment industries, with 600 hours of panels, films, and programs (including the Eisner Awards) and over 900 exhibitors who filled 52 aisles (which if placed end to end would be three miles long). Besides the comics elements, many current and upcoming television shows and films were hyped, with A-list stars appearing on panels, and many authors also appeared, including, once again, Ray Bradbury. As well-attended as it is, San Diego's Comic-Con is not the largest in the world. France's Festival International de la Bande Dessinee in Angoulême has had over 200,000 attendees, and Japan's Comiket, held twice a year in Tokyo, has attracted crowds of nearly 500,000.

A number of conventions have held panels and even tracks that appeal to librarians. San Diego Comic-Con has had several panels that consisted of librarians as well as a Comic Arts Conference for academics. The New York Comic Con includes a pre-conference sponsored by ICv2 that has included panels such as "Graphic Novel Growth and Diversification," "Superheroes and Manga: Making Room for Both at Your Library," and "Graphic Novels—The New Literature?" Panelists have included librarians, publishers, vendors, and others, and the conference itself allows librarians a free one-day pass.

Self-Review Techniques

Reviewing a book yourself is also an option and can be done in a number of ways. Some vendors, BWI with their SNAP (Selection, Notification, and Acquisition Plan) for example, will allow you to preview a book prior to purchase and also to send it back if it is unsuitable for your library. If you have a good relationship with your local comics shop, the people there might be willing to offer advice on what your patrons might like and also let you browse through the books, as will many larger bookstores. Even if you can examine only part of the book, this will help you get an idea of its contents. As immediacy is not usually a factor, you can also wait until other libraries get the title and then request it through interlibrary loan. Not only will this allow you to examine the book's contents but it will also give you an idea of how other libraries catalog and process their graphic novels.

So if you are able to personally review a graphic novel, how do you decide if it is "good"? BWI's *The Public Librarian's Guide to Graphic Novels* (2003: 14–16) has some suggestions:

- *Panel structure:* How are the panels situated on the page? Are they easy to follow? How are they shaped and how does the shape affect the story? How do they break up the artwork and do these breaks speed up, slow down, or complicate the story?
- *Images:* Is the art clear and sharp or is it muted and smudgy, and does it work for the story? How is the shading and coloring (when applicable) affecting the story?
- *Words:* Do the word balloons contain too much or too little text? Does the dialogue flow naturally when read around? Are there elements of patterned language? Do different characters have different "voices"? What is the ratio of text to art, and does the text overpower the art or crowd it out? Is the plot simple, linear, or complex?
- *Text and art together:* Do the styles of the text and the art complement each other, and if they are different, does the story still work? How does the art

relate to the story? Does it complement it or provide crucial details that add to the story?

On the other hand, if pressed for time, you may just want to do the same thing that you might do with any other book—skim through it and listen to the advice of reviewers.

There may also be someone who works in your library who is familiar with comics and graphic novels and who could advise you. This person may not necessarily work in your department or do any work with adults or with materials selection, but his or her knowledge of the subject can be very helpful. If several people are available for this, a committee can be formed to help you select titles or to select titles themselves. Your library's patrons can also be a source for recommendations that will give you an idea of what the public may be interested in.

There are some books that you will not purchase for your library because the reviews are bad, because when you personally reviewed them you felt that the stories and/or art were subpar, because you do not think there will be any interest in them, because you do not want to commit to new ongoing series or manga titles with long anticipated runs, or because they are expensive or you have allocated your budget monies elsewhere. If you are only selecting titles for adults, and the material is more suited for younger readers, then you may pass those on to the people who select materials for those ages. On the other hand, what if the material is for adults in the way that comes to mind when the adjective "adult" is most commonly used?

How Adult Is Too Adult?

A number of titles in Appendix A are rated 18+, Mature, or something similar. Many of these feature male and/or female nudity, and while in some cases it is just the case of a character being undressed, others involve sexual circumstances. For the latter, the question becomes, where is the line between erotica and pornography? How adult is too adult? Many libraries contain works in which sexual activity is described, ranging from classics such as *Fanny Hill* to the modern works of Zane to "Best Erotica of the Year" type books. And if your library owns the latter, then why should it not also own a *Best Erotic Comics* collection? In fact, that title includes excerpts from several works that are included in Appendix A.

Of course, the main difference is that if you open up the book, you'll just see words, and if you open up the graphic novel, there's a chance that you may see not only "naughty bits" but those bits doing "naughty" things. This has been referred to as the "naked buns" effect: it is a lot easier to talk about an unclothed rear end then to show one (Cary, 2004: 45). Images of nudity in a graphic novel, whether in a sexual situation or just a character bathing or changing clothes, can result in complaints from both patrons and staff; ways to deal with such complaints will be covered in Chapter 8. But if you have graphic novels in which characters are not only naked but also involved in sexual activity, there is still the question of how much is too much.

Pornographic comics have been around for a long time. Between the 1920s and the 1960s, small comics known as "Tijuana Bibles" would feature stories with sexual activity, often using the images of celebrities or characters from comics, such as Dick Tracy, Blondie, Popeye, and even Donald Duck. Some publishers today produce works that even they call pornographic, and sometimes a regular comics publisher will have a special adults-only imprint. Fantagraphics has its Eros line and NBM has its Eurotica and Amerotica titles. Other publishers, such as manga publisher Icarus Publishing, produce nothing but pornography.

Now, while no library is going to stock titles like *Kung-Fu Sex Fighter*, *Captain Hard-On*, or *Perverts of the Unknown* (unless they are part of a special collection), some pornographic titles are considered "classics" and others are written by popular "mainstream" comic writers, including Bill Willingham, Howard Chaykin, and Phil Foglio. One title of note is *Omaha the Cat Dancer* by Reed Waller and Kate Worley. While the characters in *Omaha* are anthropomorphized animals, they act and have (not counting tails) the same sort of body parts as humans.

The division between actual, meant-to-stimulate-you-sexually pornography and what has been described as "literary smut"[8] (Christina, 2008: 200) is an unsure one, and in recent years one title that had many people examining this division was Alan Moore's *Lost Girls*. Written by Moore and drawn by Melinda Gebbie over the course of 15 years (during which the pair fell in love and later married), *Lost Girls* was published by Top Shelf as a slipcased three-volume hardcover in 2006. Despite its $75.00 price, the first printing of 10,000 sold out the first day. This led to additional printings, including a cheaper one-volume edition in 2009.

In *Lost Girls*, three women of various ages and social status meet at the Austrian Hotel Himmelgarten shortly before the start of the First World War. Their names are Alice, Wendy, and Dorothy, names that are familiar to all, but whose stories are not exactly what we remember. While the women have sexual encounters in the present, including with one another, they also tell stories of their past experiences, which have parallels with the well-known versions. For Dorothy, these included her encounters with the men of the farm; for Wendy, a group of wild boys who lived in the park; and for Alice, "Mrs. Redman," a teacher who seduced her. The controversy came not only from the fact that these beloved literary characters are shown having both heterosexual and lesbian sex, but also because in many of the "flashbacks" the characters are underage.[9]

Still the reviews were impressive: *Village Voice* named it one of the top 25 books of the year, *USA Today* praised its "intelligent writing, intricate plotlines and gorgeous Victorian-style art" (Horne, 2008), and *Publishers Weekly* gave it a starred review. Commenting on its nature, Neil Gaiman, who wrote the *Publishers Weekly* review, said:[10]

> It succeeded for me wonderfully as a true graphic novel. If it failed for me, it was only as smut; the book . . . was not a one-handed read. It was too heady, dense and strange to appreciate or to experience on a visceral level. (Your mileage may vary; porn is, after all, personal.) That the material is problematic—no more so than many un-illustrated novels, but then, it is, most definitely illustrated, and the -graphy part of

pornography is what makes this a graphic novel—is obvious. Top Shelf has taken the traditional approach of a respectable publisher when faced with the problem of bringing out pornography, and has chosen to package it elegantly, expensively and beautifully, thus pricing, shaping, signaling and presenting it to the world, not as pornography, but as erotica. Whatever you call it, there has never been anything quite like this in the world before, and I find myself extraordinarily pleased that someone of Moore's ability actually has written that sort of comics for adults. (Gaiman, 2006)

And on the question of erotica versus pornography, Gaiman says that "the boundary between pornography and erotica is an ambiguous one, and it changes depending on where you're standing" (Gaiman, 2006). Libraries have purchased *Lost Girls*, though the vast majority have been academic libraries. After all, it is a little easier for an academic library to own such books as it is more unlikely that minors will have access to them. A greater worry is that due to both the content and the price, the book might be stolen. This has led some libraries not to shelve it in the open stacks but still make it available to those who request it (Green, 2008).

So what is the answer to the question of "how adult is too adult"? There might not be one. A book that one library has no problem providing to their patrons (or even making available for interlibrary loan), may be over the line for another. When it comes to the titles mentioned and recommended in this book, please remember that it is a general list, and all of the books listed are not for all libraries.

A collection development policy can be helpful in determining what you should and should not purchase for your library and if the material is challenged. Some libraries have created a special policy for graphic novels, others include a mention of graphic novels in the general policy, and still others do not specifically mention them but instead lump them in with other kinds of books. Exhibit 6-6 shows some examples of graphic-novel-specific collection development policies.

Exhibit 6-6. Examples of Collection Development Policies

Columbia University Library Collection Development Policy for Graphic Novels
www.columbia.edu/cu/lweb/services/colldev/graphic_novels.html

Purpose and Program Description
The libraries seek to support research in the literary, artistic, and cinematic aspects of graphic novels and selected comics.

Graphic novels—a recent term—have been defined as "book length collections of sequential art containing a single story, or a set of interrelated stories," although many continue to refer to such compilations simply as comics, due to their panel-art format. The libraries' collection will concentrate on titles that have won awards or otherwise received critical and/or scholarly notice—with a specific focus on the role of New York City as setting or inspiration—as well as secondary scholarly literature.

Since the late 1990s, graphic novels have become an increasingly greater influence on film both in content and style. In addition, critical recognition of graphic novels has increased dramatically.

The collection supports the needs of undergraduate, MA/MS and PhD students, the teaching faculty, postdocs, and researchers in the areas of literature, art, film, and cultural history.

(Cont'd.)

Exhibit 6-6. Examples of Collection Development Policies *(Continued)*

General Selection Guidelines
Overall, the libraries' collection is at the study and teaching level, with selected secondary literature support at the research level.

Specific Delimitations
Formats collected: We collect bound anthologies, monographs, and periodicals. We exclude individual comic issues and newspaper syndicate printings, although some such materials may be acquired in Special Collections.

Imprint Dates collected: We collect current publications selectively, and earlier 20th century publications very selectively.

Chronological focus: We collect graphic novels of the late 20th century and beyond; we collect selectively in comics of the early 20th century.

Languages collected: We collect extensively in English language, and selectively in Western-European languages.

Place of publication: We collect materials published in North America extensively, and all other areas of the world selectively. We especially concentrate on works written in or about New York City.

From the Mercer County (NJ) Library Collection Development Policy
http://webserver.mcl.org/lib/colldev6.html

Graphic Novels
According to YALSA (Young Adult Library Services Association), graphic novels are defined as "book length collections of sequential art containing a single story, or a set of interrelated stories. Not to be included are illustrated books, nonillustrated books featuring superheroes as a main character, nonfiction books about comics and graphic novels, and collections of comic strips." The use of the Graphic Novel collection is primarily recreational. The novels included in this collection span traditional age ranges—juveniles, young adults, and adults may all find titles of interest. Various subject areas are covered and one may find both fiction and non-fiction topics covered.

Various tools are used when selecting titles for the Graphic Novel collection. Review sources such as *VOYA, Library Journal,* and *Brodart TIPS*; listservs and Web sites; and patron requests all are taken into consideration when acquiring materials. Much of the collection is driven by popular culture and patron demand.

Longview (TX) Public Library
www.longview.lib.tx.us/Newweb/library_templates/CollDevPol/ColDevPolpg6.htm

Graphic Novels
The graphic novel collection is made up of recreational reading and informational titles in book form for adult readers. These are books that are primarily pictorial, with text and dialog working together to propel the narrative. Selection is based upon reviews in literary and trade journals. Preference is given to graphic novels in hardback, though paperbacks will be purchased when that is the only available format. Specific selection criteria for these materials are the same as for works of fiction but also include:
- Quality of graphics
- Public demand

St. Joseph County (Indiana) Public Library's Page
http://sjcpl.lib.in.us/policies/collectiondevelopment/

Adult Collections
We purchase graphic novels for our adult collections, but librarians may choose to shelve them with their juvenile or teen collections.

Purchasing Related Materials

You can purchase many comic-related materials for your library. Your periodical department can purchase *Comic Buyer's Guide*, *Wizard*, *The Comics Journal*, and other magazines, as well as certain comic book series. There are CD-ROMs that contain near-complete runs of various comic book series and a special version of *Maus*. In addition, Alexander Street is creating a subscribable database for academic libraries that contains various comic works from over the years. These include many underground titles, comics such as *Love and Rockets*, and work by creators such as R. Crumb. Related works, such as *Seduction of the Innocent* and transcripts from the Senate hearings on comics, are also included. The work is indexed in various ways, including by subject and content.

A large number of "text" books can also be purchased for your collection. Besides works of fiction, which have been around for over 60 years, many nonfiction books are available. These include books on creating comics (such as Eisner's *Comics and Sequential Art*) books on comics and their history (such as many of the works of Paul Gravett), spotlights on a particular creator (such as various titles from TwoMorrows Press), books on a particular title (such as the various annotations of *The League of Extraordinary Gentlemen* by librarian Jess Nevins), various kinds of encyclopedias (such as DK Books), educational views of comics (such as Douglas Wolk's *Reading Comics*), and ones that are just odd (such as *Holy Sh*t! The World's Weirdest Comic Books*). A list of some of the available books that will both inform and entertain your patrons can be found in Appendix B.

Making Your Final Decisions

You know how to order, find out what's available, evaluate a book, how to find reviews, and what you may not want to buy. The final decisions are up to you, and you must still consider some factors, including if you are selecting for a public or an academic library. Are you purchasing just for "enjoyment" reading, for scholarly research, or both? Are you the sole decider of what graphic novels are purchased, or do other departments order as well?

Obviously, budget and shelf space are factors in your purchases, but so is how often you plan to purchase graphic novels. Is this a one-time purchase of a large collection, an occasional purchase, or multiple purchases throughout the year? As mentioned earlier, the frequency of a title can affect your decisions, especially if you need to plan on two to six volumes a year. Depending on the series, an occasional volume can be skipped, but with others, especially manga, every volume is needed for the reader to fully understand what is happening. Also with manga, if the series is already out, you more than likely will also have to purchase the previous issues. This is not necessarily needed with nonmanga titles, especially superhero titles. Someone reading a new Batman story does not have to be familiar with every story of the past 70 years (though it's getting to the point that the vast majority of them have been collected, and the Internet can also help the readers with background information).

For books that have a hardcover release prior to a softcover version, you will need to decide which to get. While the softcover is cheaper, the hardcover comes out first and in the long run may be more durable, and the higher price may balance the cost of "reinforcing" a paperback (see Chapter 7). Conversely, when the larger collections come out that collect in one volume stories that had previously been collected in multiple volumes, you need to decide whether to get it if you already have those volumes. In some cases it can help to replace missing volumes or, if you have multiple branches, you can purchase it for those branches that did not get the original collections. When it comes to the Absolute Editions, they often contain additional material that make may them worth purchasing, though the higher cost may make be a negative factor. The cost may also be a factor that prevents you from getting some "Omnibus" titles, but others, such as many Dark Horse and IDW works, are more reasonably priced and, like the *Showcase and Essential* titles, provide a lot of pages for a relatively low cost.

The "event" limited series discussed in Chapter 2 can also affect how much you buy. Marvel's *Secret Invasion* (2008) continued in seven other limited series and 15

Exhibit 6-7. Author's Picks

These are my personal favorites among the titles listed in Appendix A.

B., David, *Epileptic* (p. 193)	Modan, Rutu, *Exit Wounds* (p. 194)
Bechdel, Alison, *Fun Home: A Family Tragicomic* (p. 198)	Nakazawa, Keiji, *Barefoot Gen* (p. 168)
Beland, Tom, *True Story Swear to God* series (p. 251)	Neufeld, Josh, *A.D. New Orleans After the Deluge* (p. 162)
Brown, Jeffrey, various works (p. 172)	Peeters, Frederik, *Blue Pills: A Positive Love Story* (p. 171)
Burns, Charles, *Black Hole* (p. 170)	Rabagliati, Michel, *Paul* series (p. 231)
Eisner, Will, *The Eisner Collections* (p. 192)	Satrapi, Marjane, *The Complete Persepolis* (p. 232)
Ellis, Warren, *Transmetropolitan* series (p. 250)	Schrag, Ariel, *High School Chronicles* (p. 204)
Fies, Brian, *Mom's Cancer* (p. 227)	Sfar, Joann, *The Rabbi's Cat* books (p. 234)
Gaiman, Neil, *The Sandman* series (p. 237–239)	Shaw, Dash, *Bottomless Belly Button* (p. 171)
Hernandez Brothers, *Love and Rockets* series (pp. 218–219)	Small, David, *Stitches: A Memoir* (p. 245)
Jason, various titles (pp. 207–208)	Spieglman, Art, *The Complete Maus* (p. 226)
Kazuo Koike, *Lone Wolf and Cub* (p. 217)	Stassen, Jean-Philippe, *Deogratias: A Tale of Rwanda* (p. 189)
Kirkman, Robert, *The Walking Dead* series (pp. 252–253)	Sturm, James, *James Sturm's America: God, Gold, and Golems* (p. 207)
Kubert, Joe, *Fax from Sarajevo* (p. 196)	Tezuka, Osamu, *Ode to Kirihito* (p. 229)
Mazzucchelli, David, *Asterios Polyp* (p. 167)	Thompson, Craig, *Blankets: An Illustrated Novel* (p. 170)
McCloud, Scott, *Understanding Comics* and sequels (p. 252)	Tobe, Keiko, *With the Light: Raising an Autistic Child* series (p. 255)
Miller, Frank, *Sin City* books (p. 241)	Vaughan, Brian K., *Ex Machina* series (p. 194)
Moore, Alan, *From Hell* (p. 198)	Vaughan, Brian K., *Y: The Last Man* series (pp. 255–256)
Moore, Alan, *League of Extraordinary Gentlemen* (all volumes) (p. 210)	Willingham, Bill, *Fables* series (p. 195)
Moore, Alan, *V for Vendetta* (p. 252)	Wood, Brian, *DMZ* series (pp. 189–190)
Moore, Alan, *Watchmen* (p. 253)	
Moore, Terry, *Strangers in Paradise* series (p. 245)	

ongoing titles and several one-shots and produced 25 trades that collected it all. Are all 25 needed? Not really, but if you normally get any of the ongoing titles, you probably should get the main limited series so that readers of the ongoing titles have a better idea of what's going on (and if a storyline in another trade that you normally would not get greatly affects the main limited series, you may want to get those as well).

You know why you should buy graphic novels, various ways to do so, and have an idea of how much is out there. But as the next two chapters will show, you have still more choices to make.

Notes

1. Some sources call the first issue *Fun: The Big Comic Magazine*. The title changed to *More Fun Comics* in 1936 and ran until #127 (1947).

2. The first 18 issues of this 1987 series were for all ages. The "mature audience" designation began with #19 (1989), and it is from this point that stories from this series have been recently collected.

3. Paradox Press's other works included *Road to Perdition* and the popular *"Big Books"* series.

4. This 1994 comic book was published by Archie as *Archie Meets the Punisher* and by Marvel as *The Punisher Meets Archie*.

5. For example, 2008's *Joker: Greatest Stories Ever Told* includes stories from every decade since the 1940s.

6. This refers to the 2006 *Squadron Supreme* series, not the 1985 limited series mentioned in Chapter 2.

7. There have even been celebrity presenters. The 2008 awards included Samuel L. Jackson and Gabriel Macht from *The Spirit* movie among the presenters.

8. Basically "hot sex," but with a literary and artistic quality.

9. An additional (though minor) controversy occurred because the rights to the original play of *Peter Pan* were owned by London's Great Ormond Street Hospital (given to them by the author in 1929). The debate centered on whether or not Moore had needed their permission to use his version of Wendy. Top Shelf ended up delaying the release of *Lost Girls* in the United Kingdom until the copyright expired at the end of 2007.

10. This quote is taken from Gaiman's blog at www.neilgaiman.com, where he posted his full review instead of the shortened one actually printed in *Publisher's Weekly*.

References

Anderson, Porter. 2001. "Neil Gaiman: 'I Enjoy Not Being Famous.'" Available: http://archives.cnn.com/2001/CAREER/jobenvy/07/29/neil.gaiman.focus (accessed August 22, 2009).

Baker, Bill. 2009. "The Dream Goes On: Neil Gaiman on 20 Years of *The Sandman* and *The Graveyard Book*." Available: www.worldfamouscomics.com/bakersdozen/back20090506 .shtml (accessed August 22, 2009).

Cary, Stephen. 2004. *Going Graphic: Comics at Work in the Multilingual Classroom*. Portsmouth, NH: Heinemann.

Christina, Greta (Ed.). 2008. *Best Erotic Comics 2008*. San Francisco: Last Gasp.

Gaiman, Neil. 2006. "Lost Girls Redux." Available: http://journal.neilgaiman.com/2006/
06/lost-girls-redux.html (accessed August 22, 2009).

Green, Karen. 2007. "Comic Adventures in Academia: Naughty Bits." Available:
www.comixology.com/articles/15/Naughty-Bits (accessed August 22, 2009).

Horne, Marc. 2008. "Naked Anger as Peter Pan's Wendy Gets Porno Rewrite." Available:
news.scotsman.com/uk/Naked-anger-as-Peter-Pan39s.3644511.jp (accessed August 22,
2009).

Marvel. n.d. "The Marvel Rating System." Available: http://www.marvel.com/catalog/ratings
.htm (accessed August 22, 2009).

Olbrich, Dave. 2008a. "The End of the Jack Kirby Comics Industry Awards: A Lesson in
Honesty." Available: http://funnybookfanatic.wordpress.com/2008/12/17/the-end-of-the-
jack-kirby-comics-industry-awards-a-lesson-in-honesty (accessed August 22, 2009).

Olbrich, Dave. 2008b. "The 'Origin Story of the Jack Kirby Comics Industry Awards.'" Available: http://funnybookfanatic.wordpress.com/2008/12/16/the-origin-story-of-the-jack-
kirby-comics-industry-awards (accessed August 22, 2009).

Pawuk, Michael. 2006. *Graphic Novels: A Genre Guide to Comic Books, Manga, and More.*
Westport, CT: Libraries Unlimited.

The Public Librarian's Guide to Graphic Novels. 2003. Lexington, KY: Book Wholesalers.

Thompson, Jason. 2007. *Manga: The Complete Guide.* New York: Ballentine Books.

Tokyopop. n.d. "Tokyopop Ratings System." Available: www.tokyopop.com/corporate/book
sellers/879 (accessed August 22, 2009).

VIZ Media. n.d. "Our Ratings." Available: www.viz.com/ratings (accessed August 22, 2009).

Chapter 7

How Do You Manage Your Collection?

Y ou now have selected and ordered your books, but you still must make some decisions before placing them on the shelves. How will they be cataloged? What changes must be made to the books, especially the paperbacks? Is it enough just to add your library's name, a "due date card" pocket, and, if needed, a barcode, or is additional reinforcement required? Depending on how your library works, the cataloging and physical processing may be done by an outside vendor, someone who works within your library system, someone in your own library, or perhaps even yourself.

Cataloging Options

One of the biggest debates among the supporters of graphic novels in libraries is the proper way to catalog them, particularly "fictional" graphic novels. This decision may not be up to you, having already been made by others in your library, but looking at all variations will help you to understand how to handle them in terms of both cataloging and shelving (covered in Chapter 8).

The Dewey Decimal System

Libraries that use the Dewey Decimal system (see Exhibit 7-1 for Library of Congress Cataloging) will place most fictional graphic novels in the 741.5 area or, more specifically, 741.59. To be even more specific, American trades, original graphic novels, and most original English language manga are cataloged as 741.5973, while Canadian titles are 741.5971, British books are 741.5941, and translated French works are 741.5944. For manga titles, "true" manga from Japan is cataloged as 741.5952, while both Chinese manhua and Korean manwa are cataloged as 741.5941, though manhwa can be further cataloged as 741.595195. In recent years, due in part to the great increase of graphic novels in libraries, the OCLC (Online Computer Library Center) has made additional changes to the cataloging rules, including classifying comic strip collections as 741.569XX to separate them from graphic novels.

When it comes to nonfiction graphic novels, most libraries will place them in the proper Dewey area, and nonfiction graphic novels can be found in almost every

---

Exhibit 7-1. Library of Congress Cataloging

Early LOC classification of comic books, comic strip collections, or proto-graphic novels put them in the NC area (caricature) and then briefly in the "journalism" area of the PN4700s (Scott, 1990: 69–70). In the late 1960s/early 1970s, they were placed in the PN6700s or "general literature." American graphic novels, as well as books about them, are generally in the PN6720s, while Canadian titles are in PN6731-34, British books in PN6735-38, Franco/Belgian books in PN6745-48, and manga in PN6790. Nonfiction titles are placed elsewhere in the collection; for example, *Maus* is placed in the D804 area. Chapter 9 discusses the ways that the Library of Congress has collected comic books and graphic novels.

Dewey area from the 000s to the 900s as well as in the Biography area (see Exhibit 7-2). Some libraries may decide to put these books into the 741s regardless of whether they are fiction or nonfiction, and for some titles, there are several options on where they could go. This is especially true with books in the memoir genre. Should a true-life book about a person with cancer, such as *Cancer Vixen*, go into Biography or 362? Should *Maus* and other books about Holocaust victims and survivors go into Biography or 940 with the other Holocaust books? Should Marjane Satrapi's *Persepolis* books go into Biography or 955 because they are about life in Iran? Or should they all go into the 741 area regardless?

Fiction versus Dewey

The other main school of thought for the cataloging of fictional graphic novels is to simply catalog them as "Fiction." The primary argument for this is that they are works of fiction and should be treated as such. After all, if the novels of Jodi Picoult, Brad Meltzer, and Neil Gaiman are placed in Fiction, why shouldn't the graphic

---

Exhibit 7-2. Nonfiction Dewey Locations Other Than 741

The following are some graphic novels for adults owned by the Broward County (Florida) Library system that are cataloged with a Dewey number other then 741 and their locations.

The Plot: The Secret Story of The Protocols of the Elders of Zion—305.8924 EI	*Maus*—940.5318 SP
Japan Inc.: An Introduction to Japanese Economics—330.9520480 IS	*Ethel and Ernest*—941.082092 BR
Our Cancer Year—362.196994 PE	*Macedonia*—949.7603 PE
The Mystery of Mary Rogers—364.1523 GE	*The 9/11 Report: A Graphic Adaptation*—973.931 JA
Students for a Democratic Society: A Graphic History—378.1981 PE	
The Cartoon Guide to Chemistry—540.222 GO	*Chicken with Plums*—B Kahn
	Mendel's Daughter—B Lemelman
	Cancer Vixen: A True Story—B Marchetto
The Cartoon History of the Universe—902.07 GO	*J. Edgar Hoover: A Graphic Biography*—B Hoover
	Malcolm X: A Graphic Biography—B X

In addition, a number of books that BCL has cataloged as 741 could be placed elsewhere, including *Persepolis* (955 or B), *American Splendor: Ego & Hubris* (B), *Palestine* (956), *We Are On Our Own* (940 or B), *Fallout* (355), and *Mom's Cancer* (362).

novels that they have written go in there as well? The counterargument from the pro-Dewey supporters is that placing the graphic novels in the 741s makes it easier for the patron to locate them, by eliminating the need to search throughout the fiction collection, which, depending on the library, can be a large number of rows. The counterargument to this is that a patron who is browsing the fiction area may find a graphic novel and decide to read it, which may lead to the patron reading more graphic novels, something that might not have occurred if they were "segregated" into the 741s, an area that the patron might not normally frequent. Of course, the nonfiction titles would, in most cases, still go into nonfiction.

Some libraries follow a third option by creating a special cataloging category for graphic novels. "Graphic," "GN," "Graphix," "Comix," and other prefixes are used to give graphic novels their own special classification, one that usually ties into how they are shelved. This has occurred both in libraries that use Dewey and those that use Library of Congress cataloging. However, a library using this approach will still need to decide how to handle the nonfiction titles. Of course, as is covered in Chapter 8, no matter how graphic novels are cataloged in your library, they can still have their own special area.

Cutter Choices

Regardless of whether your graphic novels are in Dewey, Fiction, or somewhere else, they still must be divided up one way or another by their cutter. In general, the normal cataloging rules apply. When there is a solo or primary author for an original graphic novel or a collected limited series, then the author's last name is used (*Blankets* is under 741.5973 TH, Fic Thompson, etc.), and for anthologies, the title is often used (the *Juicy Mother* books can be under 741.5793 JU, Fic Juicy, etc.). However, for an ongoing series, especially a long-running one, some decisions may have to be made.

Luckily, the majority of ongoing series for adults tend to be written by a single author throughout their run. The 16 volumes of *Cerebus* are all by Dave Sim, the ten volumes of *Sandman* are all by Neil Gaiman, the multiple volumes of *The Walking Dead* are all by Robert Kirkman, and so forth. The same goes for most manga titles (though make sure the English translation of the name is the same for every volume). One of the few titles with multiple authors is *Hellblazer* from DC Comics' Vertigo line. Around 30 collections have been printed as of 2009 (and that's with gaps in the run), with authors ranging from original writer Jamie Delano to Brian Azzarello, Garth Ennis, Denise Mina, and more.[1] If we use the author name as the cutter, then books in the same series might be placed in 741.5973 DE, 5973 AZ, EN, MI, etc., if Dewey is used and Fic Delano, Azzarello, Ennis, Mina, etc., when placed in Fiction (with a similar placement with special cataloging). In this case, with Dewey or special cataloging, the volumes will not be together, but unless your collection is gigantic, they also will not be too far apart (though it can still take some searching to pick out the *Hellblazer* titles). However, cataloging as "Fic Author" can mean thousands of books and several rows of bookshelves between the two collections by Denise

Mina and the trades written by her predecessor and successor, Mike Carey and Andy Diggle.

One solution is to make the series title the cutter. If all *Hellblazer* collections are cataloged 741.5973 HE, Fic Hellblazer, or any similar permutation, then the catalogers do not have to worry who the author is (or, for that matter, what to do with the trade *Rare Cuts* by multiple authors). If you choose to make superhero titles part of your adult graphic collection (or if your juvenile or young adult departments get them and your cataloging rules are in sync with theirs), then another option is to use the name of the main character as the cutter. This way all of the various Superman, Batman, Spider-Man, etc., titles would be together no matter what the title of the series, limited series, or of the "theme" trade.[2] In such cases as *Army of Darkness/Xena* or *Aliens vs. Predator*, you may have to decide who gets "top billing" in the cataloging, but this method can be helpful in leading interested readers to a particular character's adventures.

Although not an issue with original graphic novels or one-shot titles, for "series" of trades and the volumes of manga series, how they are listed in your catalog can be important in terms of making it easier for the patron to locate them. Often, along with the name of the series (or at times the name of the main character), these titles will have a subtitle (*Hellblazer: Black Flowers*), a volume number (the case with many manga titles and collections of older material, e.g., *Crying Freeman*, Vol. 1; *Batman Chronicles*, Vol. 2), or a combination of the two (*Fables*, Vol. 8: *Wolves*; *Buddha*, Vol. 6: *Ananda*).

For the latter, you will need to decide the format to use in the catalog. For example, the third collection of *Sandman*, subtitled *Dream Country*[3] can be listed as *Sandman*, Vol. 3; *Sandman*, Vol. 3: *Dream Country*; or just *Dream Country* (simply listing it as *Sandman* could be confusing unless you are cataloging it as a serial, discussed in the following).

Try to keep each volume cataloged in the same manner. It could be confusing to both staff and patrons if, for example, the Marvel Essential collections for the solo adventures of the X-Man Wolverine were each listed as follows:

Stan Lee Presents: The Essential Wolverine, Vol. 1
Wolverine, Vol. 2: *Wolverine* #24–47
Wolverine, Vol. 3
Essential Wolverine, Vol. 4
Stan Lee Presents: Wolverine, Vol. 5

And if the third volume is simply listed as *Wolverine*, Vol. 3, will it be confused with the third trade of the current *Wolverine* series, or with the third volume of the *Wolverine Classic* series of trades?[4] This is also a case where using series title or character name as the cutter would be recommended. A number of writers have works that are reprinted in these Essentials, and cataloging them as 741.5973 WO would make things easier for everyone.

Depending on your library's approach, one last issue that you may need to consider is whether a volume of an ongoing series, especially a manga series with a continuing storyline, should be cataloged as part of a serial or as an independent volume. Some think that the series trades and manga volumes are serial products and not individual books and should be cataloged as a single serial bibliographic record, with each volume distinguished by its number. However, others think that because each volume of an ongoing trade or manga series is an individual book with its own ISBN number, then each independent volume should be treated and cataloged as such. Under the first method, with all of the volumes placed in one entry, differences in the cataloged title or cutter and other similar problems can be avoided (Brenner, 2007). But, with certain online catalogs, having all volumes of a series in a single entry can make it more difficult for a librarian or patron to place a "hold" on one particular volume (and, with luck, graphic novels will be popular enough in your library that they'll regularly be off the shelf, with people signing up on waiting lists for them).

No matter which way you catalog them, what cutter you use, what format you choose for the titles, it is very important, if you have a catalog searchable by keywords or subject headings, that one of the keywords/headings be "graphic novels." That way, no matter how they are cataloged, a patron can find a title simply by doing a keyword search. Other possible keywords are "manga," the name of the primary character(s), and the name of the series, if you are listing the books by subtitle only. If graphic novels are listed correctly in your catalog, then your patrons will know how they are organized in the collection, possibly where to find them, and the number of graphic novels owned by your library, branch, or even your entire library system.

Processing

After deciding the catalog information to be placed on the book, some other processing tasks must be completed before it can be shelved. Of minor concern is the location of the "date due card" pocket. If your library tends to use the last page of the book for this purpose, then you should be aware that sometimes the end of the story appears on the final page and would obscured by the card. In other cases, that page may have "about the author/artist" information or an advertisement for future or related titles (which sometimes appears on the inside back cover). In such instances, especially if the story will be covered, the pocket should be placed on the inside back cover, the back of the book (though that may have material on it as well), the inside front cover, or a page near the front of the book. In some cases, the pocket itself could be tipped in so that it can be turned when the reader needs to see the next page. With unflopped manga, another issue is what should be considered to be the "back" of the book, something to keep in mind also when deciding where to place the barcode, sticker, label, or anything else that your library typically places on the front or back of the books in its collection. Also, if possible, try not to cover up age ratings or "mature audience" warnings, especially if your collection intermixes those titles with those for young adults or younger children. This can help to avoid some of the possible problems discussed in Chapter 8.

The other area of processing a graphic novel involves how to make the book last longer. Although recent years have seen some improvements, graphic novels are still not the sturdiest of books. Most are softcover books, and both they and the hardcover books are designed to be read occasionally, with the bulk of their existence generally spent on a shelf. The reality is that they may be read dozens of times a year and be deposited into bookdrops, sometimes opening in the process, with other, heavier books piling up on top of them. This can lead to broken spines, bent covers, loose pages, and other damage, potentially causing the library to weed the title for the collection. The books cannot be made indestructible, but some techniques can help to stave off permanent damage.

Most library vendors offer at least one method of reinforcing the book: vinabinding. With vinabinding, the original paperback cover is removed, protected by polyvinyl lamination, and then bound to binders board; additional improvements are then made to the binding and the spine. The completed process restores the book's general appearance and helps to extend its "life." Other ways of strengthening a paperback involve turning it into a hardcover book. Methods such as textbound and textmount will transform the book, and they will sometimes retain the cover art, but the bare spine (save for the title and possibly author) can lessen its shelf appeal (though vendors like McNaughton do offer a book jacket to place over it, which solves this problem). Other methods, such as BWI's "FolletBound" process, turn a paperback into a hardback while retaining the front, back, and spine artwork.

If your library does all of its own processing, or if any graphic novels are purchased from Diamond, a comic shop, a bookstore, or any other non-library vendor, then you may need to employ some in-house methods of reinforcing your paperbacks. One available option is Kapco's Easy Cover Self-Adhesive Book Covers. These can also be helpful for those rare occasions when the vendor, for various reasons, cannot bind the book.

Binding does have its drawbacks, though. Sometimes when the books are rebound, the space between the panel borders (known as the gutters) that are closest to the spine is reduced, causing some text and/or art to be obscured. And any sort of extra binding and reinforcement will cost more money, though most likely less than a replacement copy.

The Future of the Collection

With cataloging and processing behind you, the books can now be shelved and begin circulating among your patrons. Now is the time to look further ahead in terms of purchasing new books and weeding and replacing the items in the current collection.

Purchasing New Books

Some of your future purchases will be linked to what you already own and therefore involve many of the same decisions that you made with previous orders. For example, if you have a book that collects issues of an ongoing series, will you keep getting the collections for that series? As many manga titles have one story spread out over most or all of the series, buying one means that you must buy them all. This is a commitment to purchasing up to six volumes of manga a year (or more) and possibly up to three or more American titles. This will affect both your budget and your shelf space.

Do you want to add new series? Should you continue to get collected limited series and releases of older material or just those that are connected to the series that you already buy? If your budget can handle it and circulation figures back it up, then you may want to expand the collection further. This would also be a time to decide if you want to change any of your procedures or even your vendor if you are not satisfied with how things have been handled. Conversely, space and budgetary reasons may cause you to cut down on how much you buy and even drop some ongoing titles. This is also the time to see if anything in your collection needs to be replaced or, in some cases, removed.

Weeding and Replacing the Collection

No matter how you reinforce them, your graphic novels will suffer some wear and tear. Sometimes a loose page can be put back in, a rip mended, or a cover glued back on, but many times the damage will be too severe and the book will need to be weeded and, if possible/desirable, replaced. Some of the companies who provide special binding will offer a replacement warranty in case of damage, but the warranty would not apply if the books are lost, stolen, or simply not returned (see Chapter 8). When deciding whether to replace a book, you should consider a few things. Do you have the budget to replace it? Is replacement really needed? Is there enough interest in the title to warrant replacement? If the book is part of an ongoing story, as is the case with most manga, then generally it should be replaced, especially if no other copies are available in your library or library system.

If you decide to replace an item, the next question becomes, can you? In some cases, the book may be out of print or hard to get. Many publishers will keep a backlist of older volumes but not of every book that they have published, and books go out of print for various reasons. Translated manga and licensed works may end when the publisher loses the rights, and occasionally a publisher goes out of business and no other company purchases their properties. In such cases, you may be able to get a replacement copy only from a comic store or online site that still has it in stock. Also, given time, the book may be reprinted either by the original publisher or a new one, with the new edition sometimes being an improvement on the original.

When making decisions about which graphic novels should be weeded, use the same criteria that you would apply to any other item in the library. Deciding to weed for condition may be an obvious choice, especially if pages are missing or loose and unrepairable, but what are some other reasons? If, as mentioned, ongoing manga series are missing volumes and those volumes are out of print or cannot be replaced, do you wait to see if they will become available or simply get rid of the rest of the series? Some books will circulate well but over time may not go out as often as they once did and, in some cases, may even become "shelf sitters." If your shelves are getting overcrowded and you have no room to expand, clearly some books will need to be removed, and those not circulating are a good target. Circulation statistics can be the best way to decide what to cut. But in some cases weeding is not just a matter of removing the books that are not circulating, since again, there is the "all or nothing" proposition with manga, where you cannot get rid of just one volume in the series.

Hopefully both high circulation and a healthy budget will allow your library to have a great graphic novel collection for years to come. The next chapter will show you ways to use that collection to help increase circulation and patron interest. Now that you have decided how they will be cataloged, it is time to decide how they will be displayed.

Notes

1. Other writers whose issues have been collected include Warren Ellis, and Peter Milligan. Notable among those not yet collected is Paul Jenkins, who wrote the book for three years.

2. In 2008 there were 20 Superman-related, 30 Batman-related, and 27 Spider-Man-related collections published (as well as two that collected issues of the comic book *Superman/Batman*).

3. This collects *Sandman* #17–#20, including the award-winning "A Midsummer Night's Dream."

4. Both *Essential Wolverine* and *Wolverine Classic* collect the 1988–2003 *Wolverine* comic book, the latter doing so in color. The second *Wolverine* series, which began in 2003, has also been collected.

References

Brenner, Robin. 2007. *Understanding Manga and Anime*. Westport, CT: Libraries Unlimited.

Scott, Randall W. 1990. *Comics Librarianship: A Handbook*. Jefferson, NC: McFarland and Company.

Chapter 8

How Can You Display, Promote, and Work with Your Collection?

So you have all of the "behind the scenes" aspects of collection development. You have chosen what you want for your library, made sure that you had enough in your budget, picked the method of purchase, and had the books cataloged and processed in the appropriate manner. Now it is time to present them to your patrons. But how you display, publicize, and work with your collections can have an effect on how well they circulate.

Shelving Options

When it comes to shelving options, the two main choices are "as cataloged" and "special location." With the former, you would place them however they are cataloged—intermixed in the fiction or placed in the 741 or any other applicable nonfiction area (and with Library of Congress cataloging in the PN6700s or other appropriate location). If you are cataloging them in the 741s (or PN6700s) and you are bringing in a large and/or ongoing collection, then you should be prepared to shift the books that follow however far is needed. Even if titles are regularly out for periods of time, they will eventually be returned to the shelf. You may even want to perform a "preemptive shifting" and let the collection eventually fill up the empty areas.

With "special location" shelving, no matter which method of cataloging you use, you would place all of the books in one separate area. This would differ from placing them all in the 741s, as other titles with that number, such as comic strip collections and books on drawing, would not necessarily be shelved there. If you have chosen a special cataloging designation such as "Comix" or "Graphic," then they would definitely be placed on special shelves. Both public and academic libraries have used this method. In this case, additional decisions will need to be made about what to do with the graphic novels that truly are nonfiction and would be placed in that area, even if most of your titles are cataloged under "Fiction." For example, should graphic biographies, Larry Gonick's *Cartoon Guides/Histories*, the *Treasury of Victorian Murder* books, and other similar titles be placed in that section or where their

Dewey/LOC numbers indicate? Should the nonfiction titles about comics and graphic novels go there as well? If your library has special sections for science fiction, mystery, Westerns, or other literary genres, should graphic novels in those genres (remember, graphic novel is a format, not a genre) be placed in the graphic novel section or in these other sections? The same question would apply if your graphic novels are normally placed in the fiction section. If you have graphic novels in a foreign language, then you also have the option of including them in the special collection or mixed in with the other foreign-language books.

Another issue is age. Your library may have age "prefixes" for titles aimed at younger readers, such as J for juvenile, YA for young adult, or something similar, but is there age segregation in your shelving? Some libraries divide their nonfiction among the age groups, while others, sometimes due to issues of space, will interfile them. If they are intermixed, whether in the 741s or in a special graphic novel section, then you must take into consideration the fact that books with language and nudity will be right next to ones aimed at children.

If you are shelving the books in a special area, you also have the option of organizing them any way that you wish, despite how they are cataloged. You can shelve them by the cutter if you want, but you can also devise your own order. For example, you can put all the manga in one area (and since they are a smaller size, it might actually look nicer on the shelves); you can divide them by character or series instead of by author, even if the cutter is for the author; or you can put the nonfiction graphic novels apart from the fiction ones. If it's an integrated collection, you can then divide it by age listing and then subdivide it again in other ways. The most important consideration is that once you know how you want the collection organized, you have three groups of people who also need to know your decision: patrons who want to find the books, staff members whose job it is to help patrons find them, and those staff members whose duties include shelving the titles.

The location of the graphic novel shelf is also up to you and again depends on the layout of your library. If the collection is cataloged as only adult, having it near the borders of the adult fiction or nonfiction area might be best. If it's an integrated collection, then some point between the adult and youth areas would be best, if possible, or at least on the "fringes" of one of the departments. This allows easy access for adults who don't want to go into the children or teen areas for the books they want and lets children, tweens, and teens find age-appropriate works without having to go too deep into the adult section.

Promoting the Collection

No matter how you shelve the collection, you have to make sure that the patrons know that the library has graphic novels. If the majority of them are in one area (741s, PN6700s, or a special shelving spot), then you can make up your own signs ("graphic novels here," "we have graphic novels," etc.) or purchase your promotional materials. ALA Graphics has a number of "Read" posters with comic book themes. These include a popular (though slightly outdated) poster of DC Comics heroes; posters of Superman, Batman, and Wonder Woman drawn by Alex Ross; one of former librarian Barbara "Batgirl" Gordon (walking past the graphic novel section of the Gotham City Library); one of several members of the "Batman Family," one of the title character from *Sandman*; one from the manga *Canterella*; one from the OEL manga *Megatokyo*; and a poster featuring several members of the X-Men. There is also a poster that features *Sandman* creator Neal Gaiman. Some of these are shown in Figure 8-1, and the others can be found in the ALA Graphics catalog or at www.alastore.ala.org.

Demco, a supplier of library materials, has several items designed to bring attention to your collection. A simple poster (see Figure 8-2) for the wall or a standee (see Figure 8-3), which could be placed on top of the bookshelf, can attract attention, but Demco also offers special graphic-novel-related shelving (see Figure 8-4). Another way to promote the collections is to have some of the titles, especially those with eye-catching covers, facing out, either on the shelf or on top of the bookcase. If possible, you can even put them onto an "end cap."

If the graphic novels are interfiled throughout your fiction section, then posters or signs near that section can spark patron interest, as can the occasional "face out" title. In addition, both the ALA and Demco posters have bookmark counterparts (see Figure 8-5).

Figure 8-1. ALA Comics Posters

Source: © American Library Association. @ your library ® American Library Association. All Rights Reserved. Used with Permission. These posters are available through the American Library Association at www.alastore.ala.org.

Source: © American Library Association. All Rights Reserved. Used with Permission. ™ and ® DC Comics. All Rights Reserved. Used with Permission. These posters are available through the American Library Association at www.alastore.ala.org.

(Cont'd.)

Figure 8-1. ALA Comics Posters *(Continued)*

The "World's Greatest Heroes" poster is available in two sizes.

Source: © American Library Association. @ your library ® American Library Association. All Rights Reserved. Used with Permission. ™ and ® DC Comics. All Rights Reserved. Used with Permission. These posters are available through the American Library Association at www.alastore.ala.org.

The Superman, Batman, and Wonder Woman posters can be purchased as a set along with the bookmarks in Figure 8-5.

Source: © American Library Association. READ ® American Library Association. All Rights Reserved. Used with Permission. ™ and ® DC Comics. All Rights Reserved. Used with Permission. These posters are available through the American Library Association at www.alastore.ala.org.

Figure 8-2. DEMCO Poster

Source: Dist. DEMCO, Inc. demco.com. 800-356-1200. Used with permission of DEMCO.

Figure 8-3. DEMCO Standee

Source: Dist. DEMCO, Inc. demco.com. 800-356-1200. Used with permission of DEMCO.

Figure 8-4. DEMCO Shelving

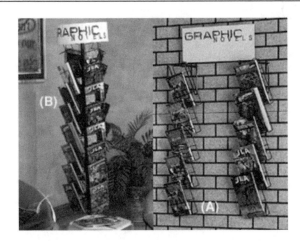

Source: Dist. DEMCO, Inc. demco.com. 800-356-1200. Used with permission of DEMCO.

Figure 8-5. ALA and DEMCO Bookmarks

The Superman, Batman, and Wonder Woman bookmarks can be purchased as a set along with the posters in Figure 8-1.

(Cont'd.)

Figure 8-5. ALA and DEMCO Bookmarks *(Continued)*

Source: Dist. DEMCO, Inc. demco.com. 800-356-1200. Used with permission of DEMCO.

Another way of catching patrons' eyes is to use stickers. Demco and Brodart are among the companies that provide stickers (see Figure 8-6) that can be placed on the spines of books, a helpful promotional approach no matter what method of shelving you use. If graphic novels are intermixed among the fiction books, then the stickers will help them stand out from the other non-graphic-novel titles. This is also true if they are intermingled with the nonfiction titles, and even if they are in the 741s (or the LOC equivalent). If you have a special section but not a special catalog designation, then the sticker can let the people who do the shelving know specifically which books should be placed in that section.

Book displays also help to attract attention. If you have just established a new collection, then a display of graphic novels would be a good approach, but once patrons are aware of the collection, you can simply include them in other displays,

Figure 8-6. DEMCO Graphic Novel Stickers

Source: Dist. DEMCO, Inc. demco.com. 800-356-1200.
Used with permission of DEMCO.

such as "what's new at the library" for different special event themes, such as national monthly celebrations such as Black History Month, Jewish American Heritage Month, National Women's History Month, etc., or for a specific theme. You can also include graphic novels on "read alike" lists: "If you liked A, then try B." Another approach for new collections is to publish a press release that your library is now carrying graphic novels and publish additional press releases about any graphic novel programs.

Besides knowing where the graphic novels are located, what gets shelved where, and ways that they can be displayed, other people on the staff, particularly those who deal with the public, should know a little something about graphic novels so that they can answer patrons' questions. This will help avoid situations like the one in which a librarian who, when asked about graphic novels for an article in *Time*, replied, "You mean like pornographic?" (Arnold, 2003). Staff members should know and understand the terms that readers might use when asking about these titles, such as "manga" or even "comics" and also know which titles may be inappropriate for younger ages, if your library serves those ages.

Using the Graphic Novel Collection for Programs and Activities

Your library can use its graphic novel collection in many events, programs, and even classes. Some of these programs are fully comics-themed, such as Free Comic Book Day (FCBD), while others incorporate graphic novels. Sponsored by Diamond, the first FCBD was held on May 4, 2002, the day after the first *Spider-Man* film premiered. With one exception, subsequent FCBDs have also been held on the first Saturday in May, a date that often has also been the same as the opening weekend of other comics-related films. A number of publishers put out a comic for the event, some of which are specially created for the day, while others are reprints of recent works. While most of the titles have been for teens and younger, there has been the occasional adult element, most notably with an excerpt from *The Salon*, which, as is discussed later, caused trouble for one Georgia comic shop owner.

The two ways in which a library can get comic books for FCBD are directly through Diamond (see www.freecomicbookday.com for more information) or from a local comic shop. If you do the latter, remember that while the books are free to the public, the comic shop is paying for them, so you should honor their donation by, at the very least, including the shop's name in any publicity. You could also mention donors as part of a display or include their names on handouts provided along with the comics. You can even purchase a graphic novel, gift certificate, or other items from donors to give out as prizes. Some comic shops will even host library-related promotions on their end; for example, a shop in San Diego gave extra comics to customers who showed a library card ("Library Cards," 2006). Good relationships with comic shops could also lead to their promotion of, and even participation in, your programs.

Other libraries have held their own comic book conventions or "anime and manga" festivals, with attendance by people in the comics industry, with some of them there to give a talk. Many comics professionals have an online presence and can be contacted through Web sites, e-mail, and social networking sites. Other ways to contact them are through their publishers' Web sites (see Appendix C) or even by asking for contact information on GNLIB-L.

You could also form a graphic novel book club, either open to all ages or limited to just adults, or even feature graphic novels as part of an existing book club. The latter approach has even been done on a larger scale by the New Hanover Country Public Library in Wilmington, North Carolina, which chose *Persepolis* as part of its "One Book, One Community" program in 2007, one of the first times that a graphic novel was chosen as the "one book" for this program (Steelman, 2007). Another graphic novel program that has appeared in libraries and universities around the United States is supported by a grant from the American Library Association. Beginning in 2007, ALA, along with Nextbook, an organization that promotes Jewish culture, arts, and ideas, offered a grant program called "Let's Talk About It: Jewish Literature—Identity and Imagination." One theme of this program is "Modern Marvels: Jewish Adventures in the Graphic Novel," in which five Jewish-themed graphic novels—*A Contract with God*; *Maus*; *Julius Knipl, Real Estate Photographer*; *The Quitter*; and *The Rabbi's Cat*—are discussed. The grant covers program costs for both books and the instructor, who is usually a professor. Dr. Andrea Greenbaum, an Associate Professor of English at Barry University, who taught the program for the Broward County (FL) Library, said of the program's benefits and of graphic novels in general:

> Invariably when I tell other academics that I'm teaching graphic novels, I am silently reproached. There's a sense of illegitimacy, like it's not "real" literature, worthy of investigation. This shouldn't surprise me, since graphic novels have evolved from their much despised counterpart, comic books. What gets confused is the form with the function; visual rhetoric is not seen as having the same rhetorical ability as traditional literature; it is seen as simplifying, reductive, a kind of intellectual short hand. Yet those of us who study graphic novels, moreover, those of us who actually *enjoy* graphic novels, recognize its potency as a literary force. In fact, in some instances, the graphic element of the storytelling makes the story more believable, more profound. I found this to be particularly true in my discussion of Jewish graphic novels at the [Library]. In Art Spiegelman's *Maus*, for instance, his experience of the Holocaust is made more vivid by the use of graphic images. His use of maps of annexed regions, diagrams of underground bunkers, and blueprints of the gas chambers, assists in creating an imaginative space that provides concrete evidence of the horrors of the Holocaust. By the library offering a series in Jewish graphic novels, I was able to reach out to non-academic readers, exposing them to a relatively young literary genre that continues to expand in both volume and in legitimacy as a genuine art form worthy of investigation. (Greenbaum, personal communication, January 25, 2009)

Dr. Greenbaum is also among a growing number of academics who are using graphic novels in college and university courses, including conducting entire classes on the subject. More on these classes can be found in the next chapter.

Graphic novels can also be used in the adult literacy and language instruction classes taught in your library. As mentioned in Chapter 1, comics and graphic novels can be used in many ways for these classes. This has been known for a long time. During World War II, comics were used to teach languages to the armed forces. And when American comics were introduced in places with low literacy, people showed an increased desire to learn to read so that they would know what the characters were saying (Elkins and Bruggemann, 1983). Comics have been found to provide "authentic language-learning opportunities for all students, regardless of a learner's second language proficiency level." In addition, "the dramatically reduced text" of many comics make them "manageable and language-profitable for even beginning reader levels" (Cary, 2004: 15). They can also improve reading development for those who are struggling with language acquisition since the illustrations help to provide contextual clues to the meaning of the written narrative (Whitworth, 2006). Also, the mix of words and images can make the lessons a little more interesting, and the students more relaxed, since they are looking at comic pages instead of straight text. While much of this instruction has been done in elementary and middle schools, and occasionally in university settings, the techniques used in the schools can be adapted for your library.

Dealing with Problems

You may have to deal with some problems concerning your graphic novel collection, but most of them will be the same sort of problems that you normally encounter with other materials in your collection, and they also will have the same solutions.

Theft and Vandalism

It has been said that graphic novels in libraries do not walk, they run. It is almost a certainty that some items in your graphic novel collection will disappear without being checked out. Popular items have a habit of being stolen, and graphic novels are popular. The question is, are they stolen at a greater rate than other popular items, such as DVDs, CDs, hot titles, and books on controversial subjects? This is hard to determine, but discussions on GNLIB-L and elsewhere seem to indicate that the theft rate for graphic novels is about the same or less than that for other popular items. With graphic novels, however, it is sometimes easier to tell when one has gone missing. For example, if the titles are all in the 741s or in a special section that you often walk by, then you may notice that a volume of a particular manga has not been there for some time. This could lead you to check the status of that title to find out if it is checked out, checked out but never returned, or listed as being on the shelf (in which case there is a strong possibility it was stolen). In other cases, you may not notice the loss until a patron asks for a particular title.

So what can you do to deter theft? You will most likely use the same antitheft devices as in all other books, such as targets that set off security gates. Of course, this tactic can be foiled by someone tearing out the book page with the target. Even if the books are shelved in a highly visible area, all a potential thief needs to do is take the book to more a secluded place in the library before tearing out the page. If you are worried about theft, you may wish to refrain from purchasing high-priced items, or, if you do buy them, keep them in the "closed stacks" or another location out of the public area, with a "dummy copy" taking its place on the shelf. Patrons would still be able to check them out, and if a book is not returned at least you have a record of who had it last. Another way to deter theft, used by some librarians, is to place a sign warning that not only will stolen titles not be replaced but future volumes will not be purchased. While this approach has not entirely prevented theft, it has, in some cases, reduced it, and some missing volumes have even found their way back to the library. In some places where this has been done, people who regularly use the graphic novel collection have even helped to keep an eye on it so their graphic novels will not be "cut off."

Then there are those patrons who, for one reason or another, cannot check out the graphic novel. They will actually hide the book that they are reading elsewhere in the library so that it will not be checked out by someone else before they can come back and finish it. Hopefully the book will be located before you have to go through the general "lost book" procedure.

Converting a graphic novel for library use—reinforcing the cover, stamping the library's name, adding stickers and call numbers, and so forth—can at least prevent thieves from selling the books to a local comic shop or used book stores or possibly even selling them online (though the buyer may not care where it came from), but, sadly, this will not stop those who want them for their own private collections.

Vandalism of comics can also be a problem, though the motives may be slightly "purer" than the simple destruction of library property. People sometimes tear or cut out a page to obtain a free poster or pictures of characters that they like. If a book is stolen, damaged beyond repair, or lost in another way, such as a patron who checks out a book and doesn't return it, you will have to decide whether to replace it. While you will make this decision based on the same criteria that you would for a book that has fallen apart, that the book was stolen once already will be on your mind. And if the replacement copy also disappears, it can be difficult to decide whether having the book is worth the cost and effort to purchase a third copy.

Complaints and Challenges

There is also the possibly that people will complain about the contents of a particular graphic novel and even ask for its removal from the library. Challenges are not common, being now far from the anti-comics feelings of the 1940s and 1950s that was discussed in Chapter 2, but they do happen. Those who do so are generally adults who are personally offended by the material and/or adults who are worried that children have seen or can see the material. Foul language, nudity, sexual content, or even certain story elements, such as homosexuality, can be among the causes for complaints, especially when a child is involved. For example, Phoebe Gloeckner's book about child abuse, *A Child's Life and Other Stories*, was banned from a library in Stockton, California, following its being checked out by an 11-year-old. The town's mayor even called it a "how-to book for pedophiles" (Olin, 2007).

However, one can never tell why someone will complain. Daniel Clowes' *Caricature* got a complaint for its content from someone who thought it was supposed to be about drawing. *Maus* was challenged in Oregon for being anti-ethnic and in Pasadena due to its portrayal of Poles (Olin, 2007). One librarian reported that she had received several informal complaints regarding *A Contract with God* from parents whose younger children had picked it up thinking that it was either Christian fiction or a manual on religious instruction (Jenson-Benjamin, 2001). In 2005, an anti-immigrant group in Denver, who had already been complaining about the library's Spanish language collection, extended their complaints to the library's collection of fotonovelas (photo-illustrated comics), giving "adult themes" as a reason ("Anti-Immigrant Criticism in Denver," 2005).

Depictions of certain ethnic groups in older materials may also lead to criticism when re-released today. For example, in 2007, after complaints of how Africans were portrayed, the children's title *Tintin in the Congo* (1931) was removed from certain bookstores or else moved to adult areas. The publisher, Little, Brown, pulled it from its catalog and decided not to include it a planned "complete" set of *Tintin* books, and the Brooklyn Public Library decided to restrict access to its copy. While Asians were also drawn stereotypically in the early years, during World War II, Japanese people were sometimes drawn as almost inhuman. When these stories are reprinted, the publishers might add a historical note, such as the one in some DC Comics Archives:

> The comics reprinted in this volume were produced in a time when racism played a larger role in society both consciously and unconsciously. They are reprinted without alteration for historical reference. (*The Seven Soldiers of Victory Archives*, 2005)

However, such a note still may not stop someone who is offended by the material and wants to complain.

Complaints from parents may happen more when the collection is intermixed for various age groups. A child, tween, or young teen may grab a book for adults that is located close to one more suitable for them. In addition, there is the case of "judging the book by its cover," such as with Frank Miller's *All-Star Batman and Robin*, which features a Batman who is "meaner" than the "regular" version (and has referred to himself as "The Goddamn Batman"), or Judd Winick's *Barry Ween*, which is about a 10-year-old genius but filled with foul language. The parent of a child who has inadvertently picked up one of these books may end up complaining to the powers that be (or even to the media).

Children are attracted to many comics written for people in their twenties, and this means that they may encounter some adult situations that a parent might find troublesome. One of the best-selling limited series of 2004, DC's Identity Crisis, contained the revelation that the wife of the superhero the Elongated Man had been raped by the villain Dr. Light. Other superhero comics have had unmarried characters engaging in sexual activity, and female characters are often shown as being "full figured" and in revealing outfits.

Even if the book is in an adult area, is cataloged as adult, and even says on the cover that it is for adults (as with Art Spiegelman's *Breakdowns*[1]), people may complain because they think that comics are only for kids. Justin Green, in an essay called "A Message to Parents" in the *Binky Brown Sampler*, said:

> I was never too crazy about the fact that the comic is primarily a children's medium. The flimsy "Adults Only" disclaimer (which was printed on every Underground production I've ever been a contributor to) was all that protected tender young minds from viewing my soul-baring and licentious extravaganzas. I took comfort in the possibility that because my drawing style is quirky, kids would be reluctant to decipher it. And the writing! Not only are the balloons much too loaded with text, but many of the expressions are no longer in common usage, and would seem like babble to their ears. (Green, 1995: 7)

A recent library challenge that made the news around the country happened in Marshall, Missouri, in 2006. A patron complained about two graphic novels—Craig Thompson's *Blankets*, which was shelved in the YA section, and Alison Bechdel's *Fun Home*, shelved in the adult area—likening them to pornography and complaining that children could have access to them. The library did not have a materials selection policy, and the board decided to temporarily remove the books from circulation until one could be created. Besides local support for the award-winning and well-reviewed books, including *Time Magazine* having named *Fun Home* the best book of the year, the Comic Book Legal Defense Fund (see Exhibit 8-1) and the National Coalition Against Censorship wrote a joint statement of support for the books. The library eventually created a policy, and the two books were returned to the shelves, though *Blankets* was moved to the adult section. This event highlights the importance of having a collection policy, even if graphic novels are not specifically mentioned in it. When asked about this in an interview with *American Libraries*, Bechdel said:

> As more graphic novels become considered more a legitimate library form, libraries are going to have to grapple with this. The issue is not, as I understand it, the content of my book, but the fact that there are pictures of people having sex—not just pictures, but comic pictures, which everyone interprets as somehow geared toward or particularly appealing to children. And that's true, kids love funny drawings. So do grown-ups. But I don't think you can use that as a reason to ban books from libraries. ("Newsmaker: Alison Bechdel," 2007: 22)

Exhibit 8-1. Comics-Related Challenges Outside of Libraries

As graphic novels are a relatively new presence in libraries, librarians are still learning how to deal with challenges to them. However publishers, creators, and, perhaps most important, comic shops have dealt with complaints for years, sometimes with legal consequences. Luckily, they do a have a source for assistance, one that, if needed, can also be of assistance to libraries.

In 1986, Michael Correa, manager of the Lansing, Illinois, comic book store Friendly Franks, was arrested and convicted on obscenity charges after selling adult comic books (including *Omaha the Cat Dancer*) to adults. The sentence was overturned on appeal only after two years and thousands of dollars in legal fees. The fees were offset after comics publisher Dennis Kitchen (of the now defunct Kitchen Sink Publishing) helped to organize support from creators, retailers, and fans.

Once the case was resolved, Kitchen and others formed the Comic Book Legal Defense Fund (CBLDF) as a nonprofit organization dedicated to protecting the First Amendment rights of comic book creators, publishers, and retailers. They often help by aiding in covering legal expenses, but they have also written "friend of the court" briefs or other letters of support. Notable cases that the CBLDF has worked on include:

- Mike Diana, a Florida cartoonist convicted of obscenity for his comic book *Boiled Angel*. His sentence included psychosocial testing at his own expense, no contact with children under 18, and the fact that his residence is "subject to inspection, without warning or warrant, to determine if he is in possession of, or is creating obscene material."
- Jesus Castillo, a comic book shop employee in Dallas, Texas, who was convicted of selling an adult comic book to an adult undercover police officer. In her closing argument, the prosecuting attorney used the reasoning that, despite what the expert testimony had claimed, comic books were for kids.
- Planet Comics. In 1995, Oklahoma City comic shop Planet Comics was the subject of an obscenity complaint from a group called Oklahomans for Children and Families. Responding to the complaint, undercover officers purchased copies of *Vertotika*, a title that was sexually explicit and for adults only, and later raided the store, confiscating certain comics. Despite the fact that the comics were sold only to adults, the owners were charged with various crimes, including displaying material harmful to minors, trafficking in adult materials, and child pornography. While all but an obscenity charge was dropped, the resulting problems caused by the arrest led to the store going out of business (Olin, 2007).
- Gordon Lee. Rome, Georgia, comic shop owner Gordon Lee was prosecuted for the misdemeanor charge of exhibition of harmful materials to a minor after a 2004 incident in which he allegedly gave a minor a free copy of *Alternative Comics #2*, which contained an excerpt from *The Salon*. This comic featured several panels in which Pablo Picasso is shown naked from the front, though there was no sexual content. Lee had previously been convicted in the 1990s for selling an adult comic to an adult. On two occasions charges were dropped, and there was even a mistrial, but new charges followed. This led to criticism of the prosecutors from many, including the local media. By the time the case was dismissed in 2008, the CBLDF had spent over $80,000 on defending Lee.

While the CBLDF has not defended librarians in court, it has joined with ALA (American Library Association), the ACLU (American Civil Liberties Union), and other groups in cases to overturn Internet filtering laws (including the Children's Internet Protection Act), material access laws, and other related issues. Board members include publishers, creators, and others in the industry, and besides membership fees and donations, additional money is raised through the sale of materials created or donated by some of the best-known people in the industry. In addition, the CBLDF puts out a quarterly publication called *Busted*! that discusses not only attacks on comic books but all free speech issues. The summer 2003 edition, created in time for Banned Books Week, had library issues as its cover story. More information can be found at www.cbldf.com.

(Cont'd.)

> **Exhibit 8-1. Comics-Related Challenges Outside of Libraries** *(Continued)*
>
> One of the most recent cases that the CBLDF was involved is one that may have an effect on libraries. In 2006, Christopher Handley, an Iowa collector, was arrested for allegedly possessing "obscene" manga. Handley had received an express mail package from Japan that contained seven Japanese comic books. That package had been intercepted by the Postal Inspector, who applied for a search warrant after determining that the package contained cartoon images of objectionable content. Agents from various agencies and organizations then went to his house where they seized his collection of over 1,200 manga books or publications along with hundreds of DVDs, VHS tapes, laser disks, and other items and documents. It is for a small amount of the manga that Handley was prosecuted under the PROTECT (Prosecutorial Remedies and Other Tools to end the Exploitation of Children Today) Act, which was designed to prevent child abuse. The prosecution's case was that among the seized material are drawings that they say appear to be depictions of minors engaging in sexual conduct (Comic Book Legal Defense Fund, 2008). Facing 20 years in prison, Handley pleaded guilty in 2009 in a plea arrangement.
>
> If the PROTECT Act is applied to drawings again in the future, then this may have ramifications for stores that sell such works as *Lost Girls* or certain works of yaoi in which the characters are teenagers. This concern has also been raised in the United Kingdom where a law has been proposed that would ban erotic drawings of minors. Libraries need to keep track of these developments, since if these ramifications affect stores, they may affect libraries as well, especially those with "adult-rated" graphic novels.

Fun Home was also the topic of a challenge in an academic setting when a teacher at the University of Utah included the title on the syllabus for the class Critical Introduction to English Literary Forms. A student objected to the assignment, in part due to a portrayal of oral sex between two women, and under UU's religious accommodation policy was given an alternate title. However, the student then contacted a local organization called No More Pornography, which started an online petition calling for the book to be removed from the syllabus, though nothing came of it. Another school-related incident involving an "older" title happened in 2007 when a high school teacher in Connecticut gave a freshman girl an issue of Daniel Clowes' comic book *Eightball* (reprinted in *Ice Haven*) which featured, among other things, foul language and brief, though not sexual, nudity.

It is not just the graphic novels themselves that are being challenged. Paul Gravett's book *Manga: Sixty Years of Japanese Comics* was challenged and then removed from a San Bernardino (CA) County library after a 16-year-old boy looked through it and found images from pornographic manga reprinted on a few pages. The order for removal came from the board of supervisors, and despite protests from the public in support of the book, it remained off the shelves.

No matter the reason for the complaint or challenge, it should be handled in the same way that you handle complaints and challenges for anything else in your collection. Sometimes it is just a matter of age classification, and all that is needed is to change it from YA to adult. On other occasions, the patron may simply wish to express concern or just want to vent. If the complaint asks for the total removal of the title from the collection, then the normal reconsideration procedures for your library should be followed. The most important thing is for your library to have some procedure for dealing with challenges.

It has become easier to defend a graphic novel from a patron complaint since the advent of more mainstream reviews of graphic novels. Many positive reviews can be found, and those from *Time, Library Journal,* or *Publishers Weekly* may have more weight with the powers-that-be than would those from a magazine on comics or from a fan-created Web site. The books on graphic novels in libraries may also provide reviews and recommendations that could be cited. The librarians at GNLIB-L can provide not only information on reviews, some of which were actually written by list members, but also information on how the title has been received by the patrons of their own libraries.

If a graphic novel is challenged, there may also be some press about it, sometimes with a "comics aren't for kids anymore" theme. The Missouri case was reported around the country (though it was often the same Associated Press article with some modifications), and the challenge to Gravett's book produced the inflammatory headline "Good Grief, Charlie Brown! Family Stunned by Porn Comics at Library" (Gonzalez, 2006).

Dealing with the media is one of the topics covered in the nine-page *Graphic Novels: Suggestions for Librarians* created by the American Library Association, the National Coalition Against Censorship, and the Comic Book Legal Defense Fund; it can be found at various Web sites, including www.ncac.org/graphicnovels.cfm. Other topics include how to field complaints and sample answers for such questions as "Why do libraries have to buy graphic novels?" and "What should I do if I find a graphic novel I don't approve of in the library?" Many of their suggestions are adapted from other ALA "dealing with challenges" documents. Here again we see that graphic novels are treated the same way as any other library material.

Publisher Self-Censorship

At times, publishers will engage in editing to make a work acceptable for younger ages. When Marvel collected the non-code-approved stories from *Tomb of Dracula* in an *Essential Edition* (which was rated "parental advisory" and not "max"), the art was altered in some stories so that the nudity from the original work was covered up (ICv2, 2006). The same has happened to certain manga, in which scenes were "toned down" for the American editions. When DC released the first volume of the manga *Tenjo Tenge* for their CMX line, it was heavily edited, with over 30 examples of nudity and fanservice items (such as "panty shots") covered up and a rape scene was tightly cropped. DC's reasoning for this was that even though the original work was for older readers, they wanted to market the book to younger teens. Since CMX was advertised as "100% the way the original Japanese creators want you to see it," fans were unhappy, and while later volumes had a higher rating, they were still edited, though this was done with the approval of the original creator (Harris, 2005).

Sometimes self-censoring includes not having the title at all. In 2007 Seven Seas Entertainment had planned to publish a translation of the seinen manga *Kodomo no Jikan* (*A Child's Time*) under the title *Nymphet*. The plot of the manga is that a third-grade teacher discovers that one of his students has a crush on him. Given that the crush is sexual in nature, there was some controversy, and Seven Seas, who was dealing with concerns from both potential readers and from vendors who were becoming wary of carrying the book, decided not to publish it after all. On some occasions, a publisher has had to reissue or even "pulp" (destroy) the comic. The first issue of the limited series *Spider-Man: Reign* (2006–2007) had an image of an elderly and naked Peter Parker (Spider-Man), and some argued that his genitals were visible. Marvel put out a "fixed" replacement issue and that version ended up in the trade collection. DC recalled, pulped, and remade an issue of *All-Star Batman and Robin* in which foul language that was meant to be blacked out in the word balloons was still visible. In the past they had also pulped (and never reissued) *Elseworlds 80-Page Giant* due to a story called "Letitia Lerner, Superman's Babysitter," which, among other things, had "Baby Superman" going into a microwave oven. Those issues that escaped the recall became collectors' items, and, ironically, the problematic story was one of only two stories from that issue to actually see print (in the pages of the original graphic novel *Bizarro Comics*) and won two Eisner Awards.

Internal Problems

One final potential problem comes not from the patrons but from those who work in your library. A survey of challenges to graphic novels conducted by ALA's Office of Intellectual Freedom found that of 149 challenges listed, 74 of them were internal (Cornog, 2008). It could be a superior who, despite all of the reasons for having them, still does not think graphic novels should be in the library. It could be co-worker who feels that limited budget resources and limited shelf-space should be devoted to other materials. Or, even worse, it could be that some staff, no matter their position, believe that the material in a graphic novel is inappropriate and either raise a fuss about it or decide on their own to simply remove the title from the collection (or conveniently "lose" it), without the consent or knowledge of the person who selected the title.

Several librarians who work with graphic novels have told of times where the person who is processing the book or is in the circulation department will prevent the title from ever even going onto the shelf. In a discussion on GNLIB-L, librarians from two different places revealed that Ellen Forney's Eisner-nominated *I Love Led Zeppelin: Panty-Dropping Comics* was the victim of internal censorship at their library. One library had removed it after someone in the library's technical services department looked through the book while processing it and found the contents to be objectionable to her. She showed it to her superior who then showed it to the library director who in turn decided against adding the book to the collection without ever consulting the librarian who ordered it in the first place. In the other case, the book was pulled by the director who felt that the title would attract a minor. While the librarian was consulted on this and attempted to argue in favor of the book, including showing positive reviews, the director's decision stood.

This shows one of the biggest problems regarding internal censorship. If a patron has an objection, then there is usually a procedure that must be followed, but most libraries have no official procedures for an internal challenge. If you become aware of internal censorship or challenges, you may be able to approach your superiors, unless you fear that this could cause additional problems for you or the collection; worse yet is when the person in charge of the library is the one with the objection, leaving you with no further appeal.

Do not be discouraged by tales of challenges and internal and external problems. The advantages of having graphic novels in your collection far outweigh the disadvantages. If your library contained nothing that *anybody* objected to, then you would have an extremely small collection, and theft, while annoying and even costly, can be an indication of the popularity of graphic novels in your library. Shelving methods and making sure the public knows what titles are appropriate for which readers can go a long way toward helping to avoid such difficulties.

Note

1. Spiegelman says that he asked for this warning because "I don't know where our culture is sexually, where the boundaries are today. It depends on the constituency. We've passed the moment where comics must be for children. But the 'pornographic strips' that I drew in 1974 were done to specifically force the issue in an underground comics. Our job was to cross the line" (Trachtenberg, 2008).

References

"Anti-Immigrant Criticism in Denver Extends to Library Fotonovelas." 2005. *Library Journal* (August 18). Available: www.libraryjournal.com/article/CA635920.html (accessed August 22, 2009).

Arnold, Andrew D. 2003. "The Graphic Novel Silver Anniversary." *Time* (November 14). Available: www.time.com/time/columnist/arnold/article/0,9565,542579,00.html (accessed August 22, 2009).

Cary, Stephen. 2004. *Going Graphic: Comics at Work in the Multilingual Classroom*. Portsmouth, NH: Heinemann.

Comic Book Legal Defense Fund. 2008. "CBLDF to Serve as Special Consultant in PROTECT Act Manga Case." Available: www.cbldf.org/pr/archives/000372.shtml (accessed August 22, 2009).

Cornog, Martha. 2008. "Graphic Novels: Challenge & Change." *Library Journal* (May 15). Available: www.libraryjournal.com/article/CA6557371.html (accessed August 22, 2009).

Elkins, Robert J., and Christian Bruggemann. 1983. "Comic Strips in the Teaching of English as a Foreign Language." In James L. Thomas (Ed.), *Cartoons and Comics in the Classroom*. Littleton, CO: Libraries Unlimited.

Gonzalez, Miguel. 2006. "Good Grief, Charlie Brown! Family Stunned by Porn Comics at Library." *[Victorville] Daily Press*, April 12.

Green, Justin. 1995. *Justin Green's Binky Brown Sampler*. San Francisco: Last Gasp.

Harris, Franklin. 2005. "Censored Book Not a Good Start." *The Decatur Daily* (online edition), February 10.

ICv2. 2006. "Marvel Edits 'Tomb of Dracula.'" Available: www.icv2.com/articles/news/9357.html (accessed August 22, 2009)

Jenson-Benjamin, Meredith. 2001. "An Irrelevant (but Amusing) Story about Challenges to GNs." E-mail post to GNLIB-L, April 25.

"Library Cards Get Bonus on Free Comic Book Day." 2006. *Library Journal* (May 11). Available: www.libraryjournal.com/article/CA6333717.html (accessed August 22, 2009).

"Newsmaker: Alison Bechdel." 2007. *American Libraries* (February): 22.

Olin, Anita. 2007. "Banned Books Week: Not Just for Prose Anymore." *Sequential Tart* 10, no. 9. Available: www.sequentialtart.com/article.php?id=665 (accessed August 22, 2009).

The Seven Soldiers of Victory Archives. 2005. New York: DC Comics.

Steelman, Ben. 2007. "Read with Us: Program Spotlights 'Persepolis.'" *StarNews Online*, September 16. Available: www.starnewsonline.com/article/20070916/NEWS/709160324/1051/NEWS (accessed August 22, 2009).

Tractenberg, Jeffrey A. 2008. "King of Cartoons." *Wall Street Journal*, September 18. Available: http://online.wsj.com/article/SB122166625405548219.html (accessed August 22, 2009).

Whitworth, Jerry. 2006. "A Case for Comics: Comic Books as an Educational Tool Pt. 2." *Sequential Tart* 9, no. 7. Available: www.sequentialtart.com/article.php?id=186 (accessed August 22, 2009).

Chapter 9

How Do Comics and Graphic Novels Fit in Academia?

In his book *Comics Librarianship: A Handbook*, Michigan State University Librarian Randall Scott recounted a meeting with a retired professor in which he told him about MSU's comic collection. The professor told Scott that when he had worked as a student library assistant in 1936, his first job had been to go through the newspapers and rip out the comics section before the papers went out into the reading room (Scott, 1990: 11). How times have changed. Today colleges and universities are using comics and graphic novels in many different ways. Their libraries are purchasing graphic novels and some also have special comics collections. Their professors are using graphic novels in their classes and even teaching courses on graphic novels that range from graphic novels and literature to graphic novels and science. Many of the nonfiction works about comics are written from an academic standpoint, and several are published by university presses. The academic world has embraced comics and graphic novels and keeps finding new ways to use and discuss them.

Comics Research Libraries

While many university libraries now carry graphic novels, others have special collections of comic books and related materials. One of the biggest and best known of these is the Comic Art Collection at the Michigan State University library in East Lansing, Michigan. The collection is part of the Russel B. Nye Popular Culture Collection and began in 1970 when Nye, a Pulitzer Prize–winning English professor, was working on the chapter "Fun in Four Colors: The Comics" for his book *The Unembarrassed Muse* and asked two undergraduates to donate their personal collections of about 6,000 comics so that people would be able to check his work (Scott, 1998). While the chapter mainly covered comic strips, it also discussed comics books, spotlighting Superman, Batman, and Marvel Comics (Nye, 1970).

The collection currently contains about 240,000 items, 200,000 of which are American comics. The rest are foreign comics, including 20,000 French titles, and books and periodicals on the subject (Harbison, 2008). The comics are preserved using acid-free packaging, such as mylar bags, and by keeping the room in which they are housed dark when titles are not being retrieved and reshelved. While many MSU professors use the collection, it is open to everyone and is often used by scholars from around the world for both the comics and for other materials, such as the periodicals, which include not only *Comics Journal* and *Comic Buyers' Guide* but also fan-created publications (Scott, 1998).

The collection's budget is around $12,000 a year, so Scott, who came to the library in 1974, does his best to get discounts and hunt for bargains (Harbison, 2008). Over the years, other collections have been purchased, including one from a collector in Sweden that formed a large percentage of the European collection. The now defunct Eclipse Comics had provided the library with not only their comics but also the "exchange copies" that they received from other publishers as well as scripts, correspondence, and other materials.

Scott has devised a way to catalog the comic collection using Library of Congress cataloging methods, placing American comics in PN6728 with additional numbers and letters depending on the decade of origin, the publisher, and the first letter of the title. PN6728.1 is for comics that began in 1935–1949, .2 for the 1950s, .3 for the 1960s, .4 for the 1970s (though the Underground titles are .45 even if they are from the 1960s), .5 for the 1980s (with .55 for "New Wave comix," minicomics, and other amateur and self-published works), .6 for the 1990s, and .7 and .8 for the first two decades of the twenty-first century (Scott, 1990).

Due to the way that comics are cataloged, related works may not be near one another. *Detective Comics* is cataloged PN6728.1.N3 D4 whereas *Detective Comics Annual* is PN6728.5.D3 because its first issue was in the 1980s, as opposed to the series, which began in 1937. In addition, when the series began, the publisher was National so its cutter number is N3, but *Annual* was published by DC Comics and so has the cutter of D3.

The same goes for series that have changed names or restarted. To use the *Legion of Super-Heroes* example from Chapter 2, Volume 1 is PN6728.4.N3 L4 (.4 for the 1970s, N for National); Volume 2, which began as *Superboy* in the 1940s and changed names three times, is PN6728.1.N3S77; Volumes 3 and 4, which are both from the 1980s, are PN6728.5.D3 L38 and L39, respectively; and the most recent version is PN6728.7.D3 L4215. When the inevitable sixth volume comes out, it will most likely be something like PN6728.8.D3 L[number].

Michigan State University is part of the Consortium of Popular Culture Collections in the Midwest (CPCCM) that includes other comics research libraries, most notably The Ohio State University in Columbus. OSU is home to the Billy Ireland Cartoon Library and Museum, founded in 1977 and formerly known as the Cartoon Research Library, until acquiring the collection of the International Museum of Cartoon Art. Its holdings include more than 450,000 original cartoons, 36,000 books, 51,000 serial titles, 3,000 linear feet of manuscript materials, and over 2.5 million comic strip clippings and tear sheets. The latter was primarily acquired from the San Francisco Academy of Cartoon Art and is the largest collection of its kind in the world.[1]

The library also has a number of collections that include the personal papers of several writers and artists as well as other materials by them. This includes the Will Eisner Collection, the Walt Kelly (*Pogo*) collection, and the Bill Watterson (*Calvin and Hobbes*) collection. There is also a collection of cartoons from Windsor McCay (*Little Nemo in Slumberland*), a collection of over 9,500 Underground Comics, and a large manga collection. The International Museum of Cartoon Art's collection added an additional 200,000 original cartoons. The museum was founded by *Beetle Bailey* creator Mort Walker, who brought the collection to OSU in 2008 after it had previously been located in museums in Stamford, Connecticut, Rye Brook, New York, and Boca Raton, Florida. The library also sponsors comics-related programs and exhibits, including a Festival of Cartoon Art.

Many other institutions have special comics collections that feature materials once owned or donated by people in the industry. These include the E. Nelson Bridwell Collection at the University of Tulsa, the Gardner F. Fox Collection at the University of Oregon, and the Stephen R. Bissette Collection at Henderson State University (whose library also has the Will Eisner Reading Room). Sometimes publishers will donate their materials. In 2008 Dark Horse Comics donated their entire catalog to Portland State University, the alma mater of its founder and president Mike Richardson. The collection includes comic books, trades, original graphic novels, and even non-comics items such as statues, lunch boxes, T-shirts, and other products put out by Dark Horse. What makes this different from many of the other collections is that two copies of each printed work are donated, one for the special collection department and one for general circulation (MacDonald, 2008).

Individual donations are also a source for collections. Brown University's John Hay Library is home to a collection donated by collector Michael J. Ciaraldi. The 60,000 items in the collection include comics, graphic novels, fan and collector's journals, reissues of classic "golden age" comics and newspaper strips, manga, European comic art, and even adult erotica. The collection also has a large amount of comics from the smaller independent publishers of the 1970s and 1980s, including the work of people like Robert Crumb and Art Spiegelman. Ciaraldi donated the collection in 1996 after moving and discovering that he had no room for his 3-ton, 255-carton comics collection. There are many other notable academic library collections, including Bowling Green State's Popular Collection and the Underground Comix collection at Iowa State. A list of these can be found at http://comics.lib.msu.edu/director/comres.htm.

Not only do academic libraries have collections of comic books, but some public libraries do as well, including the New York Public Library, which includes color microfiche reproductions of various Golden Age–era series among its holdings. However, the largest comics collection in a nonacademic library can be found at the Library of Congress, which owns approximately 120,000 comic books. The LOC, which received comics for decades due to copyright deposit rules, did almost no cataloging until the 1990s (and even then it focused more on comics that were part of a series). In 2008 the LOC's Serial and Government Publications Division began to inventory all of the comics that they held; this process included creating holdings records for all items and changing the control number for comics titles to one beginning with "Comic Book" followed by a five-digit number. This replaced the old "comic box" designation that represented more an item's location than its title. The comics, which span from the 1930s to the present, are considered to be a "high value collection," are housed in a secure vault, and require special permission from the Serial and Government Publications Division to access (Higley, personal communication, 2009).

Comics and Cartoons are among the areas for which the LOC has a collection policy statement. This statement lists the scope, research strengths, collecting policy, acquisition sources, and collecting levels for the collection. According to the statement, they collect American comics "extensively" and manga and other foreign works "selectively." The library also collects trade editions and a "comprehensive" collection of secondary sources on the topic (Library of Congress, 2008). They also have some comics-themed periodicals and other related items, including Steve Ditko's original artwork for the first-ever Spider-Man story in *Amazing Fantasy* #15, which was donated anonymously to the library in 2008. The art is part of the collection of original cartoons in the library's Prints and Photographs Division, which includes more than 125,000 caricatures, comic strips, and political and social commentaries from the 1600s to the present ("Amazing Fantasy," 2008). The LOC has held programs on comics, for example, one dealing with comics and the 9/11 attacks that featured a special display and a panel that included Will Eisner, Peter Kuper, and Trina Robbins.

The Library of Congress also administers the Caroline and Erwin Swann Foundation for Caricature and Cartoon that offers fellowships to graduate students who are conducting ongoing scholarly research and writing projects in the field of caricature and cartoon. The prize of up to $15,000 has often been awarded to a single scholar, but recent years have seen it divided up among several people due to the "number, nature, and quality of fellowship applications" (Library of Congress, n.d.). Some of the winning comics and graphic novel themed topics have included "Contemporary Graphic Narratives: History, Aesthetics, Ethics" and "Osamu Tezuka: Manga as a Site of Inter-Art Discourse in Postwar Japan (1945–1960)."

Other Academic Libraries

More and more academic libraries are actively purchasing graphic novels due to requests both from librarians interested in creating collections and professors who want to use them for classes.

For example, at New York's Columbia University, librarian Karen Green (whose primary area at the library included ancient and medieval history and modern Greek literature) was able to get a collection started after meeting with various individuals and making her case using books, reviews, a letter of support from a professor, and several examples from the MLA Bibliography. Her efforts paid off: a graphic novels fund was established with her as selector (Green, 2007). While reactions among her colleagues have been mixed, the library's users have welcomed the collection with "gusto" (Green, personal communication, 2008). Green has discussed the creation of the collection as well as the processes, perks, and pitfalls of building and maintaining an academic collection in her monthly column "Comic Adventures in Academia," which appears online at www.comixology.com.

An example of an instructor request is at the University of Memphis, where the library was asked to "consider upgrading" the library's graphic novel resources by the faculty chair of the Department of English so that the school could attract PhD-level researchers of comic books. While the library did have some graphic novels and related scholarly works, they were mainly for that professor's course, "Visual and Verbal Texts: The Graphic Novel," and many of the titles the library was supposed to have had been lost and needed to be replaced (Matz, 2004).

Classes Incorporating Comics and Graphic Novels

As is the case with the University of Memphis, part of the reason that many academic libraries seek to include graphic novels in their collections is because they are being used in the classroom. At MSU, five different professors wanted to use comics in their classrooms in the fall of 2008 (Harbison, 2008). In such cases, the comics and graphic novels are incorporated into an existing class, while in other cases, such as a literature, education, or library science course, the class may include a specific unit on them or individual books may appear on the reading list along with "text" works. *Maus* has been used in courses on the Holocaust; Paul Buhle, who has worked on nonfiction graphic novels, has used *Stuck Rubber Baby* in his survey course "Sixties Without Apologies" at Brown, and one of Buhle's books, *A People's History of the American Empire*, is being used in history courses in various schools, including Columbia University (Dooley, 2008); and *Persepolis* has been used in classes on women's literature in various places, including in an advanced composition class at the U.S. Military Academy at West Point and was chosen as the book for all incoming freshmen to read and discuss before starting their first year at Louisiana State University.

A number of schools offer courses specifically on comics and graphic novels, and it is not just "comics as literature." As shown in Exhibit 9-1, these courses cover many topics.[2]

Besides the eight listed in the exhibit, there are a number of other interesting graphic novel-themed courses and programs. One example not previously mentioned is an introductory physics class at the University of Minnesota called "Science in Comic Books" (Yang, 2003). Along with Minneapolis College of Art and Design, other art schools also offer courses on comics. The Center for Cartoon Studies in White River, Vermont, offers a Master's in Fine Arts degree, and faculty members who include many notable figures in the industry. New York City's School for the

Exhibit 9-1. Comics-Themed Courses

Example 1
North Shore Community College
The Comic Book in American Culture
Instructor: Lance Eaton

Books used include *Understanding Comics, Maus, Watchmen, Graphic Witness: Four Wordless Graphic Novels*, and *The Best American Comics 2006*. Other titles are on "recommended" list.
   The class is part of the Interdisciplinary Studies program and is a liberal arts elective. It was previously taught at Tufts University's "Experimental College," where it counted toward the Mass Communication and Media Studies minor or as a humanities elective, and it has become a "Special Topics Seminar" for their Interdisciplinary Studies Seminar at Emerson College.
   The class shows how comics work as a medium of communication and to what degree they can be considered literary art. It combines literature, history cultural studies, and other disciplines to "gain a fuller understanding of this medium of communication." Besides the books, students read articles and essays, some of which are posted on Blackboard, an online course management system that allows teachers to provide materials, such as articles and links, and interact with students via discussion boards, blogs, and other methods. Course topics include "The Forms of Comics: How Comics Communicate," "Comic Scholarship," "Comics & Ideology," and "Postmodern Concepts in the Superhero Genre."
   Student assignments include several papers, including a report on graphic novels, a report on a story from *Graphic Witness*, and a comparison of a graphic novel and its film adaptation.

Example 2
University of Texas at Austin
Special Topics in Rhetoric and Writing: The Rhetoric of Comic Books
Instructor: Andrew J. Friedenthal

Books used include *Understanding Comics, The Complete Persepolis*, and *Arguing Comics: Literary Masters on a Popular Medium*.
   This course discusses the medium and industry of comic books along with particular works to teach about the aspects and processes of rhetorical persuasion. The "Special Topics" courses are designed for graduate student instructors to "teach rhetoric and writing though the lens of their own research interests." There is also a similar class, "The Rhetoric of Cartoons," whose required reading includes *Watchmen*.
   The syllabus for this course emphasizes that "although this course is organized around the topic of comic books, it is first and foremost a course in rhetoric." It is divided into four units: Rhetoric, History, and Comic Strips; The Rhetoric About Comic Books; The Rhetoric of Comic Books (in which *Persepolis* is read and discussed); and The Rhetoric of Superhero Comic Books. Besides the primary books, handouts include photocopies of articles and excerpts from books such as *How to Read Superhero Comics and Why* and *Reading Comics: How Graphic Novels Work and What They Mean*.
   Student assignments include several papers, six rhetorical analyses, and participations in group discussions.

Example 3
Century College
Graphic Narratives: Comics as Literature
Instructor: Carl Gerriets

Books used include *Fun Home, The Fate of the Artist, Understanding Comics, Tricked, The Complete Maus, The Push Man and Other Stories, Black Cherry*, and *Jimmy Corrigan*. Honors students also use the nonfiction book *The System of Comics*.

(Cont'd.)

Exhibit 9-1. Comics-Themed Courses *(Continued)*

This is an English class for a community college designed to introduce students to the "critical study of comics literature." Students read, annotate, and discuss the works as well as write papers and do projects. The class is held partly in a classroom and partly online. Handouts are also used, and these are also available online for the students. The syllabus warns students that some of the readings may contain "adult material," and among the assignments is one in which the students visit a bookstore or library to examine how the graphic novels there are presented, organized, and marketed.

Example 4
Minneapolis College of Art & Design
History of Comic Books
Instructor: Diana Green

Books used include *The Mammoth Book of Best War Comics, Krazy & Ignatz 1925–1926, The Greatest Wonder Woman Stories Ever Told, Modesty Blaise: Bad Suki, Swamp Thing Book 1, Donna Barr's Peach Slices, Walt Disney Treasure: Disney Comics: 75 Years of Innovation,* and the anthology *Sex, Drugs, and Violence in the Comics.* Several other nonfiction books are recommended including *Understanding Comics, Reading Comics,* and *Comic Book Nation.*

   MCAD offers a major in comic book illustration and has offered classes on comics and graphic novels for over ten years. This includes a class on "Graphic Novels" and on "The History of Underground Comix." The classes have been offered both "live" and online.

   According to the syllabus, the class covers the history of comics as "an industry, a social phenomenon, and an art form" and is "intended as an overview rather than an exhaustive approach to the subject." The history is taught chronologically, and covers such topics as "the war years," the anticomics feelings of the 1950s, the beginnings of the silver age, Undergrounds, the advent of self-publishing, and the "Indy boom and bust." Besides linking to an assignment, each topic also spotlights a particular artist or artists, including Jack Kirby, Will Eisner, Robert Crumb, and Osamu Tezuka.

   Blackboard is also used. Student assignments are two research papers (one on a particular person or subject and one that either compares two items or looks at the evolution of one work to another) and a final exam.

Example 5
Henderson State University
Special Topics: Comics and Psychology
Instructor: Travis Langley

Books used include the nonfiction works *Seduction of the Innocent, Superman on the Couch: What Superheroes Really Tell Us About Ourselves and Our Society,* and *The Psychology of Superheroes.* Various comic books and graphic novels are also used but are not specified (though *Fun Home* is mentioned). HSU also offers a course titled "Comics as Communication" taught by Randy Duncan.

   Comics and Psychology is a cross-listed undergraduate/graduate-level course covering the "psychological study of sequential art literature, exploring its structure, function, and psychological value." Discussion topics include the purpose of graphic storytelling and the application of theories and concepts as well a character analysis that examines such elements as archetypes, mental illness, social interaction, and motivation. The course is part classroom seminar and part field research, and its goals include making sure that the student knows the role psychology has played in comic book history, has examined the themes that are psychologically significant in comic literature, can understand the difficulties in subjective and objective psychological writings on comics, and can discuss the need for more empirical research on the interpretation and influence of the comic arts.

(Cont'd.)

Exhibit 9-1. Comics-Themed Courses *(Continued)*

While the classroom work includes discussion and several exams, there are two research assignments of interest. The first is to do a character analysis of a specific comic/graphic novel character, primarily one who is well known and/or has a particularly important psychological significance. The other is empirical research, which has several options, including attending one of the major comic book conventions. Alternative options include doing online data collection archival research and annotated bibliographies. Students are also required to disseminate their findings as an article, a PowerPoint file, or a presentation at one of various venues, including the Comics Arts Conference and the Southwestern Psychological Association meeting.

Another alternative is doing an online survey for The ERIICA Project (http://workdaycomic .com/ERIICA) which stands for Empirical Research on the Interpretation & Influence of the Comic Arts. Current studies include "Batman Behind Bars: Simultaneous vs. Sequential Assessment of Inmates' and Students' Life Views," "Fickleness and Fascination: Findings from Interviews with Fans, Professionals, and Professional Fans," "Says the Spider or the Fly: Stigma Salience and Stereotypic Communication," "There's No Place Like Oz: Convention Attendance Bolsters Fans' Self-Esteem (aka Home Is Where the Hulk Is)," and "Who Wants to Analyze a Superhero?" Participants in the project give research presentations at the Comics Arts Conferences at Comic-Con International, WonderCon, and several Arkansas conferences.

Example 6
Seattle Central Community College
Sequential Art: History and Criticism of Comic Books and Graphic Novels
Instructor: Leonard Rifas

Books used include *An Anthology of Graphic Fiction, Cartoons,* and *True Stories*. Students are also provided with a packet of readings consisting of essays, book chapters, examples, and commentary.

This is a five-credit humanities class covering the history of comics. The purposes and goals of the course include helping students analyze comics as a composite form of art and literature and as a flexible and influential medium, to improve their skills in language proficiency and critical thinking, and to read graphic narratives that provide material for discussing larger social issues.

The course is made up of lectures, readings, guest speakers, group discussions, and other methods of learning. Besides quizzes, written assignments, and final student presentations on their self-chosen topics, students create a class mini comic. Subjects covered include Ethnic Images, Gender, Sexuality, War Comics, Horror Comics,, Underground Comix, and Manga. An introductory "preexamination" filled out by the students includes the question "Do you borrow graphic novels from the library?" Rifas has also taught a version of this course at the University of Washington, Bothell.

Example 7
Pacific Lutheran University
Special Topics: Global Comics Literature
Instructor: Alison Mandaville

Books used include *Aya, Nana, Incognegro, Understanding Comics, Shortcomings, Maggie the Mechanic, The Good Times Are Killing Me, Epileptic, Fun Home,* and *Exit Wounds*. Also recommended to students are *Maus, Persepolis, Graphic Witness,* and *The Push Man*.

The goals of this 200-level English class include making sure that the students can "use a variety of practical strategies to read a . . . visual text," that they have an introductory knowledge of the "the global field of comics and visual literatures," and that they are able to use a variety of analytical strategies to evaluate both their own and others' thinking about literary texts.

(Cont'd.)

Exhibit 9-1. Comics-Themed Courses *(Continued)*

Besides reading and discussing the graphic novels, other class assignments include writing response papers that are posted on the online academic forum Sakai and a "creative critical research project." Weekly topics include "Autobiography and Memoir," "Race in the USA," "Politics and Journalism," and "Wordless Graphic Novels."

Dr. Mandaville has also taught comics and graphic novel related courses at University of Washington, Seattle, Antioch University, and Western Washington University, and has used *Persepolis* and the works of Lynda Barry and Phoebe Gloeckner in her women's studies classes. She also wrote the article "Why I Teach Comics Literature" in *The Comics Journal* (2005, vol. 272).

Example 8
University of Alberta
Comic Books and Graphic Novels in School and Public Libraries (LIS 404/518)
Instructor: Gail de Vos

Books used include *Understanding Comics, Making Comics, Fun Home, Persepolis, Skim, Death Note, Scott Pilgrim, Castle Waiting, Ranma 1/2, Fullmetal Alchemist,* and *American Born Chinese.*

This course has been offered for both education and library science degrees and as both an undergraduate and graduate-level course. The course's objectives include students being able to "appreciate the diversity and potential of the comic book and graphic novel format, understand comic books and graphic novels as a unique medium of communication and storytelling, assess the role of comic books and graphic novels as a unique medium in Western and Japanese society and culture, [and] select and maintain a comic book and graphic library collection in a school or public library."

The class is taught online, and class assignments include one dealing with comic books and movies, an annotated bibliography of ten titles for an intended reading audience or theme, and a virtual seminar assignment. For the latter, students can suggest their own topic (with de Vos's approval), but suggested topics include manga, *Classics Illustrated,* collection development policies, marketing comics and graphic novels to female readers, online comics, and mainstream publishers versus comic book publishers for graphic novels. Graduate-level students have an additional research project or paper on a topic or theme that was not already discussed in class.

Visual Arts has a cartooning major that has seen increasing popularity, and the classes that Will Eisner taught there became the basis for his books on the subject. The Savannah College of Art and Design has both undergraduate and graduate programs in comic art (Cornwell, 2007).

Some courses are taught by people who have created graphic novels or have written books on the subject. New York University's School of Continuing and Professional Studies has offered classes taught by Peter Sanderson, who has written books about Marvel Comics, and Columbia named Art Spiegelman a "New York City Fellow" and brought Spiegelman in to teach the course "Comics: Marching into the Canon."

In most cases, professors who create comics-themed programs do get support from administrators and other members of the faculty. Lance Eaton said that faculty members were glad to be on the "cutting edge of academia" (Eaton, personal communication, 2008). Alison Mandaville found that students in the colleges where she has taught were "pretty surprised" at first, but now many of her colleagues include graphic novels in their own courses (Mandaville, personal communication, 2008).

Leonard Rifas's class in Seattle was designed at the request of the Dean of Humanities and Social Science, and the library even set up a special display promoting the class. The library has also helped students enrolled in the course who wanted to learn more than the syllabus covered (Rifas, personal communication, 2008). Many other instructors have also reported that their libraries were very helpful in providing material both for their classes and for those students who were interested in additional titles and information.

Comics-themed classes are being taught outside of North America as well. The North Wales School of Art and Design offers both a BA and an MA in illustration for graphic novels, and according to instructor Dan Berry, the students have reacted with a "mix of disbelief and joy" (Berry, personal communication, 2008).

Instructors report only minor problems in creating and teaching a course centered around graphic novels. These include working to get the proper accreditation for the course and difficulties in acquiring review copies of books they are considering for course texts. For the latter problem, libraries can be helpful, as can contacting the publisher directly for a review copy. Some publishers, such as Random House, will offer "examination" copies for instructors and free desk copies if enough copies are purchased for student use.

Some schools have even produced their own work. Duke University's Law School created a 72-page comic called *Tales from the Public Domain: Bound by Law?* which tells of filmmaker Akiko and her "tussles" with a Rights Monster as she makes a documentary. The writers are the director of Duke's Center for the Study of the Public Domain and a professor from the law school, and the artist is a professor at the University of Oregon School of Law. The comic is available both in print and online (www.law.duke.edu/cspd/comics).

Of special mention is Stanford University's course "The Graphic Novel," taught by Adam Johnson and Tom Kealey. This ten-week course has a limited enrollment of 20 students who must complete special applications to be considered (one student applied in comic strip form). Over the duration of the course, ten weeks of two weekly two-hour class sessions and a weekly three-hour drawing lab (which tends to run long), the students actually create a graphic novel. The course's first class project in 2008 was *Shake Girl*, which was based on the true-story of a woman who lived in Cambodia and was the victim of an acid attack. The comic, when completed, was made available online and reaction was very positive, and it has even attracted the attention of a mainstream publisher.[3] The 2009 class created *Virunga*, the story of a female park ranger in the Congo who is trying to protect mountain gorillas (Johnson, personal communication, 2009).

Other examples of classes and information on lesson plans, study guides, exercises, and other related information can be found on the Web site of the National Association of Comic Art Educators at www.teachingcomics.org. The NACAE is affiliated with the Center for Cartoon Studies and presided over by award-wining comic writer/artist James Sturm; its primary mission is to "effect the inclusion of comics classes" in the course catalogs of colleges and universities (Yang, 2003). Courses using graphic novels can also be found via the syllabus finder at the Center for New Media at George Mason University (http://chnm.gmu.edu/tools/syllabi). A "phrase search" on graphic novels at this site results in about 6,000 hits.

Other Academic Activities

In addition to classes and library collections, some academic institutions sponsor conferences and host databases on the comics and graphic novels. One of the most notable of these is at the University of Florida. UF is among the schools with a comics collection and comics-themed classes. Its library owns the Suzy Covey Comic Book Collection, which includes the Penny and Sol Davidson Collection containing both works by nineteenth and early twentieth century cartoonists and "special purpose" comics that are created to promote such things as employee safety, science education, and the sales of products (University of Florida, 2007a). The school offers under-graduate comics-themed courses, some of which are taught by Donald Ault, a comics scholar and writer who has also donated collections of comic strips to the library, and also a Comics and Visual Rhetoric Track for both MA and PhD students.

The school also contributes to the scholarly discussion of comics in three other ways. The first is *ImageTexT*, a peer-reviewed online journal. Besides comics and animation, the journal also covers "illustrated poetry and prose and related literary and artistic genres combining image and text, in print and digital forms" (University of Florida, n.d.). The second is the Comix-Scholars Discussion List, which is to the field of comics scholarship what GNLIB-L is to the area of graphic novels and libraries. Participants on the list include librarians, instructors, the writers of books on comics, and even comics creators. Information on how to subscribe to the list can be found in Appendix C.

The third way that UF contributes to comics scholarship is its annual conference. The conference has its origin in a 2002 symposium on Will Eisner and, except for 2005, has continued every year since. The conference sets a new topic each year with a call for papers going out several months prior. Previous topics have included "Intersections of Sex, Gender, and Sexuality," "Undergrounds," and "World Building: Seriality and History." The conferences are interdisciplinary and "examine subjects from a wide range of formal, historical, literary, sociological and economic perspectives." They are often complemented by other events and activities that appeal to the wider Gainesville community, such as gallery exhibits, book signings, and all-ages work-shops on drawing comics led by the visiting artists (University of Florida, 2007b).

Other comic-themed academic conferences are held each year at universities, hotels, and comics conventions. Some are annual events while others are "one-time" programs. The International Comic Arts Forum is an annual academic conference that is dedicated to "promoting the scholarly study and appreciation of comic art, including comic strips, comic books, comics albums and graphic novels, magazine and newspaper cartooning, caricature, and comics in electronic media." Its aims include fostering recognition of comic art as an "international phenomenon," welcoming a "multidisciplinary and pluralistic approach to the study of comic art," and providing "an accessible showcase for innovative comics scholarship and comic art, with special emphasis on traditions hitherto neglected in English-language studies" (International Comic Arts Forum, 2009). The forum began in 1997 as the International Comics and Animation Festival at Georgetown University and has since been held in various places, including the School of the Art Institute of Chicago.

The ICAF also offers a scholarship to a student who has written or is in the process of writing a "substantial" comics-themed research-based writing project. While preference is given to master's theses and doctoral dissertations, all students can apply. The winner of the scholarship must present a talk based on his or her research at an ICAF conference. The scholarship is named for Dr. John A. Lent, one of the leading proponents of the academic study of comics and the author of hundreds of articles and dozens of books on the subject (ImageText, 2008).

As mentioned in previous chapters, there have been academic tracks and programs at the San Diego Comic-Con, Wondercon, the New York Comic Con, and elsewhere. At ALA in 2008, the Association of College and Research Libraries hosted a panel on wordless books, including wordless or "Pantomime" comics and the usage of such comics in the classroom (Hatfield, 2008). This followed the ALA Midwinter conference ACRL had a panel called "Graphic Novels and Manga: Should We Add Them to Our Collections?" whose speakers included the associate curator of OSU's Cartoon Research Library (Green, 2008).

There are also special events in comics academia as well as panels on comics in other academic conferences. Recent examples include "Graven Images: Religion in Comic Books and Graphic Novels," a three-day conference at Boston University in 2008 (which led to a special collection being created at the BU library in 2009); "Reclaiming the Comic Book Canon," a panel held at the 2009 convention of the Northeast Modern Language Association (NeMLA); and "Classic and Comics," a panel at the 2008 annual meeting of the American Philological Association (APA). The latter, which included such topics as "Sin City and Hoplite Warrior" and "Wonder Woman and the Furies," received such an overwhelming response to the organizers' call for papers that a book on the subject has been planned (Green, 2008). Professional academic journals have also had comics-themed issues. For example, *English Language Notes* from the University of Colorado at Boulder had as the subject of its Fall/Winter 2008 issue "Graphica: Literary Criticism and the Graphic Novel."

Articles and Books

Of course, even without the conferences and classes, comics and graphic novels have long been discussed in academic and professional publications and have been the subject of college papers. This has been true from the beginning. Between 1935 and 1944, more than 100 critical articles about comics appeared in educational and nonprofessional periodicals and an entire volume of a 1944 edition of *The Journal of Educational Sociology* was dedicated to comics (Yang, 2003). A number of books take an academic look at comics or at comics in academia. When Randall Scott wrote *Comic Librarianship: A Handbook* in 1990, he created a list of suggested research topics that included "how comics relate to current events," "family in the comics," "how comics relate to social pathology," "language in the comics," and much more (Scott, 1990). Many students have used comics as the theme for term papers, master's theses, and doctoral dissertations for a number of majors, including library science. Some of these papers are available online while others can be acquired through interlibrary loan or have been the basis for books or other scholarly publications. Many of these are listed at the ComicsResearch.org Web site.

One important publisher of scholarly books on comics is the University Press of Mississippi, which has put out books on the topic since the 1980s. They began doing so when an acquisitions editor met English professor and comics scholar M. Thomas Inge, who convinced the editor that UPM could "make a name for itself" by covering popular culture subjects, including comics (Heer, 2008). UPM began comics-themed works in 1987 with Joseph Witek's *Comic Books as History* and Inge's essay collection *Comics and Culture* and has published many books since, including a series of "Conversations" with various writers and artists, including Stan Lee, Art Spiegelman, and Robert Crumb. A list of UPM's titles is found in Appendix B. Yale, the University of Chicago, and the University of Toronto are among the other university presses who have recently published books on the subject.

Many subjects are covered in these books and some are also produced by nonacademic publishers. As with other nonfiction subjects, some topics are covered by more than one book. For example, books on the influence of Jewish creators include *Jews and American Comics: An Illustrated History of an American Art Form*, *The Jewish Graphic Novel: Critical Approaches*, *From Krakow to Krypton: Jews and Comic Books*, *Disguised as Clark Kent: Jews, Comics, and the Creation of the Superhero*, and *Up, Up, and Oy Vey: Jews, Comics, and the Creation of the Superhero*, an award-winning book by Rabbi Simcha Weinstein. The books mentioned in this section and many others are included in Appendix B.

Research Outside the Academic World

Among those other books in Appendix B are books that take a scholarly or historical look at comics but were written not by those in the academic world but by those who are fans of the format (though in some cases the author is both a fan and an academic). Regular fans were among the earliest to explore the history of comics and write about it, often simply for other fans. One of the most important figures in comics fandom was Jerry Bails. A lifelong fan, Bails (1933–2006) began a correspondence with comics writer Gardner Fox (the creator of many classic characters, including the Flash and Hawkman), and in 1960 Fox put Bails, by then a PhD teaching science at Wayne State University, in touch with a teenager named Roy Thomas. That same year he and Thomas, a future comics writer and Marvel Editor in Chief, created the fanzine (a nonprofessional publication created for fans by fans) *Alter Ego*. During this period he also created several other publications, the most notable of which, *CAPA-alpha*, is still around today. *CAPA-alpha* was an Amateur Press Association (APA) publication that differs from a fanzine in that Amateur Press publications involve a limited number of people. These people write articles and then send them to a "central mailer" who copies them, collates the various articles, and mails them off to the other members. Bails was *CAPA-alpha*'s first "central mailer," and its members (limited to 50 people) have included many who would later work in comics.

Bails was also one of those responsible for microfilming comics from the 1940s, which made it easier for those interested in them to read those issues decades before they would be collected in book form. Additionally, he worked with others to create indexes of comics from that era as well as a "Who's Who" of people in comics. As mentioned in Chapter 2, the listing of creator credits in comic books was quite limited for several decades, and Bails' research has helped to give credit where credit was due. Bails would later computerize his data and take advantage of the Internet to further his research.

The Internet has increased the scope of fan-based comics research to the point that people from all over can contribute to the same project without having to wait for items to be physically mailed to them. One such project is the Grand Comic-Book Database (www.comics.org), on which Bails was an advisor. Begun in 1994, the GCD has indexed over 125,000 comics from around the world and lists over 2 million creator credits and character appearances. The GCD has grown to include contributors from all around the world and the contributors and the participants on the GCD e-mail lists include scholars, librarians, and comics professionals. Other cataloging databases have appeared on the Internet as well, including the Big Comic Book DataBase (www.comics-db.com) and Comic Book DB (www.comicbookdb.com). Other online databases and informational Web sites limit their scope. For example, Inducks (inducks.org) concentrates solely on Disney comics. Others concentrate on particular characters, genres, publishers, or titles. Some Web sites cover comics history and/or anecdotes, and others annotate certain comic book titles. Librarian Jess Nevins is among those who have annotated comics, most notably *The League of Extraordinary Gentlemen* and its sequels. The online *League* annotations were the early versions of what would later go into Nevins' books, and additions and corrections were provided by others online, including contributors on Usenet's rec.arts.comics.misc newsgroup, the place where Nevins first posted them in 1999.

Almost 75 years after a student library assistant was told to remove the comic strips, academia has embraced comic books and graphic novels ranging from classes in community colleges to academic events held at the Library of Congress. The acceptance into the academic world, be it classes or conferences or even simply having them in their library for recreational reading, is just one more step toward the acceptance of graphic novels as something appropriate for adults.

Notes

1. Other notable comics and cartoon-themed museums include the Cartoon Art Museum in San Francisco, the Museum of Comic and Cartoon Art in New York City, the Cartoon Museum in London, and the Musée de la bande dessinée in Angouléme.

2. Information for this section and for Exhibit 9-1 was acquired via e-mails from the instructors and from the syllabi that they provided:

Berry, Daniel, E-mail, October 6, 2008.

de Vos, Gail, E-mail, November 19, 2008; "Comic Books and Graphic Novels in School and Public Libraries (LIS 404/518)," Syllabus. University of Alberta, Edmonton, Alberta.

Eaton, Lance, E-mail, October 8, 2008; "The Comic Book in American Culture (EXP-0017-F)," Syllabus. Tufts University Medford, Massachusetts.

Friedenthal, Andrew J., E-mail, October 6, 2008; "The Rhetoric of Comic Books (RHE 309K)," Syllabus. University of Austin, Austin, Texas.

Gerriets, Carl, E-mail, October 6, 2008; "Graphic Narratives: Comics as Literature (ENG 2072)," Syllabus. Century College, White Bear Lake, Minnesota.

Green, Diana, E-mail, October 6, 2008; "History of Comic Books (HS 3657)," Syllabus. Minneapolis College of Art & Design, Minneapolis, Minnesota.

Langley, Travis, E-mail, October 6, 2008; "Special Topics: Comics & Psychology (PSY4003/5003)," Syllabus. Henderson State University Arkadelphia, Arkansas.

Mandaville, Alison, E-mail, January 8, 2009; "Global Comics Literature (English 213)," Syllabus. Pacific Lutheran University, Tacoma, Washington.

Rifas, Leonard, E-mail, October 6, 2008; "Sequential Art: History and Criticism of Comic Books and Graphic Novels (HUM 270)," Syllabus. Seattle Central Community College, Seattle, Washington.

3. *Shake Girl* can be found at www.stanford.edu/group/cwstudents/shakegirl but may be taken offline if it is published in book form.

References

"Amazing Fantasy: Library Receives Original 1962 Illustrations for First Spider-Man Story." 2008. *Library of Congress Information Bulletin* 67, no. 5. Available: www.loc.gov/loc/lcib/0805/spiderman.html (accessed August 22, 2009).

Cornwell, Lisa. 2007. "Schools Add, Expand Comics Art Classes." *USAToday*, December 15. Available: www.usatoday.com/news/education/2007-12-15-comicsclasses_N.htm (accessed August 22, 2009).

Dooley, Michael. 2008. "Power to the Panels: An Interview with Paul Buhle." *AIGA Journal of Design* (June 17). Available: www.aiga.org/content.cfm/power-to-the-panels-an-interview-with-paul-buhle (accessed August 22, 2009).

Green, Karen. 2007. "Comic Adventures in Academia: The Origin Story." Available: www.comixology.com/articles/11/The-Origin-Story (accessed August 22, 2009).

Green, Karen. 2008. "Adventures in Academia: Conventional Comics or Conference Calling." Available: www.comixology.com/articles/21/Conventional-Comics-or-Conference-Calling (accessed August 22, 2009).

Harbison, Sarah. 2008. "Fortress of Comic-tude." *The State News*, November 4. Available: www.statenews.com/index.php/article/2008/11/fortress_of_comic-tude (accessed August 22, 2009).

Hatfield, Charles W. 2008. "ALA: Reading Pictures: The Language of Wordless Books." *Thought Balloonists* (July 14). Available: www.thoughtballoonists.com/2008/07/ala-reading-pic.html (accessed August 22, 2009).

Heer, Jeet. 2008. "The Rise of Comics Scholarship: The Role of the University Press of Mississippi." Available: http://sanseverything.wordpress.com/2008/08/02/the-rise-of-comics-scholarship-the-role-of-university-press-of-mississippi/ (accessed August 22, 2009).

ImageText Newsfeed. 2008. "John A. Lent Scholarship in Comic Studies." Available: www.english.ufl.edu/imagetext/news.shtml?/cfp/lent_scholarship_in_comics_studies.shtml (accessed August 22, 2009).

International Comic Arts Forum. 2009. "ICAF's Mission." Available: www.internationalcomicartsforum.org/icaf/about-icaf.html (accessed August 22, 2009).

Library of Congress. 2008. "Library of Congress Collections Policy Statements: Comics and Cartoons." Available: www.loc.gov/acq/devpol/comics.pdf (accessed August 22, 2009).

Library of Congress. n.d. "Swann Foundations Fellowships." Available: www.loc.gov/rr/print/swann/swann-fellow.html (accessed August 22, 2009).

MacDonald, Heidi. 2008. "Every Dark Horse Comic Available at Portland State University." Available: http://pwbeat.publishersweekly.com/blog/2008/10/23/the-countrys-first-university-comic-book-archive (accessed August 22, 2009).

Matz, Chris. 2004. "Collecting Comic Books for an Academic Library." *Collection Building* 23, no. 2: 96–99.

Nye, Russell. 1970. *The Unembarrassed Muse: The Popular Arts in America*. New York: Dial Press.

Scott, Randall W. 1990. *Comics Librarianship: A Handbook*. Jefferson, NC: McFarland and Company.

Scott, Randall W. 1998. "A Practicing Comic-Book Librarian Surveys His Collection and His Craft." *Serials Review* 24, no. 1 (Spring): 49–56.

University of Florida. 2007a. "Comic Collections." Available: www.english.ufl.edu/comics/collections.shtml (accessed August 22, 2009).

University of Florida. 2007b. "Conferences." Available: www.english.ufl.edu/comics/conference.shtml (accessed August 22, 2009).

University of Florida. n.d. "ImageTexT." Available: www.english.ufl.edu/comics/imagetext.shtml (accessed August 22, 2009).

Yang, Gene. 2003. "History of Comics in Education." Available: www.humblecomics.com/comicsedu/history (accessed August 22, 2009).

Chapter 10

What Is the Future of Graphic Novels?

When he gave the keynote speech at the University of Florida symposium that would be the first of many conferences at that school, Will Eisner said:

> This seriously is a moment in time for which I have been dreaming all of my professional life, as most of those who worked around me dreamt about but weren't even aware that this was possible. We now, for the first time, we're being recognized, not yet accepted, but we're now recognized in major bookstores and in the rooms of academia—in the academic community. We're now being discussed as a form of literature, and this is what I've been hoping for in all these years. (Eisner, 2004)

Graphic novels intended for adult audiences now appear in the adult sections of public libraries, in college libraries, in college classrooms, in books by academics, in journals, in professional conferences, and on informational Web sites that are available to all. They are escaping the never-accurate description of being "only for kids," and their presence in the academic world aids in the continued growth in respect for and acceptance of comic books and graphic novels, helping to realize Eisner's dream.

So what does the future hold for graphic novels in libraries? As of this writing in 2009, both graphic novel publishers and libraries are finding themselves in a state of flux, with some publishers cutting back or going out of business and library budgets being slashed. However, the graphic novel genie is out of the bottle. High circulations and patron interest will all but ensure continued purchases by libraries, even if the amount is less. Graphic novels are being made for adults, they are being read by adults, and they are being purchased for adults. Mainstream publishers have discovered their appeal, and they have gained respect in the media, in academia, and among libraries. These trends should continue, and therefore the future looks bright indeed.

Reference

Eisner, Will. 2004. "Keynote Address from the 2002 'Will Eisner Symposium.'" *ImageTexT: Interdisciplinary Comics Studies*, 1, no. 1. Available: www.english.ufl.edu/imagetext/archives/v1_1/eisner (accessed August 22, 2009).

An Annotated List of Selected Graphic Novels

C ontained in this appendix are several hundred graphic novels titles that you may wish to consider adding to the adult graphic novels collection of your library. The list includes original graphic novels (both solo titles and OGN series), collected editions (both one-time volumes and "series of series"), manga titles and series (including manhwa, manhua, and OEL titles), and so forth. For each entry, I have either read the work, read a representational sampling of the work (primarily in the case of a series), or am familiar with the work in some other way. These titles are part of my personal collection (some of them in comic book form), have been provided to me by the publishers, have been checked out of the Broward County Library, or have been obtained from other libraries via interlibrary loan.

The following is a sample of the many titles and genres available to you. The annotations are here to inform you of the content of the work and are not necessarily meant as a review. Chapter 6 and Appendixes B and C list several sources that will provide additional information. My personal favorites are listed in Exhibit 6-7, and some recommendations are listed in the entries below. That a particular title is not on this list does not necessarily indicate that it is not a good work. A large number of age-appropriate titles were either not reviewed or were cut for reasons of space. Not every title on this list will be available from every vendor, and some may go in and out of print, be acquired by another publisher, or be collected in a newer format. All prices and the number of titles in a series are correct as of June 2009.

The titles are listed alphabetically, but in five different ways:

- **Title:** For a stand-alone work or for series without multiple names of subtitles
- **Series:** For series that include various subtitles or books with different names
- **Author:** For works by a particular author that are not given an independent entry
- **Publisher:** Titles with similar themes that are produced by the same publisher
- **Theme:** Multiple works that have the same basic theme (e.g., literary adaptations, historical biographies) but are from various creators and publishers

While this is a list of titles for an adult collection, many titles provided are perfectly appropriate for older teens (and in some cases even younger readers). These are indicated by [YR]. On the other hand, a small number are explicit enough to make them adults only. These are titles that should not be placed in a "mixed" collection and, depending on your library, may be placed somewhere other than the "open" shelves. These titles will be indicated by [AO]. The vast majority of the titles should be placed in the adult area due to either content (language, nudity, minor sexual situations, gore, intense violence, etc.) or story (aimed at adult readers), though some, depending on your library or community, may be acceptable for younger readers (or may fit in the other category). These will be indicated by [SA]. In some cases, the publisher's ratings will also be included. No matter how they are categorized, you know your patrons best and are best to judge where they should be shelved and whether or not they belong in your library at all.

A

The Acme Novelty Library. Chris Ware.
These titles by Ware have come in different sizes and shapes and from different publishers. They have contained many different stories, some of which have been collected. The most notable of these are the Jimmy Corrigan stories, which are mainly about the title character, a weak and lonely man in his thirties who, among other things, meets with his long lost father. The *Final Report* contains various short cartoons, and currently being published are the various volumes that collect the stories about "Rusty" Brown and his friend "Chalky" White. [SA]

> *Jimmy Corrigan or The Smartest Kid on Earth*. Published by Jonathan Cape. 2000 $19.95.
>
> *The Acme Novelty Library Final Report to Shareholders and Rainy Day Saturday Afternoon Fun Book*. Published by Pantheon. 2005 $27.50.

Action Philosophers. *The More-Than-Complete Action Philosophers*. Fred Van Lente and Ryan Dunlavey. Evil Twin, 2009. $24.95.
A collection of the nine-issue black-and-white comic series (previously collected in three, still available volumes) that teaches about various philosophers through humorous stories. One story portrays John Stuart Mill as Charlie Brown, another shows the life of Rousseau as a sitcom, and then there is the "Six Degrees of Francis Bacon." Also included among the over 35 "action philosophers" are Marx, Machiavelli, Plato, Sartre, Descartes, Plato, Jung, and many more. This volume includes never-before-seen stories.The creative team has also begun a series called *Comic Book Comics*, which covers the history of comic book industry. [YR]

A.D.: New Orleans After the Deluge. Josh Neufeld. Pantheon Books, 2009. $24.95.
The true story of seven residents of New Orleans and what they went through during and in the aftermath of Hurricane Katrina. Recommended. [YR]

Adolf series. Osamu Tezuka. VIZ/Cadance Books, 1996–1997. $16.95 each.
Set in the 1930s and 1940s, Tezuka's five-part story, one of his first translated into English, deals with the lives of three people named Adolf: Adolf Kamil, a younger German Jew living in Japan; Adolf Kaufmann, his German-Japanese friend who later joins the Hitler Youth; and Adolf Hitler himself. The story covers the time before, during, and after World War II and how the dealings of the older Adolf affect the lives of the younger ones. While not numbered, the volumes are subtitled. The proper reading order follows. [YR]

> *A Tale of the Twentieth Century*   *Days of Infamy*
> *An Exile in Japan*   *1945 and All That Remains*
> *The Half-Aryan*

The Adventures of Johnny Bunko: The Last Career Guide You'll Ever Need. Daniel Pink, with art by Rob Ten Pas. Riverhead, 2008. $15.00.

This is an OEL version of a business manga. Johnny Bunko works in a dead-end job, but a magical woman named Diana shows up and gives him and his coworkers helpful career advice. This title can be cataloged in the business section of the library. [SA]

The Adventures of Luther Arkwright. Bryan Talbot. Dark Horse.
The title character of these two collections is Luther Arkwright, an adventurer with the ability to travel to parallel worlds who works for an organization that protects other parallels from the action of The Disruptors. One such world, in which much of the story takes place, is an England in which Cromwell's Parliamentarians never lost control. The second book takes place 23 years later and focuses on Arkwright's daughter. Originally released in the UK, the first volume was adapted into a radio play and the second volume is also available on CD-ROM. [SA]
   Adventures of Luther Arkwright. $18.95.
   Heart of Empire: The Legacy of Luther Arkwright. $27.95.

Affair. Shiuko Kano. 801 Media, 2007. $15.95.
A one-volume yaoi manga that is rated 18+. It contains several short stories about two old friends who reunite and who are both now involved with the Yakuza. But do they now have feelings for each other? [SA]

After School Nightmare. Setona Mizushiro. Go! Comi, 2006–. $10.99.
This ten-volume Shojo manga deals with Mashiro, a teenager with a dark secret. While he considers himself a man and has the upper body of one, below the waist he is a woman. He is drawn into an odd experiment with other students that involves a shared "dreamworld" in which their secrets and "true selves" come out. The book is rated OT 16+ and was on YALSA's Great Graphic Novels for Teens List. [YR]

After the Cape. Howard Wong and Jim Valentino, with art by Marco Rudy and Manny Trembley. Image, 2007–. $12.99.
Ethan was once the Superhero Captain G, but this was all ended by his alcoholism. He has turned to crime to help his family. To date, there are two volumes. Another tale of heroes gone bad is Boom's *Irredeemable*. [YR]

Age of Bronze. Eric Shanower. Image, 2001–.
Shanower's Eisner-winning epic story of the Trojan War is told without most of the supernatural elements (Gods are mentioned but not seen). While the names are mostly in Greek style, some are given in their better-known Roman form, such as Achilles instead of Akhilleos. A glossary of names, genealogical charts, and an extensive bibliography are included in each volume. It is planned that this will be a seven-volume story, but only 27 issues were produced between 1998–2008, so it may be some time until the fourth volume is released. [SA]
   A Thousand Ships   *Betrayal Part 1*
   Sacrifice

Alan's War: The Memories of G.I. Alan Cope. Emmanuel Guibert. First Second, 2008. $24.00.
Originally published in France in three parts as *La Guerre d'Alan*, this graphic biography tells the story of Alan Cope, an American serviceman who fought in Europe in the latter part of World War II and later moved to France. [YR]

Alex. Mark Kalesniko. Fantagraphics, 2006. $19.95.
Alex, who lives in the Canadian city of Bandini, is an artist who once worked for "Mickey Walt Cartoon Studios" in California but now is living a life of frustration hanging with friends. He is drawn like a dog while everyone else is human, but no one makes mention of this. Also of note by the author is *Mail Order Bride.* [SA]

Alice in Sunderland. Bryan Talbot. Dark Horse, 2007. $29.95.
A history of the area of England known as the Sunderland and its connections to such things as *Alice in Wonderland.* A wonderful work "hosted" by Talbot that mixes drawings, photographs, and more. [SA]

Alive: The Final Evolution. Tadashi Kawashima, with art by Adachitoka. Del Rey, 2007–. $10.95.
In the wake of a global outbreak of suicides a group of teenagers find themselves with mysterious abilities. The series is rated OT (16+) and the series is still ongoing. As of April 2009, six volumes (of 16 so far) have been translated. [YR]

The Amazing Remarkable Monsieur Leotard. Eddie Campbell and Dan Best, with art by Campbell. First Second, 2008. $16.95.
When Jules Léotard (the famed "Man on the Flying Trapeze") dies in 1870 his nephew Etienne takes over the act and with his troupe of performers (including a talking bear) spend the next several decades performing and having adventures, including a voyage on the *Titanic.* [YR]

American Jesus, Vol. 1: ***Chosen.*** Mark Millar, with art by Peter Gross. Image, 2009. $9.99.
A 12-year-old boy can heal the sick, turn water into wine, and even raise the dead. Is he truly the second coming? The comic was originally put out by Dark Horse in 2004, and Milar is planning two more volumes. [SA]

American Splendor. Harvey Pekar and various artists.
Harvey Pekar began his autobiographical comic book *American Splendor* in 1976, telling about the everyday events of his life ranging from fixing a toilet to fighting cancer. This brought him some fame including appearances on *David Letterman* as well as earning him the American Book Award. His work has been adapted into both stage and film versions. His work has been published by various publishers, and many of his stories have been drawn by various artists including Joe Sacco, Joe Zabel, Eddie Campbell, Gilbert Hernandez, Ty Templeton, Hilary Barta, Ho Che Anderson, and the man who got him into writing comics in the first place, Robert Crumb. [SA]

TITLES WITH MULTIPLE ARTISTS
American Splendor: Another Day. DC/Vertigo, 2007. $14.99.
American Splendor: Another Dollar. DC/Vertigo, 2007. $14.99.
American Splendor: The Life and Times of Harvey Pekar. Ballantine Books, 2003. $20.00.
American Splendor: Our Movie Year. Ballantine Books, 2004. $16.95.
The Best of American Splendor. Ballantine Books, 2005. $17.95.
The New American Splendor Anthology: From Off the Streets of Cleveland. Running Press, 1993. $19.95.

TITLES BY ONE ARTIST
Bob and Harv's Comics. Art by Robert Crumb. Running Press, 1996. $16.00. A collection of the stories illustrated by Crumb.

Our Cancer Year. Co-written by Joyce Brabner, with art by Frank Stack. Four Walls Eight Windows, 1994. $17.95. This award winner covers Pekar's life 1990–1991 when he had cancer, his wife (Brabner) was involved with overseas peace activists, and they moved out of their apartment and into a house. Many libraries have put this in 362.area (LC area for LoC).

The Quitter. Art by Dean Haspiel. DC/Vertigo, 2005. $19.99 (HC); $12.99 (SC). An original graphic novel that covers Pekar's childhood, teens, and early adulthood.

AMERICAN SPLENDOR TITLES BY PEKAR BUT NOT ABOUT HIM

Ego & Hubris: The Michael Malice Story. Art by Gary Dumm. Ballentine Books, 2006. $19.95. Tells the true story of Michael Malice, who, among other things, helped start the blog Overheard in NY, including his youth, education, and the various jobs that he has held. Malice met Pekar after researching an obscure 1980s band.

American Splendor: Unsung Hero. Art by David Collier. Dark Horse, 2003. $11.95. Originally published as a three-issue limited series, this book recounts the experiences of Robert McNeill, an African-American soldier in Vietnam in 1969.

Non-*American Splendor* works by Pekar in this appendix include *Macedonia* and *Students for a Democratic Society: A Graphic History*.

American Virgin. Steven T. Seagle, with art by Becky Cloonan and Jim Rugg. DC/Vertigo, 2006–2008. $9.99–$17.99.

Adam Chamberlain is the spokesman for a highly popular abstinence movement. But when his girlfriend is killed while in Africa he is forced to reexamine his life, family, and relationships. [SA]

Vol. 1: *Head*	Vol. 3: *Wet*
Vol. 2: *Going Down*	Vol. 4: *Around the World*

The American Way. John Ripley, with art by Georges Jeanty and Karl Story. DC/Widstorm, 2007. $19.99.

Divisions appear in a government-formed superteam during the early 1960s, when the team gets its first black member. [YR]

American Widow. Alissa Torres, with art by Sungyoon Choi. Villard, 2008. $22.00.

On September 10, 2001, Alissa Torres' husband began working at Cantor Fitzgerald in the North Tower of the World Trade Center. The next day Torres found herself a seven-and-a-half-months-pregnant widow. This original graphic novel covers the next year of her life including how she dealt with both grief and red tape. [SA]

Angel Skin. Christian Westerlund, with art by Robert Nazeby Herzig. NBM, 2007. $11.95. Joshua Barker kills himself but finds himself in a crumbling city filled with strange people. [SA]

Anne Freaks, Vols. 1–4. Yua Kotegawa. ADV, 2006. $9.99.

Yuri, who did nothing to stop his mother from dying, Mitsuba, whose family was murdered, and Anna, an assassin who was rescued from a cult when she was a baby are drawn into even darker circumstances. The series is rated 16+. [SA]

An Anthology of Graphic Fiction, Cartoonists, & True Stories, Vols. 1–2. Edited by Ivan Brunetti. Yale University Press, 2006–. $28.00 each.

These anthologies collect previously published work from a variety of writers and artists including Peter Bagge, Phoebe Gloeckner, Harvey Kurtzman, Chester Brown, Harvey Pekar, Seth, Art Spiegelman, Chris Ware, Joe Sacco, and more. [SA]

Apocalypse Nerd. Peter Bagge. Dark Horse, 2008. $13.95.
When North Korea nukes Seattle, Perry, a software engineer who was camping with his friend Gordo must survive any way that he can in this book that contains both horror and humor. [SA]

Apollo's Song. Osamu Tezuka. Vertical, 2007. $19.95.
A 544-page collection of a 1970s Tezuka story. A man's hatred of love causes him to do cruel things that get him sent to a mental institution. During therapy a vision of a goddess tells him he must not spurn love and gives him visions of himself in other lives, ranging from historical to science fiction, in which he meets and loses love. [SA]

Archenemies: Saints and Sinners. Drew Melbourne, with art by Yvel Guichet and Joe Rubinstein. Dark Horse, 2007. $12.95.
Superhero Star Fighter and criminal Underlord are archenemies. But unknown to either they are also roommates who cannot stand each other in this "superheroes meet the Odd Couple story." [YR]

Architect. Mike Baron, with art by Andie Tong. Big Head Press, 2007. $9.95.
In the 1970s architect Roark Dexter Smith was designing a special house when he disappeared after a fire. Now the son who grew up in ignorance of his roots has been given the property only to find that Dad was hiding a dark secret. [SA]

Army of Darkness. Dynamite Entertainment.
Based on the *Evil Dead* series of films, S-Mart employee Ash Williams (played by Bruce Campbell in the film) fights the demons summoned by the Necronomicon Many of the collections cross over with other characters including Freddy Krueger, the Marvel Zombies, and characters from the television show *Xena: Warrior Princess* (including one also played by Campbell). [SA]

> *Army of Darkness/Xena*, Vol. 1: *Why Not?* John Layman and Brandon Jerwa, with art by Miguel Montenegro and Fabiano Neves, 2009. $14.99.
>
> *Xena/Army of Darkness*, Vol. 2: *What Again?* Brandon Jerwa and Elliot Serrano, with art by Miguel Montenegro. 2009. $16.99.
>
> *Army of Darkness Collected Edition.* Sam and Ivan Raimi, with art by John Bolton (movie adaptation). 2006. $14.99.
>
> *Ash vs. the Classic Monsters.* James Kuhoric, with art by Kevin Sharpe and Fernando Blanco. 2007. $19.99.
>
> *Ashes to Ashes.* Andy Hartnell, with art by Nick Bradshaw and Etienne St-Laurent. 2007. $14.95.
>
> *From the Ashes.* James Kuhoric, with art by Fernando Blanco. 2008. $14.99.
>
> *Hellbillies & Deadnecks.* Mike Raicht, James Kuhoric with art by Scott Cohn. 2009. $16.99.
>
> *Home Sweet Hell.* James Kuhoric and Mike Raicht, with art by Fernando Blanco. 2009. $14.99.
>
> *The Long Road Home.* James Kuhoric and Mike Raicht, with art by Fernando Blanco. 2008. $14.99.

Old School and More. Various writers and artists. 2009. $14.95.
Shop Till You Drop Dead. James Kuhoric, with art by Nick Bradshaw and Sanford Greene. 2005. $14.99.
There will be additional volumes, including *Ash Saves Obama.*

Army@Love. Rick Veitch, with additional art by Gary Erskine. DC/Vertigo 2007-2010 $9.99-$14.99
The U.S. soldiers fighting in the Middle Eastern country of "Afbaghistan" are part of a new army where soldiers have cell phones, war has corporate sponsors, wild parties are part of R&R, and some soldiers have entered the "Hot Zone Club" in having sex in a combat zone. This satire of war, commercialism, and sex is a fun and strange read. [SA]
Vol. 1: *The Hot Zone Club*   Vol. 3: *Art of War*
Vol. 2: *Generation Pwned*

Artesia **series.** Mark Smylie. Archaia Studios Press, 2004–. $24.95 each.
An epic fantasy series about the titular heroine. Artesia travels around the Highlands of Daradja and has been everything from a concubine to a warrior. [SA]
Artesia   *Artesia Afire*
Artesia Afield   *Artesia Besieged* (coming soon)

Asterios Polyp. David Mazzucchelli. Pantheon Books, 2009. $29.95.
Asterios Polyp is a noted architect who never actually had any of his designs built. At age 50 his house burned down, leading him to reconsider his future while remembering his past. Recommended. [SA]

Astronauts in Trouble: Master Flight Plan. Larry Young, with art by Charlie Adlard and Matt Smith. AiT/Planet Lar, 2003. $19.95.
The title that gave the company its name, the *Astronauts in Trouble* books take place both in the future (2019 and 2029) and in the past (1959) and often involve news crews covering the stories. This volume collects several *Astronauts in Trouble* collections. [SA]

Auschwitz. Pascal Croci. Harry N. Abrams, 2003. $16.95.
Originally published in France, the book begins as a couple named Kazik and Cessia are being hunted by soldiers in the war-torn Bosnia of 1993. For the first time they talk to each other about what happened to them 50 years earlier in another war. This oversized volume also includes information on how it was made, including discussing the Holocaust survivors that Croci interviewed to learn more about what happened in the concentration camp. [SA]

Autobiographix. Dark Horse Books, 2003. $14.95.
A collection of short autobiographical stories by Sergio Aragones, Matt Wagner Gabriel Ba, Frank Miller, Paul Chadwick, Eddie Campbell, Will Eisner, and more. [YR]

The Aviary. Jamie Turner. Adhouse Books, 2007. $12.95.
Odd stories that include talking animals, robots, and more. [SA]

Aya. Marguerite Abouet, with art by Clément Ouberie. Drawn & Quarterly, 2007–. $19.95 each.
1978 was a time of prosperity in Africa's Ivory Coast (Cote d'Ivorie). Aya is a "studious and clear-sighted" teenage girl, and these books tell of her adventures and the activities and

problems of her family and friends. This award-winning series was originally published in France, though some libraries catalog it in 741.596668 due the author's African origin. [YR]
Aya   *Aya: The Secrets Come Out*
Aya of Yop City

B

Ball Peen Hammer. Adam Rapp and George O'Connor. First Second, 2009. $17.99.
In a dark and dystopian world a few people are hiding out from a plague but get drawn into something even worse. [SA]

Bambi and Her Pink Gun. Atsushi Kaneko. Digital Manga Publishing, 2005–. $12.95.
Bambi is a violent 16-year-old who has been hired by the "Old Men" to kidnap a strange child in order to keep him away from the vampire pop singer Gabba King. Only two of the seven Japanese volumes have been released to date. DMP has rated this "M." [SA]

Bardín the Superrealist. Max. Fantagraphics Books, 2006. $19.95.
Originally published in Spain, this award-winning graphic novel is subtitled "His Deeds, His Utterances, His Exploits, and His Perambulations," and contains several short, odd stories about Bardin. [SA]

Barefoot Gen. *Keiji Nakazawa.* Last Gasp, 2004–. $14.95.
When he was six years old Keiji Nakazawa survived the atomic bomb drop on Hiroshima. Years later he would use his experiences to tell the tale of a young boy named Gen who went through the same thing. The bomb is dropped in the first volume and the rest cover the aftermath and later years. This is a new and more complete translation than in the earlier editions, and some parts are in the process of being translated for the first time. Recommended. [SA]
#1: *A Cartoon Story of Hiroshima*   #5: *The Never-Ending War*
#2: *The Day After*   #6: *Writing the Truth*
#3: *Life After the Bomb*   #7: *Bones into Dust*
#4: *Out of the Ashes*   #8: *Merchants of Death*
The final two volumes have not yet been translated.

Bastard: Heavy Metal Dark Fantasy. Kazushi Hagiwara. VIZ, 2004. $9.99.
This fantasy manga features angels, demons, orcs, lizardmen, and more. The protagonist is Dark Schneider, a former evil wizard now fighting his old comrades. The series has been running for over 20 years in Japan and has been collected in over 27 volumes, many of which have been translated. The series has been rated M and comes with an "explicit content" warning on the cover. [SA]

Battle Royale Ultimate Edition, Vols. 1–5. Koushun Takami and Masayuki Taguchi. Tokyopop, 2007–2009. $24.99.
Based on Takami's book, this is ultimate version of "Survivor." Forty-two students (divided evenly among boys and girls) are sent to an island where the only way to get off is to kill everyone else. Tokyopop had previously released this in 15 smaller volumes, which had some changes from the Japanese version. The series is rated "M" and has a "explicit content." A live action film has also been made. [AO]

The Beats: A Graphic History. Edited by Paul Buhle. Hill and Wang, 2009. $22.00.
A look at the Beat Movement including writers such as Jack Kerouac, Allen Ginsberg, William Burroughs, and others as well as notable places, themes, and events. Creators include Harvey Pekar, Trina Robbins, Gary Dumm, Peter Kuper, and Anne Timmons. [SA]

Beg the Question. Bob Fingerman. Fantagraphics, 2002. HC.
A "slice of life" graphic novel that collects, revises, and expands on a story that had been previously published in a graphic novel and individual comics. The book centers around Rob Hoffman, an artist who draws pornographic comics, his girlfriend Sylvia, and some of their friends. [SA]

Berlin. Jason Lutes. Drawn & Quarterly, 2000–. $19.95.
Set in Berlin between 1928–1933, this collected comic series deals with various characters during the decline of the Weimar Republic and the rise of Nazi Germany. Characters include a reporter, an art student, a black jazz band, and a family torn apart over political beliefs. At least one more volume is planned. [SA]
> *Book One: City of Stones*
> *Book Two: City of Smoke*

Berserk. Kentaro Miura. Dark Horse/Digital Manga Publishing, 2003–. $13.95–.
A "dark fantasy" sword-and-sorcery manga dealing with Guts, a one-eyed, one-armed mercenary warrior who fights demonic creatures, and Griffith, the leader of a mercenary group. Over 30 volumes are out, and there is also an anime, both of which are noted for their violence. [SA]

Best American Comics. Houghton Mifflin Co., 2006–. $22.00.
Beginning in 2006 Houghton Mifflin added comics to its series of "Best American" books, and many of the works featured are by writers and/or taken from books that are featured throughout this Appendix including Art Spiegelman, Robert Crumb, Charles Burns, Jeffrey Brown, Ben Katchor, Gilbert Hernandez, Alison Bechdel, and Adrian Tomine. Editors have included Harvey Pekar, Chris Ware, Jessica Abel, Matt Madden, and Lynda Barry. Some of the material contains nudity and may appear in other works in this appendix. [SA]

Best Erotic Comics. Edited by Greta Christina. Last Gasp, 2008 –. 19.95.
Beginning in 2008, Last Gasp published these collections, featuring stories from various years. Some stories feature heterosexual or homosexual sex, while others feature no sexual activity at all. As with the *Best American Comics* series, some artists and titles that are in this Appendix are also in these books including Phoebe Gloeckner, Ellen Forney, Peter Kuper, Gilbert Hernandez, Alison Bechdel, and Daniel Clowes. Submissions for these volumes are required to be both "hot" and "interesting in some way in addition to being hot" so that the "literary smut" featured here can contain "hot sex" but with a "literary or artistic quality." [AO]

The Best of Simon and Kirby. Edited by Steve Saffel. Titan Books, 2009. $39.95.
Some of the best stories of the 1930s and 1940s by one of comics' greatest writer/artist teams, Joe Simon and Jack Kirby. Additional volumes are planned. [YR]

Big Baby. Charles Burns. Fantagraphics Books, 2007. $16.95.
Various stories by mainly involving Tony Delmonto, the large-headed youngster known as Big Baby. Of special note is the story "Teen Plague," which is a precursor to *Black Hole*. An additional Burns collection not in this Appendix is 2001's *Skin Deep*. [SA]

Big Book of Barry Ween, Boy Genius. Judd Winick. Oni Press, 2009. $19.95.
An omnibus collection of the 12 previously collected stories about the 10-year-old super genius Barry Ween, as he deals with aliens, time travel, terrorists, talking monkeys, and the results of his own experiments. The only person who knows how smart he really is, and causes much of his problems, is his best friend Jeremy. A very funny book, but despite the character's age the language makes it for older readers. [SA]

Bigfoot. Steve Niles and Rob Zombie, with art by Richard Corben. IDW, 2005. $19.99.
Musician Zombie teams with popular writer Niles in this collected work. Thirty years earlier, Bill Fuller saw his parents killed by a creature that could only be described as Bigfoot. Now he's ready for his revenge. [SA]

Birth of a Nation: A Comic Novel. Aaron McGruder and Reginald Hudlin, with art by Kyle Baker. Crown Publishers, 2004.
In this political parody every person in East Saint Louis, Illinois, is denied the ability to vote because they all appear on a list of convicted criminals. In response they decide to secede from the United States and form the Republic of Blackland. The format of this book is art with captions below each panel. [SA]

A Bit of Madness. Emmanuel Civello and Thomas Mosdi. Checker, 2005. $24.95.
Originally in French, this graphic novel tells the adventure of the elf, Igguk, who must save the world of Faerie. This was originally serialized in the French version of *Heavy Metal*. [SA]

Black Cherry. Doug TenNapel. Image Comics, 2007. $17.99.
Tough-guy mobster Eddie Paretti agrees to steal a body from his boss, but this gets him into a situation involving aliens, demons, a priest who helped him as a boy, and Black Cherry, a stripper that he falls in love with. [SA]

The Black Diamond Detective Agency. Eddie Campbell. First Second, 2007.
In 1899, John Hardin, who at one point was part of a gang until he headed west, is framed for an explosion. He is now hunted by both the police and the famous Black Diamond Agency. He now must clear his name and get revenge. [SA]

Black Hole. Charles Burns. Pantheon Books, 2005. $27.50.
Set in 1970s Seattle, a new sexually transmitted disease is being spread around the local teenagers, a disease that causes deformities. Some can be hidden while others are more obvious. The book follows several teens—some infected, some not—and what happens to them. Recommended. [SA]

Black Jack. Osamu Tezuka. Vertical, 2008–2009, $16.95 each.
One of Tezuka's best-known works, *Black Jack* features a master surgeon who operates illegally. While he often charges high fees he also secretly gives money to those in need. His skills are extraordinary, doing surgeries that most would think impossible. VIZ had previously produced English translations of this work, which has also inspired animated adaptations. [YR]

Blankets. Craig Thompson. Top Shelf, 2005. $29.95.
An award-winning highly acclaimed graphic novel, the autobiographical work tells of Thompson's early life, growing up in a religious family, his first love, and his entering adulthood. At over 600 pages, this is one of the largest original graphic novels and it is highly recommended. [SA]

Blue Pills: A Positive Love Story. Frederik Peeters. Houghton Mifflin, 2008. $18.95.
This touching, award-winning memoir by Swiss artist Peeters tells the story of how he met his girlfriend Cati who, along with her young son, is HIV positive. Originally in French, this is a story of love and hope. Recommended. [SA]

Bond(z). Tōko Kawai. 801 Media, 2007. $15.95.
A yaoi one-shot about two friends who sleep with each other after a drunken night and despite having girlfriends think they may want to do it again. [AO]

Boneyard. Richard Moore. NBM, 2001-. $9.95 each.
Michael Paris inherited a plot of land from his grandfather that turned out to be a cemetery where the residents are anything but resting in peace. They include Abby, a 2,000-year-old vampire; Nessie, a seductive "creature from the Black Lagoon"; and Sid, an animated skeleton. But these are friendly creatures and true evil comes from other places. The series is often humorous, making fun of horror clichés. There have been six volumes published, but the first four have been rereleased in color. [YR]

The Book of Ballads. Charles Vess, with additional writers and artists. Tor, 2004. $24.95.
Adaptations of many English, Irish, and Scottish songs and folktales. Vess is the primary artist, while writers include such notable fantasy writers as Neil Gaiman, Jane Yolen, and Charles DeLint. [YR]

El Borbah. Charles Burns. Fantagraphics, 2005. $16.99.
A crude and violent individual, El Borbah is a Mexican wrestler turned private investigator who ends up with very strange cases. Many of the stories were originally written for *Heavy Metal* magazine and have previously been collected. [SA]

Bosnian Flat Dog. Max Andersson and Lars Sjunnesson. Fantagraphics Books, 2006. $13.95.
This unusual Swedish graphic novel features an absurdist trip to Bosnia where dogs have mutated to avoid being run over, zombies kidnap peacekeepers, and the corpse of Marshall Tito keeps popping up. [SA]

Bottomless Belly Button. Dash Shaw. Fantagraphics, 2008. $29.99.
This 720-page work was on the "Best of the Year" lists of various publications and tells the story of a family (the Looneys) gathered together when their parents announce they are divorcing after 40 years. While the story follows various members of the family, the focus is on Peter, who is drawn with a froglike face. Also by Shaw is *The Unclothed Man in the 35th Century A.D.* (2009). [SA]

Box Office Poison. Alex Robinson. Top Shelf.
This award-winning 600-page volume features various characters, including Sherman, a failed writer who works in a bookstore and has problems with his love life, and Ed, a cartoonist who ends up working for the elderly creator of a "Batman-like" character. Librarians will appreciate the questions that Sherman gets at the bookstore such as the person looking for the book with the "red cover." The second book contains an additional 60 pages of stories with the characters. [SA]

    Box Office Poison, 2001. $29.95.
    BOP! More Box Office Poison, 2003. $9.95.

The Boys. Garth Ennis, with art by Darick Robertson. Dynamite Entertainment, 2007–. $19.99 each.
Originally published by DC/Wildstorm, the Boys are a superpowered CIA team whose job it is to keep and eye on, and if necessary take down, the corporate controlled superheroes in America. The series often contains foul language, nudity, and sometimes disgusting images, as well as parodies of existing superhero characters. [AO]

Vol. 1: *The Name of the Game*   Vol. 3: *Good for the Soul*
Vol. 2: *Get Some*   Vol. 4: *We Gotta Go Now*

There will be additional volumes, and Dynamite has also put out "Definitive Editions" that contain the contents of two softcover collections. In addition, there is a spin-off collected limited series, *Herogasm*.

Bratpack. Rick Veitch. King Hell Press, 2009. $19.95.
A new edtion featuring parodies of several superhero archtypes and their teen sidekicks. [SA]

Breakdowns: Portrait of the Artist as a Young %@&*! Art Spiegelman. Pantheon Books, 2008. $27.50.
This book contains both new material and a reprint of the oversized version originally published in 1977 when it was subtitled "From Maus to Now. An anthology of strips by art spiegelman" [*sic*]. Included in the work is the original three-page *Maus* story as well as *Prisoner of the Hell Planet*, which also appeared in the collected *Maus*. Due to nudity and other content, the book has "adults only" printed on the cover at the author's request. [SA]

Britten and Brülightly. Hannah Berry. Metropolitan Books, 2008. $20.00.
Set in 1940s London, this noir story tracks private detective Fernandez Britten (known as the Heartbreaker for his speciality of proving infidelity) and his partner Brülightly investigate a mysterious murder. [SA]

Jeffrey Brown memoirs.
Brown has detailed many of the events of his life, especially various romantic relationships that he has had over the years. The books are generally small in height (some under six inches), and are in black and white. They are also very good and highly recommended. [SA]

TOP SHELF
Unlikely. 2003. $14.95.
Every Girl is the End of the World For Me. 2005. $8.00.
Any Easy Intimacy (AEIOU). 2005. $12.00.
Clumsy. 2006. $10.00. (originally self-published and came out first)

TOUCHSTONE/SIMON & SCHUSTER
Little Things: A Memoir in Slices. 2008. $14.00.
Funny Misshapen Body: A Memoir. 2009. $16.00.

Brownsville. Neil Kleid, illustrated by Jake Allen. NBM, 2006. $18.95.
A partially true crime novel primarily set in the 1930s in the Brownsville section of Brooklyn where Albert "Allie" Tanennbaum becomes a gangster and becomes part of "Murder Inc." The story includes the murder of Dutch Shultz and features other famous Jewish and Italian gangsters of the time. This book is part of NBM's ComicLit line, as is Kleid's 2009 work *The Big Kahn*. See *Jew Gangster* for a similar theme. [SA]

Buddha. Osamu Tezuka. Vertical, 2006 –. $14.95 each.
Tezuka's story of the life of Prince Siddhartha, who became Gautama Buddha. The series contains some violence and nudity. The 14 Japanese volumes have been collected in eight large, flopped volumes. [SA]

Vol. 1: *Kapilavastu*   Vol. 5: *Deer Park*
Vol. 2: *The Four Encounters*   Vol. 6: *Ananda*
Vol. 3: *Devadatta*   Vol. 7: *Ajatasattu*
Vol. 4: *The Forest of Uruvela*   Vol. 8: *Jetavana*

Buddy Books. Peter Bagge. Fantagraphics, 2005–. $14.95.
Consisting of *Buddy Does Seattle* (2005) and *Buddy Does Jersey* (2007), these are the complete Buddy Bradley stories that Bagge has written for the comic *Hate* and that were previously collected in six volumes. Buddy is a bit of a loser who hangs out with his friends "Stinky" and George and is in a relationship with first Val and then Lisa. The first volume discusses topics like the "Grunge scene," while the second has him moving to New Jersey with Lisa. There is a great deal of humor along with sex and drugs. [SA]

Buffy the Vampire Slayer
Taken from the popular television show, these comics portray the additional adventures of Buffy, who protects the world from vampires, demons, and other evils. Dark Horse's Omnibus collects the older comics series as well as various limited series and one-shots. The "Season Eight" titles continue the story after the show ended, with some stories written by *Buffy* creator Joss Whedon. IDW owns the rights to the spin-off series *Angel* about a good vampire and has various limited and ongoing series, some that take place after the series finale. IDW also has books with the "sometimes good, sometimes bad" vampire, Spike. [YR]

DARK HORSE
Buffy the Vampire Slayer Omnibus, Vols. 1–7. Various writers and artists. 2007–. $24.95.
Buffy the Vampire Slayer Season Eight. Unless indicated, written by Joss Whedon, art by
Georges Jeanty. 2007–. $15.95 each.
Vol. 1: *The Long Road Home*
Vol. 2: *No Future for You.* Also written by Brian K. Vaughan, with additional art by
Cliff Richards.
Vol. 3: *Wolves at the Gate.* Also written by Drew Goddard, with additional art by
Farel Dalrymple.
Vol. 4: *Time of Your Life.* Also written by Jeph Loeb, with additional art by Karl
Moline and others.
Vol. 5: *Predators and Prey.* By various writers, with additional art by Cliff Richards.
There will be additional volumes of both titles.
Fray: Future Slayer. Joss Whedon, with art by Karl Moline and Andy Owens. 2003.
$19.95. Far in the future, a teenage girl becomes the first Slayer in centuries.
IDW
Angel Omnibus. 2008. $24.99. Collects several limited series that have previously been collected on their own. Creators include Peter David, Dan Jolley, Jeff Marriotte, and others.
Angel: After the Fall (series), Vols. 1–4. 2008–$24.99. Joss Whedon and Bryan Lynch,
with art by Franco Urru.
Angel: Auld Lang Syne. Scott Tipton with David Messina. 2007. $19.99.

Angel: Blood and Trenches. John Byrne. 2009. $17.99.

Spike: After the Fall. Bryan Lynch, with art by Franco Urru. 2009. $21.99.

Spike vs. Dracula. Peter David, with art by various. 2006. $19.99.

There will be additional volumes of the series and limited series.

But I Like It. Joe Sacco. Fantagraphics, 2006. $24.95.

A collection of Sacco's various comics from over the years that recounted his days working for a punk rock band that was touring around Europe. The book also includes text pieces, early examples of the artwork, concert posters that he drew, and even a CD of one of the bands. [SA]

C

Cain Saga and **Godchild.** Kaori Yuki. VIZ. $8.99.

Set in London in the late 1800s, the *Cain Saga* is the story of Earl Cain Hargreaves, the heir to a family with dark secrets including madness, murder, and incest. The five volumes of the *Cain Saga* are followed by the eight volumes of *Godchild* in which Cain, along with his butler and 10-year-old half sister solve crimes and mysteries. The first series is rated M for mature readers, while the second is rated for a teen audience. [SA]

Cairo. G. Willow Wilson, with art by M.K. Perker. DC/Vertigo, 2007. $24.99 (HC); $17.99 (SC).

A drug-runner, a journalist, an American expatiate, a stuck-on-the-wrong-side-of-the-border Israeli soldier, and a young man with a secret plan find themselves mixed up with a genie and other strange creatures and a plot that could change the world. [SA]

Camelot 3000. Mike W. Barr, with art by Brian Bolland, Terry Austin, Bruce Patterson, and Dick Giordano. DC Comics, 2008. $34.99.

A new collection of DC's first maxiseries. In the year 3000 Earth is threatened by aliens, and with the aid of archeology student Tom Prentice, King Arthur has returned to save both England and the world. He must first awaken Merlin and find the Knights of the Round Table who have all been reincarnated in various forms, including a monstrous giant and a woman. But the aliens aren't the only threat, as Morgan LeFey has also returned. And will Lancelot and Guinevere repeat their old indiscretions? [YR]

Cancer Made Me a Shallower Person. Miriam Engelberg. HarperCollins, 2006. $14.95.

When Miriam Engelberg was 43 she was diagnosed with breast cancer. This "memoir in comics" consists of several short stories about how she dealt with it. [SA]

Cancer Vixen: A True Story. Marisa Acocella Marchetto. Alfred A. Knopf, 2006. $22.00.

The author was a cartoonist for the *New Yorker* and elsewhere and engaged to a famous restaurant owner when she learned she had breast cancer and no insurance. The book tells what she went through, including her wedding and treatment. Some of this material was originally published in *Glamour* and some of the books sales go to providing breast care to underprivileged women. [SA]

Can't Get No. Rich Veitch. DC/Vertigo. $19.99.

Chad Roe's company created the ultimate permanent marker but was sued out of business due to graffiti. A drunken night ended with his having the marker written all over his body. He goes a little crazy across America to make sense of things around the same time 9/11 happened. The book is rectangular in shape and is mainly silent except for narration boxes. [SA]

Cantarella. You Higuri. Go! Comi, 2005–. $10.99.
A fantasy historical work based on the life of Cesare Borgia, a member of the infamous Italian family. Besides family intrigue, Cesare is also haunted by demons since his father, Cardinal Rodrigo Borgia (later Pope Alexander VI) sold his soul to the devil. The title comes from the name of the poison used by the Borgias. The series has been translated in several countries and went for 10 volumes in Japan before going on hiatus. [YR]

Capote in Kansas. Andre Parks, with art by by Chris Samnee. Oni, 2005. $11.95.
The time in which Truman Capote went to Kansas to investigate the murders that he would write about in *In Cold Blood* was made into two feature films. Now the story is told in a graphic novel. [SA]

Caricature. Daniel Clowes. Fantagraphics, 1998. $29.95.
A book of nine short stories including the titular one. [SA]

Carnet De Voyage. Craig Thompson. Top Shelf, 2005. $14.95.
A memoir by Thompson in which he illustrates the three months he spent traveling in France, Spain, the Alps, and Morocco researching his next (and currently unreleased) graphic novel, *Habibi*. [SA]

Cartoon Histories and Guides. Larry Gonick.
For over 30 years, Gonick has been creating nonfiction comics covering everything from history, to science, math, and even sex. The books have been put out by various publishers, and even those that may be a little out of date are still of interest. The works are sometimes told tongue-in-cheek and are informative and entertaining. They may also be shelved various places in the library. [YR]

> *The Cartoon History of the Universe Books I–III.* Doubleday (I and II) and W.W. Norton (III). $21.95. Over 900 pages combined, covering history from the Big Bang to the Renaissance (including stories from the Bible and from Greek myths).
> *The Cartoon History of the Modern World Part 1.* HarperCollins, 2007. $17.95; and *Cartoon History of the Modern World: From the Bastille to Baghdad.* HarperCollins, 2009. $18.99. Cover the history of the New World as well as other events that happened from the fifteenth to eighteenth centuries, and from the eighteenth century to today.
> *The Cartoon History of the United States.* HarperCollins. $18.95. From the founding through the early 1990s.
> *The Cartoon Guide to Chemistry.* With Craig Criddle. Harper. $16.95.
> *The Cartoon Guide to the Environment.* With Alice Outwater.
> *The Cartoon Guide to Genetics.* With Mark Wheelis. HarperCollins. $17.95.
> *The Cartoon Guide to Physics.* With Art Huffman. HarperCollins. $17.95.
> *The Cartoon Guide to Sex.* With Christine Devault. HarperCollins. $17.99.
> *The Cartoon Guide to Stastistics.* With Woollcott Smith. HarperCollins. $12.95.

Castaways. Rob Vollmar, with art by Pablo G. Callejo. NBM. $17.95 (HC); $11.95 (SC).
Set during the Great Depression, 13-year-old Tucker Freeman is convinced by the woman who was taken in by his family that he should leave. He spends a short time "riding the rails" and learning the life of the hobo. *Kings in Disguise*, which is also in this appendix, has a similar theme. Also of interest by the same writers is *Bluesman* (NBM, 2008). [YR]

Cerebus the Aardvark. Dave Sim. Aardvark-Vanaheim. $25.00–35.00.
Almost all 300 issues of this epic and occasionally controversial title have been collected in these 16 volumes. The title character in this award-winning work is Cerebus, a three-foot-tall bipedal talking Aardvark who lives in a medieval world filled with danger and odd people, though money, power, and alcohol is enough for him. Topics such as politics, religion, and relationships are covered, and there are many parodies of familar comic book, literary, and real life characters. The books tend to run between 200–600 pages and were one of the first, if not the first, series to be collected. Beginning with the fourth volume, some background art was drawn by the artist Gerhard. [SA]

Cerebus	*Reads (Mothers and Daughters,* Vol. 3)
High Society	*Minds (Mothers and Daughters,* Vol. 4)
Church and State I	*Guys*
Church and State II	*Rick's Story*
Jaka's Story	*Going Home (Going Home,* Vol. 1)
Melmoth	*Form and Void (Going Home,* Vol. 2)
Flight (Mothers and Daughters, Vol. 1)	*Latter Days (Latter Days,* Vol. 1)
Women (Mothers and Daughters, Vol. 2)	*The Last Day (Latter Days,* Vol. 2)

Chance in Hell. Gilbert Hernandez. Fantagraphics Books, 2007. $16.95.
As a child, Empress was homeless and abused. Taken in by a kind man, she goes though her teens and adulthood but continues to hold an interest in prostitutes, criminals, and others on the bottom levels of society. A gripping and sometimes disturbing work. [SA]

Charley's War. Pat Mills, with art by Joe Colquhon. Titan Books, 2004–. $19.95 each.
These volumes collects stories originally published between 1979–1985 in the British comic *Battle Picture Weekly* about 16-year-old Charley Bourne who lies about his age and joins the army to fight in World War I. [SA]

2 June–1 August 1916	*Blue's Story*
1 August–17 October 1916	*Return to the Front*
17 October 1916–21 February 1917	*Underground and Over the Top*

More volumes are expected.

Chicken with Plums. Marjane Satrapi. Pantheon Books, 2006. $16.95 (HC).
Satrapi wrote this book about Nasser Ali Kahn, a relative of hers who was famous for playing a kind of drum known as a tar. The book has both flashbacks and flash forwards but primarily takes place in 1958 Tehran. Libraries have cataloged this both in Biography and in the 955s (ML419 for LoC). [SA]

A Child's Life and Other Stories. Phoebe Gloeckner. Revised Edition Frog Ltd., 2000. $18.95.
This occasionally controversial work has several semi-autobiographical elements. The character in many, Minnie, has a stepfather who is attracted to younger girls. [AO]

Clive Barker's Hellraiser: Collected Best, Vols 1–3. Various writers and artists. Checker, 2002–2004. $19.95–$26.95.
Originally published by Marvel comics, these are new stories based on the evil creatures in the 1980s films. Writers and artists include Neil Gaiman, Mike Mignola, Colleen Doran, Dave McKean, and Barker himself. [SA]

Closer. Antony Johnston, illustrated by Mike Norton and Leanne Buckley. Oni, 2004. $14.95.
A group of scientists and the daughter of their dead colleague are invited to a house on an island. There they are confronted by another scientist who knew about their failed teleportation experiment 30 years earlier. He has solved the problem and it leads to murder. [SA]

Clyde Fans Book 1. Seth. Drawn & Quarterly, 2004. $19.95.
This work, originally serialized in *Palookaville*, is subtitled "A Picture Novela in Two Books." In the first part of the book set in 1997, elderly Abraham Matchcard, owner of the shop Clyde Fans (founded by his father) talks about the history of the company and how to be a good salesman, which his brother Simon was not. The second part showed how Simon in 1957 Canada was unable to sell. It is not known when Book 2 will come out. [SA]

The Collected Omaha the Cat Dancer. Reed Waller and Kate Worley. NBM/Ameriotica, 2005–. $12.95.
New collections of this popular adults-only title, previous versions of which have appeared in a number of academic libraries. The main characters are anthropomorphic animals (who are very human-like when it comes to breasts and sexual organs). Popular exotic dancer Omaha gets involved in crime, conspiracies, and murder. The series had previously been collected by Kitchen Sink and Fantagraphics. NBM has collected at least seven volumes for their Ameriotica line. [AO]

The Complete Bite Club. Howard Chaykin and David Tischman, with art by David Hahn. DC/Vertigo, 2007. $19.99.
It's Dracula meets *The Sopranos*. Collecting the two *Bite Club* limited series, this collection is set in Miami where the vampire family the Del Toros control organized crime. [SA]

The Complete Crumb. R. Crumb. Fantagraphics Books, 1996–. $19.99 each.
This collection presents Crumb's work in chronological order and includes such works as reprints of the Zap Comics, the adventures of Fritz the Cat, as well as works that have not been seen in decades. The 17+ volumes tend to go in and out of print. [SA]

Vol. 1: *The Early Years of Bitter Struggle*
Vol. 2: *Some More Years of Bitter Struggle*
Vol. 3: *Starring Fritz the Cat*
Vol. 4: *Mr. Sixties*
Vol. 5: *Happy Hippy Comix*
Vol. 6: *On the Crest of a Wave*
Vol. 7: *Hot 'n Heavy*
Vol. 8: *The Death of Fritz the Cat*
Vol. 9: *R. Crumb vs. the Sisterhood*
Vol. 10: *Crumb Advocates Violent Overthrow!*
Vol. 11: *Mr. Natural Committed to a Mental Institution*
Vol. 12: *We're Livin' in the Lap of Luxury*
Vol. 13: *Season of the Snoid*
Vol. 14: *The Early 80s and Weirdo Magazine*
Vol. 15: *Mode O'Day*
Vol. 16: *The Mid-1980s: More Years of Bitter Struggle*
Vol. 17: *Cave Wimp*

The Complete Jon Sable Freelance, **Vols.** 1–8. Mike Grell. IDW, 2005–. $24.99; and ***John Sable, Freelance: Blood Trail.*** Mike Grell. IDW, 2006. $19.95.
Jon Sable is a former Olympic athlete who writes children's books under a pen name. He is also a bounty hunter and mercenary whose wife and children were murdered. IDW has been collecting the comic originally published by First Comics in the 1980s and also had Grell

create a new limited series. The collection of older material may also be listed as *The Complete Mike Grell's Jon Sable Freelance.* [SA]

Conan and Red Sonja
Since his creation by Robert E. Howard in 1932, Conan the Barbarian has appeared in stories, novels, movies, television, and, of course, comic books. In the 1970s and 1980s Marvel Comics has put out two notable publications—*Conan the Barbarian* and *Savage Sword of Conan*—that recounted his long ago adventures during the "Hyborian Age." The rights to the character are currently owned by Dark Horse, who has collected much of the Marvel Comics works as well as produced stories of their own. In both cases, some of Howard's own stories, such as *Tower of the Elephant* have been adapted. Introduced in Marvel's *Conan the Barbarian* #23, Red Sonja, the "she-devil" with a sword, has also had many adventures in that far-off time. While Dark Horse has possession of the Conan stories, the Sonja tales are currently owned by Dynamite Entertainment, who has both collected Marvel's *Red Sonja* comic titles and created new ones of their own. [YR]

The Chronicles of Conan. Dark Horse, 2003–. $15.95–$16.95.
Primarily by Roy Thomas with additional stories by J. M. DeMatteis, Bruce Jones, and Steven Grant. The main artists were Barry Windsor-Smith and John Buscema, with additional artists including Gil Kane, Neal Adams, Val Mayerik, Howard Chaykin, Ernie Chan, Tony DeZuniga, Sal Buscema, Bob McLeod, Alfredo Alcala, and Mark Silvestri. Volumes as of October 2009 are:
  Vol. 1: *Tower of the Elephant and Other Stories*
  Vol. 2: *Rogues in the House and Other Stories*
  Vol. 3: *The Monster of the Monoliths and Other Stories*
  Vol. 4: *The Song of Red Sonja and Other Stories*
  Vol. 5: *The Shadow in the Tomb and Other Stories*
  Vol. 6: *The Curse of the Golden Skull and Other Stories*
  Vol. 7: *The Dweller in Pool and Other Stories*
  Vol. 8: *Brothers of the Blade and Other Stories*
  Vol. 9: *Riders of the River-Dragons and Other Stories*
  Vol. 10: *When Giants Walk the Earth and Other Stories*
  Vol. 11: *The Dance of the Skull and Other Stories*
  Vol. 12: *The Beast King and Other Stories*
  Vol. 13: *Whispering Shadows and Other Stories*
  Vol. 14: *Shadow of the Beast and Other Stories*
  Vol. 15: *The Corridor of Mullah-Kajar and Other Stories*
  Vol. 16: *The Eternity War and Other Stories*
  Vol. 17: *The Creation Quest and Other Stories*
  Vol. 18: *Isle of the Dead*

Conan. Dark Horse, 2004–. $15.95–$24.95.
These feature new stories by Kurt Busiek (Vols. 1–4) and Tim Truman (Vols. 4–) with art by Cary Nord, Greg Ruth, Michael Wm. Kaluta, Mike Mignola, Scott Allie, Haden Blackman, Tomás Giorello, and Richard Corben.
  Vol. 0: *Born on the Battlefield*
  Vol. 1: *The Frost Giant's Daughter and Other Stories*

Vol. 2: *The God in the Bowl and Other Stories*
Vol. 3: *Tower of the Elephant and Other Stories*
Vol. 4: *The Hall of the Dead*
Vol. 5: *Rogues in the House*
Vol. 6: *The Hand of the Nergel*
Vol. 7: *Cimmeria*

Savage Sword of Conan, Vols. 1–6. Roy Thomas and Various artists. Dark Horse, 2008–. $17.95.
These 500+ page volumes includes art by as Barry Windsor-Smith, John Buscema, Alfredo Alcala, Jim Starlin, Al Milgrom, Pablo Marcos, and Walter Simonson.

OTHER CONAN COLLECTIONS
    Conan and the Demons of Khitai. Akira Yoshida, with art by Paul Lee and Pat Lee. Dark Horse, 2006. $12.95.
    Conan and the Jewels of Gwahlur. P. Craig Russell, with art by Lovern Kindzierski. Dark Horse, 2005. $13.95.
    Conan and the Midnight God. Joshua Dystart, with art by Will Conrad. Dark Horse, 2007. $14.95.
    Conan and the Songs of the Dead. Joe R. Landsdale and Timothy Truman, with art by Truman. Dark Horse, 2007. $14.95.
    Conan: The Blood-Stained Crown and Other Stories. Kurt Busiek and Fabian Nicieza, with art by Cary Nord, Eric Powell, John Severin, Bruce Timm, and Timothy Truman. Dark Horse, 2008. $14.95.
    Conan: Book of Thoth. Kurt Busiek and Len Wein, with art by Kelley Jones. Dark Horse, 2006. $17.95.
There will be additional volumes of all series.

FROM DYNAMITE ENTERTAINMENT

Adventures of Red Sonja, Vols. 1–3. Roy Thomas and Bruce Jones, with art by Frank Thorne, John Buscema, and others. $19.99.
Collections of the series originally published by Marvel Comics.

Red Sonja: She Devil with a Sword. $19.99 each.
New adventures, with authors including Michael Avon Oeming, Ron Marz, and Mike Carey, with art by Mel Rubi, Pablo Marcos, and others.

Vol. 1 (no subtitle)	Vol. 4: *Animals and More*
Vol. 2: *Arrowsmiths*	Vol. 5: *World on Fire*
Vol. 3: *Rise of Gath*	Vol. 6: *Death*

There will be additional volumes.

Crawl Space, Vol. 1: Xxxombies. Rick Rememder and Kieron Dwyer, with art by Tony Moore. Image Comics, 2008. $12.99.
It's the 1970s, there's a zombie outbreak, and the cast and crew of a pornographic film are caught in the middle of it. [SA]

Creepy Archives and Eerie Archives. Various writers and artists. Dark Horse, 2008–. $49.95.
New collections of the classic horror magazines of the 1960s. Notable creators include Gene

Colan, Steve Ditko, Joe Orlando, Wally Wood, John Severin, Archie Goodwin, E. Nelson Bridwell, and Eando Binder (who was really the science fiction writing brothers Earl and Otto Binder). At least five volumes of *Creepy* and two volumes of *Eerie* are available. [YR]

Criminal. Ed Brubaker, with art by Sean Phillips. Marvel/Icon, 2007–. $14.99–.
These Eisner-winning stories concentrate on several different criminal characters with interlinked pasts, acquaintances, and settings. Notable from the same team are Sleeper and Incognito. [SA]

Coward	*The Dead and the Dying*
Lawless	*Bad Night*

Criminal Macabre: The Cal McDonald Mysteries. Steve Niles. Dark Horse Comics, 2004–. $12.95–$14.95.
Starting off in short stories and novels, Cal McDonald is the main character of the comic *Criminal Macabre*. He is a detective who specializes in the paranormal and even works with supernatural beings including an undead ghoul. These collections include stories from the comic as well as from limited series and other titles. Artists for these volumes include Ben Templesmith, Kelley Jones, Kyle Hotz, and Nick Stakal. IDW and Dark Horse have also published prose works based on the comic (see Appendix B). [SA]

Criminal Macabre	*My Demon Baby*
Last Train to Deadsville	*Cell Block 666*
Two Red Eyes	

***Crying Freeman*, Vols. 1–5.** Kazuo Koike, with art by Ryoichi Ikegami. Dark Horse, 2006–2007. $14.95.
Yo Hinomura was hypnotized by the 108 Dragons clan of the Chinese Mafia to become the master assassin known as Crying Freeman, but he still sheds tears after each hit and falls in love with one of his targets. Dark Horse's volumes (rated 18+) collect the nine Japanese volumes. A previous translation had been published by VIZ and the work has had both animated and live-action adaptations. [SA]

Cthulhu Tales. Various writers and artists. Boom! Studios, 2008–. $15.99 each.
Anthology that deals with people who have the misfortune of dealing with Lovecraft's Elder God. See also *Fall of Cthulhu*. [YR]

Vol. 1 (no subtitle)	Vol. 3: *Chaos of the Mind*
Vol. 2: *Whispers of Madness*	

Curses. Kevin Huizenga. Drawn & Quarterly, 2006. $21.95.
A collection of stories featuring Huizenga's character of Glen Ganges and his unusual experiences, including a story where he must pluck a feather from an ogre in order to remove a curse. Along the way he meets others who need help from the feather and give him things like an "enchanted Styrofoam take-home container" to help him on his way. [SA]

CVO: Covert Vampiric Operations. IDW 2004–. $17.99–$19.99.
Not only do vampires exist but some work for the U.S. government, taking on missions for the intelligence system that only they can handle. [SA]

  CVO: Covert Vampiric Operations. Alex Garner and Jeff Mariotte, with art by Gabriel
      Hernandez and Mindy Lee.

CVO: African Blood. El Torres, with art by Luis Czerniawski.
CVO: Rogue State. Jeff Mariotte, with art by Antonio Vazquez.

D

Daddy's Girl. Debbie Drechsler. Fantagraphics Books, 2008. $14.95.
A collection of autobiographical comics by Drechsler about her childhood, including her sexual abuse by her father. [SA]

Daisy Kutter: The Last Train. Kazu Kibuishi. Viper Comics, 2005. $10.95.
A "steampunk" Western in which locomotives and robots exist side by side. Former bandit Daisy is hired to test the security of a train but gets set up. [YR]

Damn Nation. Andrew Cosby, with art by J. Alexander. Dark Horse, 2005. $12.95.
The United States has been taken over by vampire-like creatures that were once human. The borders are sealed and the U.S. government is based in London. Word has gotten out that there may be a cure, and a team must try to retrieve it. But the creatures may not be only thing working against them. [SA]

The Damned: Three Days Dead. Cullen Bunn, with art by Brian Hurtt. Oni Books, 2007. $14.95.
What happens when Prohibition-era gangsters get involved with demons from hell? [SA]

The Dark Horse Book of . . . . Various artists. Dark Horse, 2003–. $14.95–$15.95.
Short story collections with horror themes, some scary, some silly, and some with characters from other books, including Hellboy. Writers and artists include Mike Mignola, Eric Powel, Evan Dorkin, Jill Thompson, and Bob Fingerman. [YR]

> *The Dark Horse Book of Ghosts*   *The Dark Horse Book of the Dead*
> *The Dark Horse Book of Monsters*   *The Dark Horse Book of Witchcraft*

Dark Horse Omnibuses. Various writers and artists. $24.95.
Besides *Buffy* and *Star Wars*, Dark Horse has collected many ongoing series, limited series, and one-shots in Omnibus collections. Some are new stories based on the film series *Aliens, Predator, Terminator, The Mask,* and *Indiana Jones.* Others are from original works. *Barb Wire* is about a bar owner and bounty hunter in a decaying city. *Alien Legion* deals with an interplanetary "Foreign Legion." The *Dark Horse Heroes Omnibus* features the adventures of various superpowered beings. Ghost is a supernatural hero, back from the dead to fight evil. *Too Much Coffee Man* by Shannon Wheeler is a superhero parody. *X* deals with a mysterious masked killer of the corrupt. Several of these series will have additional volumes. [YR]

> *Alien Legion Omnibus*, Vol. 1
> *Aliens Omnibus*, Vols. 1–6
> *Aliens vs. Predator Omnibus*,
>   Vols. 1–2
> *Barb Wire Omnibus*, Vol. 1 [SA]
> *Dark Horse Heroes Omnibus*, Vol. 1
> *Ghost Omnibus*, Vols. 1–2
> *Indiana Jones Omnibus*, Vols. 1–2
>
> *Indiana Jones Omnibus: The Further*
>   *Adventures*, Vol. 1
> *The Mask Omnibus*, Vols. 1–2
> *Adventures of the Mask Omnibus*, Vol. 1–
> *Predator Omnibus*, Vols. 1–4
> *Terminator Omnibus*, Vols. 1–2
> *Too Much Coffee Man Omnibus*, Vol. 1 [SA]
> *X Omnibus*, Vols. 1–2

Dark Hunger. Christine Feehan, with art by Zid. Penguin/Berkeley Books, 2007. $10.00.
Riordan is a Carpathian, an ancient race who hunts vampires and may become one if they do
not find love. Julliete is an animal activist with a supernatural secret. They find themselves
drawn to each other but first must defeat a threat to them both. [SA]

David Boring. Daniel Clowes. Pantheon, 2000. $26.95.
David has a regular life. He is looking for love and finds someone, but war is looming. At one
point in the book, he and his family are on an island where they wonder if germ warfare has
killed everyone else. [SA]

DC Comics Classics

As mentioned in Chapter 6, DC has put out many books that collect older material. This
list is a sample of those titles that collect comic book stories from the 1930s through the
1980s. These include the various DC Archive Editions, which are published in hardcover,
are in color, are around 250 pages and generally cost about $50.00–$60.00, and the
Showcase Presents titles which are softcover, in black and white, are often over 500
pages, and generally cost around $19.99. A few characters also have their early adventures
in Chronicles that are in paperback, color, around 200 pages, and cost $14.99. There is
some story duplication between the Archives and Showcase editions, especially in the
earlier volumes. Stories found in other listed collections may also have been reprinted in
titles listed here as well. The prices of the titles listed vary, and more volumes of several
titles are planned. [YR]

ADAM STRANGE
Archeologist Adam Strange is transported to the planet Rann where he becomes a champion
to its inhabitants.
   Adam Strange Archives, Vols. 1–3
   Showcase Presents: Adam Strange, Vol. 1

AQUAMAN
The king of the seas fights evil both on land and under the water.
   Aquaman Archives, Vol. 1
   Showcase Presents: Aquaman, Vols. 1–3

THE ATOM
Scientist Ray Palmer can shrink down to anywhere from six inches to subatomic size and
uses his abilities to fight for justice.
   The Atom Archives, Vols. 1–2
   Showcase Presents: The Atom, Vols. 1–2

BATMAN
One of the major DC heroes, and a character who has been in books, television, and movies,
the Caped Crusader protects Gotham City alone and with partners. The first four titles listed
feature his adventures in the 1940s in chronological order. The next four contain later adventures including those from *The Brave and Bold* in which he teams up with other heroes.
Those are followed by adventures that are the "best of" that decade, overall "greatest hits,"
stories by artist Neal Adams, and collections of various themed adventures. His sidekick
Robin and occasional helper Batgirl have also had their own collections. There are also several
collections of Batman fighting various villains.

Batman Archives, Vols. 1–7

Batman Chronicles, Vols. 1–8

Batman: The Dark Knight Archives,
   Vols. 1–5

Batman in World Finest Archives,
   Vols. 1–2

Batman: The Dynamic Duo Archives,
   Vols. 1–2

Showcase Presents: Batman, Vols. 1–4

*The Brave and the Bold Team-Up
   Archives*, Vols. 1

*Showcase Presents: The Brave and
   the Bold: The Batman Team-Ups*,
   Vols. 1–3

Batman in the Forties

Batman in the Fifties

Batman in the Sixties

Batman in the Seventies

Batman in the Eighties

Batman: The Greatest Stories Ever Told,
   Vols. 1–2

Batman Illustrated by Neal Adams, Vols. 1–3

Batman: The Strange Deaths of the Batman

Batman: Secrets of the Batcave

*DC Comics Classics Library: Batman—
   The Annuals*

Robin Archives, Vols. 1–2

Showcase Presents: Robin, the Boy Wonder, Vol. 1

Showcase Presents: Batgirl, Vol. 1

The Joker: The Greatest Stories Ever Told

Batman: Scarecrow Tales

Batman vs. Two Face

THE CHALLENGERS OF THE UNKNOWN

After four adventures survive a plane crash, they decide that they are on borrowed time and vow to explore the unknown to help humanity.

Challengers of the Unknown Archives, Vols. 1–2

Showcase Presents: Challengers of the Unknown, Vols. 1–2

THE ELONGATED MAN

After Ralph Dibney takes a liquid called gingold, he becomes the ductile detective known as the Elongated Man.

Showcase Presents: The Elongated Man, Vol. 1

THE FLASH

In 1940, Jay Garrick the Golden Age (original) Flash was introduced. Sixteen years later a new Flash, Barry Allen, debuted. In *Flash of Two Worlds* the two Speedsters met for the first time, and the final book has both their adventures and that of the third Flash, the former Kid Flash, Wally West.

Golden Age Flash Archives,
   Vols. 1–2

The Flash Archives, Vols. 1–5

The Flash Chronicles, Vol. 1

Showcase Presents: The Flash, Vols. 1–3

*DC Comics Classics Library: Flash
   of Two Worlds*

The Flash Greatest Stories Ever Told

GREEN ARROW

The early adventures of DC's Battling Bowman.

Showcase Presents: Green Arrow, Vol. 1

GREEN LANTERN

In the 1940s, Allan Scott created a ring from a magical lantern. In the 1950s Hal Jordan received the ring from a dying alien. Both "ring-slingers" became warriors in the war against evil. Jordan's team-ups with Green Arrow in the 1970s are notable in comics history.

Golden Age Green Lantern Archives,
   Vols. 1–2

Green Lantern Archives, Vols. 1–6

Green Lantern Chronicles, Vols. 1–2

Showcase Presents: Green Lantern, Vols. 1–4

*Green Lantern: The Greatest Stories
   Ever Told*

Green Lantern/Green Arrow, Vols. 1–2

HAWKMAN

The Golden Age Hawkman was an archeologist who discovered Nth metal, which let him fly. The Silver Age version is an alien policeman who came to Earth with his partner Hawkgirl to catch a criminal and decided to stay.

Golden Age Hawkman Archives, *Hawkman Archives,* Vols. 1–2
  Vol. 1   *Showcase Presents: Hawkman,* Vols. 1–2

JACK KIRBY AT DC

After leaving Marvel Comics in 1970, Jack Kirby came to DC, where he created many notable characters. The Fourth World features his best known creation the New Gods, which features the heroic characters of New Genesis fighting those of Apokolips, ruled over by the evil tyrant Darkseid. OMAC is set in the future and is about an ordinary man transformed into the ultimate fighter. Set further in the future is Kamandi, the "Last Boy on Earth" trying to survive in a ruined world ruled by mutated animals. Dating back to Camelot but roaming the world today is the Demon, an otherworldly creature occasionally trapped in a mortal body. Finally, the Losers is about a four-man (and one dog) fighting squad in World War II.

Jack Kirby's Fourth World Omnibus, *Jack Kirby's the Demon Omnibus*
  Vols. 1–3   *Kamandi Archives,* Vols. 1–2
Jack Kirby's OMAC: One Man *The Losers by Jack Kirby*
  Army Corps

JUSTICE LEAGUE OF AMERICA

The major superteam of the DC Universe, with a membership that includes Superman, Batman, Wonder Woman, Green Lantern, and the Flash. The "Crisis" volumes collect stories of team-ups with their counterparts in the Justice Society who, until 1985, were on the parallel world of "Earth-2." The last volume shows how various members joined the team.

The Justice League of America Archives, *Crisis of Multiple Earths,* Vols. 1–4
  Vols. 1–9   *Crisis on Multiple Earths: The Team-Ups*
Showcase Presents: Justice League of *The Justice League Hereby Elects . . .*
  America, Vols. 1–4

JUSTICE SOCIETY OF AMERICA AND SOME GOLDEN AGE HEROES

The JSA was the first super team in comics and members have included the original Green Lantern, Flash, and Hawkman. Other 1940s characters who were on the team included a magical hero Dr. Fate, the Spectre, the ghost of a murdered policeman, and Starman, who fought evil with his "gravity rod." The Rarities and "All-Star" Archives collect the adventures of various heroes in rarely reprinted works, while the two volume *Justice Society* and "the Huntress" are from the team's 1970s adventures.

All-Star Comics Archives, Vols. 0–11 *Golden Age Starman Archives,* Vols. 1–2
The Black Canary Archives, Vol. 1 *The JSA All Star Archives,* Vol. 1
DC Comics Rarities Archives, Vol. 1 *Justice Society,* Vols. 1–2
Golden Age Doctor Fate Archive, Vol. 1 *Huntress: Dark Knight Daughter*
The Golden Age Spectre Archives, Vol. 1

THE LEGION OF SUPERHEROES

Set 1,000 years in the future, the LSH is made up of superpowered teens from many worlds who fight evil with the help of a time traveling Superboy.

Legion of Super-Heroes Archives, Vols. 1–12
Showcase Presents: The Legion of Super-Heroes, Vols. 1–3
Legion of Super-Heroes: 1,050 Years In the Future
DC Comics Classics Library: The Legion of Super-Heroes—The Life and Death of Ferro Lad

THE MARTIAN MANHUNTER
Trapped on Earth, Martian police officer J'Onn J'Onzz uses his powers to protect his new world.
Showcase Presents: Martian Manhunter, Vols. 1–2

METAL MEN
Five robots—Gold, Lead, Tin, Mercury, Iron, and Platinum—are programmed to fight evil.
Metal Men Archives, Vol. 1
Showcase Presents: Metal Men, Vols. 1–2

PLASTIC MAN
Criminal "Eel" O'Brien turns over a new leaf when a chemical gives him the power to stretch. A funny title from the 1940s.
Plastic Man Archives, Vols. 1–8

SHAZAM!
The wizard Shazam gives young Billy Batson the power to become Captain Marvel, the world's mightiest mortal. He is soon joined by Mary Marvel and Captain Marvel Jr. to become the Marvel Family. The Archives and the *Classic Library* contain stories from the 1940s and the Showcase collects the 1970s series.

Shazam! Archives, Vols. 1–4   *Showcase Presents: Shazam*, Vol. 1
Shazam! Family Archives, Vol. 1   *DC Comics Classics Library: Shazam!—*
Shazam! The Greatest Stories Ever Told   *The Monster Society of Evil*

DC Comics Fantasy, Science Fiction, and Horror
DC has had many series in the science fiction, fantasy, and horror genres. *Strange Adventures* featured science fiction adventures with some reoccurring characters. The three *House* titles are horror anthologies, hosted by Cain, Abel, and Destiny who later appear in Sandman (*House of Mystery* is also the name of a recent series from DC's Vertigo line). *The Phantom Stranger* is a mysterious man who fights the forces of magical evil. The Warlord is Travis Morgan, an air force pilot who finds himself trapped in a strange world of swords and sorcery.

Showcase Presents: Secrets of Haunted House, Vol. 1
Showcase Presents: Strange Adventures, Vol. 1
Showcase Presents: The House of Mystery, Vols. 1–3
Showcase Presents: The House of Secrets, Vols. 1–2
Showcase Presents: The Phantom Stranger, Vols. 1–2
Showcase Presents: The Warlord, Vol. 1

THE SPIRIT
Will Eisner's creation originally appeared in newspapers but have been collected here in book form. Thought dead, policeman Denny Colt takes on the crime-fighting identity of the Spirit. While not all of the work is Eisner's due to his military service, those by him have inspired artists for decades.

Will Eisner's the Spirit Archives,   *The Best of the Spirit*
    Vols. 1–26   *The Spirit: Femmes Fatale*

SUPERMAN

For over 70 years, The Man of Steel has fought for "Truth, Justice, and the American Way." The first four titles include adventures from the 1940s, while the next two are from the 1950s and 1960s. *DC Comics Presents* include team-ups and collections of stories featuring his cousin Supergirl, his girlfriend Lois Lane, and his pal Jimmy Olsen. Other collections trace his history with various villains as well as odd stories from the "Bizarro World."

Superman Archives, Vols. 1–7
Superman in Action Comics Archives, Vols. 1–5
Superman in World's Finest Archives, Vols. 1–2
Superman Chronicles, Vols. 1–6
Superman: Man of Tomorrow Archives, Vols. 1–2
Showcase Presents: Superman, Vols. 1–4
Showcase Presents: DC Comics Presents—The Team Up, Vol. 1
Superman in the Forties
Superman in the Fifties
Superman in the Sixties
Superman in the Seventies

Superman in the Eighties
DC Comics Classics Library: Superman— Kryptonite Nevermore!
Supergirl Archives, Vols. 1–2
Showcase Presents: Supergirl, Vols. 1–2
Showcase Presents: The Superman Family, Vols. 1–3
The Amazing Transformations of Jimmy Olsen
Jimmy Olsen: Adventures by Jack Kirby, Vols. 1–2
Superman vs. Brainiac
Superman vs. Lex Luthor
Superman: Tales from the Phantom Zone
Superman: Tales from Bizarro World

SUPERMAN AND BATMAN

At times Superman and Batman would team up, often in the pages of *World's Finest*. The "supersons" book is a collection of "imaginary stories" where they both have sons who take after their fathers.

World's Finest Archives, Vols. 1–3
Showcase Presents: World's Finest, Vols. 1–3

Superman/Batman: The Greatest Stories Ever Told
Batman/Superman: Saga of the Supersons

THE TEEN TITANS

The Titans were originally made of teen sidekicks Robin, Kid Flash, Aqualad, Wonder Girl, and Green's Arrow's partner Speedy. During the 1980s, newer members joined in a number of classic stories.

The Silver Age Teen Titans Archives, Vol. 1
Showcase Presents: Teen Titans, Vols. 1–2
The New Teen Titans Archives, Vols. 1–4

New Teen Titans: Terra Incognito
The New Teen Titans: The Judas Contract
New Teen Titans: Who Is Donna Troy?
The New Teen Titans: The Terror of Trigon

WONDER WOMAN

The best-known female superhero, Wonder Woman has fought everything from Nazis to supervillains. The *Archives* take place in the 1940s, the *Showcases* in the 1950s and 1960s, and the *Diana Prince* books take place in the early 1970s when she lost her powers for a time and became secret agent Diana Prince.

Wonder Woman Archives, Vols. 1–5
Showcase Presents: Wonder Woman, Vols. 1–3

Wonder Woman: The Greatest Stories Ever Told
Diana Prince: Wonder Woman, Vols. 1–4

DC Comics Miscellaneous

Action Hero Archives, Vols. 1–2. Captain Atom, Blue Beetle, the Question and other heroes originally published by Charlton Comics.

Crisis on Infinite Earths. The 1985 classic. Worlds lived, worlds died, and the DC Universe was never the same.

DC Comics Goes Ape. Various DC stories involving monkeys, gorillas, and other primates.

DC Universe Illustrated by Neal Adams, Vol. 1. Various stories drawn an noted artist.

DC Universe: The Stories of Alan Moore. Stories that Moore did for DC's superhero titles, most notably the Batman story "The Killing Joke" and the Superman tale "What Ever Happened to the Man of Tomorrow."

DC's Greatest Imaginary Stories. Stories that took place out of regular continuity including the classic "Superman Red and Superman Blue."

Seven Soldiers of Victory Archives, Vols. 1–3. During the 1940s, Green Arrow, Speedy, the Star-Spangled Kid, Stripsey, the Vigilante, the Crimson Avenger, and the Shining Knight teamed up to form this group also known as the Law's Legionnaires.

Showcase Presents Bat Lash. Adventures in the Old West.

Showcase Presents: Dial H for Hero, Vol. 1. Teenager Robby Reed becomes different heroes by dialing H-E-R-O on a magic dial.

Showcase Presents: Eclipso, Vol. 1. A modern-day Jekyll and Hyde, Dr. Bruce Gordon becomes the villainous Eclipso.

Showcase Presents: The Creeper, Vol. 1. Reporter Jack Ryder is transformed into the slightly crazy superhero the Creeper.

Showcase Presents: Metamorpho, Vol. 1. Adventurer Rex Mason was changed by the Orb of Ra into Metamorpho, who can transform his body into any element.

T.H.U.N.D.E.R. Agents Archives, Vols. 1–6. Originally published by Tower Comics in the 1960s, these archives contain the adventures of superheroes who work for The Higher United Nations Defense Enforcement Reserves.

DC Comics War Titles

DC has put out a number of war comics over the years. Blackhawk was the adventures of a team of fliers during and after World War II (the Archives, from the 1940s, feature a negative stereotype with the Chinese character "Chop Chop"). Also set in World War II are the Haunted Tank stories in which a tank commanded by Sgt. Jeb Stuart is watched over by the ghost of his Civil War namesake; Sgt. Rock and his Easy Company who fought the war without any supernatural help; and the Unknown Soldier, who was a bandaged master of disguise who infiltrated behind enemy lines. WWII soldiers found themselves on an island filled with dinosaurs and fought the "War That Time Forgot." Finally, German flier Hans Von Hammer was World War I's "Enemy Ace." Many of these characters, or updated versions of the characters, have appeared in recent DC Comics titles.

Blackhawk Archives, Vol. 1 and *Showcase Presents: Blackhawk*, Vol. 1

Showcase Presents: Haunted Tank, Vols. 1–2

Sgt. Rock Archives, Vols. 1–3 and *Showcase Presents: Sgt. Rock*, Vols. 1–2

Showcase Presents: The Unknown Soldier, Vol. 1

Showcase Presents: The War That Time Forgot, Vol. 1

Enemy Ace Archives, Vols. 1–2 and *Showcase Presents: Enemy Ace*, Vol. 1

De: Tales. Fábio Moon and Gabriel Bá. Dark Horse, 2006. $14.95.
Moon and Ba are twin brothers from Brazil who have made a splash on the comics scene in recent years. Some of the works in this collection of short stories are collaborative while others were done individually. In other cases, they both worked on the story but one wrote while the other drew. [SA]

Dead Eyes Open. Matthew Shepherd and Roy Boney Jr. SLG, 2008. $12.95.
The dead are coming back to life, but they don't want to hurt people, they just want their old lives back. But discrimination and a government roundup are forcing some to take drastic measures. [SA]

Dead High Yearbook. Various artists. Penguin/Dutton Books, 2007. $18.99.
Ivan Velez, Jennifer Camper, Ho Che Anderson, ChrisCross (SIC), and Pop Mhan are among the writers and artists who worked on this "yearbook of the dead," with zombies, vampires, and other creatures. [YR]

Dead West. Rick Spears and Rob Goodridge. Gigantic Graphic Novels, 2005. $14.95.
A bounty hunter tracking his prey in the Old West finally finds him a small town. Unfortunately the town is about to be attacked by zombies raised by a vengeful Indian. [SA]

Death by Chocolate: Redux. David Yurkovich. Top Shelf, 2007. $14.95.
"Agent Swete" was a candy store owner who discovered a dark secret and was turned into a man not only made of chocolate but who could turn other things to chocolate. After accidentally destroying the town where he lived, he was taken in by the government and eventually joined the FBI's Food Crime Division. [SA]

Death Note. Tsugumi Ohba, illustrated by Takeshi Obata. VIZ. $7.95.
In this very popular manga series student Light Yagami finds a Death Note book dropped by a bored Shinigami (death god) named Ryuk. By writing people's names in the book and picturing their faces, you can cause their deaths. Unless a particular time and cause of death is written, the person will have a heart attack after 40 seconds. Light uses the note to go after criminals, figuring that people will give up crime due to fear of being killed. He must contend with others with Death Notes as well as the super-investigator known as "L." The manga has spawned an anime series, books, video games, and live action films. There is also a thirteenth volume, subtitled "How to Read," which provides behind the scenes information on the book and characters. [YR]

Vol. 1: *Boredom*	Vol. 4: *Love*	Vol. 7: *Zero*	Vol. 10: *Deletion*
Vol. 2: *Confluence*	Vol. 5: *Whiteout*	Vol. 8: *Target*	Vol. 11: *Kindred Spirit*
Vol. 3: *Hard Run*	Vol. 6: *Give-and-Take*	Vol. 9: *Contact*	Vol. 12: *The End*

Death Valley. Andrew Cosby, Johanna Stokes, and others. Boom! 2007. $14.99.
Several short stories dealing with zombies, one of which is also in *Zombie Tales*. The title story makes up more than half of the book and deals with a group of California high school students who must escape a zombie outbreak. [YR]

Guy Delisle, travels of. Drawn & Quarterly, 2005–. $19.95 each.
Guy Delisle is a Canadian-born comic writer/artist and animator who has worked around the world. Two of his autobiographical works tell of how he went to two Asian countries while working for French animation studios. In *Pyongyang: A Journey in North Korea* (2005) he told about working in that city and how as a foreigner he could see and do things that the

average person could not in Kim Jong-Iil's North Korea. *Shenzhen: A Travelogue from China* (2006) tells of working in this city located near Hong Kong and commenting on life there. A third book *The Burma Chronicles* (2008) tells of living for a year in that country (also known as Myanmar) with his wife who works for Doctors Without Borders. [SA]

Demo. Brian Wood, with art by Becky Cloonan. DC/Vertigo, 2008. $19.99.
This black-and-white collection features 12 separate stories each about a young person, many of whom have some sort of special power, who must make a life-altering decision. The original publisher, AiT/Planet Lar, has also put out a scriptbook for the series. Another collection of 12 stories by Wood is *Local* (Oni, 2008). [YR]

Deogratias: A Tale of Rwanda. Jean-Philippe Stassen. First Second, 2006. $17.95.
Deogratias is a Hutu boy. Benina is a Tutsi girl. It is 1994 and Rwanda is about to degrade into a genocidal civil war. This harrowing tale was originally published in Belgium. Recommended. [SA]

Desolation Jones: Made in England. Warren Ellis, with art by J. H. Williams III. DC/Wildstorm, 2006. $14.99.
Jones, a British spy, altered so that he can no longer feel pain, has been "exiled" to Los Angeles where he has been allowed to become a private investigator. He has been hired for the unusual task of finding a pornographic film created by Hitler, only to find out the case is stranger than he thought. [SA]

Desperadoes Omnibus. Jeff Mariotte, with art by John Cassaday, John Lucas, John Severin, Jeremy Haun, and Alberto Dose. IDW, 2009. $24.99.
A "Weird West" series that mixes the genres of horror and Western. This omnibus collects the stories in five collections originally published by DC/Wildstorm and IDW. [SA]

The Devil Within. Ryo Takagi. Go! Comi, 2007. $10.99.
This rated OT, two-volume romantic fantasy is about Rion, who feels all men are devils and is being forced to choose one of three men as a potential husband. But she thinks that she found the right person elsewhere. [SA]

El Diablo. Brian Azzarello, with art by Danijel Zezelj. DC/Vertigo, 2008. $12.99.
Set in the old West, bounty-hunter-turned-sheriff Moses Stone has a good life, but when the outlaw El Diablo comes to town he must chase him down no matter where he may run. But Stone has a dark secret in his past. A new version appears in 2009's *El Diablo: The Haunted Horsemen.* [SA]

Diabolo. Kei Kusunoki and Kaoru Ohashi. Tokyopop, 2004. $9.99.
In this rated-OT three-volume manga, best friends Ren and Rei sell their souls to a demon in exchange for powers that allow them to fight on the side of good. But they know that soon they will turn 18, the age at which they will have reached the point of no return. [SA]

DMZ. Brian Wood, with art primarily by Riccardo Burchielli. DC/Vertigo, 2006–. $9.99–$12.99.
Set in the near future, America is in the grip of a civil war between the U.S. government and the soldiers of the "Free States." The island of Manhattan is a Demilitarized Zone stuck between the two sides with the population who couldn't or wouldn't leave, surviving however they can. Matty Roth is a journalist for *Liberty News* stuck in New York, trying to tell the

real story of the DMZ. Additional art by Wood, Danijel Zezelj, Vikto Kalvachev, Nathan Fox, Kristian Donaldson, and Nikki Cook. Recommended. [SA]

Volumes as of 2009 are:

Vol. 1: *On the Ground*   Vol. 5: *The Hidden War*

Vol. 2: *Body of a Journalist*   Vol. 6: *Blood in the Game*

Vol. 3: *Public Works*   Vol. 7: *War Powers*

Vol. 4: *Friendly Fire*

Dogs & Water. Anders Nilsen. Drawn & Quarterly, 2007. $19.95.

A man is wandering in a strange area with only his stuffed bear for company. He eventually encounters both people and wild animals on his journey, and at times his survival is in question. [SA]

The Doom Patrol. Grant Morrison, with art by Richard Case. DC/Vertigo, 2004–.

In the 1960s the Doom Patrol was formed as a group of "freaks" who used their abilities for justice. The team has had several incarnations and members, but in 1988 Grant Morrison took over and things got strange. It was this incarnation of the title that eventually became one of Vertigo's "original" books. Members of this included Crazy Jane, whose multiple personalities each have a different power, sentient roadway "Danny the Street," and Robotman, who has been a part of all of the team's incarnations. Villains included the Brotherhood of Dada and the Scissormen. Additional artists on this title included Doug Braithwaite, John Nyberg, Kim DeMulder, Kelley Jones, Steve Yeowell, Jamie Hewlett, Mark Badger, Stan Woch, Ken Steacy, Philip Bond, and Mark McKenna. [SA]

Vol. 1: *Crawling from the Wreckage*   Vol. 4: *Musclebound*

Vol. 2: *The Painting That Ate Paris*   Vol. 5: *Magic Bus*

Vol. 3: *Down Paradise Way*   Vol. 6: *Planet Love*

More volumes are expected, and also of note are *The Doom Patrol Archives*, Vols. 1–5 and *Showcase Presents the Doom Patrol*, which collect the adventures of the team's earlier incarnation.

Dork Tower. John Kovalic. Dork Storm Press, 2002–. $15.95.

These trades collect both the comic book series and strips published elsewhere. In this funny title, Matt, Ken, Igor, and Carson the talking muskrat are fans of role-playing games, movies, comics, and other "geek" interests. [YR]

In publishing order the collections are:

Dork Covenant   *1d6 Degrees of Separation*

Dork Shadows   *Dork Side of the Goon*

Heart of Dorkness   *Go, Dork, Go!*

Livin' La Vida Dorka   *Dork Decade*

Understanding Gamers   *The Tao of Igor*

Julie Doucet, works of. Drawn & Quarterly.

Born in Montreal, Doucet is an award-winning cartoonist known for her autobiographical works, many of which were first published in the comic book *Dirty Plotte*. Her work includes *My Most Secret Desire* (2006, $19.95) in which she illustrated her dreams, *My New York Diary* (2004, $15.95), which features other events from her life, and *365 Days* (2007, $29.95), originally published in France, which has her diary from October 2002–November 2003 with illustrations. [SA]

Dr. Blink Superhero Shrink. John Kovalic, with art by Christopher Jones. Dork Storm Press, 2007. $14.99.
Who do superbeings go to when they have problems? Doctor F.W. Blink, author of *Chicken Soup for the Super Soul.* Whether it's an ex-sidekick going through a midlife crisis or a scary demon with a silly name, Dr. Blink is the one. A funny book filled with super-parodies. [YR]

Drafted. Mark Powers, with art by Chris Lie. Devil's Due Publishing, 2008–. $18.99 each.
Earth has been dragged into an interstellar war, and all of humanity has been drafted one way or another. The frontline troops come from all around the world and include the President of the United States. There are several collections. [SA]

Dragon Head. Minetaro Mochizuki. Tokyopop, 2006–. $9.99.
Teen Teru Aoki is returning home from a class trip when the train derails inside a tunnel. He is only one of three survivors, and for a while they are trapped in the tunnel, but when they get out they find that a disaster has befallen all of Japan. There will be 10 volumes of this OT manga series. [SA]

The Drifting Classroom. Kazuo Umezu. VIZ, 2006–2008. $9.99.
A Japanese elementary school is transported to a strange postapocalyptic wasteland leaving the students to survive on their own. Despite the young age of many of the characters, this award-winning 11-volume work is rated M and has an explicit content warning. [SA]

Dungeon series. Joann Sfar and Lewis Trondheim, with art by various. NBM. [YR]
These humorous stories, known as Donjon in France, are parodies of the sword-and-sorcery genre. While most of the series has yet to be translated, the volumes that have been are:

Early Years, Vol. 1: *The Night Shirt*   *Twilight*, Vol. 1: *Dragon Cemetery*
Monstres, Vol. 1: *The Crying Giant*   *Twilight*, Vol. 2: *Armageddon*
Monstres, Vol. 2: *The Dark Lord*   *Zenith*, Vol. 1: *Duck Heart*
Parade, Vol. 1: *A Dungeon Too Many*   *Zenith*, Vol. 2: *The Barbarian Princess*
Parade, Vol. 2: *Day of the Toads*   *Zenith*, Vol. 3: *Back in Style*

Additional volumes will be translated and collected.

E

The Easy Way. Christopher E. Long, with art by Andy Kuhn. IDW, 2005. $17.99.
Duncan is in a drug rehabilitation center, and he knows that kicking the habit is the only way that he'll get to be with his wife and baby. But he gets caught up in a scheme to use a drug-sniffing dog to locate a stash hidden by a drug trafficker. While the plan works, the druglord soon finds out and is not happy. [SA]

Eating Steve: A Love Story. J. Marc Schmidt. SLG Publishing, 2007. $5.95.
A zombie plague is causing people to take bites of other people, and when Jill tries to eat her boyfriend's brain it ends their relationship (though not his life) and causes her to go into hiding in the countryside. A short, but fun story that, despite the basic premise, is not a horror story. [SA]

Eden: It's an Endless World. Hiroki Endo. Dark Horse, 2005–. $12.95.
This rated 18+ manga series is set in the near future after a pandemic has either killed, crippled, or disfigured a large percentage of the populations (to the point that many survivors

have had to cybernetically enhance themselves), and much of the world is in chaos. The protagonist is a teenager named Elijah and the story tells of his struggles. Eighteen volumes were published in Japan. [SA]

Will Eisner, works of.
One of the most influential figures in comics, Eisner produced a number of graphic novels beginning with the classic *A Contract with God* and ending with the posthumously published *The Plot*. Many of his stories take place in New York City, and several have autobiographical elements. The works have been put out by different publishers over the years, with most of his work currently published by W. W. Norton. Norton has also created three anthologies of his work. These anthologies are highly recommended, and the other titles should strongly be considered for your collection. Norton has also reprinted Eisner's books on creating comics (see Appendix B). [SA]

PUBLISHED BY W.W. NORTON, $15.95–$17.95
> *The Building.* The story of a NYC building and the people who live there.
> *City People Notebook.* A look at the people of New York City.
> *A Contract with God.* His first graphic novel containing four "graphic novellas."
> *The Dreamer.* A look at Eisner's early years in comics. The names are changed but a new annotation tells who was who.
> *Dropsie Avenue.* Tells how a neighborhood can change over the years.
> *Family Matter.* A family gathers for the birthday of their stroke-impaired patriarch and family greed and secrets are unearthed.
> *Invisible People.* Three stories about the kinds of people not noticed by society.
> *Life on Another Planet.* Eisner's foray into science fiction.
> *A Life Force.* Set during the Great Depression, this GN follows an out-of-work carpenter.
> *Minor Miracles.* Several short stories.
> *The Name of the Game.* A multigenerational look at various Jewish immigrant families of various social status and their interactions.
> *New York: The Big City.* The lives of people on the Lower East Side before it was a fashionable place.
> *The Plot: The Secret Story of the Protocols of the Elders of Zion.* A nonfiction work detailing the history of the anti-Semitic hoax *The Protocols of the Elders of Zion.*
> *To the Heart of the Storm.* Heading off to war, "Willy" remembers his youth and stories of his family.
> *The Will Eisner Reader.* Several short stories.
> Anthologies. $29.95 each.
>> *The Contract with God Trilogy: Life on Dropsie Avenue (Contract, Life Force, Dropsie)*
>> *Life, In Pictures: Autobiographical Stories (Dreamer, Heart, Name)*
>> *Will Eisner's New York, Life in the Big City (New York, Building, City People, Invisible)*

OTHER PUBLISHERS
> *Fagin the Jew.* Doubleday. $16.95. The "true" story of the man Charles Dickens used as a villain in *Oliver Twist* and a look at Victorian anti-Semitism.
> *Last Day in Vietnam.* Dark Horse. $10.95. Several stories about soldiers' lives in Vietnam. Some were based on what Eisner saw when he went there for *P.S. Magazine.*

Elephantmen. Richard Starkings. Image Comics, 2007–. $24.99–$29.95.
The Elephantmen stories are set in the twenty-third century where the Mappo Corporation created human/animal hybrids to work as soldiers. These transgenic creatures became known as Elephantmen when they were freed and allowed into society, but they are all kinds of animals including a hippo, crocodile, rhino, and camel. Some transgenics work for the government, while some work on their own, sometimes very successfully. Though set in the future, there are many spoofs of modern societies including parodies of Howard Stern and Katie Couric. [SA]
Elephantmen, Vol 1: *Wounded Animals.* Art by Moritat and others.
Elephantmen, Vol. 2: *Fatal Diseases.* Art by Moritat and others.
Elephantmen: Damaged Goods. Art by Martin Churchland.
Elephantmen: War Toys, Vol. 1: *No Surrender.* Art by Moritat and others.
Hip Flask, Vol 1: *Concrete Jungle.* Also written by Joe Casey, with art by Ladrönn.
Hip Flask: Unnatural Selection. Also written by Joe Casey, with art by Ladrönn.

Elk's Run. Joshua Hale Fialkov, with art by Noel Tuazon. Villard Books, 2007. $19.95.
The town of Elk's Ridge, West Virginia, was built by a group of Vietnam veterans who wanted to keep their families safe from the rest of the world. But now there are some who would do anything to leave, and others who will do anything they have to prevent that. [YR]

Embroideries. Marjane Satrapi. Pantheon Books, 2005. $16.95.
Satrapi tells a tale of the women in her family and some of their friends getting together for tea. Eventually the talk turns to sex, covering everything from failed marriages (including arranged ones to older men) to virginity (and lack thereof), plastic surgery, and more. [SA]

Empowered. Adam Warren. Dark Horse, 2007–. $14.95.
Elissa Megan Powers is a self-conscious young women who is also the superheroine Empowered. Her costume gives her powers, but unfortunately it's also easily ripped. This causes her to have a lot of exposed skin by the time she is tied up by bad guys, waiting to be rescued by her teammates, the Superhomeys. Her only friends are her boyfriend, Thugboy, a former flunky for supervillains, the former villain Ninjette, and the Caged Demonwolf, an evil mystical entity trapped in a belt. While there is a lot of flesh in this superhero spoof, there is only partial nudity, with either her hair over her breasts or just a rear view. At least five volumes have been created. [SA]

The End League. Rick Remender, with art by Mat Broome, Sean Parsons, and Eric Canete. Dark Horse Comics, 2008. $12.95.
The world's greatest heroes could not stop a disaster from ruining the world. Can they stop supervillains from destroying what's left? [YR]
Vol. 1: *Ballad of Big Nothing*
Vol. 2: *Weathered Statues*

Epileptic. David B. Pantheon Books, 2005. $17.95.
The autobiographical story of French writer/artist David B. (born Pierre-François Beauchard) who grew up in the 1960s with an epileptic brother, Jean-Christophe. The book shows the treatments their parents used to help him, including macrobiotic diets, living on a commune, mediums, magnetic therapy, and other techniques. The book also goes into his family history and his life into adulthood. The story, written between 1996–2004, had partially been earlier published in English as *Epileptic One.* Recommended. [SA]

Escape from "Special." Miss Lasko-Gross. Fantagraphics, 2006. $16.95.
Semi-autobiographical vignettes about when the author was a young girl. At times she was put both in special-ed and gifted classes while attending various schools. The book also shows her beginning to draw and some of her early cartoons. The story continues in 2009's *A Mess of Everything*. [SA]

Essex County.
The Complete Essex County. Jeff Lemire. Top Shelf, 2009. $29.95 (SC); $49.95 (HC).
Collects the three original volumes of this award-winning series of original graphic novels—*Tales from the Farm*, *Ghost Stories*, and *The Country Nurse*—and two new stories and other previously unpublished work. Lemire portrays an imaginary version of the eccentric farm community of Essex County, Canada, with characters ranging from a 10-year-old boy to a middle-aged nurse. [SA]

The Eternal Smile. Gene Luen Yang and Derek Kirk Kim. First Second, 2009. $16.95.
Three short stories, two set in "fantastic worlds" and one set in the "real" one. [SA]

Ethel & Ernest. Raymond Briggs. Pantheon Books, 1998. $15.00.
In this award-winning original graphic novel, Brigs tells the story of his parents from their first meeting the 1920s until their deaths in the 1970s. Briggs himself is a character, and he has used his parents as the model for the couple in *Gentlemen Jim* and *When the Wind Blows*. [YR]

Ex Machina. Brian K. Vaughan, with art by Tony Harris and Tom Feister. DC/Wildstorm, 2009–. $9.99–$12.99.
After being caught in the explosion of a strange device, engineer Mitchell Hundred found that he could communicate and command mechanical devices. A fan of comics, he developed a jet pack and other devices and became the superhero known as the Great Machine. While this gets him in trouble with both the police and the government, on September 11, 2001, he was able to stop the second plane from hitting the World Trade Center. Afterward Hundred runs for mayor and wins. The series is what happens to him for the next four years. Additional artwork was done by Chris Sprouse, Karl Story, and Jim Clark. Recommended. [SA]

Vol. 1: *The First Hundred Days*	Vol. 5: *Smoke Smoke*
Vol. 2: *Tag*	Vol. 6: *Power Down*
Vol. 3: *Fact V. Fiction*	Vol. 7: *Ex Cathedra*
Vol. 4: *March to War*	Vol. 8: *Dirty Tricks*

There will be additional volumes, and DC also puts out a hardcover "deluxe edition" that collected a larger number of issues for $29.99.

Exit Wounds. Rutu Modan. Drawn & Quarterly, 2007. $19.95.
This award-winning book by Israeli creator Modan was on several "best of the year" lists. Tel Aviv cab driver Koby Franco learns that his estranged father may have been killed in a suicide bombing. Now Koby and a female soldier search for the truth, and in searching for the truth of his father's death he ends up finding more about his father's life. Also of note by Modan is *Jamilti and Other Stories* (2008). Recommended. [SA]

The Exterminators. Simon Oliver, with art by Tony Moore. DC/Vertigo, 2006–2008. $9.99.
Ex-con Henry James and his co-workers at Bug-Bee-Gone are keeping Los Angeles safe from all sorts of pests. But super-intelligent roaches and an evil corporation may be pests that even

they can't handle. Additional art was by Chris Samnee, Andre Parks, Mike Hawthorne, John Lucas, Darick Robertson, and Ty Templeton. [SA]

Vol. 1: *Bug Brothers*
Vol. 2: *Insurgency*
Vol. 3: *Lies of Our Fathers*
Vol. 4: *Crossfire and Collateral*
Vol. 5: *Bug Brothers Forever*

F

Fables. Bill Willingham. DC/Vertigo, 2003–. $9.99–.
When their various homelands are conquered by a mysterious adversary, Snow White, Boy Blue, Prince Charming, King Cole, Bigby Wolf (or Big B. Wolf), Pinocchio, and other characters from fables and folklore come to live in a new world, setting up a settlement in New Amsterdam and a second one further away for giants, Lilliputians, talking animals, etc. Over the centuries as New Amsterdam became New York, the unaging Fables have lived among us, gaining new members to their communities and hoping to someday come home. The characters are a mix of the popular and the less known fables. One of them, Jack of the Tales (as in Horner, Frost, and the Beanstalk, etc.) spun-off into his own series after the events portrayed in *Homelands*. Artists on this this multi-award-winning series include Lan Medina, Steve Leialoha, Craig Hamilton, Mark Buckingham, Bryan Talbot, Linda Medley, P. Craig Russell, Tony Atkins, Jimmy Palmiotti, David Hahn, Dan Green, Andrew Pepoy, Jim Fern, Shawn McManus, Aaron Alexovich, Mike Alred, and Peter Gross. Recommended. [SA]

Vol. 1: *Legends in Exile*
Vol. 2: *Animal Farm*
Vol. 3: *Storybook Love*
Vol. 4: *March of the Wooden Soldiers*
Vol. 5: *The Mean Seasons*
Vol. 6: *Homelands*
Vol. 7: *Arabian Nights (and Days)*
Vol. 8: *Wolves*
Vol. 9: *Sons of Empire*
Vol. 10: *The Good Prince*
Vol. 11: *War and Pieces*
Vol. 12: *The Dark Ages*
Vol. 13: *The Great Fables Crossover*
(co-written by Matthew Sturges)

Fables: 1001 Nights of Snowfall. Art by Charles Vess, Brian Bolland, John Bolton, Michael Wm. Kaluta, Mark Buckingham, Jill Thompson, and others. An original graphic novel with several stories.

There will be additional collections and hardcover "Deluxe" collections as well as a prose novel, listed in Appendix B.

Jack of Fables. Bill Willingham and Matthew Sturges, with art by Tony Akins, Andrew Pepoy, Andrew Robinson, Russ Braun, and others. 2007–. $14.99 each.

Vol. 1: *The (Nearly) Great Escape*
Vol. 2: *Jack of Hearts*
Vol. 3: *The Bad Prince*
Vol. 4: *Americana*
Vol. 5: *Turning Pages*
Vol. 6: *The Big Book of War*

Fake. Sanami Matoh. Tokyopop, 2003–2004. $9.99.
This popular seven-volume manga is set in New York and deals with Randy "Ryo" Maclean, a part-Japanese rookie officer who finds himself partnered with Dee Laynter who is bisexual. The two have several cases and get into many different and sometimes humorous situations while becoming attracted to each other. While the first six volumes were rated 16+, the final volume is more explicit and is rated for adult readers. [SA]

Faker. Mike Carey, with art by Jock. DC/Vertigo, 2008. $14.99.
A group of college students with their own secrets and problems get sick after a party where they took a new drug. Now one of them has had his existence erased with only the group having any memory of him. Or is something else happening? [SA]

Fall of Cthulhu **series.** Michael Alan Nelson. Boom! Studios, 2008. $14.99–.
A horror series in which humanity must face the terror of Lovecraft's Elder Gods. Artists include Jean Ozialowski, Greg Scott, and Mat Santolouco. Also related is Boom's anthology series *Cthulhu Tales*. [YR]

Vol. 1: *The Fugue*	Vol. 4: *Godwar*
Vol. 2: *The Gathering*	Vol. 5: *Apocalypse*
Vol. 3: *The Gray Man*	Vol. 6: *Nemesis*

Fallen Angel. Peter David, with art by J.K. Woodward. IDW, 2005–.
The mysterious city of Bette Noire is a strange place filled with crime, magic, and more. But if you need help, then seek out Liandra, a former guardian angel who helps those who have been wronged. The series ran for 20 issues at DC and then restarted at IDW. [SA]

The Fallen Angel Omnibus	*Red Horse Riding.* $19.99.
(collects issues 1–21). $24.99.	*Cities of Light and Dark.* $19.99.

IDW has also put out two oversized *Premiere Collections* collecting most of the series, as well as an omnibus collecting the DC issues. Additional collections are expected, including *Fallen Angel: Reborn.*

Fallout: J. Robert Oppenheimer, Leo Szilard, and the Political Science of the Atomic Bomb. Jim Ottaviani and various artists. GT Labs, 2001. $19.95.
A "fictional nonfiction" book about the creation of the atomic bomb and what happened to some of its creators after the war. The book contains annotated notes and references and artists include Steve Lieber and Eddy Newell. [SA]

Fat Free. Jude Milner, with art by Mary Wilshire. Jeremy P. Tarcher/Penguin, 2006. $10.95.
Subtitled "Amazing All-True Adventures of a Supersize Woman," this graphic memoir tells of Milner's struggle with weight problems including diet, surgery, and self-acceptance. Another book with a similar theme is Carol Lay's *The Big Skinny: How I Changed My Fattitude: A Memoir* (Villard, 2008). [SA]

Fate of the Artist. Eddie Campbell. First Second, 2006. $15.95.
Campbell has subtitled this work "an autobiographical novel, with typographical anomalies in which the author does not appear as himself. A mix of art, photos, phony "old-time" comic strips, text pages, are among the elements that make up this well-reviewed work. Campbell has previously written semiautobiographical work about "Alec MacGarry," which has been recollected in *Alec: The Years Have Pants* (Top Shelf, 2009). [SA]

Fax from Sarajevo. Joe Kubert. Dark Horse Books, 1996. $16.95.
In this multi-award-winning work, Kubert tells the story of his friend Ervin Rustemagic who, with his family, was stuck in Sarajevo during the 1992–1993 siege. Ervin's only way to communicate with the outside world was the fax machine in a Holiday Inn. Awards include an Eisner, a Harvey, and several foreign awards. Recommended. [YR]

The Festering Season. Kevin Tinsley, with art by Tim Smith III. Stickman Graphics, 2002. $38.95.
This is a zombie title, but the classic "vodou" type as opposed to the "braaaaaains" kind. Rene Duboise returns to New York City after her mother is killed in a police shooting and finds that there are even more sinister happenings afoot. Magic, crime, racial profiling, cults, murder, and evil plots all make up this original work. [SA]

A Few Perfect Hours and Other Stories from Southeast Asia & Central Europe. Josh Neufeld. Alternative Comics, 2004. $12.95.
Neufeld has written a memoir about the travels around the world by his girlfriend and himself, including going to Thailand and Serbia (in 1993). Their experiences include working on a commune and being extras in a movie. Alternative Comics is the distributor as the book is self-published via a grant from the Xeric Foundation. [SA]

Fight for Tomorrow. Brian Wood, with art by Denys Cowan and Kent Williams. DC/Vertigo, 2008. $14.99.
Cedric Zhang was kidnapped as a young boy and put into slavery where he was forced to fight other children. Fifteen years later he was rescued along with another kidnapped girl and re-entered society. Now she is missing and he must find her. [SA]

The Filth. Grant Morrison, with Chris Weston and Gary Erkskine. DC/Vertigo, 2004. $19.95.
In this very strange collection of a 13-issue limited series, a group takes on the weird and disgusting threats to the world ranging from monsters and megalomaniacs to giant sperm. [SA]

Final Destination: Spring Break. Mike Kalvoda, with art by Lan Medina and Rodel Noora. Zenescope, 2007. $17.99.
Inspired by the film series, a group of students on the way to Cancun cheat death, but find that death could not be cheated. [SA]

The Fixer: A Story from Sarajevo. Joe Sacco. Drawn & Quarterly, 2003. $24.95.
The true story of Neven, known as "the Fixer" for his ability to get or arrange things and what he went through during the war in Bosnia, including the period when Sacco first met him in the mid-1990s. [SA]

Flower and Fade. Jesse Lonergan. NBM, 2007. $13.95.
Part of NBM's Comic Lit line, this is the story of a romance between two people who live in the same apartment building. [SA]

"For Beginners" series. Pantheon Books. $14.95.
A series of nonfiction books covering such topics as history, biography, science, philosophy, literature, and other topics. While described as a "documentary comics book" several books in this series are mainly text with a few illustrations. However, many are "hybrid" graphic novels, mixing text with comic art that adds to the story. Those that are of that nature include:
    Anarchism for Beginners. Marcos Mayer, with art by Sanyu.
    Astronomy for Beginners. Jeff Becan, with art by Sarah Becan.
    Ayn Rand for Beginners. Andrew Bernstein, with art by By Owen Brozman.
    Dada & Surrealism for Beginners. Elsa & Peter Bethanis, with art by Joseph Lee.
    The Olympics for Beginners. Brandon Toropov, with art by Joe Lee.
    Philosophy for Beginners. Richard Osborne, with art by Ralph Edney.

These works are also related to a series of "For Beginners" titles published by Pantheon books that included *Freud for Beginners* by Richard Appignanesi and Oscar Zarate, *Einstein for Beginners* by Joseph Schwartz and Michael McGuinness, and *Marx for Beginners* by Rius. All of these works would go into the appropriate nonfiction section. [YR]

Fort: Prophet of the Unexplained. Peter M. Lenkov, with art by Frazer Irving. Dark Horse, 2003. $9.95.
It's 1899 and anomalist and librarian Charles Fort and the young H. P. Lovecraft must stop a menace from beyond the stars. Both Fort and Lovecraft have appeared in other comics. [SA]

Freaks of the Heartland. Steve Niles, with art by Greg Ruth. Dark Horse, 2005. $17.95.
Trevor's little brother Billy was born with a deformity and is kept hidden in the barn. But when Billy's life is in danger, the two run off and find that Billy isn't the only secret the town is keeping. [SA]

Freshmen. Hugh Sterbakov, with art by Leonard Kirk and Andrew Pepoy. Image/Top Cow, 2006. $16.99.
Co-created by actor Seth Green, the *Freshmen* books are about a group of college students who gain superpowers after an explosion. Some abilities include being able to talk to plants and making other people drunk. And then there's the pet beaver that is now super-intelligent. But a fellow student, a comics fan who, of course, missed out on getting powers, convinces them to do more with their powers. [YR]
> *Freshman*
> *Freshmen II: Fundamentals of Fear*

From Hell. Alan Moore, with art by Eddie Campbell. Top Shelf, 2000. $35.00.
A new take on the story of Jack the Ripper, his victims, and those trying to catch him, in a story involving everything from royalty to ancient orders. It was made into a film in 2001 and includes 42 pages of annotations. Recommended. [SA]

F-Stop: A Love Story in Pictures. Antony Johnston, with art by Matthew Loux. Oni, 2005. $14.95.
Nick Stoppard wants to be a professional fashion photographer, but he is not talented enough. But when he meets supermodel Chantel, he lies to her and tells her he worked in Europe, so she recommends him for a job. Even though his shots are blurry and poorly cropped, he becomes a hit for the fashion label Gauche. But will his new fame go to his head? [SA]

Fun Home: A Family Tragicomic. Alison Bechdel. Houghton Mifflin, 2006. $13.95.
This award-winning book was named *Time Magazine*'s best book of 2006 and was on many other "best of the year" lists. In this graphic memoir Bechdel discusses her relationship with her father, including his death, and how shortly after she came out she found out that her father was also gay. Also of note by Bechdel is *The Essential Dykes to Watch Out For* (Houghton Mifflin Harcourt, 2008), which collects 20 years of her popular comic strip. Recommended. [SA]

G

Gentleman Jim. Raymond Briggs. Drawn & Quarterly, 2008. $14.95.
A new printing of Briggs' 1980 work. Jim Blogg works in a public toilet, but he has dreams of being more, including fantasies where he dreams of being a cowboy or a highwayman.

Unfortunately this lands him in trouble. This may be one of the first original graphic novels to come out of the United Kingdom. Jim and Hilda Blogg were modeled after Briggs' parents (see *Ethel and Ernest)* and also used in his classic 1982 nuclear war graphic novel *When the Wind Blows.* [SA]

Get a Life. Philippe Dupuy and Charles Berberian. Drawn & Quarterly, 2006. $19.95.
This was originally published in France as a bestselling, award-winning, three-volume collection of short stories featuring Dupuy and Berbain's character Mr. Jean. Mr. Jean is a "laconic," single writer living in Paris, and the stories discuss his work situations, love life, friends, landlady, and his life in general. [SA]

Ghost World: The Special Edition. Daniel Clowes. Fantagraphics, 2008. $39.99.
Originally serialized in the comic *Eightball, Ghost World* features several stories about two teenage girls, Enid and Rebecca, and the odd people they encounter. The special edition includes Clowes' Oscar-nominated script for the 2001 film adaptation. [SA]

Gloomcookie. Serna Valentino. SLG, 2001–2007. $15.95–$18.95.
A "goth" comic primarily dealing with Lex, a girl who has a "star-crossed" love with a former Gargoyle named Damion who has gone on through several past lives, and with Sebastian, who has an odd past of his own. Monsters, magic, and a mysterious carnival are among the elements of this spooky and fun series. Artists include Ted Naifeh, John Gebbia, Breehn Burns, and Vincent Batignole. [SA]

Vol. 1 (no subtitle)	Vol. 4: *The Carnival Wars*
Vol. 2 (no subtitle)	Vol. 5: *The Final Curtain*
Vol. 3: *Broken Curses*	

God Save the Queen. Mike Carey, with art by John Bolton. DC/Vertigo, 2007. $19.99 (HC); $12.99 (SC).
Partially related to the *Sandman* titles, this original graphic novel is about a North London teenager who gets mixed up with a group of slacker fairies and gets caught up in a war of Fairy Queens. [SA]

Golgo 13. Takao Saito. VIZ, 2006–2008. $9.99.
The 13 volumes of this "M"-rated graphic novel contain a wide range of the popular *Golgo* stories that have appeared in Japan since 1969, where they have been collected into 150 volumes and adapted into live action and animated works. The series is about master assassin Duke Togo, aka Golgo 13. Some stories focus on the killer while others are about those who hired him or his targets. Many of the stories collected by VIZ show how Golgo 13 affected modern events such as Princess Diana's death and the recount problems of the 2000 U.S. election. Each volume collects two stories published at different times. [SA]

Vol. 1: *Supergun*	Vol. 8: *Gravestone in Sicily*
Vol. 2: *Hydra*	Vol. 9: *Headhunter*
Vol. 3: *Power to the People*	Vol. 10: *Wasteland*
Vol. 4: *The Orbital Hit*	Vol. 11: *The Wrong Man*
Vol. 5: *Wiseguy*	Vol. 12: *Shadow of Death*
Vol. 6: *One Minute Past Midnight*	Vol. 13: *Flagburner*
Vol. 7: *Eye of God*	

Gorgeous Caret. You Higuri.
A yaoi-title (though with no graphic sexuality) about Florian, a beautiful but impoverished man in nineteenth-century France who agrees to be sold to moneylender Ray Balzac Courtland in order to pay off family debts. But Courtland is also the "gentleman thief" Noir, and Florian is soon drawn into his schemes. The first series is rated 16+ while the second in only rated 13+. [YR]
   Gorgeous Caret, Vols. 1–4. Tokyopop/Blu.
   Gorgeous Caret Galaxy, Vol. 1. Digital Manga Publishing/June.

Graphic Witness: Four Wordless Graphic Novels. George Walker (Ed). Firefly Books, 2007. $29.95.
A collection of four "proto-graphic novels," including the first wordless novel *The Passion of Man* (*25 Images de la Passion d'un Homme*, 1918) by Frans Masereel. Also included are *Wild Pilgrimage* (1932) by Lynd Ward, *White Collar* (1938) by Giacomo Patri, and *Southern Cross* (1951) by Laurence Hyde. These four works were created by woodcuts, not drawings. [SA]

The Grave Robber's Daughter. Richard Sala. Fantagraphics, 2006. $9.95.
Something strange is happening in the town of Obidiah's Glen, and it has something to do with clowns. It's up to girl detective Judy Drood to find out what happened. A fun and unusual story. See *Mad Night* for another of Judy's adventures. [SA]

Gravitation. Maki Murakami. Tokyopop. $9.99. Rated OT.
A yaoi manga about Shuichi Shindou, a high school student who dreams of being a rock star. He soon meets Eiri Yuki, a 22-year-old romance novelist, and the relationship between the two causes changes in both his life and his music. The story ranges from the absurd to the serious. The series is rated OT, has been collected in 12 volumes, and has a one-volume sequel *Gravitation EX*. There have also been two original novels based on the series. [SA]

Grimm Fairy Tales. Various artists. Zenescope, 2006–. $15.99.
A mysterious woman named Sela who encounters teens and others with problems and tells them or lets them read new versions of famous fairy tales. If the person is doing wrong (or having wrong done to them), then what happens in the story can come true. A woman named Belinda has also appeared, but she seems to have an opposite agenda. There have been six collections so far, along with oversized hardcover versions of the first two. The series can be violent and has had spin-offs and related works, including *Grimm Fairy Tales: The Piper, Return to Wonderland,* and *1001 Arabian Nights*. [SA]

GTO. Tohru Fujisawa.
Eikichi Onizuka is a 22-year-old former motorcycle gang member who figures if he became a teacher he might meet a teenage girl who will sleep with him. As it turns out, he is a good teacher who actually helps his students. A popular and award-winning series, GTO was 25 volumes long and spawned both a live action and an animated television show. Beginning in 2006, Tokyopop began *GTO: The Early Years*, which reprinted Fujisawa's earlier stories about Onizukua. The first series is rated OT, while the 15 volumes of the second series are rated M. [SA]
   GTO: Great Teacher Onizuka. Tokyopop, 2002–2005. $9.99.
   GTO: The Early Years. Tokyopop, 2006–. $9.99.

Gus & His Gang. Chris Blain. First Second, 2008. $16.95.
Originally published in France, this graphic novel set in the old West features several short stories, some of them humorous, about Gus and his fellow outlaws. [SA]

H

Fletcher Hanks, works of. Edited by Paul Karask. Fantagraphics, 2007–2009. $19.95–$24.95.
Fletcher Hanks was a comic book creator of the late 1930s and early 1940s who has gotten a following in recent years. His unusual characters included Fantomah, one of the first female heroes, and Stardust the Super Wizard, who, when fighting evildoers trying to take over the world, would transform them into other things or simply hurl them into space. The first book won an Eisner award and was on many "Best of the Year" lists. [YR]
> *I Shall Destroy All the Civilized Planets*
> *You Shall Die by Your Own Evil Creation*

Happy Mania. Moyoco Anno. Tokyopop, 2003–2004. $9.99.
This 11-volume series was one of Tokyopop's first "M" rated titles. 24-year-old Shigeta wants to meet the perfect man, but it's usually her own poor judgment that's stopping her. [SA]

Haunted. Philippe Dupuy. Drawn & Quarterly, 2008. $24.95.
This award-nominated solo work by Dupuy (who usually works with Charles Berberian) contains several short stories. [SA]

Hellblazer. Various artists. DC Comics/Vertigo. Various dates and prices.
John Constantine: Is he an ordinary man who acts like he is a powerful magician or is he a powerful magician who acts like he is an ordinary man? Or is it a little of both? A man who has made enemies in both Heaven and Hell and who has lost friends in the war against evil, Constantine fights on, even if he doesn't want to. *Hellblazer* is the longest running Vertigo title, having started in 1988, and a film adaptation was released in 2005 that partially adapted the *Dangerous Habits* storyline. The collections are listed in order by issue chronology, not volume publication date, and also includes stories from other sources. Some have the series title as *John Constantine: Hellblazer*. [SA]
> *Original Sins.* Jamie Delano, with art by John Ridgway and Alfredo Alcala.
> *The Devil You Know.* Jamie Delano, with art by Mark Buckingham, David Lloyd, and others.
> *The Fear Machine.* Jamie Delano and Dick Foreman, with art by Mark Buckingham, Richard Piers Rayner, and others.
> *The Family Man.* Jamie Delano and Dick Foreman, with art by Ron Tiner, Kevin Walker, Mark Buckingham, Sean Phillips, Steve Pugh, Dean Motter, and Mark Pennington.
> *Rare Cuts.* Jamie Delano, Grant Morrison, and Garth Ennis, with art by Sean Phillips, David Lloyd, Richard Piers Rayner, and Mark Buckingham various (various issues).
> *Dangerous Habits.* Garth Ennis, with art by Will Simpson and others.
> *Bloodlines.* Garth Ennis, with art by Art by Will Simpson, Steve Dillon, Mike Barreiro, and Kim DeMulder.
> *Fear and Loathing.* Garth Ennis, with art by Steve Dillon.
> *Tainted Love.* Garth Ennis, with art by Steve Dillon.
> *Damnation's Flame.* Garth Ennis, with art by Steve Dillon, Will Simpson, and Peter Snejbjerg.

Rake at the Gates of Hell. Garth Ennis, with art by Steve Dillon.

Son of Man. Garth Ennis, with art by John Higgins.

Haunted. Warren Ellis, with art by John Higgins.

Setting Sun. Warren Ellis, with art by Frank Teran, Tim Bradstreet, Marcelo Frusin, Javier Pulido, and James Romberger.

Hard Time. Brian Azzarello, with art by Richard Corben and Tim Bradstreet.

Good Intentions. Brian Azzarello, with art by Marcelo Frusin.

Freezes Over. Brian Azzarello, with art by Marcelo Frusin, Guy Davis, and Steve Dillon.

Highwater. Brian Azzarello, with art by Marcelo Frusin, Giuseppe Camuncoli, and Cameron Stewart.

Red Sepulchre. Mike Carey, with art by Steve Dillon and Marcelo Frusin.

Black Flowers. Mike Carey, with art by Jock, Lee Bermejo, and Marcelo Frusin.

Staring at the Wall. Mike Carey, with art by Marcelo Frusin and Doug Alexander Gregory.

Stations of the Cross. Mike Carey, with art by Leonardo Manco, Chris Brunner, Marcelo Frusin, and Steve Dillon.

Reasons to Be Cheerful. Mike Carey, with art by Leonardo Manco, Giuseppe Camuncoli, and others.

The Gift. Mike Carey, with art by Leonardo Manco and Frazer Irving.

Empathy Is the Enemy. Denise Mina, with art by Leonardo Manco.

The Red Right Hand. Denise Mina, with art by Leonardo Manco.

Joyride. Andy Diggle, with art by Leonardo Manco.

The Laughing Magician. Andy Diggle, with art by Leonardo Manco and Danijel Zezelj.

Roots of Coincidence. Art by Leonardo Manco and Giuseppe Camuncoli.

Scab. Peter Milligan, with art by Eddie Campbell, Goran Sudzuka, and others.

Constantine: The Hellblazer Collection. Various writers and artists. Includes film adaptation.

ORIGINAL GRAPHIC NOVELS

All His Engines. Mike Carey, with art by Leonardo Manco.

Dark Entries. Ian Rankin, with art by Werther Dell'Edera.

SPIN-OFFS

Hellblazer: Papa Midnite. Mat Johnson, with art by Tony Akins and Dan Green.

Hellblazer: Lady Constantine. Andy Diggle, with art by Goran Sudzuka (the character first appeared in issues of *Sandman*).

Hellblazer Presents: Chas: The Knowledge. Simon Oliver, with art by Goran Sudzuka.

Hellboy. Written and drawn by Mike Mignola unless indicated. Dark Horse Comics, 2002–. $17.95 and up.

During World War II the Nazis tried to conjure a demon from Hell, but it ended up in allied hands, a small, red, horned child wearing a stone glove. The authorities named him Hellboy. As he grew he joined the U.S. government's Bureau for Paranormal Research and Development, where he worked along with the aquatic Abe Sapien, the pyrokinetic Liz Sherman, and others. There have been a number of Hellboy collections and others that collect the adventures of the other members of the BPRD. Hellboy has been featured in both live action and animated films as well as original novels. The animated films have inspired a series of titles for younger readers. [SA]

Hellboy: Seed of Destruction. Additional material by John Byrne and Mark Chiarello.
Hellboy: Wake the Devil
Hellboy: The Chained Coffin and Others
Hellboy: The Right Hand of Doom
Hellboy: Conqueror Worm
Hellboy: Strange Places
Hellboy: The Troll Witch and Others
Hellboy: Darkness Calls. Art by Duncan Fegredo.
Hellboy: The Box Full of Evil
Hellboy: Library Edition. $49.95 each.
Volume 1: Collects *Seed of Destruction* and *Wake the Devil*
Volume 2: Collects *The Chained Coffin*, *The Right Hand of Doom*, and others
Volume 3: Collects *Conqueror Worm* and *Strange Places*

Hellboy Weird Tales, Vols. 1–2. $17.95. Short stories by Mignola, John Cassaday, Joe Casey, Jill Thompson, Craig Thompson, Jim Starlin, and others.

The Adventures of the B.P.R.D. Mignola, with additional creators including John Arcudi, Guy Davis, and Dave Stewart. $17.95.

B.P.R.D.: Hollow Earth and Other Stories	*B.P.R.D.: The Black Flame*
	B.P.R.D.: The Universal Machine
B.P.R.D.: The Soul of Venice and Other Stories	*B.P.R.D.: Garden of Souls*
	B.P.R.D.: Killing Ground
B.P.R.D.: Plague of Frogs	*B.P.R.D.: 1946*
B.P.R.D.: The Dead	

Abe Sapien: The Drowning. Art by Jason Shawn Alexander. $17.95.
Lobster Johnson: Iron Prometheus. Art by Jason Armstrong. $17.95.

Hero Corps: The Rookie. Jason Becker, with art by Greg Moutafis. Baby Shark Productions, 2005. $7.95.
Another look at superheroes. In a world where millions of people have superpowers, a special police force must keep order. [SA]

Hero Squared. Keith Giffen and J. M. DeMatteis, with art by Joe Abraham. Boom!, 2007–. $14.99.
A partly humorous superhero story. Milo is a slacker whose life is turned upside down by the appearance of Captain Valor, his superpowered counterpart from another reality. The two can't get along and things are made worse by the fact that Milo's girlfriend is the counterpart of a supervillain who destroyed the world. [YR]
Vol. 1 (no subtitle)   Vol. 3: *Love and Death*
Vol. 2: *Another Fine Mess*
Also of interest is *Planetary Brigade*, which is a prequel featuring Captain Valor's superteam.

Heroes. Various writers and artists. DC/Wildstorm, 2007–. $29.99 each.
Many of these original stories based on the popular NBC television show were first featured online. There have been two volumes as of 2009. [YR]

Hicksville. Dylan Horrocks. Drawn & Quarterly, 2001. $19.95.
Writer Leonard Batts is looking into the background of Dick Burger, the hottest person in comics today. His investigations bring him to Burger's birthplace, the small town of Hicksville,

New Zealand, where he finds collections of famous old comics and unreleased ones by people like Picasso. He also finds out the truth about Dick Burger. A great book for lovers of comics history. [SA]

The High School Chronicles of Ariel Schrag. Touchstone/Simon & Schuster, 2008–2009. $15.00–$16.00.
While in high school Schrag created and self-published several autobiographical comics, one for each year of high school. She would write them over summer vacation, photocopy them, and then sell them around school. In the late 1990s, SLG published the first three, *Awkward*, *Definition*, and the Eisner-nominated *Potential*, and they recently have been recollected by Touchstone (combining the first two into a single volume), which has also put out the previously unreleased senior-year volume *Likewise*. These volumes cover her high school life and includes the loss of her virginity as well as her coming out as a lesbian and her first girlfriend. Recommended. [SA]

The Hills Have Eyes: The Beginning. Jimmy Palmiotti and Justin Gray, with art by John Higgins. Fox Atomic Comics, 2007. $17.99.
An original story set between the 2006 remake of the horror film *The Hills Have Eyes* and its sequel. [SA]

***Hino Horror* series.** Hideshi Hino. DH Publishing, 2004–. $9.95.
Rated for adults, these 14 volumes feature various horror stories. [SA]

Volume 1: *The Red Snake*
Volume 2: *The Bug Boy*
Volume 3: *Oninbo and the Bugs from Hell*
Volume 4: *Oninbo and the Bugs from Hell 2*
Volume 5: *The Living Corpse*
Volume 6: *Black Cat*
Volume 7: *The Collection*

Volume 8: *The Collection 2*
Volume 9: *Ghost School*
Volume 10: *Death's Reflection*
Volume 11: *Gallery of Horrors*
Volume 12: *Mystique Mandala of Hell*
Volume 13: *Zipangu Night*
Volume 14: *Skin and Bone*

Historical Biographies
While most of the graphic novel biographies are written for children, there are several that have been written on an adult level. [YR]

A Dangerous Woman: The Graphic Biography of Emma Goldman. Sharon Rudahl. The New Press, 2007. $17.95.
A look at the life of the famous anarchist.

J. Edgar Hoover: A Graphic Biography. Rick Geary. Hill and Wang, 2008. $16.95.
This biography of the first head of the FBI tends to use captions under panels to tell the story, with word balloons used only for occasional dialogue.

King: The Special Edition. Ho Che Anderson. Fantagraphics, 2010. $34.99.
Originally produced in three volumes, this is a "warts and all" look at Martin Luther King's life between 1952–1968. Some of it is presented as interviews with "witnesses" who talked about him, both his supporters and his detractors. The special edition includes almost 100 pages not included in previous volumes.

Louis Riel: A Comic Strip Biography. Chester Brown. Drawn & Quarterly, 2003. $17.95.
Perhaps the least known figure on this list, Riel was a nineteenth-century Canadian politician

who led the rebellions of the Metis people against the recently formed Canadian government. The book also contains over 20 pages of notes.

Malcolm X: A Graphic Biography. Andrew Helfer, with art by Randy Duburke. Hill and Wang, 2006. $15.95.
Like the Hoover biography, this black-and-white work mainly uses captions under panels to tell the story, with word balloons used only for occasional dialogue.

Ronald Reagan: A Graphic Biography. Andrew Helfer, with art by Steve Buccellato and Joe Staton. Hill and Wang, 2007.
A biography of the 40th president told in the same style as the Hoover and Malcolm X titles.

Suspended in Language: Niels Bohr's Life, Discoveries, and the Century He Shaped. Jim Ottaviani, with art by Leland Purvis, Linda Medley, Jay Hosler, and others. GT Labs, 2004. $24.95.
A look at the life of the Danish physicist including his discoveries, his relationships with Einstein and Heisenberg, his escape from occupied Denmark, and his work on the Manhattan Project. The book includes references and an index.

A History of Violence. John Wagner, with art by Vince Locke. DC/Vertigo, 1997. $9.99.
The basis for the Oscar-nominated film, Tom McKenna gets unwanted publicity after stopping a robbery. This leads some gangsters who thinks that he looks familiar to pay him a visit. [SA]

Houdini: The Man from Beyond. Jeff Phillips and Brian Haberlin, with art by Haberlin and Gilbert Monsanto. Image, 2004. $16.95.
After his death, Houdini's soul is put into the body of a stockbroker. Now with the help of his old friend Arthur Conan Doyle he must stop a supernatural evil before it is too late. [YR]

House of Clay. Naomi Nowak. NBM, 2007. $12.95.
Part of NBM's Comiclit line, *House of Clay* is the story of Posy, whose family was once rich, but now circumstances have forced her to work as a seamstress in sweatshop. But with new acquaintances including a mute girl and a fortune-teller, her life may be changing even more than she thought. Another NBM title of note by Nowak is *Unholy Kinship*. [SA]

Hutch Owen. Tom Hart. Top Shelf, 2000–2004. $14.95 each.
The trials and travails of the homeless Hutch Owen. [SA]
> *The Collected Hutch Owen*
> *Hutch Owen: Unmarketable*

Hwy 115. Matthias Lehmann. Fantagraphics, 2006. $19.95.
Set in France, private investigator Rene Pluriel travels the highway looking for an escaped serial killer and meets some odd people along the way. An odd and good work. [SA]

I

I Love Led-Zeppelin: Panty-Dropping Comics. Ellen Forney. Fantagraphics, 2006. $19.95.
This collection contains various works by award-nominated writer/artist Forney, collected from various sources. They range from one-page works to longer stories as well as collaborations. Also of note by her is *Lust: Kinky Online Personal Ads from Seattle's The Stranger* (Fantagraphics, 2008), which collects the illustrations she did for adult personal ads for the site known as "Lustlab." [AO]

I Never Liked You. Chester Brown. Drawn & Quarterly, 2002. $15.95.
Canadian cartoonist Chester Brown has written several autobiographical stories that appeared in the comic book *Yummy Fur.* This volume is set in the mid-1970s during his youth and teen years and includes such things his early encounters with girls. Also by Brown and set during this period is the currently out-of-print *The Playboy.* Brown also appears in the works of his friends and fellow cartoonists Seth and Joe Matt. [SA]

I Shall Never Return, Vols 1–5. Kazuna Uchida. Aurora/Deux, 2008. $12.95.
An explicit 18+ yaoi manga, this series deals with Ritsuro who must help his old friend Ken who has fallen into hard times and sordid circumstances. Their friendship soon becomes more. [AO]

Ice Haven. Daniel Clowes. Pantheon Books, 2005. $18.95 (HC).
While there is a general story in this "Narraglyphic Picto-Assemblage" involving a missing boy, a teenage girl, a comic fan, a failed poet, and others in the town of Ice Haven, there are also some odd cartoons intermixed throughout, such as the foulmouthed Blue Bunny. [SA]

Ichigenme: The First Class Is Civil Law. Fumi Yoshinaga. 801 Media, 2007. $15.95.
An explicit, two-volume, 18+ yaoi series about Tamiya and Tohdou, former classmates whose relationship becomes much more. [AO]

IDW's Tales of Terror. Various artists. IDW, 2004. $16.99.
An anthology of horror stories including those based on *30 Days of Night* and *CVO.* Contributors include Steve Niles, Ben Templesmith, and Jeff Marriotte. Text stories are also included. [SA]

I'm Not Your Steppin' Stone. Shiuko Kano. 801 Media, 2007–. $15.95.
In this explicit, two-volume, 18+ yaoi title, Sakai Kazuya is interested in a woman who likes only well-educated men. So he asks her younger brother Ezumi to tutor him. But what Ezumi wants in return is Sakai. [AO]

In the Shadow of No Towers. Art Spiegelman. Pantheon Books, 2004. $19.95.
Oversized and on cardboard pages with art read vertically over two pages, this is Spiegelman's view of post-9/11 life. This includes telling what happened to him on that day as well as 10 pages that were first published in a German newspaper. Also included are turn-of-the-century comic strips including *The Yellow Kid* and *Little Nemo in Slumberland.* The book's cover is the one that was used on the first post–9/11 issue of the *New Yorker.* [SA]

Incognegro. Mat Johnson, with art by Warren Pleece. DC/Vertigo, 2008. $19.99.
Subtitled "A Graphic Mystery" and set in he 1930s. *Incognegro* is about Zane Pinchback who is black but light-skinned enough to "pass" for white. This allows him to go to the South and get the truth about lynchings. He then writes articles about what is happening under the name "Incognegro." But when his brother in Mississippi is accused of killing a white woman, his undercover mission finds added mysteries. [SA]

Innocent Bird. Hirotaka Kisaragi. Tokyopop/Blu, 2007–. $9.99.
In this three-volume yaoi series an angel is sent to Earth to send a demon back to hell only to find that the demon has renounced evil and wants to live as a human. [SA]

Invasion '55. Chuck Dixon, with art by Lito Fernandez. IDW, 2002. $12.99.
A fun alien invasion story. It's Halloween 1955. Hidalgo Wells, New Mexico, is about to be attacked, and its up to an air force officer, a biker, a reporter, and a 10-year-old boy to stop them. [YR]

Irredeemable. Mark Waid, with art by Peter Krause. Boom! Studios, 2009–. $9.99–.
What happens when the world's greatest superhero becomes its greatest threat? [YR]

IR$. Stephan Desberg and Bernard Vrancken. Cinebook, 2008–. $19.95.
Originally published in France, this series is about Larry B. Max who works for a little-known branch of the IRS, one that involves shoot-outs and international intrigue. Other Cinebook titles for older readers include *Largo Winch, The Worlds of Aldebraran, Alpha, Pandora Box, Lady S.*, and *The Scorpion.* [SA]

    Vol. 1: *Taxing Trails*   Vol. 3: *Silicia, Inc.*
    Vol. 2: *Blue Ice*

Isaac the Pirate. Christophe Blain. NBM, 2003–. $14.95.
This award-winning French comic is about Isaac, an eighteenth-century artist who needs money to be with the woman he loves. Unfortunately, the ship captain who hired him to come along on his voyage turns out to be a pirate, and now Isaac is stuck sailing around the world. [YR]

    Vol. 1: *To Exotic Lands*
    Vol. 2: *The Capital*

It's a Good Life, If You Don't Weaken. Seth. Drawn & Quarterly, 2003. $24.95.
This "picture novella" was selected as one of the "100 Best Comics of the 20th Century" by the editors of *Comics Journal*. While it may seem like an autobiographical work as both the author and fellow cartoonist Chester Brown appear, it is at least partially fictional. The main plot has Seth trying to find out more about an obscure cartoonist known as "Kalo." [SA]

IWGP: Ikebukuro West Gate Park. Ira Ishida, with art by Sena Aritou. Digital Manga Publishing, 2004–2006. $12.95.
A spin-off of a hit Japanese television drama, which itself was based on a mystery novel. The series deals with Makoto, who gets himself caught up in mysteries that affect his gang and the area girls. [SA]

J

James Sturm's America: God, Gold, and Golems. Drawn & Quarterly, 2007. $24.95.
This book contains three previously released stories: "The Revival," set in 1801 Kentucky at a revival meeting; "Hundreds of Feet Below Daylight," set in an 1886 Idaho mining town; and the award-winning "The Golem's Mighty Swing," which is set in the early 1920s and deals with the "Stars of David," a barnstorming Jewish Baseball Team who are convinced by a promoter to have a black player dress as the Golem. Recommended. [SA]

Jason, works of. Fantagraphics Books.
Jason is an award-winning Norwegian comics creator born John Arne Sæterøy. His stories feature anthropomorphized animals, and some are silent. The books were originally published in France and Norway and include such plotlines as a man using a time machine to kill Hitler (*I Killed*), people turning into zombies (found in *Almost Silent*), humorous short stories (*Low Moon*), a man who was framed for murder (*Why Are*), and Hemingway, Fitzgerald, Pound, and Joyce working as cartoonists in 1920s Paris (*Left Bank*). His work is enjoyable and recommended. [SA]

Hey, Wait . . . . 2001. $12.95.
Sshhh! 2002. $14.95.
The Iron Wagon. 2003. $12.95.
Why Are You Doing This? 2005. $12.95.
The Left Bank Gang. 2006. $12.95.
I Killed Adolf Hitler. 2007. $12.95.

The Last Musketeer. 2008. $12.95.
Pocket Full of Rain. 2008. $19.99.
Low Moon. 2009. $24.99.
Almost Silent. 2010. $24.99. (collects
  four additional works)
Werewolves of Montpellier. 2010. Price TBA.

Jeremiah Harm. Keith Giffen, with art by Alan Grant. Boom! 2007. $14.99.
In this science fiction title, three of the worst criminals in the galaxy have escaped from an intergalactic prison and they're headed for modern day Earth. The authorities must free another prisoner—Harm—to track them down. [YR]

Jew Gangster. Joe Kubert. Ibooks, 2005. $22.95 (HC).
It's 1930s New York City and young Reuben "Ruby" Kaplan decides that it would be better to work for crooks than to stay in school. See *Brownsville* for a similar theme. [SA]

The Jew of New York. Ben Katchor. Pantheon Books, 1998.
An odd story set in Upstate New York in 1830 involving odd schemes, mysticism, and religious fanaticism. [SA]

Jews in America: A Cartoon History. David Gantz. The Jewish Publication Society, 2006. $28.00.
Slightly oversized and updated and expanded from the 2001 edition, this nonfiction work follows the history of the Jews in the Americas from the Conversos who sailed with Columbus up through modern times. See also *The Story of the Jews: A 4,000 Year Adventure.* [SA]

Jimbo's Inferno. Gary Panter. Fantagraphics. $29.95.
This award-winning oversized title is a prequel to 2004's *Jimbo in Purgatory* and presents an odd story inspired by Dante. [SA]

Jokes and the Unconscious. Daphne Gottlieb and Diane DiMassa. Cleis Press, 2006. $17.95.
Nineteen-year-old Sasha is working at a hospital, the same one where her now dead father was a doctor. She deals with the people there and her life in general. The book also deals with Sasha's sexuality and includes the occasional joke. [SA]

Jonah Hex. DC Comics.
Jonah Hex is a scarred-faced ex-Confederate solider turned bounty hunter who travels the Old West. Hex has made guest appearances in various animated adaptations, and a feature film staring Josh Brolin came out in 2010. The Showcase edition contains stories from the 1970s while the others collect the current ongoing series. [YR]

> *Showcase Presents: Jonah Hex*, Vol. 1. John Albano & Michael Fleischer, with art by Tony DeZuniga, Doug Wildey, José Luís Garcia-López, and others. 2005–. $16.99.
>
> *Current series:* Jimmy Palmiotti and Justin Gray, with art by various including Luke Ross, Tony DeZuniga, Paul Gulacy, Jordi Bernet, Phil Noto and Val Semeiks, Russ Heath, Darwyn Cooke, Rafa Garres, and David Michael Beck. 2006–. $14.99 each.
>
> > Vol. 1: *A Face Full of Violence*   Vol. 5: *Luck Runs Out*
> > Vol. 2: *Guns of Vengeance*   Vol. 6: *Bullets Don't Lie*
> > Vol. 3: *Origins*   Vol. 7: *Lead Poisoning*
> > Vol. 4: *Only the Good Die Young*

There will be additional volumes.

Juicy Mother.
Two anthologies with gay and lesbian themed comic stories. Contributors include Ariel Schrag, Howard Cruise, Alison Bechdel, and Jennifer Camper who is also the editor. The stories and art are varied, ranging from humorous to serious to romantic to just silly. The second volume is twice as large as the first. [SA]
    Vol. 1 (no subtitle). Soft Skull Press, 2005. $10.95.
    Vol. 2: *How They Met.* Manic D. Press, 2007. $14.95.

Julius Knippl: Real Estate Photographer. Ben Katchor. Little, Brown, and Co., 1996. $16.95.
Several short, even one page, vignettes about a strange little city and the unusual people in it. [SA]

Junjo Romantica. Shungiku Nakamura. Tokyopop/Blu. 2006–. $12.99.
A high-selling, rated M yaoi title, *Junjo Romantica* deals with several relationships. Besides the couple of Junjo Romantica, there are the additional stories of the couples in Junjo Terrorist and Junjo Egoist. At least 11 volumes are available. [SA]

Just a Pilgrim. Garth Ennis, with art by Carlos Ezquerra and Mark Texeira. Dynamite Entertainment, 2009. $29.99.
After a solar event called "The Burn" ruined most of the Earth, what's left of humanity tries to survive on what was once the ocean floor. Then the former killer known as The Pilgrim arrives. [SA]

K

Kade. Sean O'Reilly, with art by Allan Otero. Arcana, 2005. $9.95.
A sword-and-sorcery epic set in the Iron Age. Kade was born with opalescent white skin and coal black hair, and now he fights demons, including the one who ordered him killed at birth. [SA]

Kickback. David Lloyd. Dark Horse, 2006. $12.95.
Most of the cops in Franklin City are on the take, but when Joe Canelli's partner is killed, he discovers that even he has his limits. [SA]

The Killer. Matz, with art by Luc Jacamon. Archaia Studios Press, 2007–. $19.95.
Originally published in France as the five-volume *Le Tueur*, these volumes tell the story of a hired killer whose profession is starting to get to him. [SA]

The King. Rich Koslowski. Top Shelf, 2005. $19.95.
Reporter Paul Erfurt used to write the "Elvis is Alive" stories for the tabloids. Now *Time Magazine* wants him to interview the biggest thing in Vegas—a golden-helmeted singer known as "The King." [SA]

King of the Lamp. Takako Shigematsu. Go! Comi, 2007. $10.99.
Long ago a king who took 1,000 girls for his harem was punished by being turned into a genie and trapped in a lamp. Now he can be free by helping 1,000 women find love. [SA]

Kingdom of the Wicked. Ian Edginton, with art by D'Israeli. Dark Horse, 2004. $15.95.
British writer Christopher Grahame is the hot children's writer hailed as a "natural successor to Rowling." As a child he dreamed about a fantasy world, and now as an adult he finds

himself back in the land of Castrovalva. But it is horribly changed after a dictator brought war, carnage, and death to it, a dictator with a strange connection to Grahame. [SA]

Kings in Disguise. James Vance, illustrated by Dan Burr. W. W. Norton, 2006. $16.95.
This award-winning, highly regarded book is set in 1932 as young Freddie Bloch becomes a hobo and rides the rails after his father walks out and his brother is put in jail. He encounters others who help or try to hurt him, and he gets mixed up with Detroit labor riots, anti-communist mobs, and people willing to burn out the hobo jungles. [SA]

Klezmer: Book One: Tales of the Wild East. Joann Sfar. First Second, 2006. $16.95.
Set in prewar Eastern Europe, where Noah Davidovich called "The Barron of my Backside," is a musician without a group who meets several other characters, including Yaacov, who was kicked out of school by the Rabbi; Vincenzo, a wandering Italian fiddler; and Tsholka, a gypsy chased by Cossacks. At least two other books may be made. [SA]

L

Lazarus Jack. Mark Ricketts and Horacio Domingues. Dark Horse, 2004. $14.95.
Once Jackson Pierce was a master magician, but now he's just an old man in a nursing home and his family mysteriously disappeared long ago. Now he has the chance to regain both his youth and his family if he can face the mystical dangers. [SA]

The League of Extraordinary Gentlemen. Alan Moore, with art by Kevin O'Neill. DC/Wildstorm, 2002–2007. $14.95–.
Alan Quatermain, Mr. Hyde, Captain Nemo, the Invisible Man, and *Dracula*'s Mina Murray are brought together to stop threats to England and the world. Moore includes not only these characters in his stories but other literary characters ranging from the well known (Poe's Inspector Dupin or Wells' Dr. Moreau) to the obscure (including characters from Victorian erotica). The first two volumes of this award-winning title take place in the 1890s, including the League dealing with the War of the Worlds, while *The Black Dossier* takes place in the post–"Big Brother" 1950s and deals with incarnations of the League throughout the centuries. Each volume also has an oversized Absolute Edition that costs $75.00–$99.00, though while the first two volumes include the original scripts and artwork, the third offers less. Top Shelf is now publishing the three volume *LOEG: Century*, which takes place in various parts of the twentieth century. Check Appendix B for the LOEG annotation by Jess Nevins. Recommended. [SA]

> *The League of Extraordinary Gentlemen*, Vol. 1
> *The League of Extraordinary Gentlemen*, Vol. 2
> *The League of Extraordinary Gentlemen: Black Dossier*

Les Bijoux. Jo Eun-Ha, with art by Park Sang-Sun. Tokyopop. $9.99.
A five-volume, rated OT fantasy mahwa set in a world where the cruel Habits oppress the commoners known as the Spars. But a child born of a hunchback and a dwarf may change all that. [SA]

Life and Times of Martha Washington in the Twenty-First Century. Frank Miller, with art by Dave Gibbons and others. Dark Horse, 2009. $99.95.
In the 1990 limited series *Give Me Liberty*, Frank Miller introduced Martha Washington, an African-American woman in the twenty-first century who escaped her poor background to

join the military and who gets caught up in events that will tear America apart. A mix of science fiction, political intrigue, war, and absurd humor make up the first story and the various sequels, which have now been collected together for the first time in this 600-page oversized, hardcovered, and slipcased edition. [SA]

Life Sucks. Jessica Abel and Gabe Soria, with art by Warren Pleece. First Second, 2008. $19.95. Dave Miller is stuck in the ultimate dead-end job. A vampire has "turned" him just so he could have someone be the night manager at the convenience store he owns. Now Dave has to learn to accept the "night life," avoid drinking people's blood directly (his choice) and figure out how to talk to the girl that he likes, especially when another, more powerful vampire has expressed an interest in her. [YR]

Life's a Bitch. Roberta Gregory. Fantagraphics, 2005. $16.95.
A collection of Gregory's "Bitchy Bitch" stories from the comic book *Naughty Bits.* Midge McCracken is a very angry woman who works in an office. She is often complaining, but it is usually in her head instead of out loud. Some stories feature her younger selves "Bitsy Bitch" and the "Hippie Bitch." Gregory worked on several Underground Comix in the 1970s, including *Wimmen's Comix.* The comic was made into an animated television show. [SA]

Line. Yua Kotegawa. ADV, 2006. $9.99.
In this one-shot manga, a high school girl named Chiko finds a cell phone on the streets and begins to receive calls telling her that people are about to commit suicide and only she can stop it. [YR]

Literary and Film Adaptations.
Comic books and graphic novels have long been a medium in which prose works have been adapted. Titles that are based on novels but contain original stories are, for the most part, elsewhere in this appendix. In addition, while films have inspired many comic book series, they too have been directly adapted into comic form. Direct adaptations include the following.

BEOWULF
There are two adaptations of this ancient work. The first, by Hinds, is primarily art with text appearing on most pages. The second is an adaptation of the 2007 film. [YR]
> *Beowulf.* Adapted by Gareth Hines. Candlewick Press, 2007. $21.99.
> *Beowulf.* Chris Ryall. Based on the screenplay by Neil Gaiman and Roger Avery, with art by Gabriel Rodriguez. IDW, 2007. $17.99.

BIBLE
Bible stories have long been adapted into comic form that includes graphic novels. Some feature a large part of both the Old and New Testament while others concentrate on one particular story.
> *The Book of Genesis.* Illustrated by R. Crumb. W. W. Norton, 2009. $24.95. From Creation to the death of Joseph as recounted by Robert Crumb. [SA]
> *The Bible: Eden.* Dave Elliott and Keith Giffen, with art by Scott Hampton. IDW, 2003. $21.99. The story of Adam and Eve (with their nudity shown), along with a few excerpts from other parts of the Bible. [SA]
> *The Manga Bible.* Siku and Akinsiku. Doubleday, 2007. $12.95. This manga version of the Bible covers Genesis to Revelation but skips parts or glides over things (Noah is only two pages). The dialogue is modern and the book also includes information on how it was made. [YR]

CITY OF GLASS. Paul Auster. Adapted by Paul Karasik, with art by David Mazzucchelli. Henry Holt, 2004. $14.00.
This adaptation off an odd detective story, originally published in 1994 as Neon Lit: Paul Auster's City of Glass, was on Comic Journal's list of the 100 Most Important Comics of the Century. [SA]

THE CURIOUS CASE OF BENJAMIN BUTTON: A GRAPHIC NOVEL. F. Scott Fitzgerald. Adapted by Nunzio DeFilippis and Christina Weir, with art by Kevin Cornell.
The story of the man born old and growing young. [YR]

DADDY COOL. Donald Goines. Adapted by Don Glut, illustrated by Alfredo P. Alcalala. Melrose Square Publishing, 2003. $9.95.
Based on the urban crime novel about a hired killer, this work contains several disturbing elements. [SA]

DARK WRAITH OF SHANNARA. Terry Brooks and Robert Place Napton, with art by Edwin David. Del Rey Books, 2008. $13.95.
A new story set in Brooks' fantasy world. [YR]

DEAN KOONTZ
> *Dean Koontz's Frankenstein: Prodigal Son*. Adapted by Chuck Dixon, with art by Brett Booth. Del Rey Books, 2008. $22.95. An adaptation of the 1995 book. It's the present, but Frankenstein's Monster is still around, as is the doctor himself, who is making new, deadly creatures. Now it's up to his first creation and a police detective to stop him. There will be several books adapting the work. [SA]
> *In Odd We Trust*. Dean Koontz and Queenie Chan, with art by Chan. Del Rey Books, 2008. $10.95. An original graphic novel prequel to Koontz's *Odd Thomas* books, which are about a 20-year-old who can see, but not hear, ghosts, and uses them to solve crimes and mysteries. [SA]

THE DISCWORLD GRAPHIC NOVELS. Terry Pratchett and adapted by Scott Rockwell, with art by Steven Ross. Harpercollins, 2008. $24.95.
A collection of two comic adaptations of the first two of Pratchett's "Discworld" fantasy novels *The Colour of Magic* and *The Light Fantastic*. [YR]

THE DRESDEN FILES. Jim Butcher. Del Rey Books, 2008–. $14.95–$22.95.
In this popular book series, Harry Dresden is a private detective who is also a powerful wizard and whose cases deal with matters that the police cannot handle. The books were first put out in comic book form by Dabel Brothers Productions. *Welcome to the Jungle* is an original story by Butcher and acts as a prequel to the first book in the series *Storm Front*, which has been adapted. Additional adaptations are planned. [YR]
> *The Dresden Files: Welcome to the Jungle*. Art by Ardian Syaf and others.
> *The Dresden Files: Storm Front*. Adapted by Mark Powers, with art by Ardian Syaf.

THE FOUNTAIN. Darren Aronofsky, with art by Kent Williams. DC/Vertigo, 2005. $19.99.
Referred to as "the ultimate directors cut" and "a sister-project to the film," it expands upon the original work. [SA]

NEIL GAIMAN
Besides his work in comics, Gaiman is also a multi-award-winning writer of short stories and novels. [YR]

From Dark Horse Comics:

Creatures of the Night. Art by Michael Zulli. 2004. $12.95. Adapts two of his short stories.

The Facts in the Departure of Miss Finch. Art by Michael Zulli. $13.95. An unusual story about and an unusual night.

Harlequin Valentine. Art by John Bolton. 2001. $10.95. A modern updating of the commedia dell' arte legend of Harlequin and Columbine.

Murder Mysteries. Art by P. Craig Russel. 2002. $14.95. An angel must solve the very first murder.

From DC/Vertigo:

Neil Gaiman's Neverwhere. Adapted by Mike Carey, with art by Glen Fabry. $19.99. *Neverwhere* began as a six-episode BBC program created by Gaiman which then expanded into a novel. Richard Madoc discovers dangers and wonders when he finds himself in "London Below."

GEORGE A. ROMERO'S DAWN OF THE DEAD. Adapted by Steve Niles, with art by Chee. IDW, 2004. $17.99; and GEORGE A. ROMERO'S LAND OF THE DEAD. Adapted by Chris Ryall, with art by Gabriel Rodriguez. IDW, 2006. $19.99.

Adaptations of two of Romero's zombie films. [SA]

GIVE IT UP! AND OTHER SHORT STORIES. Franz Kafka, with adaptation and art by Peter Kuper. NBM, 1995. $15.95.

Stories by Kafka. The text is often "narration style" with the occasional word balloon. [YR]

GRAPHIC CLASSICS. Eureka Publications. $11.95.

These books feature adapted works of many famous writers, including some of their lesser-known stories. Occasionally a story will be mostly text with a few illustrations while others are fully "graphic." Some volumes have new editions and are adapted by various writers and artists. [YR]

Each book starts with *Graphic Classics*, and the "subtitles" are:

Adventure Classics	*Gothic Classics*	*O. Henry*
Ambrose Bierce	*H. G. Wells*	*Oscar Wilde*
Arthur Conan Doyle	*H. P. Lovecraft*	*Rafael Sabatini*
Bram Stoker	*Horror Classics*	*Robert Louis Stevenson*
Edgar Allan Poe	*Jack London*	*Science Fiction*
Fantasy Classics	*Mark Twain*	

THE GREAT AND SECRET SHOW, VOLS 1–2. Clive Barker, and adapted by Chris Ryall with art by Gabriel Rodriguez. IDW, 2006–2007. $19.95.

Two men with magic powers impregnate women leading to supernatural evil. [SA]

THE GUIN SAGA MANGA: THE SEVEN MAGI. Kaoru Kurimoto, with art by Kazuaki Yanagisawa. Vertical, 2007–. $12.95.

A three-part adaptation of Kurimoto's fantasy novel. [SA]

HARLEQUIN MANGA. Dark Horse. $9.95.

Harlequin romances adapted in a manga style. The "pinks" are rated 13+ and are "Shojo" romance while the "violets" are 16+ and are more "Josei" romance. [YR]

Harlequin Pink: The Bachelor Prince. Debbie Macomber, with art by Misao Hoshiani.

Harlequin Pink: A Girl in a Million. Betty Neels, with art by Kako Itoh.

Harlequin Pink: Idol Dreams. Charlotte Lamb, with art by Yoko Hanabusa.

Harlequin Violet: Blind Date. Emma Darcy, with art by Mihoko Hirose.

Harlequin Violet: Holding on to Alex. Margaret Way, with art by Misao Hoshiani.

Harlequin Violet: Response. Penny Jordan, with art by Takako Hashimoto.

HIDEYUKI KIKUCHI'S VAMPIRE HUNTER D. Saiko Takaki. Digital Manga Publishing, 2007. $12.95.

A manga adaptation of the popular series of Japanese novels that were made into several films and set 10,000 years in the future, a world of science, sorcery, and danger. [SA]

THE LIFE EATERS. David Brin, with art by Scott Hampton. DC/Wildstorm, 2003. $19.95.

This book adapts and expands Brin's 1986 story "Thor Meets Captain America" in which the Norse Gods help the Nazis. [YR]

M. Jon J. Muth. Harry Abrams, 2008. $24.95.

A graphic adaptation of the classic 1931 Fritz Lang film about a child killer. This volume collects a 1990 limited series from the now defunct Eclipse comics. [YR]

MASTERS OF HORROR. Various Artists. IDW, 2006. $17.99.

Based on the Showtime television series, this book adapts teleplays based on the works of Joe R. Landsdale and H. P. Lovecraft. [SA]

MARVEL

Marvel Comics has adapted many novels in recent years, ranging from classic works to modern fantasy and horror titles. Some adaptations of recent works were created along with Dabel Brothers productions.

Anita Blake: Vampire Hunter. Laurell K. Hamilton. 2007–. $14.99–$19.99.

Private investigator and vampire hunter Blake gets mixed up with various supernatural evils. Additional volumes are planned. Additional adaptors on these titles include Stacie Ritchie Jonathon Green and Jessica Ruffner-Booth, with art by Brett Booth, Wellinton Alves, and Ron Lim. [SA]

> *Laurell K. Hamilton's Anita Blake: Vampire Hunter Guilty Pleasures,* Vols. 1–2
> *Laurell K. Hamilton's Anita Blake: Vampire Hunter: The First Death.*
> *Laurell K. Hamilton's Anita Blake: The Laughing Corpse Book 1—Animator*
> *Laurell K. Hamilton's Anita Blake: The Laughing Corpse Book 2—Necromancer*

The Hedge Knight. George R. R. Martin, with art by Ben Avery. 2007–2008. $14.99.

Based on a short story that is a prequel to Martin's fantasy series "A Song of Fire and Ice." Squire Dunk becomes Sir Duncan the Tall when his mentor dies and goes to the joust. There he gets on the wrong side of a Prince. [YR]

> *The Hedge Knight,* Vol. 1
> *The Hedge Knight II: Sworn Sword*

Lords of Avalon. Sherrilyn Kenyon and Robin Gillespie, with art by Tommy Ohtsuka. 2008–2009. $19.99.

An adaptation of the Arthurian fantasy work that Kenyon wrote under the name Kinley MacGregor. [YR]

> *Lords of Avalon: Sword of Darkness*
> *Lords of Avalon: Knight of Darkness*

Marvel Illustrated

These are the adaptations of classic works are primarily written by Roy Thomas 2008–. $19.99–$24.99. [YR]

These include:

The Iliad. Art by Miguel Angel Sepulveda.

Kidnapped. Art by Mario Gully.

The Last of the Mohicans. Art by Steven Kurth and Denis Medri.

The Man in the Iron Mask. Art by Hugo Petrus.

Moby Dick. Art by Pascal Alixe.

The Odyssey. Art by Greg Tocchini.

The Picture of Dorian Gray. Art by Sebastial Fiumara.

Pride and Prejudice. Art by Nancy Butler.

The Three Musketeers. Art by Hugo Petrus.

Treasure Island. Art by Mario Gully.

Magician Apprentice. Raymond E. Feist, $19.99.
In a fantasy world, young Pug becomes the apprentice to a court magician, but evidence of people from another dimension may lead to war. [YR]

Vol. 1. Adapted by Michael Avon Oeming and Bryan J. Glass, with Art by Brett Booth and Ryan Stegman.

Vol. 2. Adapted by Glass and Stegman.

Red Prophet: The Tales of Alvin Maker, Vols. 1–2. Orson Scott Card and Roland Bernard Brown, with art by Miguel Montenegro.
An adaptation of Card's first book in his fantasy/alternate history series. [YR]

Stephen King
Marvel has two series of limited series that are based on the works of Stephen King. The Dark Tower titles are an original prequel about the origin of the Gunfighter Roland Deschain of Midworld. The comics based on *The Stand* are a direct adaptation of King's novel about a killer plague and the dark force spawned in its wake. There will be additional volumes of both. [SA]

The Dark Tower. Peter David, with art by Jae Lee and Richard Isanove. 2007–. $24.99.

The Dark Tower: The Gunslinger Born   *The Dark Tower: The Fall of Gilead*
The Dark Tower: The Long Road Home   *The Dark Tower: The Battle of*
The Dark Tower: Treachery   *Jericho Hill*

The Stand. Adapted by Roberto Aguirre-Sacassa, with art by Mike Perkins.

The Stand: Captain Trips   *The Stand: Soul Survivors*
The Stand: American Nightmares

NEVERMORE: A GRAPHIC ADAPTATION OF EDGAR ALLAN POE'S SHORT STORIES. Various writers and artists. Sterling Illustrated Classics, 2008. $14.95.
Adaptations of some of Poe's stories and poems, some of which have been updated and put in different settings. [SA]

THE NIGHTMARE FACTORY, VOLS.. 1–2. Fox Atomic Comics/HarperCollins, 2007. $17.99–.
Based on the stories of Thomas Ligotti, with introductions before each story by Ligotti. Writers and artists of this award winner include Colleen Doran, Ben Templesmith, Ted McKeever, and Bill Sienkiewicz. [SA]

THE PROBABILITY BROACH: THE GRAPHIC NOVEL. L. Neil Smith and Scott Bieser. Big Head Press, 2004. $19.95.
Police Detective Edward "Win" Bear is transported from his world where America is in bad shape to a more advanced one in which a libertarian society lives in the North American Confederacy. He runs into his alternate self, talking apes, and a heavily armed society. But

even here there is danger, and it has ties to his own world. See also *Roswell, Texas* for yet another version of Bear. [SA]

RICHARD MATHESON'S I AM LEGEND. Adapted by Steve Niles, with art by Elman Brown. IDW, 2007. $19.99.
An adaptation of the classic story in which a virus turns people into monsters, and one man is left to stop them. [SA]

THE RING SERIES. Based on the novels of Koji Suzuki. Adapted by Hiroshi Takahashi. Dark Horse and Digital Manga Press, 2003–. $12.94–$14.95.
A mysterious videotape is circulating around Tokyo, and they say if you watch it you die. This series started as a novel and was made into a film, first in Japan and later in the United States. Some of the manga are adapted from the books while others are adaptations of the film sequels. Artists include Misao Inagaki, Sakura Mizuki, and Meimu. [YR]
    Vols. 0–2: *The Ring*   Vol. 4: *Birthday*
    Vol. 3: *Spiral*

ROGUE ANGEL: TELLER OF TALL TALES. Barbara Randall Kesel, with art by Renae De Liz. IDW, 2008. $19.99.
A new adventure based on the popular series by Alex Archer about Annja Creed, a globe-traveling archeologist who has strange adventures and possesses a magic sword once owned by Joan of Arc. [SA]

SPOOKHOUSE BOOKS ONE AND TWO. Adapted by Scott Hampton. IDW, 2004. $19.99 each.
Horror stories by various authors mixed in with the occasional illustrated text story, including *The Monkey's Paw* and stories by Robert E. Howard and Algernon Blackwood. [YR]

STOKER'S DRACULA. Adapted by Roy Thomas, with art by Dick Giordano. Marvel, 2005. $24.99.
An adaptation of Bram Stoker's classic horror novel. [YR]

THE TWO FACES OF TOMORROW. James P. Hogan and Yukinobu Hoshino. Dark Horse, 2006. $19.95.
A manga adaptation of the work by British science fiction writer Hogan. [SA]

UNDERWORLD. Kris Oprisko and Danny McBride, with art by Nick Postic and Nick Marinkovich. IDW, 2004. $19.99.
An adaptation of the film in which vampires fight werewolves as well as an original tale set in 1373 Africa. [SA]

Little Star. Andi Watson. Oni Press, 2006. $19.95.
Simon Adams took on less work so that he could spend more time with his wife and young daughter. He's not sure if this was what he wants, but with his "little star" things might just work out. [SA]

Little White Mouse Omnibus. Paul Sizer. Café Digital Comics, $24.95. 2006.
This 450-page edition collects the complete run of the series. In the future, 16-year-old Loo Lay Th'Eng and her sister are traveling in cryogenic suspension to the Galactic Science Academy. When she wakes up she finds the ship was destroyed, that she is the sole survivor, and that she is stuck on an abandoned mining satellite, where over 60 years earlier all of the crew suddenly died. Her only companions are two robots and the ghost of a dead scientist. The

stories also have flashbacks to her earlier years, the investigation of her family and friends into the "accident" that destroyed the ship, and stories set after she escapes the station. [YR]

Living with the Dead. Mike Richardson, with art by Ben Stenbeck. Dark Horse, 2008. $9.95.
A pair of friends have figured out how to survive the Zombie Apocalypse, mainly by putting on masks and going "braiiiiins" whenever they go out. But when a woman shows up, things may change. [SA]

Logicomix: An Epic Search for Truth. Apostolos Doxiadis and Christos H. Papadimitriou, with art by Alecos Papadatos. Bloomsbury, 2009. $22.95.
With World War II breaking out in Europe, philosopher, mathematician, and pacifist Bertrand Russell recounts his life while at a lecture in America. Part of the graphic novel includes the book's creators discussing Russell and their creation of the book, which also gives information on other notable mathematicians and philosophies. [SA]

Lone Wolf and Cub. Kazuo Koike, with art by Goseki Kojima. Dark Horse, 2000–2002. $9.95.
The 8,000+ pages of this well-known manga series tell the tale of a samurai who became an assassin who traveled around feudal Japan pushing a baby cart containing his infant son. The manga, published in Japan between 1970–1976 has influenced creators around the world and has been adapted into a series of films. Dark Horse has collected it as a small series of 28 4" x 6" books, and some of it had been released by First Comics in 1987, making it one of the first translated manga available in America. [SA]

Vol. 1: *The Assassin's Road*	Vol. 15: *Brothers of the Grass*
Vol. 2: *The Gateless Barrier*	Vol. 16: *The Gateway Into Winter*
Vol. 3: *The Flute of the Fallen Tiger*	Vol. 17: *The Will of the Fang*
Vol. 4: *The Bell Warden*	Vol. 18: *The Twilight of the Kurokuwa*
Vol. 5: *Black Wind*	Vol. 19: *The Moon in Our Hearts*
Vol. 6: *Lanterns for the Dead*	Vol. 20: *A Taste of Poison*
Vol. 7: *Cloud Dragon, Wind Tiger*	Vol. 21: *Fragrance of Death*
Vol. 8: *Chains of Death*	Vol. 22: *Heaven and Earth*
Vol. 9: *Echo of the Assassin*	Vol. 23: *Tears of Ice*
Vol. 10: *Hostage Child*	Vol. 24: *In These Small Hands*
Vol. 11: *Talisman of Hades*	Vol. 25: *Perhaps in Death*
Vol. 12: *Shattered Stones*	Vol. 26: *Battle in the Dark*
Vol. 13: *The Moon in the East,*	Vol. 27: *Battle's Eye*
the Sun in the West	Vol. 28: *The Lotus Throne*
Vol. 14: *Day of the Demons*	

In 2002, Dark Horse put out a science fiction "reimagining" of the story called *Lone Wolf 2100* written by Mike Kennedy, with art by Francisco Ruiz Velasco. The three volumes cost $12.95 and are subtitled *Shadows on Saplings, The Language of Chaos,* and *Pattern Storm.*

The Long Haul. Antony Johnston, with art by Eduardo Barreto. Oni Press, 2005. $14.95.
A Western set in 1871. Cody Plummer is a former bank robber who is trying to go straight, but his past (and a Pinkerton agent) keeps catching up to him. When he hears of a federal money train going across the country he thinks that it may be time to get the old gang together for one last job. [SA]

***Lost Colony* series.** Grady Klein. First Second, 2006–. $14.95–.
Set during the nineteenth century, on a strange island where the people keep the outside
world away and have their own peculiarities and secrets. [SA]

Vol. 1: *The Snodgrass Conspiracy*   Vol. 3: *Last Rights*
Vol. 2: *The Red Menace*

Additional volumes are planned.

Lost Girls. Alan Moore, with art by Melinda Gebbie. Top Shelf, 2009. $45.00.
Shortly before the start of World War I, three women of various ages and social status meet at
the Austrian Hotel Himmelgarten. Their names are Alice, Wendy, and Dorothy, names that are
familiar to all but whose stories are not exactly what we know. As discussed in Chapter 6, this
book, while well reviewed, includes graphic sex and nudity, including the sexual activities of
minors, and this should be remembered when considering purchase. [AO]

Love and Capes*, Vol. 1: *Would You Like to Know a Secret? Thom Zahler. IDW, 2008.
$19.99.
Bookstore owner Abby thinks her boyfriend is just a "mild-mannered" accountant until she
learns that he is also the Crusader, the world's most powerful hero in this funny and touching
title. She must learn to accept that her boyfriend is sometimes in danger (and the fact he used
to date super heroine Amazona). Additional collections are planned. [YR]

Love and Rockets. The Hernandez Brothers. Fantagraphics Book.
Notable "alternative" comics titles, these comics by brothers Jamie and Gilbert (and occasionally Mario) Hernandez (also known as "Los Bros. Hernandez") are a must-have for adult
collections and have been recollected and reformatted in recent years, making it easier to
collect all of the stories. Most of the *L&R* stories deal with one of two settings/characters. Jamie's
stories are known both as "Hoppers 13" and "Locas" and are primarily about Margarita Luisa
"Maggie" Chascarrillo and her best friend (and occasional lover) Esperanza Leticia "Hopey"
Glass, two Latina women living in California. The stories cover their lives and the lives of
various supporting characters over the years, and some have an element of science fiction to them.
Gilbert's primary works are the "Palomar" stories, also known as the "Heartbreak Soup" stories,
which are set in a fictional Latin American village and deal with its inhabitants, including
Luba who later moves to America with her family. Both series are highly recommended. [SA]

THE COLLECTIONS
There have been a number of *L&R* collections over the years. Fantagraphics has created sev-
eral "library editions" that collect some of the earlier works as well as a 700+-page hardcover
collection that reprinted much of the same material. There are also newer collections of the
Love and Rockets comic, and starting in 2008, Fantagraphics began *Love and Rockets: New
Stories*, original graphic novels that come out on a yearly basis.

BY JAMIE
Love and Rockets Library Editions, $14.95–$16.95

Maggie the Mechanic   *Perla La Loca*
The Girl from H.O.P.P.E.R.S.

Hardcover Omnibus Editions

Locas: The Maggie and Hopey Stories. $49.95.
Locas II. $39.99.

Others, $9.95–$19.99

Whoa Nellie   *Ghost of Hoppers*
Locas in Love   *The Education of Hopey Glass*
Dicks and Deedees

BY GILBERT

Love and Rockets Library Editions, $14.95

Heartbreak Soup   *Beyond Palomar*
Human Diastrophism

Hardcover Collections

Palomar: The Heartbreak Soup Stories. $39.95.
Luba. $39.99.

Others

Luba in America   *Luba: Three Daughters*
Luba: The Book of Ofelia

BY JAMIE, GILBERT, AND MARIO

Amor Y Cohetes (*Love and Rockets Library*). $16.99.
Love and Rockets: New Stories. 2008–. $14.99.

One volume each year.

***Love as a Foreign Language Collected Edition*, Vols. 1–2.** J. Torres, with art by Eric Kim. Oni, 2005–. $11.95.
In this romantic comedy, Joel is an English-as-a-second language teacher working in South Korea. He's grown tired of it and is ready to go back to his native Canada when he becomes attracted to Hana, a secretary working at the school. The title was originally released as six individual books. [YR]

***Love Is Like a Hurricane*, Vols 1–5.** Tokiya Shimazaki. 801 Media, 2007–. $15.95.
This explicit yaoi manga begins when high school student Mizuki is molested on the train by Azuma, who happens to be the student body president. But this actually leads to a relationship between the two. [AO]

Love Mode. Yuki Shimizu. Tokyopop/Blu, 2006. $12.99.
This rated M yaoi manga focuses on the employees and customers of a male escort agency. Many of the parings tend to be older client/younger worker. Eleven volumes were produced in Japan. [AO]

***Love Pistols*, Vols. 1–5.** Tarako Kotobuki. Tokyopop/Blu, 2007–2008. $12.99.
In this rated M yaoi title, Norio discovers that he is one of the rare people who have evolved from an animal other than a monkey and that the only way to pass on his genes is if *he* gets pregnant. [AO]

Lucky. Gabrielle Bell. Drawn & Quarterly, 2006. $19.95.
This volume collects three issues from Bell's memoir comic book along with new short stories. The events portrayed include her professional life including how she lost the pages for the second story and had to redo the issue. [SA]

Lynda Barry's Ernie Pook's Comeek. 2010. Price TBA.
A popular cartoonist, Barry is best known for her comic strip *Ernie Pook's Comeek*, which looks

at two families from the point of view of younger children. Some of those stories had been collected by Sasquatch Books, but Drawn & Quarterly will be creating a multivolume hardcover collection that includes the complete stories. Also of note by Barry is 2008's *What It Is*. [SA]

M

Macedonia. Harvey Pekar and Heather Roberson, with art by Ed Piskor. Villard/Random House, 2007.
A nonfiction work telling how Roberson, a UC Berkeley student getting her graduate degree in Peace and Conflict Studies went to Macedonia for her thesis to learn how they avoided the problems that many of the former Yugoslavian republics had to deal with. Issues such as the ethnic conflicts between Macedonians and Albanians are also discussed. Roberson met Pekar via her sister and he has a cameo in the book. [SA]

Mad Night. Richard Sala. Fantagraphics, 2005. $18.95.
Strange murders are happening at Lone Mountain College and a masked man, a campus cop, and a gang of "girl pirates" are all involved. It is up to girl detective Judy Drood (also seen in *The Grave Robber's Daughter*) to save the day. [SA]

***Madara*, Vols. 1–5.** Eiji Otsuka, with art by Sho-U Tajima. DC/CMX, 2004–2005. $9.95.
A young Cyborg boy from a small village finds that his mechanical limbs also work as weapons after demons working for the evil emperor attack his home. This M rated work has also appeared in book, animated, radio drama, and video game form. [SA]

The Magical Life of Long Tack Sam. Ann Marie Fleming Riverhead Books (Penguin), 2007. $14.00.
In this award-winning "Illustrated Memoir" Fleming uses comic pictures, photographs, and other types of art to tell the story of her great-grandfather Long Tack Sam, a magician considered to be one of the "greatest vaudeville acts of the early 20th century." The book expands on a Fleming's documentary film. [YR]

Maintenance. Jim Massey, with art by Robbi Rodriguez. Oni, 2007–. $9.95.
What happens when mad scientists must clean up a mess in their lab? They call for Doug and Manny, the maintenance men at the evil science think tank TerroMax Inc. The pair must deal with monsters, robots, aliens, and more as part of their daily routine. A funny and fun title. [YR]
Vol. 1: *It's a Dirty Job*   Vol. 3: *Fighting Occupants of*
Vol. 2: *Fantastic Sewage & Other Stories*   *Interstellar Craft*

Mammoth Book of . . . . Running Press, 2007–. $17.95–.
Part of the "Mammoth" series of books, these concentrate on American, British, and Japanese comics ranging from the well known to the obscure. Of note is "I Saw It" in *War*, which was the basis for *Barefoot Gen*. [SA]
The Mammoth Book of Best Crime Comics   *The Mammoth Book of Best War Comics*
The Mammoth Book of Best Horror Comics   *The Mammoth Book of Zombie Comics*
The Mammoth Book of Best New Manga

Manga Sutra. Katsu Aki. Tokyopop, 2008–.$19.99.
Makoto and Yura were introduced by a matchmaker, and at 25 they married. Both virgins, they are unsure of what do, and their early experiences are unsatisfactory. But with the advice

of others they can learn, and both their sex and love lives can improve. While there is sex and nudity in this series, there are also the facts and mechanics of making love. Tokyopop has, of course, rated this for mature audiences and it is definitely for adults only. [AO]

Vol. 1: *Futari H* Vol. 3: *Intercourse*
Vol. 2: *Foreplay*

Marvel Classics
As with DC, Marvel has put out many books that reprint comics from the 1940s–1980s (and in some collections into the 1990s). The major forms of collections are the Masterworks, which are usually hardcover, 200–300 pages, in color, and cost $49.00 and up, though a handful have been released in paperback for less. The Essential Editions are paperback, generally around 500 pages, black and white, and cost $16 and up. A new format put out by Marvel are Omnibus editions, which are hardcover works that collect a large number of issues in color and may cost up to $100.00. Again, as with DC's Archives and Showcase Presents titles, there is some redundancy between the stories included in these three formats as well as in some of the other items listed. [YR]

ANT-MAN/GIANT-MAN
Henry Pym has used his science to both shrink and grow and became both Ant-Man and Giant-Man.

Marvel Masterworks: Ant-Man/Giant-Man, Vols. 1–2
Essential Astonishing Ant-Man, Vol. 1

ATLAS AGE MARVEL
During the 1950s Marvel went by the name Atlas. Besides many anthology series of science fiction and horror stories, including *Menace*, they continued to put out a handful of superhero stories (Captain America, Human Torch, Marvel Boy, etc.) as well as stories with the medieval Black Knight, the evil Yellow Claw, Lorna the Jungle Queen, and Lorna the Jungle Girl.

Marvel Masterworks: Atlas Era Black Knight/Yellow Claw, Vol. 1
Marvel Masterworks: Atlas Era Heroes, Vols. 1–3
Marvel Masterworks: Atlas Era Journey into Mystery, Vols. 1–2
Marvel Masterworks: Atlas Era Jungle Adventure, Vol. 1
Marvel Masterworks: Atlas Era Menace, Vol. 1
Marvel Masterworks: Atlas Era Strange Tales, Vols. 1–2
Marvel Masterworks: Atlas Era Tales of Suspense, Vols. 1–2
Marvel Masterworks: Atlas Era Tales to Astonish, Vols. 1–2

AVENGERS
One of Marvel's major superteams with members that include Captain America, Iron Man, and Thor.

Marvel Masterworks: The Avengers,   *Avengers/Defenders War*
   Vols. 1–9   *The Avengers: The Kree-Skrull War*
Essential Avengers, Vols. 1–7   *Avengers: The Serpent Crown*
The Avengers: Celestial Madonna   *Avengers: Vision and the Scarlet Witch*

THE BLACK PANTHER
T'Challa, ruler of the hi-tech African land of Wakanda appears in this 1970s title by the great Jack Kirby.

Black Panther, Vols. 1–2

CAPTAIN AMERICA

Since 1941, Captain America has fought for freedom. The first Masterworks collect his World War II adventures, while the other books and the Essential cover his return in the 1960s. Also listed are several collections in which he teamed up with the African-American hero the Falcon, including the time when he gave up his identity and became Nomad, The Man Without a Country.

Marvel Masterworks: Golden Age Captain America, Vols. 1–3

Marvel Masterworks: Captain America, Vols. 1–4

Essential Captain America, Vols. 1–6

Captain America: Bicentennial Battles

Captain America and the Falcon: Madbomb

Captain America and the Falcon: Nomad

Captain America and the Falcon: The Swine

CAPTAIN MARVEL/MS. MARVEL

A member of the alien Kree race, Mar-Vell fights instead for Earth. His friend, Earthwoman Carol Danvers, later gets similar powers and becomes Ms. Marvel.

Marvel Masterworks: Captain Marvel, Vols. 1–3

Essential Captain Marvel, Vol. 1

Essential Ms. Marvel, Vol. 1

DAREDEVIL

Though blind, lawyer Matt Murdock used his enhanced other senses, including a "radar sense" to protect New York. Besides stories from the 1960s and 1970s, the classic 1980s stories by Frank Miller have also been collected, including stories with his enemy and sometimes lover Electra.

Marvel Masterworks: Daredevil, Vols. 1–5

Essential Daredevil, Vols. 1–4

Daredevil by Frank Miller, Vols. 1–4

Electra by Frank Miller

THE DEFENDERS

A team of heroes that has included Dr. Strange, the Hulk, the Sub-Mariner, and the Silver Surfer.

Marvel Masterworks: The Defenders, Vol. 1

Essential Defenders, Vols. 1–4

DR. STRANGE

Marvel's Master of Mystic Arts.

Marvel Masterworks: Doctor Strange, Vols. 1–4

Essential Dr. Strange, Vols. 1–4

THE ETERNALS

A race of immortal beings with super abilities fight their enemies the Deviants. The stories from Jack Kirby can be collected either as two paperback collections or as a hardcover omnibus.

The Eternals by Jack Kirby/The Eternals Omnibus

Thor: The Eternals Saga

THE FANTASTIC FOUR

The first team of the Marvel Age of Comics. Mr. Fantastic, the Invisible Girl/Woman, the Human Torch, and the Thing have been protecting the world since 1961. The Visionaries books collect stories written or drawn by particular creators include John Byrne and George Perez, the Human Torch titles collects his solo adventures, and *Two-in-One* has the Thing teamed up with other heroes.

Marvel Masterworks: The Fantastic Four, Vols. 1–12
Essential the Fantastic Four, Vols. 1–7
The Fantastic Four Omnibus, Vols. 1–2
Fantastic Four Visionaries

Marvel Masterworks: The Human Torch, Vol. 1
Essential the Human Torch, Vol. 1
Essential Marvel Two-in-One, Vols. 1–3

GOLDEN AGE MARVEL

These collections from the 1940s include *Marvel Comics*, the first title from the company then known as Timely, along with the adventures of various superheroes including the original, android Human Torch.

Marvel Masterworks: Golden Age All-Winners, Vols. 1–3
Marvel Masterworks: Golden Age Daring Mystery, Vols. 1-2
Marvel Masterworks: Golden Age Human Torch, Vols. 1–2
Marvel Masterworks: Golden Age Marvel Comics, Vols. 1–4 and *Marvel Comics Omnibus*
Marvel Masterworks: Golden Age USA Comics, Vol. 1
Marvel Masterworks: Golden Age Young Allies, Vol. 1

HOWARD THE DUCK

Transported to Earth from the Duckworld, Howard is now trapped in a "world he never made." A funny and popular title from the 1970s.

Essential Howard the Duck, Vol. 1
Howard the Duck Omnibus

THE HULK

Caught in the explosion of a Gamma Bomb, Bruce Banner becomes the Hulk, and the madder he gets the stronger he gets. The Visionaries books include notable stories from the 1980s by Peter David, John Byrne, and others and the other titles feature additional adventures. After Banner gave a blood transfusion to his cousin Jennifer, she became the Savage She-Hulk.

Marvel Masterworks: The Incredible Hulk, Vols. 1–5
Essential the Incredible Hulk, Vols. 1–5
Incredible Hulk Omnibus
Essential Rampaging Hulk, Vol. 1

Hulk Visionaries
Hulk: Heart of the Atom
Hulk vs. the Marvel Universe
Essential Savage She-Hulk, Vol. 1

IRON MAN

Wounded while being held captive, inventor Tony Stark built a powerful armored suit and became Iron Man. "Demon in a Bottle" is a notable story in which he dealt with his alcoholism.

Marvel Masterworks: The Invincible Iron Man, Vols. 1–6
Essential Iron Man, Vols. 1–3

The Invincible Iron Man Omnibus
Iron Man: Demon in a Bottle
Iron Man vs. Dr. Doom

Marvel Handbook

Beginning in the 1980s, Marvel has put out comic book "handbooks" that act as encyclopedias of their characters. Most have been collected in Essential editions, while the more recent ones have been collected into trade editions.

Essential Official Handbook of the Marvel Universe, Vol. 1
Essential Official Handbook of the Marvel Universe Deluxe Edition, Vols. 1–3
Essential Official Handbook of the Marvel Universe Update '89, Vol. 1

Essential Official Handbook of the Marvel Universe Master Edition, Vols. 1–2

The Official Handbook of the Marvel Universe A–Z, Vol. 1

Marvel Horror, Fantasy, and Science Fiction

Marvel has a history of characters with horror and fantasy themes. *Amazing Fantasy* was a short lived 1960s title, while licensed characters such as Godzilla and literary characters such as Dracula and the Frankenstein Monster have had their own titles. Killraven fights against alien conquerors in the near future. The Man-Thing is man turned monster that haunts the Florida swamps, Jack Russell is the "Werewolf by Night," and the Marvel Horror books feature a number of characters, including Brother Voodoo.

Amazing Fantasy Omnibus

Essential Ghost Rider, Vols. 1–3

Essential Godzilla, Vol. 1

Essential Killraven, Vol. 1

Essential Man-Thing, Vol. 1

Essential Marvel Horror, Vols. 1–2

Essential Monster of Frankenstein, Vol. 1

Essential the Tomb of Dracula, Vols. 1–4 and

  Tomb of Dracula Omnibus, Vols. 1–2

Essential Werewolf by Night, Vols. 1–2

NICK FURY

During World War II, Sgt. Fury fought the Nazis with his "Howling Commandos." In the 1960s, Col. Fury led the intelligence organization *S.H.I.E.L.D* in fighting the forces of Hydra.

Marvel Masterworks: Sgt. Fury, Vols. 1–2

Marvel Masterworks: Nick Fury, Agent of S.H.I.E.L.D., Vols. 1–2

POWER MAN AND IRON FIST

Framed for a crime he didn't commit, Luke Cage gained super-strength and invulnerability and went to work as a "Hero for Hire." He was soon joined by martial artist Iron Fist, and their two respective titles were merged into one.

Essential Iron Fist, Vol. 1

Essential Luke Cage Power Man,

  Vols. 1–2

Essential Power Man and Iron Fist,

  Vols. 1–2

THE SILVER SURFER

The Silver Surfer came to Earth as a herald for the planet-eating Galactus but betrayed his master. Now, trapped on Earth, he protects this new world.

Marvel Masterworks: The Silver Surfer,

  Vols. 1–2

Essential Silver Surfer, Vols. 1–2

Silver Surfer Omnibus

SPIDER-MAN

Probably the best-known Marvel superhero, Spider-Man has been around for almost 50 years. The first four titles collect the issues of the 1960s–1970s while the other books collect major stories or stories featuring various friends and foes. Marvel Team-Up has Spider-Man with other heroes, and while not related to Spider-Man, Spider Woman is another arachnid-based hero.

Marvel Masterworks: The Amazing

  Spider-Man, Vols. 1–11

Essential The Amazing Spider-Man,

  Vols. 1–9

Amazing Spider-Man Omnibus, $99.99

Essential Peter Parker The Spectacular

  Spider-Man, Vols. 1–4

Spider-Man: Death of the Stacys

Spider-Man: Kraven's Last Hunt

Spider-Man: A New Goblin

Spider-Man: Saga of the Sandman

Spider-Man vs. the Black Cat

Spider-Man vs. Silver Sable

Essential Marvel Team-Up, Vols. 1–3

Essential Spider-Woman, Vols. 1–2

SUB-MARINER

Prince Namor of Atlantis has fought both Nazis and criminals above and below the waters. The Golden Age volumes feature stories from the 1940s.

Marvel Masterworks: Golden Age   *Marvel Masterworks: The Sub-Mariner*, Vols. 1–3
    Sub-Mariner, Vols. 1–3   *Essential Sub-Mariner*, Vol. 1

THOR

As punishment, Thor was trapped on Earth in the body of Dr. Don Blake. But when Blake strikes his cane on the ground, he transforms back into the God of Thunder.

Marvel Masterworks: The Mighty   *Essential The Mighty Thor*, Vols. 1–4
    Thor, Vols. 1–8   *Thor Visionaries: Walt Simonson*

X-MEN

This team of mutants fights for a world that "hates and fears them." The first three collections focus on the original lineup of the 1960s and 1970s, while the next three focus on the members of the team who joined in the 1970s. Various classic stories have been collected, as those have the spin-off teams X-Factor and the New Mutants and the team's best-known member, Wolverine.

Marvel Masterworks: The X-Men,   *Uncanny X-Men Omnibus*
    Vols. 1–7   *X-Men: God Loves, Man Kills*
Essential Uncanny X-Men, Vol. 1/   *X-Men, the Dark Phoenix Saga*
    Essential Classic X-Men, Vols. 2–3   *Essential X-Factor*, Vols. 1–3
X-Men Omnibus   *New Mutants Classic*, Vols. 1–3
Marvel Masterworks: The Uncanny   *Essential Wolverine*, Vols. 1–5
    X-Men, Vols. 1–6   *Wolverine Omnibus*
Essential X-Men, Vols. 1–9

Marvel Miscellaneous

Captain Britain Omnibus. The adventures of England's greatest hero.

The Champions, Vols. 1–2. A Los Angeles–based superteam.

Essential Dazzler, Vols. 1–2. Singer Allison Blaire has the mutant power to turn sound into light.

Essential Marvel Saga, Vols. 1–2. The history of the Marvel Universe.

Essential Moon Knight, Vols. 1–3. Mercenary Marc Spector becomes the "Fist of Konshu."

Essential Nova, Vol. 1. Teenager Richard Ryder gains powers from a dying alien.

Essential Super-Villain Team-Up, Vol. 1. When two evildoers team up the world must worry.

Marvel Masterworks: Deathlok. A cyborg-soldier fights in a post-apocalyptic world.

Marvel Masterworks: Rawhide Kid, Vols. 1–2. The adventures of this Old West gunfighter.

Marvel Masterworks: The Inhumans, Vol. 1. A hidden race of superpowered beings.

Marvel Masterworks: Warlock, Vols. 1–2. Created in a lab, Adam Warlock ends up having comic adventures.

Secret Wars Omnibus and *Secret Wars II Omnibus*. Two major limited series from the 1980s are collected in hardcover along with various related comic book issues.

What If? Classic, Vols. 1–5. Stories featuring an "alternate history" of Marvel Universe.

Women of Marvel, Vols. 1–2. A look at some of Marvel's superheroines.

Marvel Zombies. Marvel Comics, $15.99 –$29.99.
Spinning off from a story in *Ultimate Fantastic Four*, an alternate version of the Marvel Universe is shown where the superheroes have been transformed into zombielike creatures. They still have their powers and minds but are consumed by an intense hunger, causing them to ravage first the Earth and then the universe. *Dead Days* contains the original UFF stories and a prequel adventure, and *Army of Darkness*, copublished with Dynamite entertainment, also takes place at this time. The third and fourth collections take place at a time in between the first two volumes. The original collection has had many printings, and one reason for its popularity is the covers by Arthur Suydam that feature zombie versions of classic Marvel Comics' covers. Unless indicated, the following is written by Robert Kirkman, with art by Sean Phillips. [YR]
  Marvel Zombies
  Marvel Zombies 2
  Marvel Zombies: Dead Days. Additional story and art by Mark Millar and Greg Land.
  Army of Darkness vs. Marvel Zombies. John Layman, with additional art by Fabiano Neves
    and Fernando Blanco.
  Marvel Zombies 3. Fred Van Lente, with art by Kev Walker.
  Marvel Zombies 4. Fred Van Lente, with art by Kev Walker.
  Marvel Zombies Return. Various writers and artists.
Additional series are planned.

Joe Matt, works of. Drawn & Quarterly.
Matt, an American cartoonist who lived for a time in Canada, is the author of the memoir comic *Peepshow*, which has been collected in three volumes. While *Fair Weather* is set during his youth, the other two books are about his adult life. He does not portray himself in the best light, showing such things as failed relationships and masturbating to pornography. The stories also feature fellow cartoonists Chester Brown and Seth. [SA]
  The Poor Bastard. 2002. $16.95.   *Peepshow: The Cartoon Diary of Joe Matt.* 2003. $14.95.
  Fair Weather. 2002. $26.95.   *Spent.* 2007. $19.95.

Maus: A Survivor's Tale. Art Spiegelman. Pantheon Books.
On of the most notable titles of the past 30 years, this Pulitzer Prize–winning work has its beginnings as a three-page story in 1971. Volume 1, *My Father Bleeds History*, was released in 1986, and the second volume, *And Here My Troubles Began*, came out in 1991. It is available as two separate volumes or in one complete work. *Maus* is the story of what happened to Spiegelman's parents during the Holocaust, with a secondary story of his relationship with his father and the interviews that he did about his fathers experiences. All characters in *Maus* are drawn as animals, with mice for Jews, cats for Germans, pigs for Poles, dogs for Americans, and so forth. This is a must for any adult graphic novel collection, and it has been used in both high school and college courses. Some libraries catalog this in the 940s along with other books on the Holocaust. Highly recommended. [YR]
  Volumes 1 and 2. $14.95 each.
  The Complete Maus. $35.00.

Maxwell Strangewell. Matthew and Shawn Fillbach. Dark Horse, 2007. $19.95.
In this goofy science fiction story, an ancient being known as the Strangewell crashes to Earth, where he's found by Anna, who names him Max. But Max is an ancient and powerful being and all sorts of aliens are coming to Earth to find him. [YR]

Maybe Later. Philippe Dupuy and Charles Berberian. Drawn & Quarterly, 2006. $16.95.
Published in France as *Journal d'un album*, this book by frequent collaborators Dupuy and
Berberian has each doing separate stories in which they discuss their lives, working in comics,
problems with publishers, and more. [SA]

Megillat Esther. JT Waldman. The Jewish Publication Society, 2005. $18.00.
A retelling of the biblical story of Esther. The actual biblical verses are written in Hebrew on
the side of the pages, and halfway through the book the artwork flips upside-down so that
while it is first read left to right it is later reversed. The title means "Scroll of Esther," which is
the original name for the Bible's "Book of Esther." [SA]

Mendel's Daughter: A Memoir. Martin Lemelman. Free Press (Simon & Schuster), 2006.
$19.95.
This holocaust memoir is taken from videotaped conversations that Lemelman had with his
mother Gusta. When she was younger she lived in the Polish town of Germakivka (now part
of the Ukraine), which at first was under Russian control but soon taken over by the Nazis.
While much of her family was taken away to the concentration camps, she, and a handful of
others, was hidden by villagers who knew and were fond of her father, Mendel. Along with the
other Holocaust memoirs in this appendix, another title of note is Bernice Eisenstein's *I Was
a Child of Holocaust Survivors* (Riverhead Books, 2006), which has illustrations and a few
pages done in a comic format. [YR]

Micrographica. Renee French. Top Shelf, 2007. $10.00.
A very small (4.8" × 4.5" × 0.9" in.) paperback book that started as a Web comic. This story
of two rodents is told with one panel on each page and dialogue printed below. [YR]

The Middleman: The Collected Series. Javier Grillo-Marxuach, with art by Les McClaine.
Viper Comics, 2008. $19.95.
Wendy Watson is an office temp finding herself at a science lab when a rampaging monster is
stopped by the Middleman, a hero who stops the things that most people think only happen
in comics. Wendy becomes his partner and the pair have many bizarre (and humorous) adventures. A number of the stories were previously collected and adapted for the short-lived television series. [YR]

Missouri Boy. Leland Myrick. First Second, 2006. $16.95.
Missouri Boy features short vignettes from the author's life, from birth as a twin, to growing
up, to family triumphs and tragedies. [SA]

Mome. Fantagraphics, 2005–. $14.99.
Mome is an award-nominated quarterly anthology from Fantagraphics whose contributors
have included Gabrielle Bell, Jeffrey Brown, Paul Hornschemeier, David B., Jim Woodring,
and Lewis Trondheim. The books also include articles and interviews with creators. Fantagraphics also has a second anthology called *Blab!* [SA]

Mom's Cancer. Brian Fies. Abrams Image, 2006. $12.95
This graphic novel began as an Eisner Award–winning Web comic telling about his mother's
bout with lung cancer and how it affected him and his family. His mother, who died as the
book was going to press, wrote the afterword. Also by Fies is *Whatever Happened to the World
of Tomorrow* (2009). Recommended. [SA]

Mother Come Home. Paul Hornschemier. Fantagraphics, 2008. $22.99.
Thomas and his father both deal with the loss of his mother—Thomas by going into fantasy and his father by checking into an asylum. This was originally published by Dark Horse Comics. [SA]

***Mushishi*, Vols. 1–10.** Yuki Urushibara. Del Rey, 2007–. $12.95.
This award-winning OT manga deals with Ginko, who wanders around Japan studying strange magical creatures called "Mushi" and helping people who have problems with them. Unlike many other manga series, each volume has a separate story instead of one continuous series-long story. [YR]

MW. Osamu Tezuka. Vertical Press, 2007. $24.95.
In this 584-page hardcover collection of a 1970s Tezuka work, a sociopath who as a boy was exposed to a chemical called MW seeks revenge. His only confidant is a priest who with him was the only survivor of the chemicals use on a village, a priest who is also his secret lover. [SA]

My Paranoid Next Door Neighbor. Kazuka Minami. 801 Media, 2007. $15.95.
In this one-volume 18+ yaoi manga, high school senior Yukito can't help the feelings that he has been having for his old friend Hokuto and has been trying to avoid him. But what happens when Hokuto makes the first move? [AO]

N

Nana. Ai Yazawa. VIZ, 2005–. $8.99.
One of the bestselling manga titles, *Nana* is about two 20-year-old women with that name—Nana Komatsu—who has had problems with love and has moved to Tokyo hoping to find the right man, and Nana Osaki, a punk rock singer looking to take her band to the top. The two eventually meet and become friends. The rest of the series follows their lives. VIZ rated earlier volumes T+ but later changed it to M. Over 20 volumes have been published in Japan, though the American collections are not too far behind. The series has been adapted into both a live action film and an anime. [YR]

Narcissa. Lance Tooks. Doubleday, 2002. $15.95.
African-American filmmaker Narcissa is angry that her new film is being messed with despite promises to the contrary. When she finds she has only a short time to live, she decides to chuck it all and visits Spain, where the new people and places open up things for her. [SA]

Narcoleptic Sunday. Jeremy Haun, with art by Brian Koschak. Oni, 2007. $14.95.
Jack Larch has met the perfect girl. But one morning he wakes up to find himself accused of her murder. Now the police are after him, criminals are after him, and unfortunately he finds himself falling asleep at the worst times. [SA]

The New Adventures of Jesus: The Second Coming. Frank Stack. Fantagraphics, 2006. $19.95.
In 1962, Stack put out *The Adventures of Jesus*, one of the earliest Underground Comics. Subsequent stories placed Jesus in modern times dealing with counterculture movement, Vietnam, and other stories set in later decades. This book is a compilation of over 40 years of work. [SA]

9/11 Titles from Hill and Wang. Sid Jacobson, with art by Ernie Colón. Hill and Wang, 2006–2008. $16.95 each. [YR]
The first book is an adaptation of the 9/11 Report put out by the National Commission on Terrorist Attacks Upon the United States that makes the report simpler for the average person to understand. The second book covers the years following the attack and concentrates on the war with some additional information on domestic and world events.
The 9/11 Report: A Graphic Adaptation
After 9/11: America's War on Terror (2001–)

Northwest Passage: The Annotated Collection. Scott Chantler. Oni, 2007. $19.95.
Set in Rupert's Land in eighteenth-century Canada. Charles Lord was once an explorer seeking the Northwest Passage, but now he has settled down as governor of the frontier trading post Fort Newcastle. But when French Privateers attack, Lord must call on old friends and old ways. Chantler annotates the volume in both historical and storytelling terms. [YR]

Notes for a War Story. Gipi. First Second, 2007. $16.95.
Originally from Italy, this award-winning graphic novel follows three young men caught up in the war being fought in an unnamed European country. They start off just trying to survive but get to the point in which they are the worst kinds of men. [SA]

Notes from a Defeatist. Joe Sacco. Fantagraphics, 2003. $19.95.
A collection of various works by Sacco. They contain both fiction and nonfiction stories, some of which appear in other titles in this appendix. Some are serious, and others are humorous (and one set in a library is a little of both). [SA]

The Number 73304-23-4153-6-96-8. Thomas Ott. Fantagraphics, 2008. $28.95.
This silent graphic novel, originally published in both France and Germany, tells the story of a man who finds a paper with a set of numbers left behind by an executed prisoner. He then finds those numbers in sequence everywhere he goes and in anything he does. [SA]

O

Object of Desire. Tomoko Noguchi. Aurora/Luv Luv, 2008. $10.95.
A collection of erotic short stories from Aurora's Josei manga line. [AO]

Ode to Kirihito. Osamu Tezuka. Vertical, 2006. $24.95.
In this 822-page volume, said to be a favorite of Tezuka among his own works, Dr. Kirihito Osanai is investigating Monmow's disease, which causes people's faces to look like that of a dog. When he is also infected, he is forced into hiding and is caught up in various scenarios that test what it means to be human. There are also side stories regarding other doctors and others who have been infected that eventually tie into his own. Recommended. [SA]

Okko **series.** Hub. Archaia Press, 2007–. $19.95.
Originally published in France, this series is set in the Japan-like Pajan Empire. Demon-hunting warrior Okko, the mysterious giant Noburo, and the magical monk Noshin have various adventures. [SA]
The Cycle of Water
The Cycle of Earth
Three more books will be translated.

100 Bullets. Brian Azzarello, with art by Eduardo Risso. DC Comics/Vertigo, 2000–2009. $9.95 and up.

In the earlier volumes of this award-winning 100 issue series, the mysterious Agent Graves offers people who have been wronged a briefcase containing an untraceable gun along with 100 bullets. Later subplots involved Graves' participation in the Minutemen, a seven-member group who serve an organization called the Trust, and how his views and the Trust's may no longer be the same. [SA]

Vol. 1: *First Shot, Last Call*
   (additional art by Dave Johnson)
Vol. 2: *Split Second Chance*
   (additional art by Dave Johnson)
Vol. 3: *Hang Up on the Hang Low*
Vol. 4: *A Foregone Tomorrow*
Vol. 5: *The Counterfifth Detective*
Vol. 6: *Six Feet Under the Gun*

Vol. 7: *Samurai*
Vol. 8: *The Hard Way*
Vol. 9: *Strychnine Lives*
Vol. 10: *Decayed*
Vol. 11: *Once Upon a Crime*
Vol. 12: *Dirty*
Vol. 13: *Wilt*

One Thousand and One Nights. Jeon JinSeok, illustrated by Han Seunghee. Yen Press, 2005–. $10.95.

This Korean Mahwha adds a yaoi element to the classic story in which a boy takes his sister's place when she is summoned to the palace, and it is he who mollifies the king by telling stories. Some early volumes are listed as being published by ICEkunion who has since been absorbed by Yen. This series is rated OT and has at least six volumes. [SA]

1000 Steps to World Domination. Rob Osborne. AIT/Planet Lar, 2004. $12.95.

In this award-winning work, Osborne discusses how he wants to conquer the world through comics. This funny book includes many fantasy sequences. [SA]

Orbiter. Warren Ellis, with art by Colleen Doran. DC/Vertigo, 2003. $27.95.

The space shuttle *Venture* disappeared, putting an end to manned space travel. Now 10 years later, Cape Canaveral has become a tent city and the *Venture* has come home. But where has it been? [YR]

Ordinary Victories. Manu Larcenet. NBM. $15.95.

Originally from France, this award-winning series is part of NBM's ComicsLit line. The books deal with Marc, a photographer and how he deals with life, love, and his family. [SA]

   Ordinary Victories. 2005.
   Ordinary Victories: What Is Precious. 2008.

The Originals. Dave Gibbons. DC/Vertigo, 2004. $17.99 (SC).

This original graphic novel is set in a domed city that is both futuristic and retro. Lel and Bok want to join the Originals, the gang who enjoy nice clothes and music and ride hover-scooters and are the rivals of the leather-clad hoverbike-riding "Dirt." The book hearkens back to the "Mods vs. Rockers" of the mid-1960s England. [SA]

The Other Side. Jason Aaron, with art by Cameron Stewart. DC/Vertigo, 2007. $12.99.

Two soldiers, Private Billy Everette of the United States and Vo Binh Dai of the NVA, are in Vietnam of the same time, and both have to deal with the horrors of war. [SA]

Out of Picture: Art from the Outside Looking In, Vols. 1–2. Villard, 2007–. $19.95–$26.00.
A collection of short stories and illustrations from artists whose works include children books and animation, all who also work for Blue Sky Studios, which specializes in CGI Animation. [SA]

P

Palestine: The Special Edition. Joe Sacco. Fantagraphics, 2007. $29.95.
In this "journalistic" work, Sacco interviews Palestinians living in the West Bank and Gaza strip in the early 1990s and shows their lives. There have been several editions of this book and some libraries place it in the 956 area. [SA]

Parasyte. Hitoshi Iwaaki. Del Rey, 2007. $12.95.
Alien parasites have invaded Earth and have the ability to take over people's bodies and transform them any way they wish. High school student Shin was infected but prevented the alien from taking over any more than his hand. The two have come to an uneasy agreement, and now Shin must try to save the human race from these deadly invaders. Tokyopop had previously put out a translation of this title, but the eight volumes from Del Rey are closer to the original Japanese version. [SA]

Paris. Andi Watson, with art by Simon Gane. SLG, 2007. $10.95.
Paris in the 1950s. Juliet is a penniless American art student who earns money by painting portraits of socialites. That's how she meets Deborah, who is visiting from England. Can class differences stop them from being friends and maybe something more? [SA]

Past Lies. Christina Weir and Nunzio DeFilippis, with art by Christopher Mitten Oni. $14.95.
Millionaire Trevor Schalk underwent hypnotherapy in the belief that he would be reincarnated, and he wanted to remember his old life while in his new one. That same night he was murdered. Twenty-five years later Timothy Gilbraight begins to believe he was Schalk. It is up to Amy Devlin, a private investigator with a secret of her own, to find out the truth. [SA]

Paul series. Michel Rabagliati. Drawn & Quarterly, 2003–. $16.95–$19.95.
These semiautobiographical stories by French-Canadian cartoonist Rabagliati cover various points in Paul's life, sometimes via flashbacks, ranging from working as a camp counselor when he was younger to the attempts of he and his wife to have a baby. Rabagliati had won a "best new talent award" for his first Paul comic book. Recommended. [SA]
    Paul Has a Summer Job   *Paul Goes Fishing*
    Paul Moves Out

A People's History of the American Empire. Howard Zinn and Paul Buhle, with art by Mike Konopacki. Metropolitan Books/Henry Holt and Co., 2008. $17.00.
A graphic adaptation of Zinn's *A People's History of the United States*, this nonfiction book looks at some parts of American history that do not show the country in the best light, including anti-union activities and the prevention of women's and civil rights as well as overseas activities. [SA]

Percy Gloom. Cathy Malkasian. Fantagraphics, 2007. $18.95.
The short and odd Percy just wants to work for a place that issues safety warnings, but Percy gets caught up in even more strangeness. [SA]

La Perdida. Jessica Abel. Pantheon, 2006. $19.95.
The story of Carla, an American of Mexican descent who stays in Mexico with her ex-boyfriend. They begin to have problems, and each has a different circle of friends, but then things take a tragic turn. At first the dialogue is in English, with any Spanish translated at the bottom of the panel, but soon it is primarily translated Spanish used in the word balloons. A glossary of particular terms, phrases, people, and places used or mentioned in the book is included. [SA]

Persepolis (The Complete Persepolis). Marjane Satrapi. Pantheon, 2007. $24.95.
Marjane Satrapi was 10 years old and living in Tehran when the Islamic Revolution occurred. *Persepolis* tells both of her teenage years under the new regime, her time studying abroad, and her return for a time as an adult. This award-winning work has been translated into more the 20 languages (it was originally in French) and was turned into an award-winning animated film. *Persepolis* has also been produced in two separate volumes subtitled *The Story of a Childhood* and *The Story of a Return.* Recommended. [YR]

Pet Noir: An Anthology of Strange but True Pet Crime Stories. Edited by Shannon O'Leary. Manic D Press, 2006. $13.95.
Odd true stories about crimes that involved pets from the tragic to the odd. [SA]

The Photographer: Into War-Torn Afghanistan with Doctors Without Borders. Emmanuel Guibert. First Second, 2009. $29.95.
The true story of photographer Didier Lefèvre's 1986 journey with Doctors Without Borders into war-torn Afghanistan. Lefèvre's actual photos are seen along with Guibert's art. [SA]

Postcards: True Stories That Never Happened. Edited by Jason Rodriguez. Villard, 2008. $21.95 (HC).
Rodriguez took various postcards from the early 1900s and had various writer/artist teams make up stories based on the messages written on the cards. Creators include Tom Beland, Harvey Pekar and Joyce Brabner, Matt Kindt, Stuart Moore, Neil Kleid, and others. [YR]

Powers. Brian Michael Bendis, with art by Michael Avon Oeming. 2000–. $13.95–.
In a world with superheroes and supervillians the police must find ways to deal with their activities. Christian Walker and Deena Pilgrim are homicide detectives who investigate cases involving "Powers," whether they were the perpetrators or the victims. Walker was a superhero who lost his powers and Pilgrim is hiding a secret. The award-winning series series originated at Image but later moved to Marvel's Icon imprint. [SA]

COLLECTIONS FROM IMAGE
Who Killed Retro Girl?	*Supergroup*
Roleplay	*Anarchy*
Little Deaths	

COLLECTIONS FROM MARVEL/IXON
The Sellouts	*Psychotic*	*The 25 Coolest Dead Superheroes*
Forever	*Cosmic*	*of All Time*
Legends	*Secret Identity*	

Marvel has also put out two hardcover *Definitive Collections* that collect larger amounts of issues.

Preacher. Garth Ennis, with art by Steve Dillon and Glenn Fabry. DC/Vertigo, 1996–2001. $14.99–$17.99.
A reverend with a disturbing past who has been possessed by offspring of an angel and a demon, his ex-girlfriend who wants to be a hired killer, and an alcoholic Irish vampire. These are actually the good guys and the most normal people seen in *Preacher*. The others include the Saint of All Killers, the reverend's family, Herr Star and his secret order The Grail, fallen angels, and a deformed teenager who calls himself Arseface. The complete series has been collected along with additional limited series and specials, and there are also hardover editions that collect a larger number of issues. Peter Snejbjerg, Steve Pugh, Carlos Ezquerra, and Richard Case provided additional artwork. [AO]

Vol. 1: *Gone to Texas*	Vol. 6: *War in the Sun*
Vol. 2: *Until the End of the World*	Vol. 7: *Salvation*
Vol. 3: *Proud Americans*	Vol. 8: *All Hell's a'Coming*
Vol. 4: *Ancient History*	Vol. 9: *Alamo*
Vol. 5: *Dixie Fried*	

***Pretty Face,* Vols 1–6.** Yasuhiro Kano. VIZ, 2007–2008, $7.99 each.
After he is disfigured in a car crash, teenage boy Rando has plastic surgery but is given the face of a picture he had—the girl he has a crush on. Now he's mistaken for her twin sister and taken in by her family. [SA]

Pride of Baghdad. Brian K. Vaughan and Niko Henrichon. DC/Vertigo, 2006. $19.99 (HC); $12.99 (SC).
Set during the 2003 invasion of Iraq, this original graphic novel was inspired by a true event in which a pride of lions escaped from the Baghdad Zoo. While the animals are shown talking, it is only a "translation." [SA]

Priest. Min-Woo Hyung. Tokyopop, 2002–. $9.99 each.
A Korean Manhwa that mixes the Western and horror genres. Ivan Isaacs is a nineteenth-century priest who sold his soul in order to battle and defeat fallen angels. There have been at least 16 volumes. [SA]

The Professor's Daughter. Joann Sfar, illustrated by Emmanuel Guibert. First Second, 2007. $16.95.
This enjoyable French import recounts what happened when, in Victorian London, the mummy of Pharaoh Imhotep IV decides to leave the museum because he has fallen in love with the daughter of the Egyptologist who found him and who resembles his long-dead wife. She also falls for him, but will this do in Victorian times, especially when he is 3,000 years old and technically museum property? [YR]

Project Romantic. Various artists. Adhouse Books, 2006. $19.95.
An anthology of romance-themed stories of all kinds. [SA]

Pulpatoon Pilgrimage. Joel Priddy. Adhouse Books, 2002. $12.95.
The strange adventures of a Minotaur, a robot, and a plant man. [SA]

The Punisher. Various writers, artists, and prices. Marvel Comics.
Frank Castle is Vietnam War veteran whose family was killed by the mob after witnessing a gangland execution. Vowing revenge, he has waged war on them, occasionally encountering

the superpowered beings of the Marvel Universe. While many Punisher stories involve people being killed, often by the Punisher, it is the Marvel Max stories, especially those by Garth Ennis, that are the most violent and appropriate for the adult section. Notable collections include the following: [SA]

Essential Punisher, Vols. 1–3   *Punisher: From First to Last*
The Punisher by Garth Ennis Omnibus   *Punisher vs. Bullseye*

Pussey! Daniel Clowes. Fantagraphics Books, 2006. $19.95.
A new collection of one of Clowes' earlier works dealing with Dan Pussey (pronounced "Poo-say") and his ups and downs as a comic book creator. [SA]

Q

Queen and Country: The Definitive Editions. Greg Rucka, with various artists. 2007–. $19.95.
Remastered and reformatted collections of the Eisner Award–winning series about the agents of the Special Operations Sections of Britain's Secret Intelligence Service (SIS), primarily agent Tara Chase. The four Definitive Editions collect a number of previously collected stories. There are also two *Q&C* prose novels by Rucka. [SA]

The Question. Dennis O'Neil, with art by Denys Cowan, Rick Magyar, and others. DC Comics, 2007–. $19.99 each.
A recent collection of the 1980s series about Vic Sage, aka the Question, the faceless fighter of crime in Hub City. [SA]

Vol. 1: *Zen and Violence*   Vol. 4: *Welcome to Oz*
Vol. 2: *Poisoned Ground*   Vol. 5: *Riddles*
Vol. 3: *Epitaph for a Hero*

R

The R. Crumb Handbook. R. Crumb and Peter Poplaski. MQP Publications, 2005. $25.00.
An autobiography of Crumb's life, intermixed with pictures and examples of his comics from over the year. [SA]

Rabbi Harvey. Stephen Sheinkin. Jewish Lights, 2006–2008. $16.99.
Featuring rather simplistic art, old Jewish folktales are retold in these humorous adventures of a frontier Rabbi. [SA]

The Adventures of Rabbi Harvey: A Graphic Novel of Jewish Wisdom in the Wild West
Rabbi Harvey Rides Again: A Graphic Novel of Jewish Folktales Let Loose in the Wild West

Rabbi's Cat. Joann Sfar. Pantheon.
These award-winning French works are set in the 1930s Algeria where the cat of an elderly Rabbi eats a parrot, gains the ability to talk, and begins to explore his spiritual side. Both books tell of the adventures of the cat and the rabbi as well as other characters such as the rabbi's cousin Malka of the Lions. Stories are set in Algeria, the Congo, Paris, and elsewhere. The stories are good and art is beautiful. Recommended. [SA]

The Rabbi's Cat 1. 2005. $16.95.
The Rabbi's Cat 2. 2008. $22.95.

Ted Rall, travels of. NBM.
A hybrid work with pages of text, pages of cartoons, and some pages with both, these "graphic travelogues" discuss Rall's travels in Afghanistan, Tajikistan, Turkmenistan, and other central Asian places. Both books could be cataloged in the 958s [SA]
  To Afghanistan and Back
  Silk Road to Run: Is Central Asia the New Middle East?

Recess Pieces. Bob Fingerman. Dark Horse, 2006. $14.95.
At the K–8 Ben Turpin School, a science experiment gone wrong turns students and teachers into zombies, and it's up to a small group of unaffected kids to get out. While some characters are stereotypes, it is an enjoyable work. [YR]

Red Blinds the Foolish. est em. Aurora/Deux, 2008. $12.95.
In this one-shot yaoi manga, Rafita is a rising star in the bullfighting world, but his confidence wavers when he meets and falls in love with Mauro, a butcher who rends the bulls he kills, and like the bulls, is colorblind. [AO]

Red Colored Elegy. Seiichi Hayashi. Drawn & Quarterly, 2008. $24.95.
An underground manga from the early 1970s tells of the relationship between two artists, Sachiko and Ichiro, who are not sure what they want from life. [SA]

Red Eye, Black Eye. K. Thor Jensen. Alternative Comics, 2007. $19.95.
Jensen's memoir of how he spent 60 days traveling around the country on a Greyhound bus staying with people he had met online. [SA]

Red Menace. Danny Bilson, Paul DiMeo, and Adam Brody, with art by Jerry Ordway DC/Wildstorm, 2007. $17.99.
During the 1950s, a superhero is accused of being a communist by the House Un-American Activities Committee and is forced to give up his costumed identity. [SA]

Regards from Serbia. Aleksandar Zograf. Top Shelf, 2007. $15.95.
Subtitled "A Cartoonist's Diary if a Crisis in Serbia," this work is a mixture of comics and print. Zograf is a Serbian cartoonist who created diary entries in comic form during the problems in the former Yugoslavia. Much of the printed material consists of copies of e-mails that he sent during NATO's bombing of his hometown of Pančevo in 1999. [SA]

Remains. Steve Niles, with art by Kieron Dwyer. IDW, 2004. $19.99.
An atomic blast has turned much of the world into zombies, but now they are getting smarter and stronger. This makes things even worse for two survivors, a blackjack dealer and a waitress/stripper who survived because they were fooling around in the vault and are now stuck in Reno, Nevada. [SA]

Revere: Revolution in Silver. Edward Lavalee, with art by Grant Bond. Archaia Studios Press, 2007. $19.95.
Everyone knows about Paul Revere's midnight ride, but what most people don't know is that he also was part of an organization that kills werewolves, some of who are in the Redcoats. [SA]

Rex Libris: Librarian. James Turner. SLG, 2007–. $14.95–$17.95.
Middleton Public Library has several unusual staff members, but none more than Rex Libris.

He is over 2,000 years old, works for the god Thoth, and will face monsters, demons, or aliens if it means tracking down an overdue book. [YR]

    Vol. 1: *I, Librarian*
    Vol. 2: *Book of Monsters*

Rex Mundi. Arvid Nelson, with art by Juan Ferreyra Dark Horse. 2006–2009. $16.95 each. A mystery and adventure set in an alternate historical France of the 1930s where magic works, Louis the XXII is on the throne, and the Church has great power. Master Physician Julien Saunière gets caught up with ancient secrets and political intrigue. The first two volumes were originally published by Image before being reprinted by Dark Horse. [SA]

    Vol. 1: *The Guardian of the Temple*   Vol. 4: *Crown and Sword*
    Vol. 2: *The River Underground*   Vol. 5: *The Valley at the End of the World*
    Vol. 3: *The Lost Kings*   Vol. 6: *Gate of God*

Road to Perdition. Max Allan Collins, with art by Richard Piers Rayner. Pocket Books, 1998. $20.95.
Set during the depression, mob hitman Michael O'Sullivan is betrayed by his boss John Rooney, resulting in the death of his wife and youngest son. Now he must go on the run with his older son, protecting him and getting his revenge. This was the basis for the 2002 award-winning film, and Collins has written two novels that act as sequels. [YR]

Robotika. Alex Sheikman. Archaia Studios Press, 2006. $19.95.
Set in the far future, Niko the "Steampunk Samurai" is ordered by his queen to recover a new discovery that can bring a reconciliation between regular humans and cyborgs. [YR]

Rocky. Martin Kellerman Fantagraphics, 2005–. $12.95.
Collection of the semi-autobiographical Swedish comic strip about a dog who is a cartoonist living in Stockholm. [SA]

    Vol. 1: *The Big Payback*
    Vol. 2: *Strictly Business*

Ronin. Frank Miller. DC, 1995. $19.99.
This classic early 1980s limited is set in a dystopian New York of the twenty-first century where a disgraced thirteenth-century samurai is reborn to fight the same demon he fought 800 years earlier. An enlarged, hardcovered, and slipcased Absolute edition was released in 2008. [SA]

Roswell, Texas. L. Neil Smith and Rex F. May, with art by Scott Bieser and Jen Zach. Big Head Press, 2008. $12.95.
In the 1947 of an alternate timeline, Texas remained independent, California is run by Emperor-for-life Walt Disney, and Europe is controlled by the British-run Third-and-a-half Reich. When a flying disc crashes in the Texas town of Roswell, agents of various governments, some who are very familiar, come to try to find out its secrets. Another alternate worlds story by the author of *The Probability Broach*. [SA]

Run, Bong-Gu Run! Byun Byung-Jun. NBM, 2007. $15.95.
This ComicsLit title is subtitled "a little manhwa graphic novel." Young Bong-Gu comes to Seoul with his mother from their small island village. They meet a little girl and her grandfather who are homeless but may be able to help them. A sweet story. [YR]

S

Sachs & Violens. Peter David, with art by George Perez and various inkers. DC Comics, 2006. $14.99.
Model J. J. Sachs and soldier-turned-photographer Ernie "Violens" Schultz go after a group of pornographers who made a snuff film and are also kidnapping children. The pair later appeared in *Fallen Angel*. [SA]

Safe Area Goražde: The War in Eastern Bosnia 1992–1995. Joe Sacco. Fantagraphics, 2000. $19.95.
A journalistic graphic novel by Sacco, telling the story of people who were trapped in the enclave of Goražde during the war, the only town in the area to avoid ethnic cleansing. [SA]

The Salon. Nick Bertozzi. St. Martin's Griffin, 2007. $19.95.
Set in 1907 Paris, the characters in this graphic novel include Gertrude Stein, Matisse, Braque, Alice Toklis (who meets Gertrude here), and Picasso. A strange blue woman is killing artists and their friends, and this all may be connected to a special kind of absinthe that allows people to go into paintings. Also co-written by Bertozzi is *Stuffed!* [SA]

Sandman. Neil Gaiman and various artists. DC/Vertigo, 1993. Various prices.
The flagship title of the Vertigo line and winner of several awards, the *Sandman* titles are a must-have for any adult collection. The series primarily deals with Dream of the Endless, the actual personification of dreams, though in many stories he is a secondary character to those mortals who end up encountering him. The series, along with a special and some short stories printed elsewhere have been collected in 10 volumes, but the four volumes of the *Absolute Sandman* books (2007–2008, $99.00) have recolored them, improved the inking on one issue, and include scripts and works that have not previously been collected. Two other *Sandman* titles are *Endless Nights*, a short story collection, and *The Dream Hunters*, an adaptation of a "text" *Sandman* story that had featured illustrations by Yoshitaka Amano. The series, in whatever form you collect it, is highly recommended. There have also been a number of limited and ongoing series that have spun-off from the original *Sandman* title, the descriptions of which can be found below. Artists on the series include Sam Keith, Mike Dringenberg, Malcolm Jones III, Charles Vess, Colleen Doran, Kelley Jones, Matt Wagner, Bryan Talbot, P. Craig Russell, Jill Thompson, Vince Locke, Michael Allred, Mark Buckingham, Dick Giordano, Mark Hempel, Teddy Kristiansen, Michael Zulli, and Jon J. Muth. [all items are SA]

Vol. 1: *Preludes and Nocturnes*	Vol. 9: *The Kindly Ones*
Vol. 2: *The Doll's House*	Vol. 10: *The Wake*
Vol. 3: *Dream Country*	*The Sandman: The Dream Hunters.*
Vol. 4: *Season of Mists*	Adapted by P. Craig Russell.
Vol. 5: *A Game of You*	*The Sandman: Endless Nights.* Art by
Vol. 6: *Fables and Reflections*	P. Craig Russell, Bill Sienkiewicz,
Vol. 7: *Brief Lives*	Barron Storey, Glenn Fabry, and others.
Vol. 8: *World's End*	

SPIN-OFFS
One of the most popular supporting characters in the series was Dream's older sister, Death. *The High Cost of Living* tells of a day in which she becomes mortal, while *Time of Your Life* features characters from *A Game of You*. Both were collected in *Absolute Death* along with

additional material from other sources. *At Death's Door* is a digest-sized manga-style adaptation of *Season of Mists* that tells the story from her point of view. Unless indicated, the following titles are by Gaiman, with art by Chris Bachalo, Mark Buckingham, and Dave McKean.

   Death: The High Cost of Living. 1994. $12.99.

   Death: The Time of Your Life. 1997. $12.99.

   Absolute Death. Additional art by Jeffrey Jones and Mark Pennington.

   Death: At Death's Door. Written and drawn by Jill Thompson. 2003. $9.99.

Lucifer. Mike Carey and various artists. 2001–2007. $14.99 each. In the storyline *Season of Mists*, Lucifer abdicates as ruler of Hell. This collection of the 75-issue series tells what happened next. Peter Gross and Ryan Kelly were the main artists, and additional art was provided by Scott Hampton, Chris Weston, James Hodgkins, Dean Ormston, Craig Hamilton, David Hahn, P. Craig Russell, Ted Naifeh, Marc Hempel, Ronald Wimberly, Colleen Doran, and Michael Wm. Kaluta.

Vol. 1: *Devil in the Gateway*	Vol. 7: *Exodus*
Vol. 2: *Children and Monsters*	Vol. 8: *The Wolf Beneath the Tree*
Vol. 3: *A Dalliance with the Damned*	Vol. 9: *Crux*
Vol. 4: *The Divine Comedy*	Vol. 10: *Morningstar*
Vol. 5: *Inferno*	Vol. 11: *Evensong*
Vol. 6: *Mansions of the Silence*	

The Sandman Presents: Taller Tales. Bill Willingham with art by various.
A collection of stories that Willingham wrote for several *Sandman*-related one-shots, limited series, and other works.

The Sandman Presents: Thessaly—Witch for Hire. Bill Willingham, with art by Shawn McManus.
This is about a character first introduced in *A Game of You* and is a sequel to a story that appears in *Taller Tales.*

The Sandman Presents: Dead Boy Detectives. Ed Brubaker, with art by Art By Bryan Talbot and Steve Leialoha.

The Dead Boy Detectives. Jill Thompson.
A collected limited series and a manga-style original work featuring two dead teenage boys who become detectives instead of moving on to the next world. Based on characters introduced in *A Season of Mists.*

Sandman Presents: The Furies. Mike Carey, with art by John Bolton.
A follow-up to the events of *The Kindly Ones*, this original graphic novel with beautiful artwork is about Lyta Hall, known as the super heroine the Fury, who has lost her child and now must deal with gods and creatures from Greek myths.

Sandman Mystery Theatre. DC Comics/Vertigo.
Introduced in 1939, the Sandman, aka Wesley Dodds, debuted wearing a suit, cape, fedora, and gas mask before soon changing to a more "typical" crimefighting costume. When the modern Sandman was introduced with a helmet that resembled a gas mask, a link was made between the two. These adventures take place early in Dodds' career and have him solving mysteries and stopping criminals in pre–WWII New York and taking on issues that the comics couldn't talk about 60 years ago. These recent volumes collect stories by Matt Wagner and Steven T. Seagle from the 1990s as well as a 2007 limited series by John Ney Reiber and

Eric Nguyen. Guy Davis is the primary artist on the series with additional art by Vince Locke, Warren Pleece, John Watkiss, and R. G. Taylor. [SA]

Vol. 1: *The Tarantula*	Vol. 5: *Dr. Death and the Night of the Butcher*
Vol. 2: *The Face and the Brute*	Vol. 6: *The Hourman and the Python*
Vol. 3: *The Vamp*	Vol. 7: *The Mist and the Phantom of the Fair*
Vol. 4: *The Scorpion*	*Sandman Mystery Theatre: Sleep of Reason*

Also of note is the *Golden Age Sandman Archives*, Vol. 1 (2005; $49.99), which features Gardner Fox's original stories featuring the character, and *Neil Gaiman's Midnight Days* (2000, $17.99), which contains various stories by Gaiman, including one in which the two "Sandmen" both appear.

Savage Brothers. Andrew Cosby and Johanna Stokes, with art by Rafael Albuquerque. Boom! Studios, 2007. $14.99.
Redneck country boys Dale and Otis Savage work as freelancers during a zombie apocalypse. [YR]

Scalped. Jason Aaron, with art by R. M. Guera. DC/Vertigo, 2007–. $9.99–$14.99.
Dashiell Bad Horse is recruited by the FBI to return to Prairie Rose Indian Reservation where he grew up to investigate criminal activity tied in with organized crime, a new casino, and past members of a radical movement. Additional art is by John Paul Leon, Davide Furno, and Francesco Francavilla. There will be additional volumes. [SA]

Vol. 1: *Indian Country*	Vol. 4: *The Gravel in Your Guts*
Vol. 2: *Casino Boogie*	Vol. 5: *High Lonesome*
Vol. 3: *Dead Mothers*	

Scarlet Traces and **Scarlet Traces: The Great Game.** Ian Edginton, with art by D'Israeli. Dark Horse, 2003–. $14.95.
In these award-nominated stories, England has recovered from the "War of the Worlds" of 1898 and has used the Martian technology for themselves. But a new problem has emerged. In the second book, the counterinvasion of Mars is ongoing, but an increasingly authoritarian England has a greater threat. Much like *The League of Extraordinary Gentlemen*, which also featured the Martian invasions, these books also include references to other works. [YR]

Scott Pilgrim series. Bryan Lee O'Malley. Oni Press, 2004–2010. $11.95.
Twenty-three-year-old Scott Pilgrim is having a good life and has just met a great girl named Ramona Flowers. However, in order to be with her, he must defeat her seven evil ex-boyfriends. A film adaptation is due out in 2010. [YR]

Scott Pilgrim's Precious Little Life	*Scott Pilgrim Gets It Together*
Scott Pilgrim vs. the World	*Scott Pilgrim vs. the Universe*
Scott Pilgrim & the Infinite Sadness	*Scott Pilgrim #6* (title TBA)

Scream Queen. Brendan Hay, with art by Nate Watson. Boom! Studios, 2009. $15.99.
Wrighty, a deformed psychopath who lives at the mall, has fallen in love with high school student Molly. He will do anything to make her happy, including eliminating her rivals. But Molly is definitely not happy with his gifts. [YR]

Scream Queen: Sand and Fury. Ho Che Anderson. Fantagraphics, 2010. $16.99.
A tale of sex, depravity, and supernatural revenge. [SA]

Scrublands. Joe Daly. Fantagraphics, 2005. $16.95.
A collection of odd short stories by South African cartoonist Daly. These works are in both color and black and white and includes one long, mostly wordless tale. [SA]

The Secret. Mike Richardson, with art by Jason Shawn Alexander. Dark Horse, 2007.
Teens randomly call people and say, "I know your secret." But tragedy happens when one person has a dark secret that he'll do anything to protect. [YR]

Seduce Me After the Show. est em. Aurora/Deux, 2008. $12.95.
An M-rated one-shot collection of five yaoi stories. [SA]

Sensitive Pornograph. Ashika Sakura. 801 Media, $15.95.
An explicit 18+ yaoi about a manga artist who meets an artist that he admires and is amazed to find out it is a man. [AO]

Sentences: The Life of M. F. Grimm. Percy Carey, with art by Ronald Wimberly. DC/Vertigo, 2007. $19.99 (HC); $14.99 (SC).
As a child, Percy Carey was on *Sesame Street*. When he was older he got into rap music and was known by various names, including M. F. Grimm. Unfortunately, his life led to a murder attempt that left him in a wheelchair and drug charges that put him in prison for three years. Today he has produced both music and this award-winning original graphic novel. [SA]

Se7en. Various artists. Zenescope, 2007. $34.95.
A prequel to the feature film, showing exactly how and why serial killer "John Doe" went after his victims. [SA]

Sexy Voice and Robo. Iou Kuroda. VIZ, 2005. $19.99.
Fourteen-year-old Nico Hayashi works as a telephone dating operator, though her clients don't know how young she is. She wants to be a spy and gets involved in a world of mysteries using the code name "Sexy Voice." "Robo" is Iichiro Sudo, a 20-something man who doesn't know that she was who he spoke to on the phone, likes to collect toy robots, and gets caught up in Nico's adventures. This prize-winning manga was also a television show in Japan. [YR]

Shadowland. Kim Deitch. Fantagraphics, 2006. $18.95.
Several strange stories, originally published in various places, involving a carnival owner, his son, a group of midgets, and alien creatures called Grey Ones. [SA]

Shooting War. Anthony Lappé, with art by Dan Goldman. Grand Central Publishing, 2007. $21.99 (HC); $13.99 (SC).
In 2011 the Iraq War has gotten worse. Jimmy Burns is a video blogger who became famous by getting live footage of the suicide bombing of a Brooklyn Starbucks. This gets him a job with cable news network Global News who makes him their Iraq correspondent, where he gets himself caught up in all sorts of trouble. Interestingly, the book, written before the 2008 election, has John McCain as president. [SA]

Shortcomings. Adrian Tomine. Drawn & Quarterly, 2007. $19.95 (HC); $14.95 (SC).
Ben Tanaka is living in California and is dating a girl named Miko. But can their relationship survive her going to New York and her fear that he has a wandering eye. *Shortcomics* was originally serialized in the comic book *Optic Nerve*, and other collections from this title include *Sleepwalk and Other Stories* and *Summer Blonde*. [SA]

Siberia. Nikolai Maslov. Soft Skull Press, 2006. $19.95.
The autobiographical story of the author's life, including being drafted into the army to serve in Mongolia, attempts to become an artist, and even time in a mental hospital. Maslov was able to get interest in his book when, working as a night watchman in Moscow, he handed sample pages to the editor of the Russian translation of *Tintin*, who was visiting from France. [SA]

Silent Dragon. Andy Diggle, with art by Leinil Yu, Gerry Alanguilan, and Richard Friend. DC/Wildstorm, 2006. $19.99.
Tokyo, 2063. Japan is ruled by a military junta, but the Yazuka wants to take over. Renjiro is caught between the two sides when he is transformed into a Cyborg and made the ultimate weapon. [SA]

Silverfish. David Lapham. DC/Vertigo, 2007. $17.99.
Mia Fleming does not get along with her new stepmother Suzanne, but when she looks through her possessions she finds that Suzanne has a dark secret that may endanger Mia's family. Lampham is also well known for his comic *Stray Bullets*. [SA]

Posy Simmonds, works of.
Originally serialized in the British paper *The Guardian*, these works mix text with illustrations and word balloons. In *Gemma*, Baker Raymond Joubert remembers Englishwoman Gemma Bovery and the uncanny parallel between her life and that of the literary Madame Bovary. *Tamara Drewe* is inspired by Thomas Hardy's *Far from the Madding Crowd* and is about gossip columnist Tamara who has returned to her family home and how this various men. [SA]
   Gemma Bovery. Pantheon Books, 2005. $19.95.
   Tamara Drewe. Houghton Mifflin, 2008. $16.95.

Sin City. Frank Miller. Dark Horse, various dates. $12.00–$28.00.
In Basin City things are often in black and white, and that's exactly how Miller portrays this world, black and white and no shades of grey. The stories are told in a film noir style and involve gangsters, killers, prostitutes, and the corruption of those in power. The *Sin City* stories have been put out in various forms, and characters who make a small appearance in one story can be the focus of another. The 2005 movie was based on several of these volumes, with many scenes taken directly from the comics. New reformatted editions were released around the same time as the film. Recommended. [SA]

The Hard Goodbye	*Family Values*
A Dame to Kill For	*Booze, Broads, & Bullets*
The Big Fat Kill	*Hell and Back (a Sin City Love Story)*
That Yellow Bastard	

Singularity 7. Ben Templesmith. IDW, 2005. $19.99.
Microscopic machines called nanites have destroyed most of the Earth, disassembling the majority of the people on a molecular level. The remaining humans hide in underground cities, but the nanites and their robotic footsoldiers have destroyed almost all of them. It is up to a small band of humans to save what is left of the day. [SA]

The Sky Over My Spectacles. Mio Tennohji. 801 Media, 2006–. $15.95.
In this one-volume 18+ yaoi manga, Azuma makes passes at girls who wear glasses, but a boy named Azuma stirs feelings in him as well. [AO]

Skyscrapers of the Midwest. Joshua Cotter. Adhouse Books, 2008. $19.95.
This award-winning and well-reviewed title is about two young brothers (drawn as animals) with overactive imaginations, and their stories of "childhood hope, panic, and loss." [SA]

Sloth. Gilbert Hernandez. DC/Vertigo, 2006. $19.99 (HC); $14.99 (SC).
After awakening from a year-long coma, Miguel finds that things have slowed down for him and strange things are happening involving a mysterious lemon orchid. Additional works by Gilbert Hernandez include *The Troublemakers*, *Speak of the Devil*, and the *Love and Rockets*-related *The High Soft Lisp*. [SA]

Slow News Day. Andi Watson. SLG. $12.95.
Katherine Washington has come from America to work at a newspaper in a small British town. The story also features the lives and problems of her co-workers, her relationship with her mother, who has a link to the paper, and what happens when she returns home. [SA]

Smoke. Alex De Campi, with art by Igor Kordney. IDW, 2005. $24.99.
In a London of the near future, a soldier-turned government assassin gets caught up in political intrigue, government corruption, terrorists, problems in his love life, and an old betrayal. [SA]

Squadron Supreme and Supreme Power. Marvel Comics, 2003–. $10.99–.
The original incarnation of the Squadron Supreme were a team of superheroes who lived on a different "Earth" than that of the mainstream Marvel Universe. As an in-joke, the members each had counterparts to DC's Justice League. For example Hyperion was like Superman, Power Princess was Wonder Woman, Nighthawk was Batman, and so forth. They made various appearances, including in the limited series mentioned in Chapter 2. In 2003, Marvel introduced a "reimagining" of the characters in a more mature story line as part of their "Max" line under the title *Supreme Power*. Marvel has since continued their adventures in two *Squadron Supreme* titles that are not as adult, but because reading *Supreme Power* is helpful to understand the events, it is best if this is all in an adult collection. Unless indicated, the collections are written by J. Michael Straczynski, with art by Gary Frank. [SA]

> *Supreme Power: Contact*
> *Supreme Power: Powers and Principalities*
> *Supreme Power: High Command*
> *Squadron Supreme: The Pre-War Years*
> *Squadron Supreme: Hyperion vs. Nighthawk.* Marc Guggenheim, with art by Paul Gulacy.
> *Ultimate Power.* Co-written by Brian Michael Bendis, with art by Greg Land.
> *Squadron Supreme: Power to the People.* Howard Chaykin, with art by Marco Turini.
> *Squadron Supreme: Bright Shining Lies.* Howard Chaykin, with art by Marco Checchetto.

Stagger Lee. Derek McCulloch, with art by Shepherd Hendrix. Image, 2006. $17.99.
In 1895 Lee Shelton, an African-American cab driver and pimp shot and killed William Lyon. He soon became the subject of a folk song that over the years has been known as Stagger Lee, Stack O'Lee, Stackalee, and other versions and in the past 100 years has been recorded by dozens of performers including Wilson Pickett, Fats Domino, Neil Diamond, and the Grateful Dead. This award-winning original graphic novel gives one version of what may or may not have happened. [SA]

Star Trek
There have been *Star Trek* comics published for over 40 years, with all series except for *Enterprise* turned into a comic by one publisher or another. There have also been a number of titles set in the *Star Trek* universe but featuring new or secondary characters. [YR]

Star Trek: The Key Collection. Checker. $22.95 each.
A collection of the *Star Trek* comics published Gold Key. These were the first *Trek* comics and are known for their odd stories and the artistic mistakes of the early issues (such as portraying African Lt. Uhura as being Caucasian). At least six volumes have been produced.

Star Trek from IDW. All $19.99.
IDW is the current rights holder for *Star Trek* and usually presents their stories as either a series of themed-one shots or of five-issue limited series. Some of their collections are the following.

Star Trek: Alien Spotlight. Various artists. $19.99.
A collection of one-shots dealing with the alien races in the *Star Trek* Universe.

Star Trek Archives. $19.99.
Theme-based collections with material from the Marvel, Malibu, and DC *Star Trek Comics*

Vol. 1: *The Best of Peter David*   Vol. 5: *The Best of James T. Kirk*
Vol. 2: *The Best of the Borg*   Vol. 6: *The Best of Alternate Universes*
Vol. 3: *The Best of Gary Seven*   Vol. 7: *The Best of Klingons*
Vol. 4: *The Best of Star Trek:*   Vol. 8: *The Best of Mr. Spock*
        Deep Space Nine

There are also the *Star Trek Omnibuses* ($24.99), which collected various Marvel series as well as film adaptations.

Star Trek: Assignment Earth. John Byrne. $19.99.
Based on an episode from the original series and set in the twentieth century, an agent of an alien race helps Earth with his human assistant. This is the same character from the third archive.

Star Trek: Countdown. Mike Johnson and Tim Jones, with art by David Messina.
A prequel to the 2009 film.

Star Trek: Klingons—Blood Will Tell. Scott and David Tipton, with art by David Messina.
A look at the best-known *Star Trek* alien race, with one a special issue in the Klingon language.

Star Trek: Mirror Images. Scott & David Tipton, with art by David Messina.
Set in the Evil Mirror Universe.

Star Trek: New Frontier. Peter David, with art by Stephen Thompson.
A new story featuring characters from Peter David's series of novels.

Star Trek: The Next Generation: Intelligence Gathering. Scott and David Tipton, with art by David Messina.

Star Trek: The Next Generation: The Space Between. David Tischman, with art by Casey Maloney.

New Adventures of the Next Generation
   Star Trek: The Next Generation: The Last Generation. Written in conjunction with Pocket
   Books' "Myriad Universe" line, an alternate history version of Star Trek.

Star Trek: Year Four. David Tischman, with art by Steve Conley.

Star Trek: Year Four—The Enterprise Experiment. Dorothy "D.C." Fontana and Derek Chester, with art by Gordon Purcell. New adventures of the original series crew. Fontana wrote episodes of various *Star Trek* shows.

FROM TOKYOPOP

Star Trek: Ultimate Edition. 2009. $19.99. Collects the three *Star Trek Manga* volumes including a story by Wil "Wesley Crusher" Wheaton. There is an OEL Manga based on *Star Trek: The Next Generation.*

Star Wars. Dark Horse Comics. Various writers and artists.

Like *Star Trek, Star Wars* has been in comics form since it began. Dark Horse has had the license for a long time, and the settings of their stories have ranged from thousands of years before *Episode I* to decades after *Return of the Jedi.* Stories have dealt with the main characters, other members of the rebellion, villains, and other supporting characters. Many of these stories have been collected into trades, but both many trades and various uncollected stories have also been placed into omnibus editions. The omnibuses were created as "a way to showcase actual novel-length stories or series and to provide homes for 'orphaned' series, single-issue stories, and short stories which would otherwise never be collected, or which might fall out of print." Dark Horse has also reprinted the first *Star Wars* series that was published by Marvel Comics under the name *A Long Time Ago.* [YR]

Star Wars: A Long Time Ago. 2002–.$29.95.

Vol. 1: *Doomworld*
Vol. 2: *Dark Encounters*
Vol. 3: *Resurrection of Evil*
Vol. 4: *Screams in the Void*

Vol. 5: *Fool's Bounty*
Vol. 6: *Wookie World*
Vol. 7: *Far, Far Away*

OMNIBUS SERIES, $24.95

Star Wars Omnibus: Droids
Star Wars Omnibus: Early Victories (2008)
Star Wars Omnibus: Emissaries and Assassins
Star Wars Omnibus: Menace Revealed
Star Wars Omnibus: Rise of the Sith
Star Wars Omnibus: Shadows of the Empire
Star Wars Omnibus Tales of the Jedi, Vols. 1–2
Star Wars Omnibus: X-Wing Rogue Squadron, Vols. 1–3

OTHER STAR WARS COLLECTIONS

Several series have multiple volumes, including the following.

Star Wars: Dark Times
Star Wars: Empire
*Star Wars: Knights of the
    Old Republic*

Star Wars: Legacy
Star Wars: Rebellion
Star Wars Tales
Star Wars: The Force Unleashed

Check the Dark Horse Web site at www.darkhorse.com for prices and subtitles.

Stephen Colbert's Tek Jansen. John Layman, Tom Peyer, and Jim Massey, with art by Scott Chantler and Robbi Rodriguez. Oni, 2009. $19.95.

These humorous science fiction adventures are based on the cartoon occasionally shown on Comedy Central's popular *Colbert Report.* [YR]

Steve Niles' Cellar of Nastiness. Steve Niles with various artists. IDW, 2005. $24.99.
Various stories by Niles, including the story of a boy trying to help "classic" movie monsters make a comeback and a new take on Jekyll and Hyde. [SA]

Steve Niles Omnibus. Steve Niles. IDW, 2008. $24.99.
This edition collects four stories by Niles that were previously published in the graphic novels *Aleister Arcane*, *The Lurkers*, *Secret Skull*, and *Wake the Dead*. [SA]

Stitches: A Memoir. David Small. W.W. Norton, 2009. $23.95.
In this autobiographical work, the Caldecott-winning illustrator tells of his life and his troubled relationship with his parents. One major event retold is how, after what he thought was going to be a routine operation, he awoke with one vocal cord removed and large stitches down the side of his throat. Recommended. [YR]

Stonehaven series. Kevin Tinsley. Stickman Graphics, 2004–. $38.95 (HC); $19.95 (SC).
In an alternate-reality version of New York, magical creatures live alongside humans. But there is still crime and danger and people who have help save the day, including half-elf detective Victor Jardine. There is also a prose novel listed in Appendix B. [SA]
  Milk Cartons & Dog Biscuits. Art by Phil Singer.
  Subterranean Hearts. Art by Tinsley

Stop Forgetting to Remember: The Autobiography of Walter Kurtz. By Peter Kuper. Crown Publishers, 2008. $19.95.
Through his "alter-ego" Kurtz, Kuper talks about his life, including flashbacks to his younger days, having a child, 9/11, and trying to get the book published. [SA]

The Story of the Jews: A 4,000-Year Adventure. Stan Mack. Villard, 1998. $19.95.
An illustrated, cartoon history of the Jewish people from Abraham to the present. See also *Jews in America: A Cartoon History*. [YR]

Strangers in Paradise, Vols. 1–6. Terry Moore. Abstract Studio, 2004–2007. $17.95.
These large collections include over 100 stories from this award-winning comic book series (which had previously been collected in 19 softcover and eight hardcover editions). The series is primarily about two old friends, Francine Peters and Katina "Katchoo" Choovanski, the latter of whom has a troubled past. With stories that deal with everything from relationships to conspiracies, these are a must-have for an adult collection and are highly recommended. A two-volume complete hardcover omnibus edition is also availible for $159.95. A new series from Abstract Studies by Moore is *Echo*. [SA]

Strawberry 100%. Mizuki Kawashita. VIZ, 2007 –. $7.99.
This romantic comedy is about Manaka, a high school student and aspiring film director who accidentally startles a girl who falls in front of him, exposing her strawberry-patterned panties. Although he was not able to see her face, he was instantly smitten with her and has become determined to find her identity. There will eventually be 19 volumes of this title which also inspired an anime. [SA]

Stuck Rubber Baby. Howard Cruse. DC Comics, 2000. $14.99.
Set in the American South of the 1960s, this award-winning graphic novel deals with both racism and homophobia. The main character is Toland, who must deal with his emerging homosexuality, the feelings he may have for a woman, and the growing civil rights movement. [SA]

Students for a Democratic Society: A Graphic History. Harvey Pekar and others, with art by Gary Dumm and others. Hill and Wang, 2008. $22.00.
A look at the history of the SDS from its origins, to the radical "Weather Underground" to its resurgence today. Pekar and Dumm have created a 50-page history followed by stories of individual people involved in the movement written and drawn by various people. [SA]

The Summer of Love. Debbie Drechsler. Drawn & Quarterly, 2001. $24.95.
Set in 1967, ninth-grader Lily Maier's family moves to a small town and she and her younger sister learn about love (though for her sister it is for another girl). There are some autobiographical elements to the story. [SA]

Supermen! The First Wave of Comic Book Heroes 1939–1941. Fantagraphics, 2009. $24.99.
A new collection of rarely seen superhero stories from the early Golden Age featuring tales from Will Eisner, Jerry Siegel and Joe Shuster, Jack Cole, Jack Kirby, Fletcher Hanks, and others as well as the introduction of The Clock. [YR]

Supernatural Law. Batton Lash. Exhibit A Press. $14.95–$16.95.
Beware the creatures of the night—for they have lawyers. Alanna Wolff and Jeff Byrd are experts in supernatural law. Whether it getting a restraining order against a slayer on behalf of the vampire she's hunting, defending a muse against the writer she inspired to commit plagiarism, or representing a guardian angel facing charges of negligence, the "Counselors of the Macabre" will take the case. This is a funny series and is filled with parodies of all sorts. [YR]
> *Tales of Supernatural Law*
> *The Soddyssey and Other Tales of Supernatural Law*
> *Sonovawitch! and Other Tales of Supernatural Law*
> *The Vampire Brat! and Other Tales of Supernatural Law*
> *Mister Negativity, and Other Tales of Supernatural Law*

Surrogates and ***Surrogates: Flesh and Blood.*** Robert Venditti, with art by Brett Weldele. Top Shelf, 2006–2009. $19.95 each.
In 2054 people are able to stay at home and transmit their minds into artificial bodies and many prefer to interact in that way. But there is still crime and unrest and detective Harvey Greer must investigate a radical movement that could move society backward. *The Surrogates* was made into a 2009 film with Bruce Willis as Greer, and both volumes are collected in the $75.00 hardover *The Surrogates Operator Manual.* [SA]

Swallow Me Whole. Nate Powell. Top Shelf. $19.95.
This award-winning work shows the problems faced by Ruth and Perry, two teenage stepsiblings with psychological problems. [YR]

Swamp Thing. DC Comics/Vertigo. $17.99–$24.99.
For many years it was thought that the Swamp Thing was scientist Alec Holland who was turned into a strange creature. But when Alan Moore took over, his true nature and potential was revealed. New editions of older collection are currently being produced and may simply be listed by volume number without a subtitle. Moore wrote the first six volumes and was followed by Rick Veitch. Artists include Veitch Stephen Bissette, John Totleben, Shawn McManus, Alfredo Alcala, Tom Yeates, Jamie Delano, and Tom Mandrake. [SA]

Vol. 1: *Saga of the Swamp Thing*   Vol. 4: *A Murder of Crows*   Vol. 7: *Regenesis*

Vol. 2: *Love and Death*   Vol. 5: *Earth to Earth*   Vol. 8: *Spontaneous Generation*

Vol. 3: *The Curse*   Vol. 6: *Reunion*   Vol. 9: *Infernal Triangles*

Also of note is *DC Comics Classics Library: Roots of the Swamp Thing* by Len Wein, with art by Berni Wrightson and Nestor Redondo. This features some of the character's early adventures and costs $39.99.

T

Tag. Boom! Studios, 2007–. $14.99.

Mitch has been "tagged" by someone who he had wronged turning him into a zombie-like creature and the only way to reverse the curse is to tag someone else. In the second book, another victim, Ed, explores the origins of the curse. Book one includes an unrelated story, *10*. [SA]

     Vol. 1 (no subtitle). Keith Giffen, with art by Kody Chamberlain and Chee.

     Vol. 2: *Cursed.* Michael S. Leib, with art by Chee.

Talent. Christopher Golden and Tom Sniegoski, with art by Paul Azaceta. Boom! Studios, 2007. $14.99.

The sole survivor of a plane crash, Nicholas Dane finds that he suddenly has the skills of everyone else who was on that plane. Now the people who caused the crash are after him and Dane must use his newfound skills to survive. [SA]

Tales from the Cornerstone: The Midnight Shift. Andrew Charipar. Misfit Corner Press, 2006. $12.95.

Vampires, zombies, and other monsters live in Cornerstone City, and the populace has grown to accept them. But some of the creatures get into trouble, and so a special police force of supernatural creatures is formed. [SA]

Tales of the Zombie. Marvel Comics.

A main character in the 1970s publication *Tales of the Zombie* was Simon Garth, a businessman who was killed and turned into a zombie but who still encounters and protects his love ones. Marvel revamped the character for two limited series for their "Max" line beginning in 2006. Garth was now a bankteller who was infected by a "zombifying" gas. The original stories were collected in an Essential Edition that included other stories with zombies as well as the heroic Brother Voodoo and some text pieces. [SA]

     Essential Tales of the Zombie. Various artists. 2006. $16.99.

     Zombie. Mike Raicht, with art by Kyle Hotz. 2007. $13.99.

     The Zombie: Simon Garth. Kyle Hotz and Eric Powell, with art by Hotz. 2008. $13.99.

Yoshihiro Tatsumi, works of. Drawn & Quarterly. 2005–. $19.95–$29.95.

Credited for creating the term "gekiga," Tatsumi is considered to be the "grandfather of Japanese alternative comics" and has influenced generations of manga-ka. Since 2005, Drawn & Quarterly has been putting out collections of short manga stories that previously had been translated into poorly done unauthorized editions. Although they are flopped, they have been personally rearranged by the author and edited by Adrian Tomine. The first three collections listed contain his work from 1969–1971, while *A Drifting Life* is an 820-page autobiographical work. D&Q will be putting out additional works by Tatsumi in the future. [SA]

The Push Man and Other Stories (2005)   *Good-Bye* (2008)
Abandon the Old in Tokyo (2006)   *A Drifting Life* (2009)

Therefore Repent! Jim Munroe, with art by Salgood Sam. IDW, 2007. $14.99.
Subtitled "A Post-Rapture Graphic Novel." The Rapture has happened and those left behind must deal with magic, talking dogs, and heavily armed angels. But a couple known as Raven and Mummy are more worried about the state of their relationship. [SA]

Things Just Get Away from You. Walt Holcombe. Fantagraphics Books, 2007. $24.95.
A collection of various stories by Holcombe that includes his Eisner award-winning *King of Persia* in which King Faisal Al-Ghazali searches for a giant emerald in order to win a woman's love. [SA]

30 Days of Night **series.** IDW, 2003–. $17.99 –.
Barrow, Alaska, is a small town so far north that in the wintertime they have one month of total darkness. This makes them a prime target for vampires looking for a month-long feast. The town's sheriff, his wife, and a few others survivors must find a way to survive. This collected limited series was adapted into a 2007 film and has resulted in a number of sequels that have also been collected. Some of these sequels feature characters from the original while others feature other doings by the vampires of that world in both the past and the present. Two related novels appear in Appendix B. [SA]

COLLECTIONS
Some collections are available in both hard- and softcover. Unless otherwise indicated, the author is Steve Niles, with art by Ben Templesmith. In order of publication they are:

30 Days of Night
Dark Days
30 Days of Night: Return to Barrow
30 Days of Night: Bloodsucker Tales. Additional story and art by Matt Fraction and Kody Chamberlain.
30 Days of Night: Three Tales. Additional story and art by Dan Wickline, Nat Jones, and Milx.
30 Days of Night: Spreading the Disease. Dan Wickline, with art by Alex Sanchez.
30 Days of Night: Eben & Stella. Additional story and art by Kelly Sue DeConnick and Justin Randall.
30 Days of Night: Red Snow. Story and art by Ben Templesmith.
30 Days of Night: Beyond Barrow. Art by Bill Sienkiewicz.
30 Days of Night: 30 Days Till Death. Story and art by David Lapham.

Three Fingers. Rich Koslowski. Top Shelf, 2002. $14.95.
The horrifying truth of cartoon characters revealed. Written as a "documentary," old-time "toon" actors like Ricky Rat, Dapper Duck, Portly Pig, and Buggy Bunny discuss their past, including the rumor that many of them altered their hands to have only three fingers in order to duplicate Ricky's successes. A fun, though sometimes disturbing, award-winning work. [YR]

300. Frank Miller. Dark Horse, 2006. $30.00.
The source of the 2007 film took many of its images from the original comic. This new edition of Miller's classic story recounts the Battle of Thermopylae in which 300 Spartans fought

against thousands of invaders. *300* has won many awards and the collected work has gone through 11 printings in ten years. Of note is the rectangular shape of the book (12.9 × 9.8 × 0.5 inches), which may affect how it stands on your bookcases. [SA]

The Three Paradoxes. Paul Hornschemier. Fantagraphics Books, 2007. $14.95.
An autobiographical comic framed with conversations between Paul and his father mixed in with flashbacks to his past as well as additional cartoons. An additional and more humorous collection of cartoons by the same author is *Let Us Be Perfectly Clear.* [SA]

The Ticking. Renee French. Top Shelf, 2005. $19.95.
An unusual, award-nominated work with one or two panels per page and text below them instead of word balloons. Edison Steelhead's mother dies in childbirth and he inherits his father's deformity. The book covers several years of his life. [SA]

Tokko, Vols. 1–3. Tohru Fujisawa. Tokyopop, 2008. $10.99.
The general public thinks that the main duty of the organization known as Tokko is public safety. But the truth is they are sword-wielding law enforcers with special abilities whose job it is to take down demons. [SA]

Too Cool to Be Forgotten. Alex Robinson. Top Shelf, 2008. $14.95.
When middle-aged Andy Wicks undergoes hypnosis to stop smoking he finds himself in his own body as it was in 1985, when he was an awkward teenager. Is this real? And if it is can he change things? And if he can, should he? [SA]

Top 10. DC/Wildstorm, 2000–.
Described by some as *Hill Street Blues* with superheroes, the *Top 10* stories deal with the officers of the 10th Precinct who are based in Neopolis, a city where all of the inhabitants are "super" in some way. Besides those with powers, other city residents include robots, aliens, monsters, and even gods, and in this city even the cops need to have powers. One fun element of the books, especially in the first two volumes, is the various "Easter eggs" that have been put into the artwork. The books have won various awards. Other notable Wildstorm titles by Moore are *Tom Strong* and *Promethea.* [YR]

    Top 10, Vols. 1–2. Alan Moore, with art by Gene Ha and Zander Cannon. $14.99–
      $17.99.

    Top 10: The Forty-Niners. Alan Moore, with art by Gene Ha. $24.99 (HC); $17.99 (SC).
      A prequel to the series told how the city was founded.

    Top 10: Beyond the Farthest Precinct. Paul Di Filippo, with art by Jerry Ordway. $14.99.

Torso: A True Crime Graphic Novel. Brian Michael Bendis, with art by Marc Andreyko Image Comics, 2001. $24.95.
In 1935 Cleveland was rocked by a serial killer. Fresh off of his success in Chicago, Elliot Ness has been brought in to try to catch him. Other crime-related works that Bendis has produced for Image include *Jinx*, *Goldfish*, and *Fire.* [SA]

Tough Love: High School Confidential. Abby Denson. Manic D Press, 2006. $12.95.
Described as an American shounen-ai story, *Tough Love* is the story of a teenager named Brian who falls in love with another boy, Chris, whose former boyfriend was sent away by his disapproving parents. Gay bashing, suicide, and other themes are covered in this work. [YR]

Town of Evening Calm, Country of Cherry Blossoms. Fumiyo Kouno. Last Gasp, 2006, 2009. $14.95.
These two stories take place in the author's home of Hiroshima. The first takes place in 1955 and deals with a survivor of the atomic bomb. The second takes place in 1987 and 2004 and deals with the survivor's relatives. The book was a bestseller in Japan and has won awards there and abroad. [SA]

Transmetropolitan. Warren Ellis, with art by Darick Robertson and Rodney Ramos. DC/Vertigo, 1998–. $14.99.
Set in an unspecified future, Gonzo journalist Spider Jerusalem reports from "The City" exposing both its problems and those of the President. A strange and entertaining series, though one that's not for everyone, that has been collected in its entirety. DC has recently begun rereleasing the trades with new formatting. Jerome K. Moore, Keith Aiken, Ray Kryssing, Dick Giordano, Kim DeMulder, and others provided additional artwork. Recommended. [SA]

Vol. 1: *Back on the Street*   Vol. 5: *Lonely City*   Vol. 9: *The Cure*
Vol. 2: *Lust for Life*   Vol. 6: *Gouge Away*   Vol. 10: *One More*
Vol. 3: *Year of the Bastard*   Vol. 7: *Spider's Thrash*   *Transmetropolitan: Tales*
Vol. 4: *The New Scum*   Vol. 8: *Dirge*   *of Human Waste*

The Treasury of Victorian Murder. Rick Geary. NBM. $8.95–.
Part of NBM's ComicsLit line, Geary's award-winning series tells of some of the nineteenth century's most notorious events, ranging from presidential assassinations to lesser-known cases such as the family of killers known as "The Bloody Benders." Geary has also begun a new series of murder cases from the twentieth century. The books are available in both hard- and softcover. [YR]

Vol. 1: *The Treasury of Victorian*   Vol. 5: *The Mystery of Mary Rogers*
    Murder   Vol. 6: *The Beast of Chicago*
Vol. 2: *Jack the Ripper*   (H.H. Holmes)
Vol. 3: *The Borden Tragedy*   Vol. 7: *The Murder of Abraham Lincoln*
Vol. 4: *The Fatal Bullet* (murder   Vol. 8: *The Case of Madeleine Smith*
    of Pres. Garfield)   Vol. 9: *The Saga of the Bloody Benders*

The Treasury of XX Century Murder.
Vol. 1: *The Lindbergh Child*
Vol. 2: *Famous Players* (murder of William Desmond Taylor)

Tricked. Alex Robinson. Top Shelf, 2005.
In 50 chapters the lives of a reclusive rock star, a waitress, a counterfeiter, a "lost daughter," a crank, and a "frustrated lover" are intertwined. [SA]

Trigun. Yasuhiro Nightow. Dark Horse/Digital Manga, 2003–. $14.95.
A "space Western comedy" set on a desert planet settled by Earthmen, the main character is Vash the Stampede, a man who has a reputation for trouble but is actually a pacifist. Two insurance agents follow him trying to minimize the damage, which often is actually caused by people out to get Vash. [SA]

Trigun, Vols. 1–2. $14.95 each.
Trigun Maximum. $9.95.

Vol. 1: *Hero Returns*	Vol. 6: *The Gunslinger*	Vol. 11: *Zero Hour*
Vol. 2: *Death Blue*	Vol. 7: *Happy Days*	Vol. 12: *The Gunslinger*
Vol. 3: *His Life as a . . .*	Vol. 8: *Silent Ruin*	Vol. 13: *Double Duel*
Vol. 4: *Bottom of the Dark*	Vol. 9: *LR*	Vol. 14: *Mind Games*
Vol. 5: *Break Out*	Vol. 10: *Wolfwood*	

The Trouble with Girls, Vols. 1–2. Will Jacobs and Gerard Jones and various artists. Checker, 2006–2007. $17.95.

These volumes collect the humorous 14-issue comic series of the 1980s and 1990s. For super adventurer Lester Girls, action, riches, women, and fame are his, but all he ever wanted was a regular job and a station wagon. A great spoof of the "secret agent" genre. [SA]

True Story Swear to God. Tom Beland. Image.

When Beland, who lived in California, was at "The Magical Kingdom" he met Lily Garcia, a Puerto Rican radio personality. They fell in love and for a while tried a long-distance relationship, but eventually he moved to Puerto Rico to be with her. He has put the story of how they met and their relationship into a comic book. The comic was originally put out by AIT/Planet Lar but has moved to Image, which has collected the original issues and continued Tom and Lily's story. Recommended. [SA]

> *True Story Swear to God Archives*, Vol. 1. 2008. $19.99. Collects the original 17 issues, some of which have been previously collected.
> *New series:* Vol. 1. $14.99.

12 Reasons Why I Love Her. Jamie S. Rich, with art by Joëlle Jones. Oni, 2006. $14.95.
Twelve nonchronological vignettes detailing the relationship between Gwen and Evan. [SA]

Twentieth-Century Eightball. Daniel Clowes. Fantagraphics Books, 2002. $19.00.
Like many other works by Clowes in this appendix, the stories were originally featured in his comic book *Eightball*. Of note is the four-page *Art School Confidential*, which inspired the 2006 film. [SA]

28 Days Later: The Aftermath. Steve Niles, with art by Dennis Calero, Diego Olmos, Nat Jones, and Ken Branch. Fox Atomic, 2007. $17.99.
New stories set before, during, and after the events of the 2002 film about a disease that turns people into zombielike creatures. Boom! Studios has also created an ongoing series set during this period. [SA]

Twilight of the Dark Master. Saki Okuse. Digital Manga Publishing, 2005. $12.95.
Set in the year 2019, mysterious murders of girls in the sex industry are investigated by a mysterious detective with unusual powers. This rated M title was also made into an anime. [SA]

Two-Fisted Science. Jim Ottaviani and various artists. GT Labs. $14.95.
Biographies and "fictionalized science" stories about many scientists including Galileo, Neils Bohr, and Heisenberg, but mostly about Richard Feynman. Artists include Donna Barr, Coleen Doran, and Steve Lieber. The book comes with notes and references. [YR]

U

The Umbrella Academy: Apocalypse Suite. Gerard Way, with art by Gabriel Bá. Dark Horse, 2008. $17.95.
This award-winning title, written by musician Way, tells of a millionaire inventor who adopted

seven children with unusual abilities. Years later, the grown children must reunite to stop the end of the world. But which side will one of them be on? Their adventures continue in *The Umbrella Academy: Dallas* (2009). [YR]

Understanding Comics and sequels. Scott McCloud. HarperCollins, 1993–. $22.00–.
Scott McCloud has written several books in graphic novel form that discuss comics. *Understanding Comics* discusses the medium's history, forms, and other areas. This was followed by *Reinventing Comics* in which he examined new changes in the medium, and *Making Comics*, which discusses the process. All three are recommended. [YR]
 Understanding Comics: The Invisible Art.
 Reinventing Comics: How Imagination and Technology Are Revolutionizing an Art Form
 Making Comics: Storytelling Secrets of Comics, Manga and Graphic Novels

V

V for Vendetta. Alan Moore, with art by David Lloyd. DC Comics. $29.99 (HC); $19.99 (SC).
Set in a fascist 1997 England, a teenage girl gets caught up in the activities of a masked anarchist seeking revenge. This acclaimed work began in Brittan's *Warrior* magazine before being reprinted, colored, and completed by DC in 1988. A 2006 film adapted much of the story though made several changes. DC has also put out an oversized "Absolute Edition" (2009; $99.00). Highly recommended. [YR]

Vagabond. Takehiko Inoue. VIZ, 2001–. $9.95.
Based on the Japanese novel *Musashi*, this long-running manga is a fictionalized version of the life of the great swordmaker Miyamoto Musashi, especially when he was younger and known as Takezo. Over 28 volumes have been produced as of 2009, and some of the earlier volumes have been repackaged into larger "VIZbig" editions for $19.99. [SA]

Valentine. Daniel Cooney and various inkers. Red Eye Press, 2003–. $14.95.
The adventures of assassin Dana Valentine, who can't leave her old life behind. [SA]
 Vol. 1: *Fully Loaded*   Vol. 3: *The Killing Moon*
 Vol. 2: *Red Rain*

Vampire Loves. Joann Sfar. First Second, 2006. $16.95.
Ferdinand is a timid vampire. He bites only enough to feed, leaving a mark that can be mistaken for a mosquito bite. But he is lonely having broken up with his girlfriend. This collection of the four *Grand Vampire* stories from France also tells of his other friends, would-be loves, and adventures and has connections to *The Professor's Daughter* as well as Sfar's juvenile *Little Vampire* books. [YR]

W

The Walking Dead. Robert Kirkman, with art by Tony Moore, Charlie Adlard, and Cliff Rathburn. Image Comics. $9.99–$12.99.
Police officer Rick Grimes awakes in a hospital to find that there has been a zombie outbreak. He has encountered other survivors and they are traveling together for protection. For several volumes they are based in an abandoned prison. Characters have been killed throughout the course of the series, and its not just the zombies doing the killing. A dark and entertaining ongoing series. Recommended. [SA]

Vol. 1: *Days Gone Bye*   Vol. 5: *The Best Defense*   Vol. 9: *Here We Remain*
Vol. 2: *Miles Behind Us*   Vol. 6: *This Sorrowful Life*   Vol. 10: *What We Become*
Vol. 3: *Safety Behind Bars*   Vol. 7: *The Calm Before*   Vol. 11: *Fear the Hunters*
Vol. 4: *The Heart's Desire*   Vol. 8: *Made to Suffer*

There will be additional volumes, and there are also hardcover editions, each of which collects the contents of two softcover columns. Two hardcover omnibus editions have also collected the contents of four editions each. They have no subtitles other than Volume 1, Volume 2, etc. In addition a Compendium Edition collects the contents of the first eight volumes.

Wanted. Mark Millar, with art by J. G. Jones. Image/Top Cow, 2008. $19.99.
Wesley Gibson was just a cubicle worker with a lousy life until he learned the truth. Supervillians (who may seem familiar) secretly rule the world, having taken out the heroes and making the world forget. His father was one of them, and with his death Wesley takes over his role as "The Killer," the world's greatest assassin. But there is a war brewing between the villains and he is caught in the middle. The 2008 movie was very loosely based on the comic, keeping only the "great assassin" aspect. [SA]

***War Stories,* Vols. 1 and 2.** Garth Ennis and various artists including Dave Gibbons, and David Lloyd. DC/Vertigo, 2004–2006. $19.99 each.
A collection of eight stories about the members of various militaries during both the Spanish Civil War and World War II. Ennis also provides the factual background behind each story. [SA]

War's End: Profiles from Bosnia 1995-1996. Joe Sacco. Drawn & Quarterly, 2005. $14.95.
Two stories set in Bosnia after the cease-fire. "Soba" is about a Sarajevo musician while "Christmas with Karadzic" is about the attempt to locate a local leader who is now wanted for war crimes. Some libraries cataloged this in 949.74203/ DR1313.3.S23. [SA]

Wasteland. Antony Johnson, with art by Christopher Mitten. Oni, 2007. $11.95–.
Set 100 years after the disaster known as "The Big Wet," people fight to survive in a devastated America. [SA]

Vol. 1: *City of Dust*   Vol. 3: *Black Steel in the Hour of Chaos*
Vol. 2: *Shades of God*   Vol. 4: *Dog Tribe*

Watchmen. Alan Moore, with art by Dave Gibbons. DC Comics. $39.99 (HC); $19.99 (SC).
On *Time Magazine*'s list of the greatest books since 1923, *Watchmen* is set in an alternate 1985 where Nixon is still president, people drive electric cars, and the United States won in Vietnam. Superheroes have been outlawed except for two, government operative the Comedian and Dr. Manhattan, a blue, incredibly powerful (and often naked) individual who has helped to keep the Russians in check. But now the Comedian has been murdered and former heroes must discover who did it before it is too late for them and the world. *Watchmen* is an excellent work, and the reader will discover new things about it with each reading. DC has also published a $75.00 oversized Absolute Edition that includes 48 pages of supplemental material. No matter which version you buy, this work is highly recommended. [SA]

We Are On Our Own. Miriam Katin. Drawn & Quarterly, 2006. $19.95 (HC).
An memoir of how in 1944, the author, a small child at the time, and her mother, who were Jews living in Budapest, escaped being sent to the camps. The story also tells of how their father who had been separated from them was able to find them. [SA]

Wet Moon **series.** Ross Campbell. Oni, 2004–. $14.95.
Set in the Southern town of Wet Moon, this series of original graphic novels deals with Cleo Lovedrop and her friends, many of whom are into the Goth subculture. [SA]

Vol. 1: *Feeble Wanderings*   Vol. 4: *Drowned in Evil*
Vol. 2: *Unseen Feet*   Vol. 5: *Where All Stars Fail to Burn*
Vol. 3: *Further Realms of Fright*

More volumes may come out.

We3. Grant Morrison, with art by Frank Quitely. DC/Vertigo, 2005. $12.99.
A cat, dog, and rabbit are tested on by the government to make them cybernetic killing machines, but when the project is to be shut down, the animals escape. [SA]

When I'm Old and Other Stories. Gabrielle Bell. Alternative Comics, 2002. $12.95.
Various short stories by Bell, some of which are semiautobiographical. Many of these stories were originally in Bell's self-published comics. See also *Lucky* for more of her work. [SA]

Whiteout. Greg Rucka, with art by Steve Lieber. Oni, 2007. $13.95 each.
U.S Marshall Carrie Stetko is sent to Antarctica where she must solve a murder before winter sets in. In *Melt*, she must find weapons stolen from a nearby Russian base. These books have been remastered and reformatted from the earlier collections of the two limited series. A film version of the first book came out in 2009 with Kate Beckinsale as Carrie. [SA]

Whiteout, Vol. 1: *The Definitive Edition*
Whiteout, Vol. 2: *Melt—The Definitive Edition*

Wildstorm Television and Movie-Based Comics

DC's imprint Wildstorm has produced a number of series, limited series, and specials based on films and television programs mainly based on science fiction and horror works. Besides the titles listed below, they have also put out comics based on *Chuck* and *The X-Files*. [SA]

Freddy vs. Jason vs. Ash. Jeff Katz and James Kuhoric, with art by Jason Craig. $17.99.
Co-published by Dynamite who has the license for Ash (of Army of Darkness), three horror stars do battle. A sequel, *Freddy Jason Ash: Nightmare Warriors* came out in 2009.

Friday the 13th. 2007–. $14.99 each.
In the first volume yet another group of teens go to Camp Crystal Lake and encounter (and are killed by) Jason. The second volume has several short stories. Like the films, the comic includes gory violence, sex, and nudity.

Vol. 1. Justin Gray and Jimmy Palmiotti, with art by Adam Archer and Peter Guzmen.
Vol. 2. Marc Andreyko, Jason Aaron, Ron Marz, and Joshua Hale Fialkov, with art by Adam Archer, Andy B, Shawn Moll, and Mike Huddleston.

Lost Boys: Reign of Frogs. Hans Rodionoff, with art by Joel Gomez. 2008. $17.99.
What happened to the Frog Brothers between the original *Lost Boys* film and its sequel?

A Nightmare on Elm Street. Chuck Dixon, with art by Kevin West and Bob Almond. $14.99.
The newest adventures of Freddy Krueger.

Supernatural Origins. Peter Johnson with art by Matthew Dow Smith. $14.99.

Supernatural: Rising Son. Peter Johnson and Rebecca Dessertinem with art by Diego Olmos. $14.99.
Two prequels to the popular CW Network television show.

Texas Chainsaw Massacre. $14.99 each.
Volume 1 contains a prequel while Volume 2 collects several short stories.
    Vol. 1. Dan Abnett and Andy Lanning, with art by Wes Craig.
    Vol. 2. Will Pfeifer, Bruce Jones, Dan Abnett, and Andy Lanning, with art by Stefano Raffaele, Chris Gugliotti, Joel Gomez, and Wes Craig.

Wimbledon Green: The Greatest Comic Book Collector in the World. Seth. Drawn & Quarterly, 2005. $19.95.
These short stories tell of the experiences of the mysterious and strange Green who has a large and notable comic book collection. His rival collectors are also shown discussing him and trying to beat him to the best finds. [SA]

With the Light: Raising an Autistic Child, Vol. 1–. Keiko Tobe. Yen Press, 2007–. $14.99.
The story of Sachiko Azuma who finds out that her son Hikaru is autistic. She must deal with the reaction of her husband who soon comes around, a mother-in-law who at first blames her, and the reaction of people who do not understand autism. Much of the series also deals with Hikaru's years in school and the problems of his parents to get certain teachers to understand more about their child. The series has won awards in Japan and was made into an award-winning television program. There will most likely be at least five volumes, each of which is over 500 pages long. Recommended. [YR]

The World Below. Paul Chadwick. Dark Horse, 2007. $12.95.
Six people are sent to explore a strange underground world by businessman Charles Hoy who made his fortune 15 years earlier with items that came from there. The "team of six" encounters strange creatures and even greater threats in "The World Below." [YR]

X

X Isle. Andrew Cosby and Michael Alan Nelson, with art by Greg Scott. Boom! $14.99.
A group of researchers investigating a strange creature are marooned on an island containing even stranger creatures and more. [YR]

X-Kai. Asami Tohjoh. Tokyopop, 2006–. $9.99.
A two-volume OT crime manga about Kai, who works in a flower ship by day and as an assassin at night, though only so he can pay for his brother's medical care. [SA]

Xombie, Vol 1: ***Reanimated.*** James Farr, with art by Nate Lovett. Devil's Due, 2008. $18.99.
Based on an online animated series, this title is set in 2052, nearly 20 years after zombie attacks left humans hiding in a few isolated cities. But there are some "variant" zombies who can think and have a moral compass, and one of them once helped to keep six-year-old Zoe safe. Now 10 years later, she needs his help to save the city from destruction. [YR]

Y

Y: The Last Man. Brian K. Vaughan, with art by Pia Guerra and José Marzán Jr. DC/Vertigo, 2003–2008. $12.99–$14.99.
At one moment, every male mammal—human and animal—on the face of the Earth dies, except for two. One is a campuchean monkey being trained to be a helper animal. The other is his trainer, a would-be escape artist in his early twenties named Yorick Brown, who

finds himself the last man on Earth. After getting in touch with his mother, a congress-woman, he ends up traveling with a government agent and a scientist, both of whom may have been linked to the "gendercide," in order to find its true cause and how to help the survival of the human race. Their journey takes them across the country and the world, encountering dangers ranging from foreign armies to a violent ultra-feminist group of "Amazons," but all Yorick truly wants is to find Beth, the woman he loves. The complete series has been collected in 10 paperbacks, and new $30.00 "deluxe editions" contain larger amounts. Paul Chadwick and Goran Sudzuka provided additional artwork throughout the series. Recommended. [SA]

Vol. 1: *Unmanned*	Vol. 5: *Ring of Truth*	Vol. 8: *Kimono*
Vol. 2: *Cycles*	Vol. 6: *Girl on Girl*	Vol. 9: *Motherland*
Vol. 3: *One Small Step*	Vol. 7: *Paper Dolls*	Vol. 10: *Whys and Wherefores*
Vol. 4: *Safeword*		

Yossel April 19, 1943. Joe Kubert. Ibooks, 2003. $13.95.
Kubert's family came to America from Poland in 1926 when he was two months old. But what if he didn't? Teenaged Yossel is in the Warsaw ghetto but still wants to be an artist. The art is in pencil, but with no ink, the way a boy with only a pencil might have drawn in the period leading up the this point and the ongoing ghetto uprising. [SA]

Z

The Zombie Survival Guide: Recorded Attacks. Max Brooks, with art by Ibraim Roberson. Random House/Three Rivers Press, 2009. $17.00.
A companion to Brooks' bestselling book, this contains tales of zombie attacks throughout history. [SA]

Zombie Tales. Boom! Studios, 2007–. $14.99–$15.99.
These volumes collect Boom! Studios' first title and features several short stories about people dealing with Zombies. Some of these stories also appear in *Death Valley*. [SA]

Vol. 1 (no subtitle)	Vol. 3: *Good Eatin'*
Vol. 2: *Oblivion*	Vol. 4: *This Bites*

Zombies. Edited by Dave West and Colin Mathieson. Accent UK Comics, 2007. $10.00.
An anthology of zombie stories from the United Kingdom, some quite humorous. [SA]

Zombies! Eclipse of the Undead. El Torres, with art by Yair Herrera. IDW, 2008. $19.99.
The zombies have invaded Los Angeles, law and order has broken down, and the LA Coliseum has become a refugee camp that is about to be overrun. A small band of diverse people must escape the city before it's too late. [SA]

Zombieworld. Dark Horse, 2005–. $8.95.
Various stories involving zombies and other supernatural terrors. [SA]
  Zombieworld: Champion of the Worms. Mike Mignola with art by Pat McEown.
  Zombieworld: Winter Dregs and Other Stories. By various including Bob Fingerman.

Recommended Additional Books for Your Collection

As covered in Chapter 6, the titles in Appendix A are not the only comic- and graphic-novel-related books that you can purchase. Some are of primary interest to teachers and librarians while others will also be enjoyed by your patrons. Some may even be used in classes on the subject.

For Your Information

These are titles that you may use as either a librarian or a teacher to learn more about graphic novels, get bibliographic information and book lists, and learn more of how they are being used in library settings.

Brenner, Robin. *Understanding Manga and Anime*. Libraries Unlimited, 2007. $40.00.

Cornog, Martha, and Timothy Perper (Ed.). *Graphic Novels Beyond the Basics: Insights and Issues for Libraries*. *Libraries Unlimited*, 2009. $45.00.

Goldsmith, Francisca. *Graphic Novels Now: Buiding, Managing, and Marketing a Dynamic Collection*. American Library Association, 2005. $38.00.

Miller, Steve. *Developing and Promoting Graphic Novels Collections*. Neal-Schuman, 2005. $49.95.

Pawuk, Michael. *Graphic Novels: A Genre Guide to Comic Books, Manga, and More*. Libraries Unlimited, 2007. $65.00.

Serchay, David S. *The Librarian's Guide to Graphic Novels for Children and Tweens*. Neal-Schuman, 2008. $55.00.

Thompson, Jason. *Manga: The Complete Guide*. Ballentine Books, 2007. $19.95.

Weiner, Stephen. *The 101 Best Graphic Novels: A Guide to This Exciting New Medium*, Revised Edition. NBM, 2006. $9.95.

Books for Both You and Your Patrons

These titles, divided by publisher, list just some of the many related books that you can purchase for your library. They range from the informative (books about graphic novels, their characters, and their creators), instructive (writing and drawing books), scholarly, and just plain fun. This is just some of the many titles available to libraries.

About Comics
www.aboutcomics.com

Panel One. 2002. $19.95.
Panel Two. 2003. $20.95.
Simone, Gail. *You'll All Be Sorry*. 2009. $11.99.

Adams Media
www.adamsmedia.com

Ellis, Mark, and Melissa Martin Ellis. *The Everything Guide to Writing Graphic Novels: From Superheroes to Manga—All You Need to Create and Sell Your Graphic Works*. 2008. $14.95.

Allworth Press
www.allworth.com

Dooley, Michael, and Steven Heller (Eds). *The Education of a Comics Artist*. 2005. $19.95.

Alpha Books
us.penguingroup.com

Forbeck, Matt, and Yair Herrera. *The Complete Idiot's Guide to Drawing Superheroes and Villains Illustrated*. 2008. $19.95.

Forbeck, Matt, and Tomoko Taniguchi. *The Complete Idiot's Guide to Manga Fantasy Creatures Illustrated*. 2007. $19.95.

Forbeck, Matt, and Tomoko Taniguchi. *The Complete Idiot's Guide to Manga Shoujo Illustrated*. 2008. $19.95.

Gertler, Nat, and Steve Lieber. *The Complete Idiot's Guide to Creating a Graphic Novel*. 2008. $18.95.

Layman, John, and David Hutchison. *The Complete Idiot's Guide to Drawing Manga Illustrated*. 2008. $19.95.

Aurum Press
www.aurumpress.co.uk

Gravett, Paul, and Peter Stanbury. *Great British Comics: Celebrating a Century of Ripping Yarns and Wizard Wheezes*. 2006. $35.00.

Barricade Books
www.barricadebooks.com

Weinstein, Simcha. *Up, Up, and Oy Vey: How Jewish History, Culture, and Values Shaped the Comic Book Superhero*. 2009. $19.95.

Barron's Educational Books
www.barronseduc.com

Chinn, Mike. *Writing and Illustrating the Graphic Novel*. 2004. $23.99.

Basic Books
www.perseusbooksgroup.com/basic

Jones, Gerard. *Men of Tomorrow: Geeks, Gangsters, and the Birth of the Comic Book*. 2005. $15.00.

Benbella Books
www.benbellabooks.com

Conway, Gerry (Ed). *Webslinger: SF and Comic Writers on Your Friendly Neighborhood Spider-Man*. 2007. $17.95.

O'Neil, Dennis. *Batman Unauthorized: Vigilantes, Jokers, and Heroes in Gotham City.* 2008. $17.95.

Rosenberg, Robin (Ed). *The Psychology of Superheroes: An Unauthorized Exploration.* 2008. $14.95.

Wein, Len, and Leah Wilson (Eds). *The Unauthorized X-Men: SF and Comic Writers on Mutants, Prejudice, and Adamantium.* 2006. $17.95.

Yeffeth, Glenn (Ed.). *The Man from Krypton: A Closer Look at Superman.* 2006. $17.95.

Chicago Review Press
www.chicagoreviewpress.com

Kaplan, Arie. *Masters of the Comic Book Universe Revealed!* 2006. $18.95.

Raphael, Jordan, and Tom Spurgeon. *Stan Lee and the Rise and Fall of the American Comic Book.* 2004. $16.95.

Chronicle Books
www.chroniclebooks.com

Cain, Chelsea and Marc Mohan. *Does This Cape Make Me Look Fat? Pop Psychology for Superheroes.* 2006. $12.95.

Daniels, Les. *Batman: The Complete History.* 2004. $19.95.

Daniels, Les. *Superman: The Complete History.* 2004. $18.95.

Daniels, Les. *Wonder Woman: The Life and Times of the Amazon Princess.* 2001. $40.00.

Collins and Brown
www.anovabooks.com/imprint/collinsbrown

Pilcher, Tim, and Brad Brooks. *The Essential Guide to World Comics.* 2005. $19.95.

Continuum
www.continuumbooks.com

Duncan, Randy, and Matthew J. Smith. *The Power of Comics: History, Form and Culture.* 2009. $24.95.

Fingeroth, Danny. *Superman on the Couch: What Superheroes Really Tell Us About Ourselves and Our Society.* 2004. $26.95.

Klock, Geoff. *How to Read Superhero Comics and Why.* 2002. $29.95.

Versaci, Rocco. *This Book Contains Graphic Language: Comics as Literature.* 2007. $22.95.

Corwin Press
www.corwinpress.com

Frey, Nancy, and Douglas Fisher (Eds.). *Teaching Visual Literacy: Using Comic Books, Graphic Novels, Anime, Cartoons, and More to Develop Comprehension and Thinking Skills.* 2008. $33.95.

Da Capo Press
www.perseusbooksgroup.com/dacapo

Hajdu, David. *Heroes and Villains.* 2009. $17.95.

Wolk, Douglas. *Reading Comics: How Graphic Novels Work and What They Mean.* 2007. $22.95.

Dark Horse
www.darkhorse.com

Brownstein, Charles. *Eisner/Miller: A One-on-One Interview.* 2005. $19.95.

DC Comics
www.dccomics.com

Bender, Hy. *Sandman Companion.* 1999. $14.99.
Couch, N. C. Christopher, and Stephen Weiner. *The Will Eisner Companion.* 2004. $19.95.
Fleischer, Michael. *The Original Encyclopedia of Comic Heroes,* Vol. 1: *Batman.* 2007. $19.99.
Fleischer, Michael. *The Original Encyclopedia of Comic Heroes,* Vol. 2: *Wonder Woman.* 2007. $19.99.
Fleischer, Michael. *The Original Encyclopedia of Comic Heroes,* Vol. 3: *Superman.* 2007. $19.99.

Del Rey
www.randomhouse.com/delray

Greenberger, Robert. *The Essential Batman Encyclopedia.* 2008. $29.95.

DK
www.dk.com

Irvine, Alex. *The Vertigo Encyclopedia.* 2008. $30.00.
Sanderson, Peter. *The Marvel Chronicle.* 2008. $50.00.
Teitelbaum, Michael, et al. *The DC Comics Encyclopedia: The Definitive Guide to the Characters of the DC Universe.* 2008. $40.00.
Thomas, Roy. *Conan: The Ultimate Guide to the World's Most Savage Barbarian.* 2006. $24.99.
Wallace, Daniel, et al. *The Marvel Encyclopedia.* 2006. $45.00.

Fantagraphics Books
www.fantagraphics.com

Bell, Blake. *Stranger and Stranger: The World of Steve Ditko.* 2008. $39.99.
Feiffer, Jules. *The Great Comic Book Heroes.* 2003. $8.95.
George, Milo (Ed.). *The Comics Journal Library,* Vol. 1: *Jack Kirby.* 2002. $18.95.
George, Milo (Ed.). *The Comics Journal Library,* Vol. 3: *R. Crumb.* 2003. $18.95.
Levin, Bob. *Outlaws, Rebels, Free Thinkers, and Pirates.* 2005. $16.95.
McCabe, Joseph (Ed.). *Hanging Out with the Dream King: Conversations with Neil Gaiman and His Collaborators.* 2005. $17.95.
Nadel, Dan, and Glenn Bray (Eds.). *So That's Where the Demented Wented: The Comics and Art of Rory Hayes.* 2008. $22.99.
Rosenkranz, Patrick. *Rebel Visions: The Underground Comix Revolution, 1963–1975.* 2003. $39.95.
Sanders, Joe (Ed.). *The Sandman Papers.* 2006. $18.95.
Schelly, Bill. *Man of Rock: A Biography of Joe Kubert.* 2008. $19.99.
Spurgeon, Tom (Ed.). *The Comics Journal Library,* Vol. 5: *Classic Comics Illustrators.* 2005. $22.95.
Spurgeon, Tom (Ed.). *The Comics Journal Library,* Vol. 6: *The Writers.* 2006. $19.95.

Farrar, Straus, and Giroux

us.macmillan.com/FSG.aspx

Hajdu, David. *The Ten-Cent Plague: The Great Comic-Book Scare and How it Changed America.* 2008. $26.00.

First Second Books

www.firstsecondbooks.com

Abel, Jessica, and Matt Madden. *Drawing Words & Writing Pictures.* 2008. $29.95.

Sturm, James, Andrew Arnold, and Alexis Frederick-Frost. *Adventures in Cartooning: How to Turn Your Doodles into Comics.* 2009. $12.95.

Flammarion

www.flammarion.com

Koyama-Richard, Brigitte. *One Thousand Years of Manga.* 2008. $49.95.

Gemstone Publishing

www.gemstonepub.com

Overstreet, Robert M. *The Official Overstreet Comic Book Price Guide.* Annual. Prices vary.

Gotham Books

us.penguin.com

Kakalios, James. *The Physics of Superheroes*, 2nd edition. 2009. $16.00.

Greenwood Press

www.greenwood.com

The Greenwood Encyclopedia of Graphic Novels. 2010. Price TBA.

HarperCollins (Collins Design)

www.harpercollins.com

Casaus, Fernando. *The Monster Book of Manga: Draw Like the Experts.* 2006. $24.95.

Geissman, Grant. *Foul Play! The Art and Artists of the Notorious 1950s E.C. Comics!* 2005. $29.95.

Goulart, Ron. *Comic Book Encyclopedia: The Ultimate Guide to Characters, Graphic Novels, Writers, and Artists in the Comic Book Universe.* 2004. $49.95.

Gravett, Paul. *Graphic Novels : Everything You Need to Know.* 2005. $29.95.

Kannenberg, Gene. *500 Essential Graphic Novels: The Ultimate Guide.* 2008. $24.95.

Lehmann, Timothy R. *Manga: Masters of the Art.* 2005. $24.95.

Sparrow, Keith. *Bishoujo Manga: Easel-Does-It.* 2007. $18.95.

Sparrow, Keith. *Drawing Action Manga: Easel-Does-It.* 2005. $18.95.

Sparrow, Keith. *Drawing Shoujo Manga: Easel-Does-It.* 2006. $18.95.

Harry N. Abrams/Abrams ComicArts

www.abramsbooks.com

Daniels, Les. *The Golden Age of DC Comics: 365 Days.* 2004. $29.95.

Danky, James, and Dennis Kitchen. *Underground Classics: The Transformation of Comics Into Comix.* 2009. $29.95.

Evanier, Mark. *Kirby: King of Comics.* 2008. $40.00.

Kitchen, Dennis, and Paul Buhle. *The Art of Harvey Kurtzman*. 2009. $40.00.

Nadel, Dan. *Art Out of Time: Unknown Comics Visionaries, 1900–1969*. 2006. $40.00.

Pilcher, Tim, and Gene Kannenberg Jr. *Erotic Comics: A Graphic History from Tijuana Bibles to Underground Comix*. 2008. $29.95.

Pilcher, Tim, and Gene Kannenberg Jr. *Erotic Comics 2: A Graphic History from the Liberated '70s to the Internet*. 2009. $29.95.

Yoe, Craig. *Secret Identity: The Fetish Art of Superman's Co-creator Joe Shuster*. 2009. $24.95.

Heinemann
www.heinemann.com

Cary, Stephen. *Going Graphic: Comics at Work in the Multilingual Classroom*. 2004. $32.50.

Hermes Press
www.hermespress.com

Andrae, Thomas. *Creators of Humor in Comics*. 2009. $39.00.

Andrae, Thomas. *Creators of the Superheroes*. 2009. $39.99.

Goulart, Ron. *Good Girl Art*. 2008. $29.99.

Herman, Daniel. *Gil Kane: The Art of the Comics*. 2007. $49.99.

Herman, Daniel. *Gil Kane: Art and Interviews*. 2002. $49.99.

Herman, Daniel. Silver Age: *The Second Generation of Comic Book Artists*. 2005. $29.00.

Irving, Christopher. *From Four Color to Silver Screen: The First Movie Superheroes*. 2009. $39.99.

Porter, Alan J. *Star Trek: A Comic Book History*. 2009. $39.99.

I. B. Tauris
www.ibtaurus.com

Kaveney, Roz. *Superheroes! Capes and Crusaders in Comics and Films*. 2008. $18.95.

Impact Books
www.impact-books.com

David, Peter. *Writing for Comics and Graphic Novels with Peter David*, 2nd edition. 2009. $22.99.

Doran, Colleen. *Girl to Grrrl Manga: How to Draw the Hottest Shoujo Manga*. 2006. $19.99.

Giordano, Dick. *Draw Comics with Dick Giordano*. 2005. $19.99.

Hernandez, Lea. *Manga Secrets*. 2005. $19.99.

McKenzie, Alan. *How to Draw and Sell Comics*. 2005. $22.99.

Ryall, Chris, and Scott Tipton. *Comic Books 101: The History, Methods, and Madness*. 2009. $22.99.

Schmidt, Andy. *The Insider's Guide to Creating Comics and Graphic Novels*. 2009. $19.99.

J. Wiley/For Dummies
www.wiley.com

Farrington, Brian. *Drawing Cartoons and Comics For Dummies*. 2009. $19.99

Gresh, Lois and Robert Weinberg. *The Science of Superheroes*. 2003. $16.95.

Gresh, Lois and Robert Weinberg. *The Science of Supervillains*. 2004. $24.95.

Irwin, William (Ed.). *Batman and Philosophy: The Dark Knight of the Soul*. 2008. $17.95.

Irwin, William (Ed.). *X-Men and Philosophy: Astonishing Insight and Uncanny Argument in the Mutant X-Verse*. 2009. $17.95.

Okabayashi, Kensuke. *Manga for Dummies*. 2006. $19.99.

Jewish Publication Society of America
www.jewishpub.org

Kaplan, Arie. *From Krakow to Krypton: Jews and Comic Books*. 2008. $25.00.

Johns Hopkins University Press
www.press.jhu.edu

Wright, Bradford W. *Comic Book Nation: The Transformation of Youth Culture in America*. 2003. $21.00.

Zehr, E. Paul. *Becoming Batman: The Probability of a Superhero*. 2008. $26.95.

Krause Publications
www.krausebooks.com

Isabella, Tony. *1,000 Comic Books You Must Read*. 2009. $29.99.

Last Gasp
www.lastgasp.com

Yoe, Craig. *Clean Cartoonists' Dirty Drawings*. 2007. $19.95.

Laurence King Publishing
www.laurenceking.com

Gravett, Paul. *Manga: Sixty Years of Japanese Comics*. 2004. $24.95.

Linworth Publishing
www.linworth.com

Gorman, Michele. *Getting Graphic: Using Graphic Novels to Promote Literacy with Preteens and Teens*. 2003. $36.95.

M Press
www.mpressbooks.com

Andleman, Bob. *Will Eisner: A Spirited Life*. 2005. $14.95.

McFarland and Co.
www.mcfarlandpub.com

DeTora, Lisa (Ed.). *Heroes of Film, Comics, and American Culture: Essays on Real and Fictional Defenders of Home*. 2009. $39.95.

Jones, William Jr. *Classics Illustrated: A Cultural History with Illustrations*. 2002. $55.00.

Kahan, Jeffrey, and Stanley Stewart. *Caped Crusaders 101: Composition Through Comic Books*. 2006. $35.00.

LoCicero, Don. *Superheroes and Gods: A Comparative Study from Babylonia to Batman*. 2007. $39.95.

Muir, John Kenneth. *The Encylopedia of Superheroes on Film and Television*, 2nd edition. 2008. $75.00.

Nolan, Michelle. *Love on the Racks: A History of American Romance Comics*. 2008. $49.95.

Scivally, Bruce. *Superman on Film, Television, Radio, and Broadway*. 2007. $49.95.

Sheyahshe, Michael A. *Native Americans in Comic Books: A Critical Study*. 2008. $49.95.

Wandtke, Terrance R. (Ed.). *The Amazing Transforming Superhero: Essays on the Revision of Characters in Comic Books, Film, and Television*. 2007. $35.00.

Weiner, Robert G. *Marvel Graphic Novels and Related Publications: An Annotated Guide*. 2007. $49.95.

Monkey Brain Books
www.monkeybrainbooks.com

Coogan, Peter. *Superhero: The Secret Origin of a Genre*. 2006. $15.95.

Nevins, Jess. *A Blazing World: The Unofficial Companion to the Second League of Extraordinary Gentlemen*. 2004. $15.95.

Nevins, Jess. *Heroes & Monsters: The Unofficial Companion to The League of Extraordinary Gentlemen*. 2003. $15.95.

Nevins, Jess. *Impossible Territories: An Unofficial Companion to The League of Extraordinary Gentlemen: The Black Dossier*. 2008. $15.95.

National Council of Teachers of English
www.ncte.org

Carter, James Bucky (Ed.). *Building Literacy Connections with Graphic Novels: Page by Page, Panel by Panel*. 2007. $30.95.

NBM
www.nbmpub.com

Talbot, Bryan. *The Art of Bryan Talbot*. 2007. $19.95.

Weiner, Stephen. *Faster Than a Speeding Bullet: The Rise of the Graphic Novel*. 2004. $9.95.

New Press
www.thenewpress.com

Buhle, Paul (Ed.). *Jews and American Comics: An Illustrated History of an American Art Form*. 2008. $29.95.

Omnigraphics
www.omnigraphics.com

Misiroglu, Gina. *The Superhero Book*. 2004. $29.95.

Misiroglu, Gina. *The Supervillain Book*. 2004. $29.95.

Open Court
www.opencourtbooks.com

Morris, Tom, and Matt Morris (Eds.). *Superheroes and Philosophy: Truth, Justice, and the Socratic Way*. 2005. $19.95.

Palace Press
www.palacepress.com

Robbins, Trina. *The Great American Superheroines*. 2010. Price TBA.

Pantheon
pantheon.knopfdoubleday.com

Kidd, Chip. *Bat-Manga! The Secret History of Batman in Japan*. 2008. $29.95.
Ross, Alex. *Mythology: The DC Comics Art of Alex Ross*. 2005. $25.95.

Penguin/Plume
us.penguin.com

Cronin, Brian. *Was Superman a Spy? And Other Comic Book Legends Revealed*. 2009. $14.95.

Praeger
www.praeger.com

Booker, M. Keith. *May Contain Graphic Material: Comic Books Graphic Novels and Film*. 2007. $44.95.
Lent, John A. *Comic Books and Comic Strips in the United States through 2005: An International Bibliography*. 2006. $104.95.

Quirk Books
www.chroniclebooks.com

Beatty, Scott. *The Batman Handbook: The Ultimate Training Manual*. 2005. $15.95.
Beatty, Scott. *The Superman Handbook: The Ultimate Guide to Saving the Day*. 2005. $15.95.
Grahame-Smith, Seth. *The Spider-Man Handbook: The Ultimate Training Manual*. 2006. $15.95.

Rough Guides
us.penguin.com

Fingeroth, Danny. *Rough Guide to Graphic Novels*. 2007. $35.00.
Yadao, Jason. *The Rough Guide to Manga*. 2009. $18.99.

Rutgers University Press
rutgerspress.rutgers.edu

Baskand, Samantha, and Ranen Omer-Sherman. *The Jewish Graphic Novel: Critical Approaches*. 2008. $49.95.

St. Martin's Press
http://us.macmillan.com/smp.aspx

Gravett, Paul, and Peter Stanbury. *Holy Sh*t!: The World's Weirdest Comic Books*. 2008. $12.95.
Wagner, Hank, Christopher Golden, and Stephen R. Bissette. *Prince of Stories: The Many Worlds of Neil Gaiman*. 2008. $29.95.

Stickman Graphics
www.stickmangraphics.com

Tinsley, Kevin. *Digital Prepress for Comic Books*. 2009. $38.95.

Stonebridge Press
www.stonebridge.com

Schodt, Frederik L. *The Astro Boy Essays: Osamu Tezuka, Mighty Atom, and the Manga/Anime Revolution.* 2007. $16.95.

Schodt, Frederik L. *Dreamland Japan: Writings on Modern Manga.* 1996. $19.95.

Titan Books
www.titanbooks.com

DeFalco, Tom. *Comics Creators on Fantastic Four.* 2005. $17.95.

DeFalco, Tom. *Comics Creators on Spider-Man.* 2004. $16.95.

DeFalco, Tom. *Comics Creators on X-Men.* 2006. $17.95.

Gibbons, Dave, Chip Kidd, and Mike Essl. *Watching the Watchmen: The Definitive Companion to the Ultimate Graphic Novel.* 2008. $39.95.

Saffel, Steve. *Spider-Man: The Icon—The Life and Times of a Pop Culture Phenomenon.* 2007. $49.95.

Salisbury, Mark. *Writers on Comics Scriptwriting*, Vols. 1–2. 2002–2004. $16.95.

TwoMorrows Publishing
twomorrows.com

Alter Ego Collection, Vol. 1. 2006. $21.95.

The Best of Draw, Vols. 1–4. 2005– . $17.95–$29.95.

Cadigan, Glenn (Ed.). *Best of the Legion Outpost.* 2004. $17.95.

Cadigan, Glenn (Ed.). *Titans Companion*, Vols. 1–2. 2005– . $24.95–$26.95.

Comtois, Pierre. *Marvel Comics in the 1960s: An Issue-by-issue Field Guide.* 2009. $27.95.

Cooke, Jon B. (Ed.). *T.H.U.N.D.E.R. Agents Companion.* 2005. $24.95.

Dallas, Keith. *Flash Companion.* 2008. $26.95.

Eury, Michael. *Batcave Companion* (with Michael Kronenberg). 2009. $26.95.

Eury, Michael. *Comics Gone Ape.* 2007. $16.95.

Eury, Michael. *Justice League Companion*, Vol. 1. 2005. $24.95.

Eury, Michael. *Krypton Companion.* 2006. $24.95.

Fingeroth, Danny (Ed.). *The Best of Write Now.* 2008. $19.95.

Fingeroth, Danny, and Mike Manley. *How to Create Comics from Script to Print.* 2006. $13.95.

Irving, Christopher. *Blue Beetle Companion.* 2007. $19.95.

Irving, Christopher. *Comic Introspective*, Vol. 1: *Peter Bagge.* 2007. $16.95.

Khoury, George. *Extraordinary Works of Alan Moore.* 2003. $29.95.

Khoury, George. *Image Comics: The Road to Independence.* 2007. $34.95.

Khoury, George (Ed.). *True Brit: A Celebration of the Great Comic Book Artists of the UK.* 2004. $21.95.

Lowe, John. *Working Methods: Comic Creators Detail Their Storytelling and Creative Processes.* 2007. $21.95.

Nolen-Weathington, Eric (and others). *The Modern Masters Series.* 2003– . $14.95–$15.95. (Over 20 volumes, each concentrating on a particular creator.)

Silver Age Sci-fi Companion. 2007. $19.95.

Thomas, Roy. *All-Star Companion*, Vols. 1–3. 2004–2007. $24.95–$26.95.

Thomas, Roy, and Jim Amash. *John Romita and All That Jazz.* 2007. $18.95.
Zawisza, Doug. *Hawkman Companion.* 2008. $24.95.

University of Hawaii Press
www.uhpress.hawaii.edu

Kinsella, Sharon. *Adult Manga: Culture and Power in Contemporary Japanese Society.* 2000.
$54.95.

University of Texas Press
www.utexas.edu/utpress

Aldama, Frederick Luis. *Your Brain on Latino Comics: From Gus Arriola to Los Bros Hernandez.*
2009. $24.95.

University of Toronto Press
www.utpress.utoronto.ca

Beaty, Bart. *Unpopular Culture: Transforming the European Comic Book in the 1990s.* 2007.
$32.95.

University Press of Mississippi
www.upress.state.ms.us

Alaniz, José. *Komiks: Comic Art in Russia.* 2010. $38.00.
Andrae, Thomas. *Carl Barks and the Disney Comic Book: Unmasking the Myth of Modernity.*
2006. $22.00.
Ault, Donald (Ed.). *Carl Barks: Conversations.* 2002. $20.00.
Barker, Martin. *A Haunt of Fears: The Strange History of the British Horror Comics Campaign.*
1992. $25.00.
Brown, Jeffrey A. *Black Superheroes, Milestone Comics, and Their Fans.* 2001. $22.00.
Campbell, Bruce. *¡Viva la historieta! Mexican Comics, NAFTA, and the Politics of Globalization.*
2009. $25.00.
Di Liddo, Annalisa. *Alan Moore: Comics As Performance, Fiction As Scalpel.* 2009. $22.00.
Gabilliet, Jean-Paul. *Of Comics and Men: A Cultural History of American Comics Books.* 2009.
$55.00.
Gordon, Ian, Mark Jancovich, and Matthew P. McAllister (Eds.). *Film and Comic Books.*
2007. $25.00.
Groensteen, Thierry. *The System of Comics.* 2007. $25.00.
Hatfield, Charles. *Alternative Comics: An Emerging Literature.* 2005. $22.00.
Harvey, Robert C. *The Art of the Comic Book: An Aesthetic History.* 1995. $30.00.
Heer, Jeet, and Kent Worcester. *Arguing Comics: Literary Masters on a Popular Medium.*
2004. $25.00.
Heer, Jeet, and Kent Worcester. *A Comics Studies Reader.* 2008. $25.00.
Holm, D. K (Ed.). *R. Crumb: Conversations.* 2004. $20.00.
Inge, M. Thomas. *Comics As Culture.* 1992. $25.00.
McKinney, Mark (Ed.). *History and Politics in French-Language Comics and Graphic Novels.*
2008. $50.00.
McLaughlin, Jeff (Ed.). *Comics as Philosophy.* 2005. $25.00.
McLaughlin, Jeff (Ed.). *Stan Lee: Conversations.* 2007. $22.00.

Nyberg, Amy Kiste. *Seal of Approval: The History of the Comics Code.* 1998. $20.00.

Power, Natsu Onoda. *God of Comics: Osamu Tezuka and the Creation of Post–World War II Manga.* 2009. $25.00.

Pustz, Matthew J. *Comic Book Culture: Fanboys and True Believers.* 1999. $25.00.

Reynolds, Richard. *Super Heroes: A Modern Mythology.* 1994. $25.00.

Rhode, Michael G. (Ed.) *Harvey Pekar: Conversations.* 2008. $22.00.

Royal, Derek. *The Hernandez Brothers: Conversations.* 2010. Price TBA.

Varnum, Robin, and Christina T. Gibbons (Eds.). *The Language of Comics Word and Image.* 2002. $25.00.

Witek, Joseph (Ed.). *Art Spiegelman: Conversations.* 2007. $20.00.

Witek, Joseph. *Comic Books As History: The Narrative Art of Jack Johnson, Art Spiegelman, and Harvey Pekar.* 1990. $25.00.

U-X-L/Thompson-Gale
www.gale.cengage.com/uxl

Pendergast, Tom, and Sara Pendergast. *U-X-L Graphic Novelists.* 2006. $165.00.

Vanguard Productions
www.creativemix.com/vanguard

Buckler, Rich. *How to Draw Dynamic Comic Books.* 2007. $19.95.

Golden, Michael. *Excess: The Art of Michael Golden: Comics Inimitable Storyteller (and How He Does It).* 2007. $24.95.

Kronenberg, Michael, and J. David Spurlock. *Spies, Vixens & Masters of Kung Fu: The Art of Paul Gulacy.* 2005. $24.95.

Kubert, Joe. *How to Draw from Life.* 2009. $34.95.

Simon, Joe, and Jim Simon. *The Comic Book Makers.* 2003. $34.95.

Zeno, Eddy. *Curt Swan: A Life in Comics.* 2002. $19.95.

W.W. Norton
www.wwnorton.com

Eisner, Will. *Comics and Sequential Art.* 2008. $22.95.

Eisner, Will. *Graphic Storytelling.* 2008. $22.95.

Eisner, Will. *Expressive Anatomy for Comics and Narrative: Principles and Practices from the Legendary Cartoonist.* 2008. $22.95.

Watson-Guptill Publications
www.randomhouse.com/crown/watsonguptill.html

Chiarello, Mark and Todd Klein. *The DC Comics Guide to Coloring and Lettering Comics.* 2004. $21.95.

Daniels, Les. *DC Comics: A Celebration of the World's Favorite Comic Book Heroes.* 2003. $29.95.

Hart, Christopher. *Manga for the Beginner.* 2008. $21.95.

Hart, Christopher (and others). *Manga Mania Series.* 2001–. $19.95 each.

Hart, Christopher. *Simplified Anatomy for the Comic Book Artist.* 2007. $19.95.

Hart, Christopher (and others). *Xtreme Art Series.* 2009. $6.95 each.

Janson, Klaus. *The DC Comics Guide to Inking Comics.* 2003. $21.95.

Janson, Klaus. *The DC Comics Guide to Penciling Comics*. 2001. $22.95.
Martinbrough, Shawn. *How to Draw Noir Comics: The Art and Technique of Visual Story-telling*. 2007. $19.95.
O'Neil, Dennis. *The DC Comics Guide to Writing Comics*. 2001. $21.95.
Rollins, Prentis. *The Making of a Graphic Novel*. 2006. $19.95.
Smith, Andy. *Drawing American Manga Superheroes*. 2007. $19.95.

Weiser Books
www.weiserbooks.com

Knowles, Christopher. *Our Gods Wear Spandex*. 2007. $19.95.

Fiction Based on Comics, Novelizations, or with Comic Themes

Some books are "novelizations" of comic book stories, much in the way that movies are made into books. Others feature characters from comic books in new stories. Some incorporate comics themes and concepts ranging from books with superheroes to books in which comic books or comic book creators are a important part of the story. Some of the titles listed may also be available in other formats.

Anderson, Kevin J. *Enemies and Allies*. William Morrow, 2009. $26.99.
Anderson, Kevin J. *Last Days of Krypton*. Harper, 2007. $25.95.
Chabon, Michael. *The Amazing Adventures of Kavalier & Clay*. Random House, 2000. $16.00.
Cox, Greg. *52: The Novel*. Ace, 2007. $15.00.
Cox, Greg. *Countdown: The Novel*. Ace, 2009. $15.00.
Cox, Greg. *Infinite Crisis: The Novel*. Ace, 2006. $15.00.
David, Peter. *Wolverine: Election Day*. Pocket, 2008. $7.99.
DeHaven, Tom. *It's Superman*. Chronicle Books, 2005. $15.00.
Golden, Christopher. *Hellboy: The Dragon Pool*. Dark Horse, 2007. $7.99.
Golden, Christopher (Ed.). *Hellboy: Odd Jobs*. Dark Horse, 1999. $14.95.
Golden, Christopher (Ed.). *Hellboy: Odder Jobs*. Dark Horse, 2004. $14.95.
Golden, Christopher (Ed.). *Hellboy: Oddest Jobs*. Dark Horse, 2008. $14.95.
Grossman, Austin. *Soon I Will Be Invincible*. Vintage, 2008. $22.95.
Hodge, Brian. *Hellboy: On Earth as It Is in Hell*. Dark Horse, 2005. $6.99.
King, Owen, and John McNally. *Who Can Save Us Now? Brand-New Superheroes and Their Amazing (Short) Stories*. Free Press, 2008. $16.00.
Lang, Jeffrey. *Fantastic Four: Doomgate*. Pocket Star Book, 2008. $7.99.
Lebbon, Tim. *Hellboy: The Fire Wolves*. Dark Horse, 2009. $12.95.
Lebbon, Tim. *Hellboy: Unnatural Selection*. Dark Horse, 2006. $7.99.
Mariotte, Jeff. *Spider-Man: Requiem*. Pocket Books, $7.99.
Mayer, Robert. *Superfolks*. St. Martin's Griffen, 2005. $13.95.
Meltzer, Brad. *The Book of Lies*. Grand Central Publishing, 2008. $7.99.
Moore, Perry. *Hero*. Hyperion, 2007. $16.99.
Morris, Mark. *Hellboy: The All-Seeing Eye*. Dark Horse, 2008. $12.95.
Niles, Steve, and Jeff Mariotte. *30 Days of Night: Immortal Remains*. IDW, 2007. $7.99.
Niles, Steve, and Jeff Mariotte. *30 Days of Night: Rumors of the Undead*. IDW, 2006. $7.99.

Niles, Steve, and Jeff Mariotte. *Criminal Macabre: The Complete Cal McDonald Stories*. Dark Horse, 2008. $12.95.

Niles, Steve, and Jeff Mariotte. *Guns, Drugs, and Monsters*. IDW, 2005. $6.95.

NISIOSIN. *Death Note: Another Note*. VIZ, 2008. $17.99.

Piccirilli, Tom. *Hellboy: Emerald Hell*. Dark Horse, 2008. $12.95.

Rogers, Rob. *Devil's Cape*. Wizards of the Coast, 2008. $14.95.

Rucka, Greg. *Queen and Country: A Gentlemen's Game*. Bantam, 2004. $6.99.

Rucka, Greg. *Queen and Country: Private Wars*. Bantam, 2006. $6.99.

Schwartz, David J. *Superpowers: A Novel*. Three Rivers Press, 2008. $14.95.

Sniegoski, Thomas E. *Hellboy: The God Machine*. Dark Horse, 2006. $7.99.

Tinsley, Kevin. *Stonehaven: Fruits of the Poisonous Vine*. Stickman Graphics, 2008. $14.95.

Willingham, Bill. *Peter and Max: A Fables Novel*. Titan Books, 2009. $22.99.

Wolfman, Marv. *Crisis on Infinite Earths*. Ibooks, 2006. $22.95.

Non-comics-themed books by Peter David, Warren Ellis, Neil Gaiman, Greg Rucka, and others who have written graphic novels in your collection may also be of interest to your patrons. In addition, if you purchase graphic adaptations of novels, you may wish to have to have the original work in your collection as well. The same applies to series such as *Odd Thomas* or *The Dresden Files*, which have had original graphic novel stories based on them.

Recommended Online Sources for Information and Purchasing

The Internet can be very helpful to the librarian starting a graphic novel collection, whether checking publisher Web sites to see upcoming releases, finding vendors, getting reviews, or getting ideas for classroom activities. Besides Web sites, many publishers, reviewers, professionals, and scholars are also on MySpace, Facebook, and Twitter. Many sites also update via RSS feed.

Publishing Companies

Abacus Comics
www.abacuscomics.com

Abstract Studio
www.strangersinparadise.com

Accent UK Comics
www.accentukcomics.com

Adhouse Books
www.adhousebooks.com

ADV
www.advmanga.com

AiT/Planet Lar
www.ait-planetlar.com

Alfred A. Knopf
www.randomhouse.com/knopf

Alternative Comics
www.indyworld.com/altcomics

Antarctic Press
www.antarctic-press.com

Arcana
www.arcanacomics.com

Archaia Studios Press
www.archaiasp.com

Aurora Publishing
www.aurora-publishing.com

Ballentine Books
www.randomhouse.com

Barbour Publishing
www.barbourbooks.com

Barron's
barronseduc.com

Big Head Press
www.bigheadpress.com

Blu
blumanga.com

Boom! Studios
www.boom-studios.net

Café Digital
www.paulsizer.com

Candlewick Press
www.candlewick.com

Checker Book Publishing Group
www.checkerbpg.com

Cinebook
www.cinebook.com

Cleis Press
www.cleispress.com

Crown Publishing
www.randomhouse.com/crown

Dark Horse Comics
www.darkhorse.com

DC Comics
www.dccomics.com

Del Rey Manga
www.randomhouse.com/delrey/manga

Deux Press
www.deux-press.com

Devil's Due Publishing
www.devilsdue.net

DH Publishing
www.dhp-online.com

Digital Manga Publishing
www.dmpbooks.com

Dork Storm Press
archive.gamespy.com/comics/dorkstorm

Doubleday Press
doubleday.knopfdoubleday.com

Drawn & Quarterly
www.drawnandquarterly.com

Dynamite Entertainment
www.dynamiteentertainment.com

801 Media
www.801media.com

Eureka Productions
www.graphicclassics.com

Exhibit A Press
www.exhibitapress.com

Fantagraphics
www.fantagraphics.com

Firefly Books
www.fireflybooks.com

First Second
www.firstsecondbooks.com

For Beginners
www.forbeginners.com

Gigantic Graphic Novels
www.giganticgraphicnovels.com

GoComi
www.gocomi.com

Grand Central Publishing
www.hachettebookgroup.com/publishing_
    grand-central-publishing.aspx

GT Labs
www.gt-labs.com

HarperCollins
www.harpercollins.com

Harry N. Abrams
www.abramsbooks.com

Henry Holt
us.macmillan.com/HenryHolt.aspx

Hill and Wang
us.macmillan.com/HillAndWang.aspx

Houghton Mifflin
www.hmco.com

IDW
www.idwpublishing.com

Image Comics
www.imagecomics.com

Jewish Publication Society
www.jewishpub.org

Last Gasp
www.lastgasp.com

Little, Brown, and Co.
www.hatchettebookgroup.com

Manic D Press
www.manicdpress.com

Marvel Comics
www.marvel.com

Misfit Corner Press
misfitcorner.blogspot.com

Moonstone Books
www.moonstonebooks.com

NBM
www.nbmpub.com

New Press
www.thenewpress.com

Oni Press
www.onipress.com

Pantheon Books
pantheon.knopfdoubleday.com

Penguin
us.penguingroup.com

Random House
www.randomhouse.com

Redeye Press
www.redeyepress.net

Riverhead Books
www.riverheadbooks.com

Running Press
www.perseusbooksgroup.com/runningpress/
    home.jsp

Simon & Schuster/Atheneum Books
www.simonsays.com

Slave Labor/SLG/Amaze Ink
www.slavelabor.com

Soft Skull Press
www.softskull.com

St. Martin's Griffin
us.macmillan.com/smp.aspx

Stickman Graphics
www.stickmangraphics.com

Titan Books
www.titanbooks.com

Tokyopop
www.tokyopop.com

Top Cow Productions
www.topcow.com

Top Shelf
www.topshelfcomix.com

Tor
www.tor-forge.com

Vertical Publishing
www.vertical-inc.com

Villard Books
www.randomhouse.com/rhpg/villard

Viper Comics
www.vipercomics.com

VIZ Media
www.viz.com

W.W. Norton
www.wwnorton.com

Yale University Press
yalepress.yale.edu/yupbooks/home.asp

Yen Press
yenpress.us

Zenescope Entertainment
www.zenescope.com

Resources for Purchasing

American Library Association
www.alastore.ala.org

Amazon
www.amazon.com

Baker & Taylor
www.btol.com

Barnes and Noble
www.barnesandnoble.com

Brodart
www.brodart.com and
www.graphicnovels.brodart.com

BWI
www.bwibooks.com

CBR Comic Shop Locator
www.comicbookresources.com/resources/
    locator

CBR New Comics List
www.comicbookresources.com/resources/
    ncl

Demco
www.demco.com

Diamond Comic Shop Locator
www.comicshoplocator.com

Diamond Comics
www.diamondcomics.com (main)
http://bookshelf.diamondcomics.com
    (library page)

Ingram
www.ingrambook.com

Kapco
www.kapco.com

The Master List of Comic Book and
Trading Card Stores
www.the-master-list.com

New Comic Book Release List
www.comiclist.com
This also links to information on reviews,
publishers, and comics professionals and is
also available via e-mail.

Additional Sites

These sites include source for news, reviews,
recommendations, academic resources, and
some sites that are just fun to read. Many
sites include links to other sites, and some,
such as Comic Book Resources, include a
number of columns.

Anime News Network
www.animenewsnetwork.com

The Beat
pwbeat.publishersweekly.com/blog

Bleeding Cool
www.bleedingcool.com

Center For Cartoon Studies
www.cartoonstudies.org

Comic Book Awards Almanac
users.ren.com/aardy/comics/awards

Comic Book Conventions
www.comicbookconventions.com

Comic Book Legal Defense Fund
www.cbldf.com

The Comic Book Periodic Table of
Elements
www.uky.edu/Projects/Chemcomics

Comic Book Resources
www.comicbookresources.com

Comic Buyer's Guide
www.cbgxtra.com

ComicMix
www.comicmix.com

Comicon.com
www.comicon.com

Comics Scholarship Annotated
Bibliographies
www.comicsresearch.org

Comics Bulletin
www.silverbulletcomicbooks.com

Comics in the Classroom
www.comicsintheclassroom.net

Comics Continuum
www.comicscontinuum.com

Comics Radar
http://comicsradar.com

Comics Reporter
www.comicsreporter.com

Comics Research Bibliography
www.rpi.edu/~bulloj/comxbib.html

Comics Worth Reading
www.comicsworthreading.com

Comixology
www.comixology.com

Free Comic Books Day
www.freecomicbookday.com

Friends of Lulu
http://friendsoflulu.wordpress.com

Grand Comic Book Database
www.comics.org

Graphic Novel Reporter
www.graphicnovelreporter.com

ICv2
www.icv2.com

Journalista
www.tcj.com/journalista

The Librarian's Guide to Anime and Manga
www.koyagi.com/Libguide.html

Library Journal
www.libraryjournal.com

Michigan State University Comic Art
Collection
www.lib.msu.edu/comics

National Association of Comic Art
Educators
www.teachingcomics.org

Newsarama
www.newsarma.com

No Flying, No Tights
www.noflyingnotights.com

Ohio State University Cartoon Library and
Museum
http://cartoons.osu.edu

PopCultureShock
popcultureshock.com

Precocious Curmudgeon
precur.blogspot.com

The Pulse
www.comicon.com/pulse

Recommended Graphic Novels for Public
Libraries
my.voyager.net/~srateri/graphicnovels.htm

The Secret Origins of Good Readers
www.night-flight.com/secretorigin/SOGR2004.pdf

Sequential Tart
www.sequentialtart.com/home.shtml

Superdickery
www.superdickery.com

Syllabus Finder
chnm.gmu.edu/tools/syllabi

University of Florida Comics Studies
www.english.ufl.edu/comics

Unshelved
www.unshelved.com

Wizard: The Guide to Comics
www.wizardworld.com

E-Mail Resources

GNLIB-L
GNLIB-L is a listserv for librarians dealing
with the subject of graphic novels in libraries.

Originally on Topica, the list moved to
Yahoo Groups in 2007. To subscribe, e-mail
GNLIB-L-subscribe@yahoogroups.com
or go to http://groups.yahoo.com/group/
GNLIB-L.

Scholars Discussion List
Comixschl, the Comix-Scholars list is "an
academic forum that serves the interests of
those involved in research, criticism, and
teaching related to comics art." To join, send
an e-mail to comix-scholars-request@clas
.ufl .edu with "subscribe" in the body of the
message. The list is also available in digest
form. For more information go to www
.english.ufl.edu/comics/scholars/index
.shtml.

Anime and Manga Research Circle
The AMRC describes itself as a "diverse
community of scholars engaged in the
academic study of anime and manga, their
associated (sub)cultures worldwide, and
(tangentially) Japanese popular culture in
general." To join and for more information
go to http://tech.groups.yahoo.com/group/
amrc-l.

PW Comics Week: A Weekly E-newsletter from *Publishers Weekly*
Go to www.publishersweekly.com/subscribe
.asp and scroll down to the "e-mail news-
letters" section.

Graphic Novel Reporter
Information is available at their Web site, and
a newsletter is available via e-mail. Go to
www.graphicnovelreporter.com and click on
the link to sign up.

Bibliography

"Amazing Fantasy: Library Receives Original 1962 Illustrations for First Spider-Man Story." 2008. *Library of Congress Information Bulletin* 67, no. 5. Available: www.loc.gov/loc/lcib/0805/spiderman.html (accessed August 22, 2009).

Anderson, Porter. 2001. "Neil Gaiman: 'I Enjoy Not Being Famous.'" Available: http://archives.cnn.com/2001/CAREER/jobenvy/07/29/neil.gaiman.focus (accessed August 22, 2009).

Andleman, Bob. 2005. *Will Eisner: A Spirited Life*. Milwaukee, WI: M Press.

Anime News Network. 2007. "Hong Kong Artist Wins Japan's 1st Manga Nobel Prize." Available: www.animenewsnetwork.com/news/2007-06-30/hong-kong-artist-wins-japan's-1st-manga-nobel-prize (accessed August 22, 2009).

"Anti-Immigrant Criticism in Denver Extends to Library Fotonovelas." 2005. *Library Journal* (August 18). Available: www.libraryjournal.com/article/CA635920.html.

Arnold, Andrew D. 2003. "The Graphic Novel Silver Anniversary." *Time* (November 14). Available: www.time.com/time/columnist/arnold/article/0,9565,542579,00.html (accessed August 22, 2009).

Auden, W. H. 1973. *Forewords and Afterwords*. New York: Random House.

Baker, Bill. 2009. "The Dream Goes On: Neil Gaiman on 20 Years of *The Sandman* and *The Graveyard Book*." Available: www.worldfamouscomics.com/bakersdozen/back20090506.shtml (accessed August 22, 2009).

Bechdel, Alison. 2008. "Life Drawing." *Entertainment Weekly* (June 27): 110–113.

Beerbohm, Robert, Richard Samuel West, and Richard D. Olsen. 2007. "Comic Strips and Books 1646–1900." In Robert Overstreet, *Overstreet Comic Book Price Guide*, 37th edition (pp. 318–338). New York: House of Collectibles/Gemstone.

Brady, Matt. 2008. "Watchmen: One Million Copies in 2008." Available: www.newsarama.com/comics/080814-WatchmentOneMillion.html (accessed August 22, 2009).

Brenner, Robin. 2007. *Understanding Manga and Anime*. Westport, CT: Libraries Unlimited.

"Broccoli Books Shuts Down." 2008. Available: www.icv2.com/articles/news/13785.html (accessed August 22, 2009).

Buchanan, Rebecca. 2006. "A Case for Comics: Comic Books as an Educational Tool, Part 3." Available: www.sequentialtart.com/article.php?id=234 (accessed August 22, 2009).

Callahan, Bob. 2004. "No More Yielding but a Dream." In *The New Smithsonian Book of Comic-Book Stories*. Washington, DC: Smithsonian Books.

Campbell, Eddie. 2004. "Graphic Novel Manifesto." Available: www.donmacdonald.com/archives/000034.html (accessed August 22, 2009).

Caren, Eric. C. 2007. "The American Comic Book: 1500–1828." In Robert Overstreet, *Overstreet Comic Book Price Guide*, 37th edition (pp. 308–317). New York: House of Collectibles/Gemstone.

Cary, Stephen. 2004. *Going Graphic: Comics at Work in the Multilingual Classroom*. Portsmouth, NH: Heinemann.

Comic Book Legal Defense Fund. 2008. "CBLDF to Serve as Special Consultant in PROTECT Act Manga Case." Available: www.cbldf.org/pr/archives/000372.shtml (accessed August 22, 2009).

Chinn, Mike. 2004. *Writing and Illustrating the Graphic Novel*. New York: Barron's.

Cho, Grace, Hong Choi, and Stephen Krashen. 2005. "Hooked on Comic Book Reading: How Comic Books Made an Impossible Situation Less Difficult." *Knowledge Quest* 33, no. 4 (March/April): 35–38.

Chow, Natsuko. n.d. "Comics: A Useful Tool for English as a Second Language (ESL)." Available: http://bookshelf.diamondcomics.com/public/default.asp?t=1&m=1&c=20&s=182&ai=37714&ssd=. (accessed August 22, 2009).

Christina, Greta (Ed.). 2008. *Best Erotic Comics 2008*. San Francisco: Last Gasp.

Cinebook Catalog #6, Winter/Spring 2009. 2008. Canterbury, Kent, UK: Cinebook. Available: www.cinebook.co.uk/cinebook_catalogue_dec08.pdf.

Cornog, Martha. 2008. "Graphic Novels: Challenge & Change." *Library Journal* (May 15). Available: www.libraryjournal.com/article/CA6557371.html (accessed August 22, 2009).

Cornwell, Lisa. 2007. "Schools Add, Expand Comics Art Classes." *USAToday*, December 15. Available: www.usatoday.com/news/education/2007-12-15-comicsclasses_N.htm (accessed August 22, 2009).

Cronin, Brian. 2006. "Comic Book Urban Legends Revealed #39." Available: http://goodcomics.comicbookresources.com/2006/02/23/comic-book-urban-legends-revealed-39/ (accessed August 22, 2009).

Daniell, Mark. 2009. "T.O. Surprises Don't Stop for Neil Gaiman." Available: http://jam.canoe.ca/Books/2009/06/22/9890516-ca.html (accessed August 22, 2009).

DC Comics Rarities Archive, Vol. 1. 2004. New York: DC Comics.

de Vos, Gail. 2005. "From ABCs of Graphic Novels by Gail de Vos." *Resource Links* 10, no. 3. Retrieved from (no longer available): www.resourcelinks.ca/features/feb05.htm.

Dooley, Michael. 2008. "Power to the Panels: An Interview with Paul Buhle." *AIGA Journal of Design* (June 17). Available: www.aiga.org/content.cfm/power-to-the-panels-an-interview-with-paul-buhle (accessed August 22, 2009).

Eisner, Will. 1996. *Graphic Storytelling & Visual Narrative*. Tamarac, FL: Poorhouse Press.

Eisner, Will. 2004. "Keynote Address from the 2002 'Will Eisner Symposium.'" *ImageTexT: Interdisciplinary Comics Studies* 1, no. 1. Available: www.english.ufl.edu/imagetext/archives/v1_1/eisner (accessed August 22, 2009).

Elkins, Robert J., and Christian Bruggemann. 1983. "Comic Strips in the Teaching of English as a Foreign Language." In James L. Thomas (Ed.), *Cartoons and Comics in the Classroom*. Littleton, CO: Libraries Unlimited.

Gaiman, Neil. 2006. "Lost Girls Redux." Available: http://journal.neilgaiman.com/2006/06/lost-girls-redux.html (accessed August 22, 2009).

Gertler, Nat, and Steve Lieber. 2004. *The Complete Idiot's Guide to Creating a Graphic Novel*. New York: Alpha Books.

Gonzalez, Miguel. 2006. "Good Grief, Charlie Brown! Family Stunned by Porn Comics at Library." *[Victorville] Daily Press*, April 12.

Goulart, Ron. 2004. *Comic Book Encyclopedia: The Ultimate Guide to Characters, Graphic Novels, Writers, and Artists in the Comic Book Universe.* New York: HarperCollins.

Gravett, Paul. 2004. *Manga: Sixty Years of Japanese Comics.* London: Laurence King Publishing.

Gravett, Paul, and Peter Stanbury. 2006. *Great British Comics.* London: Aurum Press.

Green, Justin. 1995. *Justin Green's Binky Brown Sampler.* San Francisco: Last Gasp.

Green, Karen. 2007. "Comic Adventures in Academia: The Origin Story." Available: www.comixology.com/articles/11/The-Origin-Story (accessed August 22, 2009).

Green, Karen. 2008. "Adventures in Academia: Conventional Comics or Conference Calling." Available: www.comixology.com/articles/21/Conventional-Comics-or-Conference-Calling (accessed August 22, 2009).

Green, Karen. 2008. "Comic Adventures in Academia: Naughty Bits." Available: www.comixology.com/articles/15/Naughty-Bits (accessed August 22, 2009).

Hajdu, David. 2008. *The Ten-Cent Plague: The Great Comic-Book Scare and How It Changed America.* New York: Farrar, Straus, and Giroux.

Harbison, Sarah. 2008. "Fortress of Comic-tude." *The State News*, November 4. Available: www.statenews.com/index.php/article/2008/11/fortress_of_comic-tude (accessed August 22, 2009).

Harris, Franklin. 2005. "Censored Book Not a Good Start." *The Decatur Daily* (online edition), February 10.

Harvey, Robert C. 2001. "Comedy at the Juncture of Word and Image: The Emergence of the Modern Magazine Gag Cartoon Reveals the Vital Blend." In Robin Varnum and Christina T. Gibbons (Eds.), *The Language of Comics: Word and Image* (pp. 77–78). Jackson: University Press of Mississippi.

Hatfield, Charles W. 2008. "ALA: Reading Pictures: The Language of Wordless Books." *Thought Balloonists* (July 14). Available: www.thoughtballoonists.com/2008/07/ala-reading-pic.html (accessed August 22, 2009).

Heer, Jeet. 2008. "The Rise of Comics Scholarship: The Role of the University Press of Mississippi." Available: http://sanseverything.wordpress.com/2008/08/02/the-rise-of-comics-scholarship-the-role-of-university-press-of-mississippi (accessed August 22, 2009).

Horne, Marc. 2008. "Naked Anger as Peter Pan's Wendy Gets Porno Rewrite." Available: news.scotsman.com/uk/Naked-anger-as-Peter-Pan39s.3644511.jp (accessed August 22, 2009).

ICv2. 2006. "Marvel Edits 'Tomb of Dracula.'" Available: www.icv2.com/articles/news/9357.html (accessed August 22, 2009).

ImageText Newsfeed. 2008. "John A. Lent Scholarship in Comic Studies." Available: www.english.ufl.edu/imagetext/news.shtml?/cfp/lent_scholarship_in_comics_studies.shtml (accessed August 22, 2009).

Inge, M. Thomas. 1990. *Comics as Culture.* Jackson: University Press of Mississippi.

International Comic Arts Forum. 2009. "ICAF's Mission." Available: www.international comicartsforum.org/icaf/about-icaf.html (accessed August 22, 2009).February 10, 2009).

"Japan Plans 'Nobel Prize of Manga'." CNN.Com (May 23, 2007).

Jenson-Benjamin, Meredith. 2001. "An Irrelevant (but Amusing) Story about Challenges to GNs." E-mail post to GNLIB-L, April 25.

Kavanagh, Barry. 2000. "The Alan Moore Interview." Blather.net (October 17). Available: www.blather.net/articles/amoore/northampton.html (accessed August 22, 2009).

Kinsella, Sharon. 2000. *Adult Manga: Culture and Power in Contemporary Japanese Society.* Honolulu: University of Hawaii Press.

"Library Cards Get Bonus on Free Comic Book Day." 2006. *Library Journal* (May 11). Available: www.libraryjournal.com/article/CA6333717.html (accessed August 22, 2009).

Library of Congress. 2008. "Library of Congress Collections Policy Statements: Comics and Cartoons." Available: www.loc.gov/acq/devpol/comics.pdf (accessed August 22, 2009).

Library of Congress. n.d. "Swann Foundations Fellowships." Available: www.loc.gov/rr/print/swann/swann-fellow.html (accessed August 22, 2009).

MacDonald, Heidi. 2003. "Bookstore Revolution: Graphic Novels Get Their Own Category." *Pulse News*, January 20. Retrieved from (no longer available): www.comicon.com/ubb/ultimatebb.php/ubb/forum/f/36.html.

MacDonald, Heidi. 2008. "Every Dark Horse Comic Available at Portland State University." Available: http://pwbeat.publishersweekly.com/blog/2008/10/23/the-countrys-first-university-comic-book-archive (accessed August 22, 2009).

Marsh, Rufus K. 1983. "Teaching French with the Comics." In James L. Thomas (Ed.), *Cartoons and Comics in the Classroom.* Littleton, CO: Libraries Unlimited.

Marvel. n.d. "The Marvel Rating System." Available: www.marvel.com/catalog/ratings.htm (accessed August 22, 2009).

Matz, Chris. 2004. "Collecting Comic Books for an Academic Library." *Collection Building* 23, no. 2: 96–99.

McCabe, Joseph (Ed.). 2004. *Hanging Out with the Dream King: Conversations with Neil Gaiman and His Collaborators.* Seattle: Fantagraphics Books.

McCloud, Scott. 2000. *Reinventing Comics: How Imagination and Technology Are Revolutionizing an Art Form.* New York: HarperCollins.

Nakazawa, Keiji. 2004. *Barefoot Gen: A Cartoon Story of Hiroshima.* San Francisco: Last Gasp.

"Newsmaker: Alison Bechdel." 2007. *American Libraries* (February): 22.

Nyberg, Amy Kiste. 1998. *Seal of Approval: The History of the Comics Code.* Jackson: University Press of Mississippi.

Nye, Russell. 1970. *The Unembarrassed Muse: The Popular Arts in America.* New York: Dial Press.

Olbrich, Dave. 2008. "The End of the Jack Kirby Comics Industry Awards: A Lesson in Honesty." Available: http://funnybookfanatic.wordpress.com/2008/12/17/the-end-of-the-jack-kirby-comics-industry-awards-a-lesson-in-honesty (accessed August 22, 2009).

Olbrich, Dave. 2008. "The Origin Story of the Jack Kirby Comics Industry Awards. Available: http://funnybookfanatic.wordpress.com/2008/12/16/the-origin-story-of-the-jack-kirby-comics-industry-awards/) (accessed August 22, 2009).

Olin, Anita. 2007. "Banned Books Week: Not Just for Prose Anymore." *Sequential Tart* 10, no. 9 (September). Available: sequentialtart.com/article.php?id=665 (accessed August 22, 2009).

O'Neil, Dennis. 2001. *The DC Comics Guide to Writing Comics.* New York: Watson-Guptill Publications.

Overstreet, Robert. 2007. *Overstreet Price Guide,* 37th edition. New York: House of Collectibles/Gemstone.

Pawuk, Michael. 2006. *Graphic Novels: A Genre Guide to Comic Books, Manga, and More.* Westport, CT: Libraries Unlimited.

Pekar, Harvey, and Joyce Brabner. 1994. *Our Cancer Year.* New York: Four Walls Eight Windows.

Pilcher, Tim, and Brad Brooks. 2005. *The Essential Guide to World Comics.* London: Collins and Brown.

Pilcher, Tim, and Gene Kannenberg Jr. 2008. *Erotic Comics: A Graphic History from Tijuana Bibles to Underground Comix.* New York: Harry N. Abrams.

The Public Librarian's Guide to Graphic Novels. 2003. Lexington, KY: Book Wholesalers.

Reese, Jennifer, et al. 2008. "The New Classics: Books." *Entertainment Weekly* (June 27): 96–107.

Rollins, Prentis. 2006. *The Making of a Graphic Novel.* New York: Watson-Guptill Publications.

Rosen, Judith. 2006. "Comics Shops Turn to Book Distributors for Graphic Novels." *PW Comic Week—Publishers Weekly* (July 18). Available: www.publishersweekly.com/article/CA6354132.html (accessed August 22, 2009).

Russell, Michael. 2005. "History of Comic Books Part II." Available: http://ezinearticles.com/?History-of-Comic-Books—-Part-II&id=114701 (accessed August 22, 2009).

Schodt, Frederik L. 1998. "Henry Yoshitaka Kiyama and *The Four Immigrants Manga.*" Available: www.jai2.com/HK.htm (accessed August 22, 2009).

Scott, Randall W. 1990. *Comics Librarianship: A Handbook.* Jefferson, NC: McFarland and Company.

Scott, Randall W. 1998. "A Practicing Comic-Book Librarian Surveys His Collection and His Craft." *Serials Review* 24, no. 1 (Spring): 49–56.

The Seven Soldiers of Victory Archives. 2005. New York: DC Comics.

Spiegelman, Art. 1995. "Symptons of Disorder/Signs of Genius." In *Justin Green's Binky Brown Sampler.* San Francisco: Last Gasp.

Steelman, Ben. 2007. "Read with Us: Program Spotlights 'Persepolis.'" *StarNews Online,* September 16. Available: www.starnewsonline.com/article/20070916/NEWS/70916 0324/1051/NEWS (accessed August 22, 2009).

Talbot, Bryan. 2007. *Alice in Sunderland: An Entertainment.* Milwaukee, OR: Dark Horse.

Thompson, Don, and Dick Lupoff. 1973/1998. *The Comic-Book Book,* revised edition. Iola, WI: Krause Publications.

Thompson, Jason. 2007. *Manga: The Complete Guide.* New York: Ballentine Books.

Tokyopop. n.d. "Tokyopop Ratings System." Available: www.tokyopop.com/corporate/book sellers/879 (accessed August 22, 2009).

Tractenberg, Jeffrey A. 2008. "King of Cartoons." *Wall Street Journal,* September 18. Available: http://online.wsj.com/article/SB122166625405548219.html (accessed August 22, 2009).

Twiddy, David. 2007. "Pictures Causing Problems." *[Cedar Rapids–Iowa City] Gazette,* January 14: 5L.

University of Florida. 2007. "Comic Collections." Available: www.english.ufl.edu/comics/collections.shtml (accessed August 22, 2009).

University of Florida. 2007. "Conferences." Available: www.english.ufl.edu/comics/conference.shtml (accessed August 22, 2009).

University of Florida. n.d. "ImagetexT." Available: www.english.ufl.edu/comics/imagetext.shtml (accessed August 22, 2009).

Versaci, Rocco. 2007. *This Book Contains Graphic Language: Comics as Literature*. New York: Continuum.

VIZ Media. n.d. "Our Ratings." Available: www.viz.com/ratings (accessed August 22, 2009).

Weiner, Stephen. 1996. *100 Graphic Novels for Public Libraries*. Northampton, MA: Kitchen Sink Press.

Whitworth, Jerry. 2006. "A Case for Comics: Comic Books as an Educational Tool, Part 2." *Sequential Tart* 9, no. 7 (July). Available: www.sequentialtart.com/article.php?id=186 (accessed August 22, 2009).

Whitworth, Jerry. 2006. "A Case for Comics: Comic Books as an Educational Tool, Part 3." *Sequential Tart* 9, no. 7 (July). Available: www.sequentialtart.com/article.php?id=234 (accessed August 22, 2009).

"Will Eisner Spirit of Comics Retailer Award." 2008. Available: www.comic-con.org/cci/cci_eisners_spirit.shtml (accessed August 22, 2009).

Yang, Gene. 2003. "History of Comics in Education." Available: www.humblecomics.com/comicsedu/history (accessed August 22, 2009).

Yaoi Press. 2008. "Yaoi Press Blog." Available: www.yaoipress.com/2008/10/yaoi-press.html (accessed August 22, 2009).

Title, Series, Creator, Character, and Publisher Index

Note: For the titles in this index, I have listed both the series name and the subtitles of the original works. For example, for *Hellblazer: Hard Time*, both *Hellblazer* and *Hard Time* have entries. Subtitles are listed with their series in parenthesis.

Due to space limitations, in some cases when parts of a series begin with the same word, their entries have been combined, and some character listings have been merged with titles that begin with that character's name or with the listing for the *Essential, Showcase Presents, Archives,* and/or *Marvel Masterworks* editions. In addition, some creators, publishers, and titles that are not in the appendixes have not been included here, though some of them may appear in the general index. Also, some titles are shortened or appear without their subtitles.

Page numbers followed by the letter "e" indicate exhibits; those followed by the letter "f" indicate figures. Page numbers in boldface indicate main entries in Appendixes A and B.

Subject Index

Page numbers followed by the letter "e" indicate exhibits; those followed by the letter "f" indicate figures. Due to space limitations, certain creators and works are listed only in the previous index.

About the Author

D avid S. Serchay is a youth services librarian for the Broward County Library System in South Florida, where he is on the graphic novel selection committee. He has been reading comic books all of his life and has a personal collection of over 25,000 comics and graphic novels. He has previously written about the subject in *Thinking Outside the Book*, *The Greenwood Encyclopedia of Graphic Novels*, *Magazines for Libraries*, *Library Journal*, *Serials Review*, *Florida Living*, *Animato!*, *Comics Source*, and *The Librarian's Guide to Graphic Novels for Children and Tweens*. He has also lectured extensively on the subject and has contributed to the Grand Comic Book Database and Graphicnovelreporter.com. He lives in Coral Springs, Florida, with his wife, Bethany, and can be reached at davidserchay@yahoo.com.